SCOTLAND: AN ANTHOLOGY

By the same author

SCOTLAND

An Anthology

MAURICE LINDSAY

ROBERT HALE · LONDON

Copyright © Maurice Lindsay 1974
First published in Great Britain 1974
This paperback edition 1989

Robert Hale Limited
Clerkenwell House
Clerkenwell Green
London ECIR OHT

British Library Cataloguing in Publication Data
Scotland, an anthology.
  1. English literature. Scottish writers, to 1973.
Anthologies
I. Lindsay, Maurice, *1918*
820.8'09411

ISBN 0–7090–3786–4

Printed and bound in Great Britain by
Mackays of Chatham PLC, Chatham, Kent

Contents

HISTORY

PEOPLE

A SHEAF O BALLANTS

CREATURES

PURSUITS AND PASTIMES

MYSTICISM

RELIGION

COUNTRYSIDE CONCERNS

LOVERS

HUMOUR

THE SCOTS CHARACTER

L'ENVOI

Introduction

The purpose of this book is to bring within the confines of two covers a selection of poetry and prose designed to give the general reader as varied as possible an experience of Scotland. I particularly hope that it will afford young people a valid yet pleasurable impression of much that has gone to make up the fabric of their own country.

To some, anthologies are anathema. To others, any interference with an original text, however riddled it may be with vagaries of orthography or elementary spelling errors, is a kind of corruption. This book is not for them. While I have made no alterations at all where the meaning was clear, and I have tried not to alter a syllable of the middle Scots pieces where either sound or sense might have been affected, I have discreetly modernized the spelling where not to do so would have resulted in the possibility of unintelligibility. In particular, the 'thorn' and 'yok' letters have been transcribed. Where the *is* ending cannot have been meant to be sounded, it has been altered by me to *s*, thus leaving only *is* endings the sounding of which is essential to the metre.

I have recorded the sources from which virtually all my extracts have been taken, and given the dates of my authors wherever ascertainable. The index by authors acknowledges the publishers of copyright material.

I have not reflected those events after 1764 which were British rather than Scottish. Since this is a reprint of the original anthology, corrections apart, it has not been possible to include work by writers who have come before the public since 1974.

Within the compass of a single volume it is not possible to include everything one likes, nor indeed to produce a selection which will please every taste. Many authors whose work I enjoy or admire could not be represented. However, I hope I have at least managed to reflect the breadth of my own Scottish tastes and interests.

I particularly wish to thank those who have assisted me in various ways: Miss Marion Stewart of Register House, Edinburgh, who drew my attention to some hitherto unpublished material; Colonel Pat Thomas, a descendant of James Watt, who made available to me the manuscript account of the inventor's childhood, written by his cousin and early companion, Marion Campbell; those who shared with me the burden of typing, especially my daughter Kirsteen and Mrs Brenda Ewing; Morven Cameron, who helped me proof-read; and my daughter Seona, who prepared the Index.

Speaking of Scotland

What do you mean when you speak of Scotland?
The grey defeats that are dead and gone
behind the legends each generation
savours afresh, yet can't live on?

Lowland farms with their broad acres
peopling crops? The colder earth
of the North East? Or Highland mountains
shouldering up their rocky dearth?

Inheritance of guilt that our country
has never stood where we feel she should?
A nagging threat of unfinished struggle
somehow forever lost in the blood?

Scotland's a sense of change, an endless
becoming for which there was never a kind
of wholeness or ultimate category.
Scotland's an attitude of mind.

Maurice Lindsay

PLACES

North of Berwick

Slowly the sea is parted from the sky:
The light surprises, crinkling on the water.
The white sun hardens; cliffs solidify.
A long coast of red rock where three swans fly
Engraves itself in calm, deceptive weather.

Three swans fly north, a diesel thumping south
Draws out of sight along the rusting railway,
All windows clouded with a communal breath.
Fields flash in the sunlight, far beneath
The sea turns in its scales, well in a seal's way.

No boat invades that shining emptiness.
Because the waves are distant, the sky windless,
That pale line round the shore looks motionless.
Hearing such border warfare lost in space
You say the breathing of the sea is endless.

What is the one thing constant? Can you say?
The loneliness that we are born to merges
Perhaps with such a place on such a day.
No stones cry out because we cannot stay.
Through all our absences the long tide surges.

Sydney Tremayne (1912–1980)

The Tweed

The Tweed did not inspire the unknown poets in the magic way of the spring Hippocrene, but it was an indirect cause of inspiration. Forming with the Liddel Water a doubtful boundary between two hostile nations, it gave rise to strife, set the stage for real alarms and excursions, in which they found inspiring subjects. The Scots often crossed the Border, in private raids or, as Shakespeare knew, in open invasion, if the English were elsewhere engaged. To King Henry V, contemplating war with France, Westmoreland points out,

> ... the eagle England being in prey,
> To her unguarded nest the weasel Scot
> Comes sneaking, and so sucks her princely eggs.

But everything shows that the Scots suffered more in the end. King David I founded large abbeys, Melrose, Kelso and Jedburgh the most notable, and while we cannot doubt the piety of saintly Queen Margaret's son in doing so, it may have been with the hope that their lands would be respected as sanctuaries by the English. But a ruin like Jedburgh Abbey tells a different story. Enough remains to make it impressive, but little is left of Jedburgh Castle, where at the marriage of Alexander III, presaging his death, the dancing skeleton appeared; like Roxburgh Castle it was destroyed by the Scots themselves to prevent its further occupation by the English. The Crown gave grants of land to the Border towns in the hope that it would be in the citizens' interest to defend them; the citizens still proudly keep up their Common Ridings, but apart from a few odd buildings, such as Queen Mary's House in Jedburgh, these towns themselves are gone. We need not look for old towns in the Border country; only the names are ancient. Roxburgh, the largest of them, was never rebuilt; as it had a convent, a mint and a palace, it is a remarkable case of a town disappearing to, literally, its last stone.

Andrew Young (1885–1971)
A Prospect of Britain

Living in Edinburgh

Kilmarnock-born Alexander Smith followed his father's trade of pattern designer in Glasgow, but was appointed Secretary of Edinburgh University in the wake of the reputation created by his poems, particularly 'A Life Drama' and 'City Poems'. W. E. Aytoun, however, attacked him in 'Firmillian' for those qualities which led him to be dubbed the leader of the 'spasmodic' school of poetry. 'A Summer in Skye', first published in 1865, is one of the finest Scottish travel books written, and has rarely been out of print since it appeared.

Living in Edinburgh there abides, above all things, a sense of its beauty. Hill, crag, castle, rock, blue stretch of sea, the picturesque ridge of the Old Town, the squares and terraces of the New—these things seen once are not to be forgotten. The quick life of to-day sounding around the relics of antiquity, and over-shadowed by the august traditions of a Kingdom, makes residence in Edinburgh more impressive than in any other British city. I have just come in—surely it never looked so fair before! What a poem is that Princes Street! The puppets of the busy, many-coloured hour move about on its pavements, while across the ravine Time has piled up the Old Town, ridge on ridge, grey as a rocky coast washed and worn by the foam of centuries; peaked and jagged by gable and roof; windowed from basement to cope; the whole surmounted by St Giles' airy crown. The New is there looking at the Old. Two Times are brought face to face, and are yet separated by a thousand years. Wonderful on winter nights, when the gully is filled with darkness, and out of it rises, against the sombre blue and the frosty stars, that mass and bulwark of gloom, pierced and quivering with innumerable lights. There is nothing in Europe to match that, I think.

Alexander Smith (1830–67)
A Summer in Skye

An Edinburgh Day

In this extract from Robert Fergusson's poem 'Auld Reekie', the progress of an Edinburgh day about the year 1770 is described. Only the beginnings of the New Town were then in existence, the bustling life of the City still centring around the Old Town, with its cadies or messengers, its chairmen to light the progress of sedan chairs, and its close-packed mixture of the wealthy, including the 'macaronies' or young dandies, the rogues, and what the nineteenth century came to call the 'deserving poor'. A distant echo of this bustling, smelly life—the citizens still emptied the contents of their chamber-pots, called 'Edina's roses', into the street—is outwardly preserved in some of the buildings on present-day High Street.

Now morn, with bonny purpie-smiles,
Kisses the air-cock o' St Giles;
Rakin their ein, the servant lasses   [eyes
Early begin their lies and clashes: [arguments
Ilk tells her friend of saddest distress,   [each
That still she brooks frae scouling mistress;
And wi' her joe in turnpike stair
She'd rather snuff the stinking air,
As be subjected to her tongue,
When justly censur'd in the wrong.

On stair wi' tub, or pat in hand,
The barefoot housemaids looe to stand,
That antrin fock may ken how snell   [other people . . . sharp
Auld Reikie will at morning smell: [The Nor' Loch lay
Then, with an inundation big as   where the railway
The burn that 'neath the nore loch brig is,   line to Waverley
They kindly shower Edina's Roses,   Station is now.

To quicken and regale our noses.
Now some for this, wi' satyr's leesh
Ha'e gi'en auld Edinburgh a creesh:
But without souring nocht is sweet;
The morning smells that hail our street,
Prepare, and gently lead the way,
To simmer canty, braw and gay:
Edina's sons mair eithly share,
Her spices and her dainties rare,
Then he that's never yet been call'd
Aff frae his plaidie or his fauld.

Now stairhead critics, senseless fools,
Censure their aim, and pride their rules,
In Luckenbooths, wi' glouring eye,
Their neighbours sma'est faults descry:
If ony loun should dander there,
Of aukward gate, and foreign air,
They trace his steps, till they can tell
His pedigree as weel's himsell.

Whan Phoebus blinks wi' warmer ray
And schools at noonday get the play,
Then bus'ness, weighty bus'ness comes;
The trader glours; he doubts, he hums:
The lawyers eke to Cross repair,
Their wigs to shaw, and toss an air;
While busy agent closely plies,
And a' his kittle cases tries.

Now Night, that's cunzied chief for fun,
Is wi' her usual rites begun;
Thro' ilka gate the torches blaze,
And globes send out their blinking rays.
The usefu' cadie plies in street,
To bide the profits o' his feet;
For by thir lads Auld Reikie's fock
Ken but a sample, o' the stock
O' thieves, that nightly wad oppress,
And make baith goods and gear the less . . .

Near some lamp-post, wi' dowy face,
Wi' heavy ein, and sour grimace,
Stands she that beauty lang had kend,
Whoredom her trade, and vice her end.
But see wharenow she wuns her bread

By that which Nature ne'er decreed;
And sings sad music to the lugs,
'Mang burachs o' damn'd whores and rogues . . .

Frae joyous tavern, reeling drunk,
Wi' fiery phizz, and ein half sunk,
Behad the bruiser, fae to a'
That in the reek o' gardies fa':
Close by his side, a feckless race
O' macaronies shew their face,
And think they're free frae skaith or harm,
While pith befriends their leaders arm:
Yet fearfu' aften o' their maught,
They quatt the glory o' the faught
To this same warrior wha led
Thae heroes to bright honour's bed;
And aft the hack o' honour shines
In bruiser's face wi' broken lines;
Of them sad tales he tells anon,
Whan ramble and whan fighting's done;
And, like Hectorian, ne'er impairs
The brag and glory o' his sairs.

Whan feet in dirty gutters plash,
And fock to wale their fitstaps fash;
At night the macaroni drunk,
In pools or gutters aftimes sunk;
Hegh! what a fright he now appears,
Whan he his corpse dejected rears!
Look at that head, and think if there
The pomet slaister'd up his hair!
The cheeks observe where now cou'd shine
The scancing glories o' carmine?
Ah, legs! in vain the silk-worm there
Display'd to view her eidant care;
For stink, instead of perfumes, grow,
And clarty odours fragrant flow.

Now some to porter, some to punch,
Some to their wife, and some their wench,
Retire, while noisy ten-hours drum
Gars a' your trades gae dandring home.
Now mony a club, jocose and free,
Gie a' to merriment and glee,
Wi sang and glass, they fley the pow'r

O' Care that wad harrass the hour:
For wine and Bacchus still bear down
Our thrawart Fortune's wildest frown:
It makes you stark, and bauld and brave,
Ev'n whan descending to the grave.

Robert Fergusson (1750–74)
from *Auld Reekie*

The Uniqueness of Edinburgh

*John Gibson Lockhart married Scott's daughter, Sophia. Educated as a lawyer,
Lockhart became a brilliant journalist, and a penetrating, though sometimes
savage, critic.*

   *The book from which this view of Edinburgh is taken is couched in the form of a
series of letters by an imaginary Welsh doctor.*

Edinburgh, even were its population as great as that of London, could never
be merely a city. Here there must always be present the idea of the comparative littleness of all human works. Here the proudest of palaces must be
content to catch the shadows of mountains; and the grandest of fortresses to
appear like the dwellings of pigmies, perched on the very bulwarks of creation. Everywhere—all around—you have rocks frowning over rocks in
imperial elevation, and descending, among the smoke and dust of a city, into
dark depths. such as nature alone can excavate. The builders of the old city
too, appear as if they had made nature the model of their architecture. Seen
through the lowering mist which almost perpetually envelops them, the
huge masses of these erections, so high, so rugged in their outlines, so heaped
together, and conglomerated and wedged into each other, are not easily to
be distinguished from the yet larger and bolder forms of cliff and ravine,
among which their foundations have been pitched. There is a certain gloomy
indistinctness in the formation of these fantastic piles, which leaves the eye
that would scrutinize and penetrate them, unsatisfied and dim with gazing.

John Gibson Lockhart (1794–1854)
Peter's Letters to his Kinsfolk

The Winds of Edinburgh

As this Town is situated on the borders of the sea, and surrounded by hills
of an immense height, the currents of air are carried down between them

with a rapidity and a violence which nothing can resist. It has frequently been known, that in the New Town at Edinburgh three or four people have scarce been able to shut the door of the house; and it is a very common accident to hear of sedan chairs being overturned . . .

At other times, the winds, instead of rushing down with impetuosity, whirl about in eddies, and become still more dreadful. On these occasions it is almost impossible to stir out of doors, as the dust and stones gathered up in these vortices not only prevent your seeing, but frequently cut your legs by the velocity with which they are driven. The Scotch have a peculiar appellation for this, '*The Stour*'.

The chief scene where these winds exert their influence, is the New Bridge, which, by being thrown over a long valley that is open at both ends, and particularly from being ballustraded on each side, admits the wind in the most charming manner imaginable; and you receive it with the same force you would do, were it conveyed to you through a pair of bellows. It is far from unentertaining for a man to pass over this bridge on a tempestuous day. In walking over it this morning I had the pleasure of adjusting a lady's petticoats which had blown almost entirely over her head, and which prevented her disengaging herself from the situation she was in: but in charity to her distresses, I concealed her charms from public view. One poor gentleman, who was rather too much engaged with the novelty of the objects before him, unfortunately forgot his own hat and wig, which were lifted up by an unpremeditated puff, and carried entirely away.

Edward Topham (1751–1819)
Letters from Edinburgh

Haar in Princes Street

The heicht o the biggins is happit in rauchens o haar,   [sea-mist
    The statues alane
  Stand clearlie, heid til fit in stane,
And lour frae *then* and *thonder* at *henceforth* and *here*.

The past on pedestals, girnan frae ilka feature,
    Wi granite frouns
  They glower at the present's feckless loons,
Its gangrels tint i the haar that fankles the future.

The fowk o flesh, stravaigan wha kens whither,
    And come frae whar,
  Hudder lik ghaists i the gastrous haar,
Forfochten and wae i the smochteran smore o the weather.

They swaiver and flirn i the freeth like straes i the sea,
        An artless swither,
    Steeran awa the t'ane frae t'ither,
Alane, and lawlie aye to be lanesome sae.

But heich i the lift (whar the haar is skailan fairlie
        In blufferts o wind)
    And blacker nor nicht whan starns are blind,
The Castle looms, a fell, a fabulous ferlie.

Dragonish, darksome, dourlie grapplan the Rock
        Wi claws o stane
    That scart our historie bare til the bane,
It braks like Fate throu Time's wanchancy reek.

                                    Alexander Scott (*b.* 1920)

Edinburgh

The ancient and famous metropolis of the North sits overlooking a windy
estuary from the slope and summit of three hills. No situation could be more
commanding for the head city of a kingdom; none better chosen for noble
prospects. From her tall precipices and terraced gardens she looks far and
wide on the sea and broad champaigns. To the east you may catch at sunset
the spark of the May lighthouse, where the Firth expands into the German
Ocean; and away to the west, over all the carse of Stirling, you can see the
first snows upon Ben Ledi.

But Edinburgh pays cruelly for her high seat in one of the vilest climates
under heaven. She is liable to be beaten upon by all the winds that blow, to
be drenched with rain, to be buried in cold sea fogs out of the east, and
powdered with the snow as it comes flying southward from the Highland
hills. The weather is raw and boisterous in winter, shifty and ungenial in
summer, and a downright meteorological purgatory in the spring. The delicate die early, and I, as a survivor, among bleak winds and plumping rain,
have been sometimes tempted to envy them their fate. For all who love
shelter and the blessings of the sun, who hate dark weather and perpetual
tilting against squalls, there could scarcely be found a more unhomely and
harassing place of residence. Many such aspire angrily after that Somewhere-
else of the imagination, where all troubles are supposed to end. They lean
over the great bridge which joins the New Town with the Old—that windiest
spot, or high altar, in this northern temple of the winds—and watch the
trains smoking out from under them and vanishing into the tunnel on a
voyage to brighter skies. Happy the passengers who shake off the dust of
Edinburgh, and have heard for the last time the cry of the east wind among

her chimney-tops! And yet the place establishes an interest in people's hearts; go where they will, they find no city of the same distinction; go where they will, they take pride in their old home.

R. L. Stevenson (1850–94)
Picturesque Notes on Edinburgh

November Night, Edinburgh

The night tinkles like ice in glasses.
Leaves are glued to the pavement with frost.
The brown air fumes at the shop windows,
Tries the doors, and sidles past.

I gulp down winter raw. The heady
Darkness swirls with tenements.
In a brown fuzz of cottonwool
Lamps fade up crags, die into pits.

Frost in my lungs is harsh as leaves
Scraped up on paths.—I look up, there,
A high roof sails, at the mast-head
Fluttering a grey and ragged star.

The world's a bear shrugged in his den.
It's snug and close in the snoring night.
And outside like chrysanthemums
The fog unfolds its bitter scent.

Norman MacCaig (*b.* 1910)

A New Town Memory

Now that we have learned to appreciate the beauty and the order and the decency and the nobility of the New Town (and incidentally have turned it into a conglomeration of business premises, offices, flats, hotels and lodging houses) it is easy to dismiss as stuffy, late and post-Victorians those who once actually lived in these buildings as houses. It is easy, because there would be a certain amount of justice and reason in that desire to smile. After all, they were late-Victorian or post-Victorian, and they were a trifle stuffy.

Let it not be thought, however, that the present chronicler smiles (if he smile at all) in anything but affectionate remembrance of that now half-forgotten world in which the houses of the New Town really were houses. He recalls with nostalgia that is not wholly sentimental those vast green doors at the top of a wide flight of steps, the bell-pull, long and solid, framed in a wide square of gleaming and always polished brass, the number of the house standing out also in bold and equally new polished brass Roman figures upon the woodwork of the door. He remembers how, when the door was opened to him by a maid in stiff starched linen, he was admitted into a hall which, to his childish eyes, seemed as large and as dark as a church. He remembers the size of the hat rack, of the press for the men's overcoats, the huge round dinner gong standing by the stairs, whose polished surface caught and reflected only the most transient gleams of Edinburgh daylight. He remembers the dining-room to the right of the hall, again huge, brown and ill-lit, with dark curtains over the enormous windows. He sees once more that long dining-table of dully gleaming mahogany, capable of being lengthened even more by the insertion of flaps so that it could seat twenty of a family at Christmas time, New Year, or upon reunions. It is a room which to him recalls domestic devotion as much as domestic festivity; for it was here, every morning, that family prayers were held.

How vividly the memory of those large Edinburgh New Town family prayers return to mind. Daily domestic devotions were of course not uncommon at that time in Scotland, and even in England—though it is true that in the first decade of this century the custom was on the decline—but surely few family prayers elsewhere could have acquired quite the rich and solemn ceremonial of those held in the dining-rooms of the New Town. Himself the head of the family would be seated at the end of the table nearest the huge curtained windows. On either side, flanking him in crescent form, were the members of his family, his wife on his right hand, his eldest daughter on his left, and at the ends of the crescent were the children. When the family was seated, a bell was rung, and the servants trooped in in reverse order of seniority, the butler or manservant (if there was one) bringing up the rear, marching his female brood before him like a barnyard fowl with his hens. There would be the solemn reading of God's word; then, upon the injunction 'Let us pray' there would be a scraping of chairs, a susurration of skirts, and the whole company of twenty or more would, with one exception, turn, kneel, and bury their faces in the chairs on which they had been sitting. The one exception was the head of the house. He, still seated, would but bend his head over the open Bible on the table before him and, with clasped hands and closed eyes, address our Creator on behalf of his family and his servants in the New Town of Edinburgh. Permeating the atmosphere, like incense in a cathedral, there was the scent of sausages, bacon, fresh coffee and old leather. How evocative, even now, is that combination of almost forgotten smells.

Moray McLaren (1901–72)
The Capital of Scotland

An Edinburgh Childhood

I was born in this city of grey stone and bitter wind,
Of tenements sooted up with lying history:
This place where dry minds grow crusts of hate, as rocks
Grow lichens. I went to school over the high bridge
Fringed with spikes which, curiously, repel the suicides;
And I slept opposite the rock-garden where the survivors,
Who had left Irving and Mallory under the sheet of snow,
Planted the incarvillea and saxifrages of the Himalayas.

And, as I grew in childhood, I learned the knack to slip
The breech-block of the field-gun in the park, peering
Along the rifled barrel I would enclose a small circle
Of my world, marked out for death; death as unreal
As the gun's forgotten action under the hot African sun.
Growing older, I met other and more frequent ghosts,
Lying to preserve the remnants of a reputation.

Knox spoke sweetly in the Canongate—'I was not cruel
To gaunt Mary, the whore denying the hand that lit the fuse.'
Charles Stuart returned, alive only to the past, his venture
That was little but a dream, forgetting the squat bottle,
Quivered in the lace-veined hand and the unseeing sharpness of his eyes.
Bruce could not stir the cobwebs from his skeleton,
And the editor spoke regretfully, but firmly, of poor Keats.

Here the boy Rimbaud paused, flying love and lust,
Unnoticed on his journey to the Abyssinian plains
And the thick dropsy of his tender leg. Here the other Knox,
Surgeon and anatomist, saw the beauty of the young girl
Smothered by Burke and Hare. And here, O certainly,
God was the private property of a chosen few
Whose lives ran carefully and correctly to the grave.

This, deny it as I like, is still my city and these ghosts,
Sneer as I may, have helped to make me what I am.
A woman cried in labour and Simpson inhaled his vapour
Falling, anaesthetized, across the drawing-room table.
John Graham, laird of Claverhouse, did not have tears
For those he killed, nor did the silver bullet weep for him.
This city, bulwark of the eastwind, formed me as I am.

Ruthven Todd (1914–1978)
In Edinburgh 1940

A European City

It is a northern town, there is no doubt of that. We have to think of it as compared, for instance, with Copenhagen. And what an individuality it has! To an Englishman, whose first sight of Edinburgh came nearly last of all the cities in Europe that he had visited, the tall houses in the wynds are unlike anything else in experience. Can old Paris have been like this, before the Revolution? But if the colour of the houses may have been the same on rainy winter days, the very material is different. Paris was always a city of dilapidated paint and stucco. Edinburgh, by contrary, is a town of dark, grey stone. The inhabitants of Edinburgh were flat dwellers long before this economy had dawned upon the minds of other races. There are but few towns still retaining such a nucleus of mediaeval buildings. And the system of wynds is a Scottish or north-country contrivance. It is even to be seen in its beginnings in towns like Leeds or Sheffield, where, in their older parts, an infinity of courts and obscure passages lead off from the street. It is this plan of building which was developed and heightened in old Edinburgh.

The long extent of the High Street and Canongate, leading down to Holyrood, has traits about it that recall both Naples and Nuremburg. In no other city but Naples is such a degree of poverty to be found so near a royal palace; while nowhere else but in Nuremburg is there such an assembly of ancient dwellings. In the time of Sir Walter Scott it was said that the High Street was the loveliest street in any town of Europe. This is an opinion with which few contemporary persons would be found to concur. Those who appreciate mediaeval houses would prefer those of Chester, or Shrewsbury; of Hildesheim and Dinkelsbühl, but not of Rothenburg in Germany. Rothenburg is too suggestive of the comic drawings of Heath Robinson. But Chester and Shrewsbury, or the best German mediaeval towns such as the aforementioned Hildesheim or Dinkelsbühl, have a wealth of exterior decoration which is altogether lacking in the High Street or Canongate of Edinburgh. Elaborate interiors these houses did certainly possess, some few of which are still preserved, unspoilt; but this tract of the old town is chiefly interesting historically. It has an historical, and not an aesthetic, interest.

Nothing, it is certain, could be more romantic than the associations of Holyrood. It is for ever haunted for us by Mary, Queen of Scots, and by the Young Chevalier. Is it, though, as interesting as the chain of circumstances would lead one to suppose? This question is easily answered. Holyrood is of absorbing interest; but not, again, of any artistic importance. It is of no use to compare Holyrood with the Doge's Palace, or even with Hampton Court or Windsor Castle. And the same stricture applies, perhaps, to the churches of Edinburgh. Few churches, anywhere in Europe, have more drama in association with their history than St. Giles's; but iconoclasm has removed most of the vestiges, and certainly all the ornaments, of that history. However, the façade of the Parliament building, close by, is a reminder of the other, or classical Edinburgh. It is this which constitutes the beauty of the capital. Charlotte Square should be, in itself, sufficient evidence that this is true. It may be that Moray Place and Ainslie Place have become too familiar a sight to their inhabitants; but to the eyes of a stranger they present, as do many of the streets in their vicinity, the appearance of a more sober and solid Bath. To one writer, at any rate, this part of Edinburgh has a human, as well as an aesthetic interest, which is not shared by the mere historical association of the other town. Robert Adam, Playfair, or Gillespie, the architects of the 'Modern Athens' are, according to this opinion, the persons to whom the true beauty of Edinburgh is due.

And there is, of course, Edinburgh Castle. It is undeniably magnificent, even if this same heretical opinion can see nothing to admire in the Scottish War Memorial, except in the spirit in which it was built and the emotion with which it is regarded. Let us turn, then, from the Memorial to the Castle. This cliff or hill, has been besieged on more occasions, it is probable, than any other castle in Europe. This spot is, in fact, the history of Scotland. And the view from here, looking down over Edinburgh, is a thing not easily forgotten. Once again, the thickness of those grey stone walls is impressive, and the Castle looks as if it could once more withstand a siege. We may hope and trust that this will never happen, but the lesson of the Alcazar, in Toledo, goes to prove how long such ancient fortifications can still resist.

Down below, at the foot of the hill, there is Princes Street. And how is it possible to write of Edinburgh without extolling Princes Street! There is to a foreigner in Edinburgh—for an Englishman does feel a foreigner in Edinburgh, even if a favoured one—the charm of seeing so many peculiarly Scottish products exposed for sale in the shop windows. We refer, not only to the tartans, but to the tea shops and sweet shops, and this must be, to ourselves, the peculiar attraction in Princes Street. It is, also, almost a pleasure to be able, without reservation, to admire a railway line; and this, upon mature reflection, is our considered opinion of the mass of lines uniting the Waverley and Caledonian Stations. A garden along the whole of that ravine would not have the glamour and modernity of this, it must be admitted, exceptionally quiet and well behaved railway line. In any case, it is too late, now, to complain, for this railway is, to Edinburgh, what the Grand Canal is to Venice. The only sadness comes when we think how gladly the Venetians would hand over their Grand Canal in exchange for this congery of lines. But this cannot be accomplished. Venice has to keep her canal and Edinburgh her railway line. It is better thus, and none should regret it. And, if we accept that, then Princes Street becomes, as is really the truth, perhaps the finest street in Europe.

Sacheverell Sitwell (1897–1988)
Edinburgh (with Francis Bamford)

How Glasgow Cathedral was Saved

Situated in a populous and considerable town, this ancient and massive pile has the appearance of the most sequestered solitude. High walls divide it from the buildings of the city on one side; on the other it is bounded by a ravine, at the bottom of which, and invisible to the eye, murmurs a wandering rivulet, adding, by its gentle noise, to the imposing solemnity of the scene. On the opposite side of the ravine rises a steep bank, covered with fir-trees closely planted, whose dusky shade extends itself over the cemetery with an appropriate and gloomy effect. The churchyard itself has a peculiar character; for though in reality extensive, it is small in proportion to the number of respectable inhabitants who are interred within it, and whose graves are almost all covered with tombstones. There is therefore no room for the long rank grass, which, in most cases, partially clothes the surface of those retreats, where the wicked cease from troubling, and the weary are at rest. The broad flat monumental stones are placed so close to each other, that the precincts appear to be flagged with them, and, though roofed only by the heavens, resemble the floor of one of our old English churches, where the pavement is covered with sepulchral inscriptions. The contents of these sad records of mortality, the vain sorrows which they preserve, the stern lesson which they teach of the nothingness of humanity, the extent of ground which they so closely cover, and their uniform and melancholy tenor, reminded me of the roll of the prophet, which was 'written within and without, and there was written therein lamentations and mourning and woe.'

The Cathedral itself corresponds in impressive majesty with these accompaniments. We feel that its appearance is heavy, yet that the effect produced would be destroyed were it lighter or more ornamental. It is the only metropolitan church in Scotland, excepting, as I am informed, the Cathedral of Kirkwall, in the Orkneys, which remained uninjured at the Reformation; and Andrew Fairservice, who saw with great pride the effect which it produced upon my mind, thus accounted for its preservation. 'Ah! it's a brave kirk; nane o' yere whigmaleeries and curliewurlies and opensteek hems about it—a' solid, weel-jointed masonwark, that will stand as lang as the warld, keep hands and gunpowther aff it. It had amaist a douncome lang syne at the Reformation, when they pu'd doun the kirks of St Andrews and Perth, and there-awa', to cleanse them o' Papery, and idolatry, and image worship, and surplices, and sic-like rags o' the muckle hure that sitteth on seven hills, as if ane wasna braid eneugh for her auld hinder end. Sae the commons o' Renfrew, and o' the Barony, and the Gorbals, and a' about, they behoved to come into Glasgow ae fair morning, to try their hand on purging the High Kirk o' popish nick-nackets. But the townsmen o' Glasgow, they were feared their auld edifice might slip the girths in gaun through siccan rough physic, sae they rang the common bell, and assembled the train-bands wi' took o' drum. By good luck, the worthy James Rabat was Dean o' Guild that year—(and a gude mason he was himsell, made him the keener to keep

up the auld bigging)—and the trades assembled, and offered downright
battle to the commons, rather than their kirk should coup the crans, as others
had done elsewhere. It wasna for luve o' Paperie—na, na!—nane could ever
say that o' the trades o' Glasgow. Sae they sune came to an agreement to
take a' the idolatrous statues of sants (sorrow be on them) out o' their neuks.
And sae the bits o' stane idols were broken in pieces by Scripture warrant,
and flung into the Molendinar burn, and the auld kirk stood as crouse as a
cat when the flaes are kaimed aff her, and a'body was alike pleased. And I hae
heard wise folk say that if the same had been done in ilka kirk in Scotland,
the Reform wad just hae been as pure as it is e'en now, and we wad hae mair
Christian-like kirks; for I hae been sae lang in England, that naething will
drived out o' my head that the dog-kennel at Osbaldistone Hall is better than
mony a house o' God in Scotland.'

Thus saying, Andrew led the way into the place of worship.

Sir Walter Scott (1771–1832)
Rob Roy

Glasgow in the Eighteenth Century

Hail, Glasgow! famed for ilka thing
That heart can wish or siller bring!
May Peace, wi' healing on her wing,
   Aye nestle here;
And Plenty gar thy childer sing
   The lee-lang year!

Within the tinkling o' they bells,
How mony a happy body dwells!
Where they get bread they ken themsels;
   But I'll declare
They're aye bien-like, and, what precels,   [comfortable-looking
   Hae fouth to spare.

If ye've a knacky son or twa,
To Glasgow College send them a',
Wi' whilk, for gospel, or for law,
   Or classic lair,
Ye'll find few places herawa'
   That can compare . . .

In ilka house, frae man to boy,
A' hands in Glasgow find employ;
Even little maids, wi' meikle joy,
   Flower lawn and gauze,

Or clip wi' care the silken soy
　　For ladies' braws.

Their fathers weave, their mothers spin
The muslin robe, so fine and thin
That, frae the ankle to the chin,
　　It aft discloses
The beauteous symmetry within—
　　Limbs, neck, and bosies.

Look through the town! The houses here
Like noble palaces appear;
A' things the face o' gladness wear—
　　The market's thrang,
Business is brisk, and a's asteer
　　The streets alang.

Clean-keepit streets! so lang and braid,
The distant objects seem to fade;
And then, for shelter or for shade
　　Frae sun or shower,
Piazzas lend their friendly aid
　　At ony hour.

Wond'ring, we see new streets extending,
New squares wi' public buildings blending,
Brigs, stately brigs, in arches bending
　　Across the Clyde,
And turrets, kirks, and spires ascending
　　In lofty pride. . . .

'Tween twa and three wi' daily care,
The gentry to the cross repair—
The politician, wi' grave air,
　　Deliberating;
Merchants and manufacturers there
　　Negotiating.

It's not by slothfulness and ease
That Glasgow's canty ingles bleeze;
To gi'e her inland trade a heeze
　　As weel's her foreign,
She's joined the east and western seas
　　Together, roaring.

Frae Forth, athort the land, to Clyde,
Her barks a' winds and weathers glide,
And on the bosom o' the tide,
   Wi' gentle motion,
Her vessels like a forest ride
   And kiss auld Ocean. . . .

Hence commerce spreads her sails to a'
The Indies and America:
Whatever mak's ae penny twa,
   By wind or tide
Is wafted to the Broomielaw
   On bonnie Clyde.

O Glasgow! famed for ilka thing
That heart can wish or siller bring!
May nowther care nor sorrow ding
   Thy childer dear,
But peace and plenty gar them sing
   Fra'e year to year!

                                                John Mayne (1759–1836)
                                                Glasgow

Glasgow

*In Smollett's novel 'The Expedition of Humphry Clinker', young Jerry Melford
writes to an Oxford friend, and Matthew Bramble, his uncle, to his family
doctor. The university referred to is, of course, the mediaeval College, abandoned
in 1870 in favour of the present Gothic structure on Gilmorehill. John Golborne
carried out the first deepening operation on the upper Clyde. Subsequent
operations opened the Clyde to up-river traffic, and Port Glasgow then became
a shipbuilding and engineering town.*

Glasgow is the pride of Scotland, and indeed it might very well pass for an
elegant and flourishing city in any part of Christendom. . . . Considering the
trade and opulence of this place, it cannot but abound with gaiety and
diversions. Here is a great number of young fellows that rival the youth of
the capital in spirit and expense; and I was soon convinced, that all the
female beauties of Scotland were not assembled at the hunters' ball in
Edinburgh. The town of Glasgow flourishes in learning as well as in commerce. Here is an university, with professors in all the different branches of
science, liberally endowed, and judiciously chosen. . . . Their mode of
education is certainly preferable to ours in some respects. The students are
not left to the private instruction of tutors, but taught in public schools or

classes, each science by its particular professor or regent. My uncle is in raptures with Glasgow. . . .

His Uncle writes:

I am so far happy as to have seen Glasgow, which, to the best of my recollection and judgment, is one of the prettiest towns in Europe; and without all doubt, it is one of the most flourishing in Great Britain. In short, it is a perfect bee-hive in point of industry. It stands partly on a gentle declivity; but the greatest part of it is in a plain, watered by the river Clyde. The streets are straight, open, airy, and well paved; and the houses lofty and well built, of hewn stone. At the upper end of the town, there is a venerable cathedral, that may be compared with York-minster or Westminster; and, about the middle of the descent from this to the Cross, is the College, a respectable pile of building, with all manner of accommodation for the professors and students, including an elegant library, and an observatory well provided with astronomical instruments. The number of inhabitants is said to amount to thirty thousand; and marks of opulence and independency appear in every quarter of this commercial city, which, however, is not without its inconveniences and defects. The water of their public pumps is generally hard and brackish, an imperfection the less excusable, as the river Clyde runs by their doors, in the lower part of the town; and there are rivulets and springs above the cathedral, sufficient to fill a large reservoir with excellent water, which might be thence distributed to all the different parts of the city. It is of more consequence to consult the health of the inhabitants in this article than to employ so much attention in beautifying their town with new streets, squares and churches.

Another defect, not easily remedied, is the shallowness of the river, which will not float vessels of any burden within ten or twelve miles of the city; so that the merchants are obliged to load and unload their ships at Greenock and Port-Glasgow, situated about fourteen miles nearer the mouth of the firth, where it is about two miles broad. The people of Glasgow have a noble spirit of enterprise.

Tobias Smollett (1721-1771)
The Expedition of Humphry Clinker

Glasgow Through French Eyes

Faujas St Fond, the French lawyer and geologist who became Professor of Geology at the Muséum d'Histoire Naturelle in Paris, made an extensive tour of England and Scotland, stimulated by the writings of Sir Joseph Banks and Thomas Pennant, in which they described Staffa and its geological characteristics.

I was greatly astonished, in a climate so cold and moist as that of Glasgow, to see the greater part of the lower class of women, and even many of those in easy circumstances, going about with bare feet and bare heads, their bodies covered only with a bodice, petticoat and a cloak of red stuff, which descends to the middle of their legs; their fine long hair hanging down without any other ornament than a simple curved comb to keep back what would otherwise fall over their faces. This garb of the females, quite simple as it is, is not without grace, and since nothing impedes their movements, they have an elegance and agility in their gait so much the more striking, as they are in general tall, well made, and of a charming figure. They have a bright complexion, and very white teeth. It is not to be inferred, because they walk bare-legged, that they are neglectful of cleanliness; for it appears that they wash frequently, and with equal facility, both their feet and their hands. . . .

The vicinity of the mountains attracts a considerable number of High-landers to this city. Their antique costume, much resembling that of the Roman soldiers, forms a remarkable contrast with the dress of the women and the other inhabitants. . . . In the environs of Glasgow a considerable number of mines yield coal of excellent quality. These make manufacturers and commerce to prosper; and thereby increase the happiness of the inhabitants.

Bartholomew Faujas St Fond (1741–1819)
Travels in England and Scotland

Victorian Glasgow

City! I am true son of thine;
Ne'er dwelt I where great mornings shine
    Around the bleating pens;
Ne'er by the rivulets I strayed,
And ne'er upon my childhood weighed
    The silence of the glens.
Instead of shores where ocean beats,
I hear the ebb and flow of streets.

Black Labour draws his weary waves.
Into their secret-moaning caves;
    But with the morning light,
The sea again will overflow
With a long weary sound of woe,
    Again to faint in night.
Wave am I in that sea of woes;
Which, night and morning, ebbs and flows.

I dwelt within a gloomy court
Wherein did never sunbeam sport;

Yet there my heart was stirr'd—
My very blood did dance and thrill,
When on my narrow window-sill,
    Spring lighted like a bird.
Poor flowers—I watched them pine for weeks,
With leaves as pale as human cheeks.

Afar, one summer, I was borne;
Through golden vapours of the morn,
    I heard the hills of sheep:
I trod with a wild ecstasy
The bright fringe of the living sea:
    And on a ruined keep
I sat, and watched an endless plain
Blacken beneath the gloom of rain.

O fair the lightly sprinkled waste,
O'er which a laughing shower has raced!
    O fair the April shoots!
O fair the woods on summer days,
While a blue hyacinthine haze
    Is dreaming round the roots!
In thee! O City! I discern
Another beauty, sad and stern.

Draw thy fierce streams of blinding ore,
Smite on a thousand anvils, roar
    Down to the harbour-bars;
Smoulder in smoky sunsets, flare
On rainy nights, with street and square
    Lie empty to the stars.
From terrace proud to alley base
I know thee as my mother's face.

When sunset bathes thee in his gold,
In wreathes of bronze thy sides are rolled,
    Thy smoke is dusky fire;
And, from the glory round thee poured,
A sunbeam like an angel's sword
    Shivers upon a spire
Thus have I watched thee, Terror! Dream!
While the blue night crept up the stream.

The wild Train plunges in the hills,
He shrieks across the midnight rills;
    Streams through the shifting glare,

The roar and flap of foundry fires,
That shake with light the sleeping shires;
   And on the moorlands bare,
He sees afar a crown of light
Hang o'er thee in the hollow night.

At midnight, when thy suburbs lie
As silent as a noonday sky,
   When larks with heat are mute,
I love to linger on thy bridge,
All lonely as a mountain ridge,
   Disturbed but by my foot;
While the black lazy stream beneath,
Steals from its far-off wilds of heath.

And through my heart, as through a dream,
Flows on that black disdainful stream;
   All scornfully it flows,
Between the huddled gloom of masts,
Silent as pines unvexed by blasts—
   'Tween lamps in streaming rows.
O wondrous sight! O stream of dread!
O long dark river of the dead!

Alexander Smith (1830–67)
from *Glasgow*

Glasgow Football

The players trotted limberly to their positions. For a moment there was
dead silence over Ibrox Park. Then the whistle blew. . . .
   For nearly two hours thereafter Danny Shields lived far beyond himself
in a whirling world of passion. All sorts of racial emotions were released by
this clash of athletic young men; the old clans of Scotland lived again their
ancient hatreds in the struggle for goals. Not a man on the terraces paused to
reflect that it was a spectacle cunningly arranged to draw their shillings, or to
remember that the twenty-two players were so many slaves of a commercial
system, liable to be bought and sold like fallen women, without any regard
for their feelings as men. Rangers had drawn their warriors from all corners of
Scotland, lads from mining villages, boys from Ayrshire farms, and even an
undergraduate from the University of Glasgow. Celtic likewise had ranged
the industrial belt and even crossed to Ulster and the Free State for men fit
to win matches so that dividends might accrue. But for such as Danny they

remained peerless and fearless warriors, saints of the Blue or the Green as it might be; and in delight in the cunning moves of them, in their tricks and asperities, the men on the terraces found release from the drabness of their own industrial degradation.

That release they expressed in ways extremely violent. They exhorted their favourites to dreadful enterprises of assault and battery. They loudly questioned every decision of the referee. In moments of high tension they raved obscenely, using a language ugly and violent in its wealth of explosive consonants—f's and k's and b's expressing the vehemence of their passions.

The young man behind Danny . . . was notable in foulness of speech. His commentary on the game was unceasing, and not an observation could he make but one primitive Anglo-Saxon epithet must qualify every noun—and serve frequently, as a verb. It was as if a fever of hate had seized that multitude, neutralizing for the time everything gracious and kindly.

Yet that passionate horde had its wild and liberating humours. Now and again a flash of rough jocularity would release a gust of laughter, so hearty it was as if they rejoiced to escape from the bondage of their own intensity of partisanship. Once in a while a clever movement by one of the opposition team would evoke a mutter of unwilling but sincere admiration. They were abundantly capable of calling upon their favourites to use their brawn, but they were pontifical in the observation of the unwritten laws that are called those of sportsmanship. They constituted, in fact, a stern but ultimately reliable jury, demanding of their entertainers the very best they could give, insisting that the spectacle be staged with all the vigour that could be brought to it.

The old Firm—thus the evening papers conventionally described the meeting of Rangers and Celtic.

George Blake (1893–1961)
The Shipbuilders

Glasgow Green

Clammy midnight, moonless mist.
A cigarette glows and fades on a cough.
Meth-men mutter on benches,
pawed by river fog. Monteith Row
sweats coldly, crumbles, dies
slowly. All shadows are alive.
Somewhere a shout's forced out—'No!'—
it leads to nothing but silence,
except the whisper of the grass
and the other whispers that fill the shadows.

'What d'ye mean see me again?
D'ye think I came here jist for that?
I'm no finished with you yet.
I can get the boys t'ye, they're no that faur away.
You wouldny like that eh? Look there's no two ways aboot it.
Christ but I'm gaun to have you Mac
if it takes all night, turn over you bastard
turn over, I'll—'

                                    Cut the scene.

Here there's no crying for help,
it must be acted out, again, again.
This is not the delicate nightmare
you carry to the point of fear
and wake from, it is life, the sweat
is real, the wrestling under a bush
is real, the dirty starless river
is the real Clyde, with a dishrag dawn
it rinses the horrors of the night
but cannot make them clean,
though washing blows
                        where the women watch
by day,
          and children run,
                                on Glasgow Green.
And how shall these men live?
Providence, watch them go!
Watch them love, and watch them die!
How shall the race be served?
It shall be served by anguish
as well as by children at play.
It shall be served by loneliness
as well as by family love.
It shall be served by hunter and hunted in their endless chain
as well as by those who turn back the sheets in peace.
The thorn in the flesh!
Providence, water it!
Do you think it is not watered?
Do you think it is not planted?
Do you think there is not a seed of the thorn
as there is also a harvest of the thorn?
Man, take in that harvest!
Help that tree to bear its fruit!
Water the wilderness, walk there, reclaim it!
Reclaim, regain, renew! Fill the barns and vats!

Longing,
          longing
               shall find its wine.

Let the women sit in the Green
and rock their prams as the sheets
blow and whip in the sunlight.
But the beds of married love
are islands in a sea of desire.
Its waves break here, in this park,
splashing the flesh as it trembles
like driftwood through the dark.

                              Edwin Morgan (b. 1920)

Catholic and Protestant

You're either a dirty Orangeman or a Papish bastard. It's much more subtle
than anti-Semitism, and it must be understood that most people in Glasgow
don't spend much time thinking about it at all from one year's end to
another. But it's there, and even the most impartial Glaswegian is likely to
have some feelings based on religion in this restricted sense.

I don't like the Catholic Church myself, on the whole. A religion based on
authority and infallibility seems silly to me, as a philosophical idea, although
its strength as an institution in the political sense must command respect.
Obviously it has something that a lot of people want, and along with its gory
history and its fondness for bigotry and repression (the Protestant Church in
Scotland has a fair amount of blood on its historical hands too) it obviously
has spread a lot of Christian charity and goodwill towards men in the bygoing.

In Glasgow, it represents a very large minority population group which has
a history of social underprivilege. The bulk of Glasgow's Catholics are
descended from Irish immigrants as I am myself. They fled from Irish unemployment and famines and were accepted as a new lower class in Glasgow,
and you can still see it. Whatever the situation is elsewhere, there's nothing
chic about Glasgow Catholicism. It's the religion of the lower classes,
however obsolete the description may sound. The Catholics have a bigger
proportion of poor people than the Protestants. The average child in a
Glasgow Catholic school looks less kempt than the average child in a Glasgow
Protestant school. Absenteeism is commoner among Catholic children than
among Protestants. On the average, Glasgow Catholics probably grow up
more ignorant educationally than Glasgow Protestants.

There are no published statistics covering such facts. There's a lot of
exaggerated conjecture instead. Alarmed Protestants, the brooding kind, are
perpetually afraid of the Roman peril because the Catholic birthrate, as a
result of Rome's rigorous attitude to contraception, is higher than the

Protestant. It is also a fact that people lower down the educational ladder usually reproduce faster in any case. Protestants in Glasgow suspect that the Catholic Church doesn't want its adherents too highly educated. Well, the Church is more concerned with good Catholics than with breeding successful businessmen or eggheads.

On the other hand, you can disprove any generalization about Glasgow Catholics by choosing examples. A rough Protestant school is just as rough as a rough Catholic school. The crack Catholic schools, St Aloysius for example, do just as well in external examinations as the crack Protestant schools like Hutcheson's Grammar. Most of the Protestants who make the generalizations reject the exceptions, if they have heard of them.

Still most of the smartish businessmen's bars in the city contain fewer Catholics at lunch time than Protestants—a lot fewer than the relative population figures justify. And it isn't because Catholics are more temperance-minded than Protestants. There are too few Catholics in the newspaper industry in Glasgow, for instance. Freemasonry is strong among the printing craftsmen, of course, but even in the editorial departments the proportion of Catholics is fairly tiny. It's hard to say that there is any kind of bar against them, because there are notable exceptions. But Protestants tend to mix with Protestants, and to employ Protestants rather than Catholics, other things being even roughly equal. The average Glaswegian isn't bigoted, but he's aware of the fact of religion in this restricted sense. The difficulty is that many Protestants make assumptions about all individual Catholics on the basis of some generalized hostility to the Catholic idea. And Catholics are fairly active assumers too, when the situation arises.

The whole thing is a fearful tangle and it will never be sorted out.

Cliff Hanley (b. 1922)
Dancing in the Streets

Glasgow Nocturne

Materialized from the flaked stones of buildings
dank with neglect and poverty, the pack,
thick-shouldered, slunk through rows of offices
squirting anonymous walls with their own lack

of self-identity. *Tong ya bass*, *Fleet*,
Fuck the Pope, spurted like blood: a smear
protesting to the passing daylight folk
the prowled-up edge of menace, the spoor of fear

that many waters cannot quench, or wash
clean from what hands, what eyes, from what hurt hearts?

O Lord! the preacher posed at the dark gates,
what must we do to be whole in all our parts?

Late on Saturday night, when shopfronts doused
their furniture, contraceptives, clothes and shoes,
violence sneaked out in banded courage,
bored with hopelessness that has nothing to lose.

A side-street shadow eyed two lovers together;
he, lured from the loyalties of the gang
by a waif who wore her sex like a cheap trinket;
she, touched to her woman's need by his wrong

tenderness. On the way from their first dance,
the taste of not enough fumbled their search
of hands and lips endeared in a derelict close.
Over the flarepath of their love, a lurch

thrust from the shadow, circling their twined bodies.
It left them clung before its narrowing threat,
till she shrieked. They peeled her from her lover,
a crumpled sob of a doll dropped in the street,

while he received his lesson: ribs and jaw
broken, kidneys and testicles ruptured, a slit
where the knife licked his groin. Before he died
in the ambulance, she'd vanished. Shops lit

up their furniture, contraceptives, clothes and shoes
again. Next morning, there was a darker stain
than *Tong ya bass* and *Fleet* on the edge of the kerb;
but it disappeared in the afternoon rain.

Maurice Lindsay (b. 1918)

Scotland's Black Country

This picture of the drab environment of industrial Scotland just before the Second World War has since than lightened a little. While post-1965 council housing now and again manages to reconcile good design with the stringent cost restriction made necessary because the Scot often resents having to pay what would be regarded as a reasonable rent by English standards, too often a new kind of unimaginative drabness has replaced the old.

It happened over and over again, notably in Glasgow, that two or three tenement buildings would be set up in close-gathered rows on a feu originally intended for one, the property-owner carrying on the work of social ruination at a time when accommodation had to be provided for the hordes of incomers to the industrial field and nobody had the time or knowledge or enlightenment to give thought to the future. The result, of course, was overcrowding, with all its resultant effects on health and morals. Thus the slums of Glasgow, for instance, became notorious, too many of the people stunted in bodily and mental growth, and a problem established that is not yet solved. So also about the pits something very like slavery put the colliers and their families into those long, bleak, squat insanitary rows that were virtually barracks and still house too large a proportion of the population. The dearness of land finally produced that most characteristic feature of the Scottish urban landscape, the tenement.

That the tenement is an undesirable form of communal dwelling it would be quite absurd to maintain. In the inner suburbs of Glasgow, for instance, it is easily seen that it can be a clean, attractive, convenient and not ungracious item in a city's housing equipment. Manifestly it can be a horror where the constituent apartments are small, the number of the tenants to the block high, and the landlord a mere collector of rents. Otherwise its influences are spiritual. Plainly built of dark, grey stone, long rows of tenements make many Scottish streets seem like canyons in a deserted land of gloom. They oppress the spirit. The domestic life that glows so warmly within would seem to acquire its qualities of cosiness and kindliness from sheer reaction to the unfriendliness of the cliff-like exteriors.

The dullness of the average small town in industrial Scotland suggests one of fate's most cynical conspiracies. It is hard to find one of the lesser places depending on coal and iron that differs much from another. In Lanark and Fife they seem to be all length and no breadth—small houses and tenements strung along an endless Main Street, with an outcrop of Old Red Sandstone on an ambitious shop frontage breaking the monotony here and there and a certain liveliness about the inevitable Cross. There will be a few small villas to house the officials and foremen of local enterprises and the more prosperous shopkeepers, notably the manager of the Co-operative Society. One large villa houses the doctor, another is at once the office and dwelling-house of the banker. Churches in various versions of bogus Gothic testify to the denominational zeal of the Scot, and in most mining districts the Chapel, as the Presbyterian describes the Roman Catholic Church, is liable to be a prominent landmark. (Writings on the walls, referring unpleasantly to the Pope, testify to the abiding strength of religious passions in the descendants of the Covenanters.) There will be a football field somewhere behind the tedious rows of dwellings and probably a bald quoiting pitch. Throw in a public park with some iron swings for the children and a picture-house with a façade in battered stucco, and the picture is more or less complete.

4

Such towns are the creation of the industrial age, and a good deal more sorrow than anger must be brought to the contemplation of them.

George Blake (1893–1961)
The Heart of Scotland

Kirkcudbright

'KIRKCUDBRIGHT COUNTY is very beautiful, very wild with craggy hills somewhat in the Westmorland fashion,' wrote Keats in a letter; and he went on, 'the Country is very rich—very fine—and with a little of Devon.' Though he wrote from the pleasant village of Auchencairn, he may have made the comparisons at Kippford, for there you are in sight of curious craggy hills such as you might see in Westmorland, and the inlet on which it stands has a striking resemblance to a Devon estuary. Such comparisons suggest the rich variety of the Solway coast; nothing appears to be lacking; there are cliffs and rocky headlands, shady coves and isle-studded inlets, all backed by wooded or heathy slopes, and also by a dominating mountain, Cairnsmore of Fleet.

Along with its variety there is a wide variation according to the state of the tide. For some eyes the coast will lose much of its charm, taking on a forlorn air, when a vast expanse of water gives place to an equally vast expanse of sand or mud. Their gay colours do not save the yachts at Kippford from having a depressed look as they recline on mud-banks, and Rockcliffe's beach, forsaken by the sea, is not half as pretty as when white waves mingle with its silver cockle shells. 'The Venice of Scotland,' Lord Cockburn calls the town of Kirkcudbright, but he admits that 'a world of waters' changed at low tide to 'a world of squelch'.

But when Lord Cockburn speaks of the mud as 'a dreadful composition', he is imagining himself walking on it; he is not letting his eyes rest on its rich sheen, remarkable in the evening light. And the views from the heathery path between those neighbours, Kippford and Rockcliffe, need be none the worse for low tide, the wet empty Solway shot with glancing lights. The emptiness itself is a singular, almost mysterious spectacle; there is neither land nor sea, and you look on a part of the earth which is still in process of creation. The invasion of the water may be announced by a distant sound; then you see it, a long low wall of surf, moaning to itself as it is pushed on by a multitude of impatient waves. When it comes closer, it is so swift and yet so stealthy in its race, and so deliberate in its infiltration, that you have the queer feeling of something more than water, a live creature, snaky and sinister.

Andrew Young (1885–1971)
A Prospect of Britain

Loch Lomond

Loch Lomond is a beautiful, noble stretch of water and it is quite fitting that it should be called 'the King of the Lakes', but the real meaning is 'the Lake with many Islands'. It is large and rich in water and the islands float on it like great water-lilies. Even the mountains surrounding its shores seem not to dam it in as though they were its masters, but are more like satellites which surround it and accompany it, for the position of these lovely mountains, which sometimes attain a height of three thousand feet, is such that one always remains in the centre of their circular dance and has always got them around one—like the moon when on a clear night you drive for miles through the fields.

Theodor Fontane (1819–89)
Jenseit des Tweed, Bilder und Briefe aus Schottland

A French View of Loch Lomond

The superb Loch Lomond, the fine sunlight that gilded its waters, the silvery rocks that skirted its shores, the flowery and verdant mosses, the black oxen, the white sheep, the shepherds beneath the pines, the perfume of the tea poured into cups that had been given by kindness, and received with gratitude, will never be effaced from my memory, and make me cherish the desire not to die before again seeing Tarbet. I shall often dream of Tarbet, even in the midst of lovely Italy with its oranges, its myrtles, its laurels, and its jessamines.

B. Faujas St Fond (1741–1819)
Travels in England and Scotland

The Low Road

Bohannan held onto a birch branch
by yon bonny banks and looked down
through several strata of liquid
—there is someone somewhere
aiming a missile at me (he thought)
for the mountain behind him
was drilled with caves
each one crammed with nuclear hardware
and the sea-loch over the mountain
lay easy with obsolescent new submarines.

Would an underwater burst at Faslane
kill me (Walter Bohannan)
and for how many seconds/split seconds
would its bubble of steam swell and rupture
and swell and rupture again as it rose
to its final spiflification
sending fission products skimming
across the surface to Rhu and Roseneath
and Garelochhead and Greenock and Rothesay?

But no doubt they'll have arranged
for an airburst over Glen Douglas
the fireball of which will deforest Inchlonaig,
vaporize Cailness and Rowchoish, fry
the Glasgow councillors fishing for free
on Loch Katrine and kill all the spiders
and earwigs between here and Crianlarich
and me (he thought) as through the soft air
trucks, cars, buses and articulated lorries
accelerated their loads of Omo, people and bricks
towards Oban and Inveraray.

Tom Buchan (b. 1931)

Loch Katrine

And now, to issue from the glen,
No pathway meets the wanderer's ken,
Unless he climb, with footing nice,
A far projecting precipice.
The broom's tough roots his ladder made,
The hazel saplings lent their aid;
And thus an airy point he won,
Where, gleaming with the setting sun,
One burnished sheet of living gold,
Loch Katrine lay beneath him rolled,
In all her length far winding lay,
With promontory, creek and bay,
And islands that, empurpled bright,
Floated amid the livelier light,
And mountains, that like giants stand,
To sentinel enchanted land.
High on the south, huge Benvenue

Down on the lake in masses threw
Crags, knolls, and mounds, confusedly hurled,
The fragments of an earlier world;
A wildering forest feathered o'er
His ruined sides and summit hoar,
While on the north, through middle air,
Ben-an heaved high his forehead bare.

Sir Walter Scott (1771–1832)
The Lady of the Lake

The Trossachs

Theodore Fontane, the German poet and novelist (and, incidentally, one of Ibsen's first defenders) visited Scotland in 1858, producing an account of his journey two years later. It was the romantic Scotland of 'Ossian' MacPherson and Sir Walter Scott that attracted him. Indeed, his visit to the Trossachs was a direct outcome of his enjoyment of 'The Lady of the Lake', Scott's poem published in 1810, which not only laid the foundations of his own fame and fortune but might be said to have provided the keystone of the Scottish tourist industry.

What exactly *are* the Trossachs? They are a pass, a gorge, a hollow way that stretches out beside a little river between the two masses of rock, those of Ben A'an and Ben Venue, which stand like watchmen next to Lock Katrine with their broad backs stretching to Loch Achray.... The road through the Trossachs proper does not follow the course of the little river that foams in the depths beneath us, but goes along at a level that is about half way up the ridge of the northward-facing rock—a pure work of artifice. Immediately to our right Ben A'an's heavy masses of rock rise into the air with varying degrees of steepness, while on our left we have a kind of double neighbour—first of all the precipitous drop into the valley, and then, beyond that, the mighty flanks of Ben Venue. The height of this mountain wall is very remarkable, and the rich forests which grace it up to its highest point contribute not a little to the beauty of the picture. There is layer upon layer of differing vegetation, and while birch trees and aspens almost cover the gorge, there greets us from the centre of the mountain an oak forest above whose verdant crowns black pine trees begin to shoot up, covering the rest of the mountainside up to its peak. . . .

Such are the Trossachs, but such is not that place known as Beal-an-Duine which rises up in front of Loch Katrine between the peaks of the two mountains. The mountains here approach so close to each other that their green-clad walls form a huge arbour which is almost closed at the rear but from the front gives one a glimpse of the lake which, if thus seen, seems to be surrounded by a frame of green branches. As a picture the whole thing is quite perfect, and Walter Scott knew very well what he was doing when he made Ellen Douglas put her boat ashore and made the King step forth from the undergrowth by the lakeside just at this particular point. The place seems positively to compel the poet to speak in a romantic vein, and no maiden could here step ashore from the lake without being immediately taken for the Lady of the Lake herself.

It was the least romantic hour of the world (two o'clock in the afternoon and everybody hungry) when we descended the mountain path and embarked on the steamer which had drawn up along the shore and which plies back and forth across the lake. Everybody and everything is here called MacGregor. The bare-legged boy who presses his services as a guide upon us, the two old men who carry our luggage on to the steamer, and needless to say the steamer itself. But a certain amount of rather obvious intention, a certain amount of speculation on the Southrons' thirst for the Highlands, is something that one can put up with in such a spot as this.

The beeches at the foot of Ben Venue stretch forth their branches far into the lake, while our steamer lies under a roof of foliage and from time to time squirts out a shimmering rain of water through all the branches and leaves above. Now comes a signal with the bell and we glide forth from the shady coolness upon the glittering surface of the water between walls covered with foliage. Then, passing through the green frame of the rocky gateway, we move towards Loch Katrine proper. At the very beginning of the lake and close to the right bank lies Ellen Island. Everybody is at pains to recognize the place where the house of old Douglas, which has been described with such a wealth of poetic effort, is said to have stood. But only birches and young pines tower above the inhospitable plain.

At the moment when we have left Ellen Island behind us, it is all up with our interest in Loch Katrine. The voyage across this much-sung lake is like a dinner that begins with champagne and, after a great deal of dallying over plain claret, ends up with sugar-water.

Theodor Fontane (1819–98)
Jenseit des Tweed, Bilder und Briefe aus Schottland

Stirling

From the field of Bannockburn you obtain the finest view of Stirling. The Ochils are around you. Yonder sleeps the Abbey Craig, where, on a summer day, Wight Wallace sat. You behold the houses climbing up, picturesque, smoke-feathered; and the wonderful rock, in which the grace of the lily and the strength of the hills are mingled, and on which the castle sits as proudly as ever did rose on its stem. Eastward from the castle ramparts stretches a great plain, bounded on either side by mountains, and before you the vast fertility dies into distance, flat as the ocean when winds are asleep. It is through this plain that the Forth has drawn her glittering coils—a silvery entanglement of loops and links—a watery labyrinth. Turn round, look in the opposite direction, and the aspect of the country has entirely changed. It undulates like a rolling sea. Heights swell up into the blackness of pines, and then sink into valleys of fertile green. At your feet the Bridge of Allan sleeps in azure smoke. Beyond are the classic woods of Keir; and ten miles further on, what see you? A multitude of blue mountains climbing the heavens! The heart leaps up to greet them— the ramparts of a land of romance, from the mouths of whose glens broke of old the foray of the freebooter; and with a chief in front, with banner and pibroch in the wind, the terror of the Highland war. Stirling, like a huge brooch, clasps Highlands and Lowlands together.

Alexander Smith (1830–67)
A Summer in Skye

At the East Port, St Andrews

Pause stranger at the porch: nothing beyond
This framing arch of stone, but scattered rocks
And sea and these on the low beach
Original to the cataclysm and the dark.

Once one man bent to the stone, another
Dropped the measuring line, a third and fourth
Together lifted and positioned the dressed stone
Making wall and arch; yet others
Settled the iron doors on squawking hinge
To shut without the querulous seas and men.
Order and virtue and love (they say)
Dwelt in the town—but that was long ago.
Then the stranger at the gate, the merchants,
Missioners, the blind beggar with the dog,
The miscellaneous vendors (duly inspected)
Were welcome within the wall that held from sight
The water's brawl. All that was long ago.
Now the iron doors are down to dust,
But the stumps of hinge remain, the arch
Opens to the element—the stones dented
And stained to green and purple and rust.

Pigeons settle on the top. Stranger,
On this winter afternoon pause at the porch,
For the dark land beyond stretches
To the unapproachable element; bright
As night falls and with the allurement of peace,
Concealing under the bland feature, possession.
Not all the agitations of the world
Articulate the ultimate question as do those waters
Confining the memorable and the forgotten;
Relics, records, furtive occasions—Caesar's politics
And he who was drunk last night:
Rings, diamants, snuff boxes, warships.
Also the less worthy garments of worthy men.

Prefer then this handled stone, now ruined
While the sea mists wind about the arch.
The afternoon dwindles, night concludes,
The stone is damp, unyielding to the touch,
But crumbling in the strain and stress
Of the years: the years winding about the arch,
Settling in the holes and crevices, moulding
The dressed stone. Once, one man bent to it,
Another dropped the measuring line, a third
And fourth positioned to make wall and arch
Theirs. Pause, stranger, at this small town's edge—
The European sun knew those streets
O Jesu parvule; Christus Victus, Christus Victor,
The bells singing from their towers, the waters
Whispering to the waters, the air tolling
To the air—the faith, the faith, the faith.

All this was long ago. The lights
Are out, the town is sunk in sleep.
The boats are rocking at the pier,
The vague winds beat about the streets—
Choir and altar and chancel are gone.
Under the touch the guardian stone remains
Holding memory, reproving desire, securing hope
In the stop of water, in the lull of night
Before dawn kindles a new day.

George Bruce (*b.* 1909)

St Andrews in Decline

A few years before Boswell and Dr Johnson arrived in Scotland, Thomas Pennant, the Flintshire naturalist who published accounts of his several tours throughout Britain, penetrated as far north as the Pentland Firth. He made two tours of Scotland, on the second of which he visited St Andrews, then in sad decline, as Johnson was also to discover. His 'Tour of Scotland' appeared between 1771 and 1775 and provoked from Johnson the remark that Pennant 'observes more things than anyone else does'.

Full in front, at the bottom of a long descent, appears the city, placed at the extremity of a plain at the water's edge. Its numerous towers and spires give it an air of vast magnificence, and serve to raise the expectation of strangers to the highest pitch. On entering the west port, a well-built street, straight, and of a vast length and breadth, appears; but so grass-grown, and such a dreary solitude lay before us, that it formed the perfect idea of having been laid waste by the pestilence.

On a further advance, the towers and spires, which at a distance afforded such an appearance of grandeur, on the near view shewed themselves to be the aweful remains of the magnificent, the pious works of past generations. A foreigner, ignorant of the history of this country, would naturally enquire, what calamity has this city undergone? Has it suffered a bombardment from some barbarous enemy? Or has it not, like Lisbon, felt the more inevitable fury of a convulsive earthquake? But how great is the horror on reflecting that this destruction was owing to the more barbarous zeal of a minister, who, by his discourse, first enflamed, and then permitted a furious crowd to overthrow edifices, dedicated to the very Being he pretended to honour by their ruin. The cathedral was the labour of a hundred and sixty years, a building that did honour to the country: yet in June 1559, John Knox effected its demolition in a single day.

Thomas Pennant (1726–98)
Tour in Scotland

St Andrews

Andrew Lang, the Selkirk-born scholar, poet, historian and journalist— Stevenson's 'Dear Andrew, with the brindled hair'—was a graduate both of the Universities of St. Andrews and Oxford. He honoured the town with a delightful history and a poem which celebrates both his almæ matres. In turn, they both honoured him with doctorates.

Not in summer, among crowds of holiday-making strangers, but in winter, when the scarlet gowns of the students brighten the streets, and the waves fill the roofless fanes with their monotone, is the time to see St Andrews.

The world alters; new cries ring above the unceasing brawl of men, but the northern sea, with its changeless voice, we hear as Eadmer heard it, and St Margaret, Beaton, and Queen Mary, Knox in his chamber in the besieged castle, and Bruce in the priory. Even so forlorn, when St Andrews is but a fishing village again, men will hear the tide as they stand on the wave-worn promontory whence the great broken towers shall have fallen. Have all our revolutions, all our changes of creed, all the bloodshed and the burning, made men happier? Is the truth as near now as it was when the Pictish king died here in religion, or when Knox held, as he deemed, the actual vertiy and secret of the world? We grow grey like the 'dear city of youth and dream', the city of our youth: like her, we have seen many disappointments. Her shattered monuments yet behold the sea, the sun, the sky; to have done so much, says the Greek, is not to have failed. So some may muse as the pale winter sunset fades beyond the sands.

Andrew Lang (1844–1912)
St Andrews

Almae Matres

St Andrews by the Northern Sea,
   A haunted town it is to me!
A little city, worn and grey,
   The grey North Ocean girds it round,
And o'er the rocks, and up the bay,
   The long sea-rollers surge and sound,
And still the thin and biting spray
   Drives down the melancholy street,
And still endure, and still decay,
   Towers that the salt winds vainly beat.
Ghost-like and shadowy they stand
Dim mirrored in the wet sea-sand.

St Leonard's chapel, long ago
   We loitered idly where the tall
Fresh-budded mountain ashes blow
   Within thy desecrated wall:
The tough roots rent the tomb below,
   The April birds sang clamorous,
We did not dream, we could not know
   How hardly Fate would deal with us!

O, broken minster, looking forth
   Beyond the bay, above the town,

O, winter of the kindly North,
　O, college of the scarlet gown,
And shining sands beside the sea,
　And stretch of links beyond the sand,
Once more I watch you, and to me
　It is as if I touched his hand!

And therefore art thou yet more dear,
　O, little city, grey and sere,
Though shrunken from thine ancient pride
　And lonely by thy lonely sea,
Than these fair halls on Isis' side,
　Where Youth an hour came back to me!

A land of waters green and clear,
　Of willows and of poplars tall,
And, in the spring-time of the year,
　The white may breaking over all,
And Pleasure quick to come at call,
　And summer rides by march and wold,
And Autumn with her crimson pall
　About the towers of Magdalen rolled;
And strange enchantments from the past,
　And memories of the friends of old,
And strong Tradition, binding fast
　The 'flying terms' with bands of gold,—
All these hath Oxford: all are dear,
　But dearer far the little town,
The drifting surge, the wintry year,
　The college of the scarlet gown.
　　St Andrews by the Northern Sea,
　　　That is a haunted town to me!

Andrew Lang

Killiecrankie

I am just returned from a Highland expedition, and was much delighted
with the magnificence of nature in her awful simplicity. These mountains,
and torrents, and rocks, would almost convince one that it was some being
of infinite power that had created them. Plain corn countries look as if men
had made them; but I defy all mankind put together to make anything like
the Pass of Gilliecranky (Killiecrankie).

Mrs Alison Cockburn (1713–94)
Letters

Aberdeen Receives a Royal Visit

On 4th May 1511, the magistrates of Aberdeen decided 'to ressave our soverane lady, the Queyne, als honourablie as ony burgh of Scotland, except Edinburgh allanerlie [only].' Two hundred pounds was raised to meet the expenses of a visit celebrated in a set of 'thank you' verses by King James IV's court poet, William Dunbar.

Blyth Aberdeen, thou beriall of all tounis,   [beryl
   The lamp of bewtie, bountie and blythness;
Unto the heaven ascendit thy renoun is
   Of virtue, wisdom, and of worthiness;
   High noted is thy name of nobliness,
Into the coming of our lusty Queen,   [beautiful
   The wall of welth, guid cheir, and mirriness:
Be blyth and blissful, burgh of Aberdeen . . .

The Streetis were all hung with tapestrie,
   Great was the press of people dwelt about,
And pleasant pageants playit prettily;
   The lieges all did to their Lady loutt,   [bow down
   Wha was convoyed with ane royal rout
Of great barons and lusty ladies schene: [bright
   Welcome, our Queen! the commons gave ane shout;
Be blyth and blissful, burgh of Aberdeen.

At hir coming great was the mirth and joy,
   For at their Cross abundantly ran wine;
Untill hir ludging the toun did her convoy;   [over to
   Hir for to treit they set their hail ingyne   [ingenuity
   Ane rich present they did til hir propyne,   [give
Ane costly coup that large thing wald contain,
   Coverit and full of cunyeitt gold richt fine:
Be blyth and blissful, thou burgh of Aberdeen.

O potent princess, pleasant and preclair,   [famous
   Great cause thou hes to thank this noble toun,
That, for to do thee honour, did not spare
   Their geir, riches, substance and persoun,
   Thee to receive in most fair fashioun;
Thee for to please they socht all way and mein;
   Thairfoir, sa lang as Queen thou beiris croun,
Be thankful to this burgh of Aberdeen.

William Dunbar (1465?–1530?)
from *To Aberdein*

The Two Aberdeens

Old Aberdeen is about a mile from the New City. It has something of a collegiate character—an air of quietness and permanence—of old times; long walls well built in former days; a few old trees, and houses standing separately, each in its garden. Gibbs states its population at 1,500; that of the New City is 40,000. Here all is life, bustle, business and improvement, for in outward and visible improvement this place may almost be said to keep pace with Edinburgh. Union Street, where our hotel stands, is new, and many houses are still building—the appearance is very good, because they have the finest granite close at hand. But the Town-Council has become bankrupt thro' these improvements: for having to purchase and demolish old houses to make room for the new streets they let pass the opportunity of disposing of the ground to advantage, asking too much for it, when the spirit of enterprise was on the alert. But they had borrowed money to make the purchase, and the interest of this debt ran on, while the ground was lying unproductive. Of late, since mercantile adventures have proved so hazardous, monied men have thought it safer to embark their property in building; and thus the number of houses which are here in progress becomes, like the high price of stocks, a fallacious measure of the general prosperity. The capital, however, is well employed for the public and for the town, whatever it may be for the owners.

Robert Southey (1774–1843)
Journal of a Tour in Scotland in 1819

Aberdeen, The Granite City

The brown land behind, south and north
Dee and Don and east the doubtful sea,
The town secured by folk that warsled
With water, earth and stone; quarrying,
Shaping, smoothing their unforgiving stone,
Engineering to make this sufficient city
That takes the salt air for its own.
The pale blue winter sky, the spring green trees,
The castigating thunder rain, the wind
Beating about the midnight streets,
The hard morning sun make their change
By the white unaltered granite—
Streets of it, broad roadways, granite pavemented
To the tall tenements, rectangular wide-walled stores,
To the kirks and pillared Assembly Rooms;
Streets with drinking troughs for the animals,
And at the port quays crowded,

Overfed with horses, lorries, men and boys,
And always and at every point
Clatter on the causies.
Business is good, will be good here
At the dead end of time. Record then
This people who purposive and with strategy
Established a northern city, a coast town
That stands and stares by the waters,
Dee and Don and the sea.

George Bruce (*b.* 1909)

With the Herring Fishers

'I see herrin'.'—I hear the glad cry
And 'gainst the moon see ilka blue jowl
In turn as the fisherman haul on the nets
And sing: 'Come, shove in your heids and growl.'

'Soom on, bonnie herrin', soom on,' they shout,
Or 'Come in, O come in, and see me,'
'Come gie the auld man something to dae.
It'll be a braw change frae the sea!'

O it's ane o' the bonniest sichts in the warld
To watch the herrin' come walkin' on board
In the wee sma' 'oors o' a simmer's mornin'
As if o' their ain accord!

For this is the way that God sees life,
The haill jing-bang o's appearin'
Up owre frae the edge o' naethingness
—It's his happy cries I'm hearin'.

'Left, right—O come in and see me,'
Reid and yellow and black and white
Toddlin' up into Heaven thegither
At peep o' day frae the endless night.

'I see herrin',' I hear his glad cry,
And 'gainst the moon see his muckle blue jowl,
As he handles buoy-tow and bush raip
Singin': 'Come, shove in your heids and growl!'

Hugh MacDiarmid (1892–1978)

Royal Deeside

Queen Victoria and her Consort showed much sagacity and real sense of country when they leased the old house of Balmoral in 1848. They had been first enchanted by the Highlands when entertained at Taymouth Castle by the Marquis of Breadalbane in 1842, but, despite her affection for Perthshire, the Queen chose Deeside to be her very own. Old Balmoral was no sooner leased than loved. It was bought outright in 1852 and then began the construction of the new Castle, which was ready for habitation in 1855. The work was done in the towered style deemed proper at the time. That style observed a tradition and those who think that every period must have its own architectural idiom, defying tradition and irrespective of the site, can join McKnocker in his groans about Balmoralism and bogus antiques. Doubtless that style does not suit modern needs of internal convenience, but the tower of the Victorian castle, on that superb site beside the Dee's northward bend to Crathie, need affront nobody. What, by the way, would McKnocker have had the Queen build? Functional cubic stuff? That would ill beseem the natural baroque of Lochnagar's soaring background, or the tartans and the Landseer canvases that were to decorate the walls within.

The emotions roused by Balmoral in Queen Victoria's descendants have naturally varied with their tastes and temperaments. But one thing is certain. In one long life that contained much unhappiness Balmoral was an abode of serene and supreme delight. Here, wrote Lytton Strachey, his irony disarmed, 'her happiest days passed. In after years, when she looked back on them, a kind of glory, a radiance as of an unearthly holiness, seemed to glow about these golden hours. Each hallowed moment stood out clear, beautiful, eternally significant. For, at the time, every experience there, sentimental, or grave, or trivial, had come upon her with a peculiar vividness, like a flashing of marvellous lights.' *Leaves from our Journal of Life in the Highlands* and the subsequent *More Leaves* are necessary reading for those who visit Deeside. These are books of complete sincerity, complete simpleness, and, up to the death of Albert, complete felicity. There is no doubt that Deeside continually evoked in Queen Victoria the word of which she was so fond in her uninhibited, unpretentious authorship, ecstasy . . .

Deeside was not only beautiful; it had in abundance everything that the Highland sportsman wanted, the stags, the salmon, the grouse. Albert found the scenery agreeably like that of Switzerland; he also acquired some proficiency in the pursuit of game. Inevitably the royal example was followed, the royal tastes and sentiments re-echoed. Deeside became the centre of great houses, entertaining the eminent with the most expensive reaches of the river and the most coveted grouse-moors and deer-forests on the hills. The Deeside season became the smartest season and the Braemar Gathering and Games, royally supported, became the high assembly of the September sports. Queen Victoria was spared the age of petrol which has turned the roadsides of the Dee into Aberdeen's back-garden and a swarming ground of motor-coaches. In these conditions I would hardly recommend the Braemar Gathering as a good occasion for butting in. But all this crowding and peering have happened without royal encouragement, not because of it. McKnocker, who so detests what he calls Balmorality, must turn his wrath against the motor-car. It is the penalty of a monarch's life that, not even in the shadow of the highest Highlands, is a total escape possible. The Royal Family cannot now cross the road on a Sunday to attend Crathie Church, where Queen Victoria had been 'much edified' and given 'lumps in the throat' by the simple eloquence of Dr Macleod and other Scottish divines, without attracting a crowd of several thousands. It is not royalty that has created Balmorality but the eagerness of its subjects, now able to defeat distance, to be numerous, ardent and intrusive Balmoralists.

Ivor Brown (*b.* 1891–1974)
Summer In Scotland

Scottish Mountains

Each year a race is run up and down Ben Nevis, starting from Fort William, a mile or so away; as the time taken is usually less than two hours, Scotland's highest mountain may seem of no great height. Nor will it seem steep, for motor-cycles and cars have reached the ruined observatory on the summit. And consider the Cairngorms, the highest group of Scottish hills; travelling in a train through Aviemore and looking at them across Rothiemurchus Forest, you might regard them as little higher than the South Downs. And if you were to land among them from an aeroplane, perhaps on the broad back of Beinn a Bhuird, you might imagine at a first glance you were on an extensive plain. Indeed, it is often said there are no mountains in the Highlands, only deep valleys, called by their Gaelic name, glens.

But if the Scottish mountains are not to be respected for their height, they are for their age, being relics of vast and ancient mountains, compared with which the Alps are modern upstarts. They were so disintegrated and washed away, that where is now a high ridge may have been the bed of a valley. In effect, the land was reduced to a deeply and widely trenched plateau where height is really depth. Much of the plateau remains in the granite Cairngorms, but elsewhere only protuberances are left, rounded, peaked or ridgy. Their rock varies in age, but a few of them, as Ben More Assynt and The Clisham in Harris, are composed of the most primeval rock, Lewisian gneiss, familiarly called Old Boy. The world has no more ancient mountains.

It is told of an Alpine guide, who proposed to climb a Scottish mountain, that he selected a site for a night camp, from which he would assault the summit on the following morning. The point of the story is that Scottish mountains have an illusory height. It is partly due to their structure, but even more to the atmosphere . . . Ben Loyal in Sutherland, rising from low ground, draws with its four peaks a magnificent line across the sky; but on climbing it you feel it is a fraud, the peaks no more impressive than Dart-moor tors. But what gives a quite extraordinary illusion of height is mist, cliffs and pinnacles soaring dimly till they are lost in apparent distance. And it is so volatile that at times it is startling. I have seen in Coire Ardair a mist which was hanging on Creag Meaghaidh, a precipice towering more than a thousand feet above the lonely lochan, swoop down with such a sudden hawklike speed that, vapour as it was, the effect was alarming. But if atmos-phere, architecture and mist lend an illusory height, they also, with cloud and flying cloud-shadow, give what is no illusion, an enchanting beauty.

Andrew Young (1885–1971)
A Prospect of Britain

The Wordsworths Visit Glencoe

In 1803 William Wordsworth and his sister Dorothy made an extensive tour of Scotland in an Irish jaunting car. Dorothy later wrote a varied account of the journey.

Our road frequently crossed large streams of stones, left by the mountain-torrents, losing all appearance of a road. After we had passed the tarn the glen became less interesting, or rather the mountains, from the manner in which they are looked at; but again, a little higher up, they resume their grandeur. The river is, for a short space, hidden between steep rocks: we left the road, and, going to the top of one of the rocks, saw it foaming over with stones, or lodged in dark black dens; birch-trees grew in inaccessible banks, and a few old Scotch firs towered above them. At the entrance of the glen the mountains had been all without trees, but here the birches climbed very far up the side of one of them opposite to us, half concealing a rivulet, which came tumbling down as white as snow from the very top of the moun-tain. Leaving the rock, we ascended a hill which terminated the glen. We often stopped to look behind at the majestic company of mountains we had left. Before us was no single paramount eminence, but a mountain waste, mountain beyond mountain, and a barren hollow or basin into which we were descending.

We parted from our companion at the door of a whisky hovel, a building which, when it came out of the workmen's hands with its unglassed windows, would, in that forlorn region, have been little better than a howling place for the winds, and was now half unroofed. On seeing a slope, I exclaimed, 'Is it possible any people can live there?' when at least half a dozen men, women and children, came to the door. They were about to rebuild the hut, and I suppose that they, or some other poor creatures, would dwell there through the winter, dealing out whisky to the starved travellers. The sun was now setting, the air very cold, the sky clear; I could have fancied that it was winter-time, with hard frost. Our guide pointed out King's House,

5

our resting-place for the night. We could just distinguish the house at the bottom of the moorish hollow or basin—I call it so, for it was nearly as broad as long, lying before us, with three miles of naked road winding through it, every foot of which we could see. The road was perfectly white, making a dreary contrast with the ground, which was of a dull earthy brown. Long as the line of road appeared before us, we could scarcely believe it to be three miles—I suppose owing to its being unbroken by any one object, and the moor naked as the road itself; but we found it the longest three miles we had yet travelled, for the surface was so stony we had to walk most of the way.

The house looked respectable at a distance—a large square building, cased in blue slates to defend it from storms; but when we came close to it the outside fore-warned us of the poverty and misery within. Scarce a blade of grass could be seen growing upon the open ground; the heath-plant itself found no nourishment there, appearing as if it had but sprung up to be blighted. There is no enclosure for a cow, no appropriated ground but a small plot like a church-yard, in which were a few starveling dwarfish potatoes, which had, no doubt, been raised by means of the dung left by travellers' horses: they had not come to blossoming, and whether they would either yield fruit or blossom I know not. The first thing we saw on entering the door was two sheep hung up, as if just killed from the barren moor, their bones hardly sheathed in flesh. After we had waited a few minutes, looking about for a guide to lead us into some corner of the house, a woman, seemingly about 40 years old, came to us in a great bustle, screaming in Erse, with a most horrible guinea hen or peacock voice I ever heard, first to one person and then another. She could hardly spare time to show us up stairs, for crowds of men were in the house—drovers, carriers, horsemen, travellers, all of whom she had to provide with supper, and she was, as she told us, the only woman there.

Never did I see such a miserable, such a wretched place,—long rooms with ranges of beds, no other furniture except benches, or perhaps one or two crazy chairs, the floors far dirtier than an ordinary house could be if it were never washed,—as dirty as a house after a sale on a rainy day, the rooms being large, and the walls naked, it looked as if more than half the goods had been sold out. We sate shivering in one of the large rooms for three quarters of an hour before the woman could find time to speak to us again; she then promised a fire in another room, after two travellers, who were going a stage further, had finished their whisky, and said we would have supper as soon as possible. She had no eggs, no milk, no potatoes, no loaf-bread, or we should have preferred tea. With length of time the fire was kindled and, after another hour's waiting, supper came—a shoulder of mutton so hard that it was impossible to chew the little flesh that might be scraped off the bones, and some sorry soup made of barley and water, for it had no other taste.

After supper, the woman, having first asked if we slept on blankets, brought in two pairs of sheets, which she begged that I would air by the fire, for they would be dirtied below-stairs. I was very willing, but behold! the sheets were so wet, that it would have been at least a two-hours' job before a far better fire than could be mustered at King's House—for, that nothing might be wanting to make it a place of complete starvation, the peats were not dry, and if they had not been helped out by decayed wood dug out of the earth along with them, we should have had no fire at all. The woman was civil, in her fierce, wild way. She and the house, upon that desolate and extensive Wild, and everything we saw, made us think of one of those places of a rendezvous which we read of in novels—Ferdinand Count Fathom or Gil Blas—where there is one woman to receive the booty, and prepare the supper at night. She told us that she was only a servant, but that she had now lived there five years, and that, when but a 'young lassie' she had lived there also. We asked her if she had always served the same master, 'Nay, nay, many masters, for they were always changing'. I verily believe that the woman was attached to the place like a cat to the empty house when the family who brought her up are gone to live elsewhere. The sheets were so long in drying that it was very late before we went to bed. We talked over our day's adventures by the fireside, and often looked out of the window towards a huge pyramidal mountain at the entrance of Glen Coe. All between, the dreary waste was clear, almost, as sky, the moon shining full upon it. A rivulet ran amongst the stones near the house, and sparkled with light: I could have fancied that there was nothing else, in that extensive circuit over which we looked, that had the power of motion.

> Dorothy Wordsworth (1771–1855)
> *A Tour in Scotland*

Dr Johnson in the Hebrides

A country that has no money is by no means convenient for beggars, both because such countries are commonly poor, and because charity requires some trouble and some thought. A penny is easily given upon the first impulse of compassion, or impatience of opportunity; but few will deliberately search their cupboards or their granaries to find out something to give. A penny is likewise easily spent; but victuals, if they are unprepared, require houseroom, and fire, and utensils, which the beggar knows not where to find.

Yet beggars there sometimes are, who wander from Island to Island. We had, in our passage to Mull, the company of a woman and her child, who had exhausted the charity of *Col* [Coll]. The arrival of a beggar on the Island is accounted a sinistrous event. Every body considers that he shall have the less for what he gives away. Their alms, I believe, is generally oatmeal . . .

Life is here, in some respects, improved beyond the condition of some other Islands. In *Sky* [Skye] what is wanted can only be bought, as the arrival of some wandering pedlar may afford an opportunity; but in *Col* there is a standing shop, and in *Mull* there are two. A shop in the Islands, as in other places of little frequentation, is a repository of every thing requisite for common use. Mr Boswell's journal was filled, and he bought some paper in *Col*. To a man that ranges the streets of London, where he is tempted to contrive wants for the pleasure of supplying them, a shop affords no image worthy of attention; but in an Island, it turns the balance of existence between good and evil. To live in perpetual want of little things, is a state not indeed of torture, but of constant vexation. I have in *Sky* had some difficulty to find ink for a letter; and if a woman breaks her needle, the work is at a stop. As it is, the Islanders are obliged to content themselves with succedaneous means for many common purposes. I have seen many a chief man of a very wide district riding with a halter for a bridle and governing his hobby with a wooden curb.

Samuel Johnson (1709–84)
Journey to the Western Isles of Scotland

The Lord of the Isles Sails By

Merrily, merrily goes the bark,
  Before the gale she bounds;
So darts the dolphin from the shark,
  Or the deer before the hounds.
They left Loch-Tua on their lee,
And they waken'd the men of wild Tiree
  And the Chief of sandy Coll;
They paus'd not at Columba's isle,
Though peal'd the bells from the holy pile
    With long and measured toll;
No time for matin or for mass,
And the sounds of the holy summons pass
    Away in the billows' roll.
Lochbuie's fierce and warlike lord
Their signal saw, and grasped his sword,
And verdant Ilay call'd her host,
And the clans of Jura's rugged coast
    Lord Ronald's call obey,
And Scarba's isle, whose tortured shore
Still rings to Corrievrekan's roar,
    And lonely Colonsay;
Scenes sung by him who sings no more!
His bright and brief career is o'er.

Sir Walter Scott (1771–1832)
from *The Lord of the Isles*

Iona

We were now treading that illustrious island, which was once the luminary of the Caledonian regions, whence savage clans and roving barbarians derived the benefits of knowledge, and the blessings of religion. To abstract the mind from all local emotion would be impossible, if it were endeavoured, and would be foolish, if it were possible. Whatever withdraws us from the power of our senses; whatever makes the past, the distant, or the future predominate over the present, advances us in the dignity of thinking beings. Far from me and from my friends be such frigid philosophy, as may conduct us indifferent and unmoved over any ground which has been dignified by wisdom, bravery, or virtue. That man is little to be envied, whose patriotism would not gain force upon the plain of Marathon, or whose piety would not grow warmer among the ruins of Iona.

Samuel Johnson (1709–84)
Journey to the Western Isles

The Genesis of the 'Hebrides' Overture

Iona, one of the Hebrides-sisters—there is truly a very Ossianic and sweetly sad sound about that name—when in some future time I shall sit in a madly crowded assembly with music and dancing round me, and the wish arises to retire into the loneliest loneliness, I shall think of Iona, with its ruins of a once magnificent cathedral, the remains of a convent, the graves of ancient Scottish Kings, and still more ancient pirate-princes—with their ships rudely carved on many a monumental stone. If I had my home on Iona, and lived there upon melancholy as other people do on their rents, my darkest moment would be when in that wide space that deals in nothing but cliffs and seagulls, suddenly a curl of steam should appear, followed by a ship, and finally by a gay party in veils and frock-coats, who would look for an hour at the ruins and graves and the three little huts for the living, and then move off again. This highly unjustifiable joke, occurring twice a week, and being almost the only thing to make one aware that there are such things as time and clocks in the world, would be as if the inhabitants of these old graves haunted the place in a ludicrous disguise. Opposite Iona stands a rocky island which, to complete the effect, looks like a ruined city.

Felix Mendelssohn-Bartholdy (1809–47)
from Sebastian Hensel's *The Mendelssohn Family*

Queen Victoria Off Iona

Prince Albert, the Prince of Leinengen, the Duke of Norfolk, Earl Grey and Sir James Clark landed on the island in August, 1847, while the Queen herself was contiguous on the royal yacht, at the time of the progress northward to Ardverikie; and they had a reception from the people so primitive and decorous as was probably given anywhere to any ancient Lord of the Isles. A few plainly dressed islanders stood on the shore, carrying tufted willow-wands, and prepared to act as an escort; the body of the people, for the most part decently dressed, stood behind, looking eagerly on as spectators, yet all maintaining a respectful distance; only a few children, in the usual fashion of the island, offered pebbles and shells for sale; and when the august visitors, after quietly surveying the curiosities of the place, returned to the barge, all the population gave loud voice in a hearty farewell cheer.

from *The Imperial Gazette*

Mithich Domh Triall Gu Tigh Pharais (It is time for me to go up unto the House of Paradise)

An I mo chridhe, I mo ghràidh
An àit' guth manaich bidh geum bà;
Ach mu'n tig an Saoghal gu crìch
Bithidh I mar a bha.

In Iona of my heart, Iona of my love,
Instead of monks' voices shall be lowing of cattle;
But ere the world come to an end,
Iona shall be as it was.

Anonymous

Skye

Twentieth-century communications may have taken from the islanders some of the self-sufficiency, described by Alexander Smith in 1856, in return for material comforts and benefits. But his observations on the quality of rural life in Skye still seem to describe a continuing kind of satisfaction.

A Skye family has everything within itself. The bare mountains yield mutton, which possesses a flavour and delicacy unknown in the south. The copses swarm with rabbits; and if a net is set over-night at the Black Island, there is abundance of fish to breakfast. The farmer grows his own corn, barley, and potatoes, digs his own peats, makes his own candles; he tans leather, spins cloth shaggy as a terrier's pile, and a hunchbacked artist in the place transforms the raw materials into boots or shepherd garments. Twice every year a huge hamper arrives from Glasgow, stuffed with all the little luxuries of housekeeping—tea, sugar, coffee and the like. At more frequent intervals comes a ten-gallon cask from Greenock, whose contents can cunningly draw the icy fangs of a north-easter, or take the chill out of the clammy mists. ... And once a week the *Inverness Courier*, like a window suddenly opened on the roaring sea, brings a murmur of the outer world, its politics, its business, its crimes, its literature, its whole multitudinous and unsleeping life, making the stillness yet more still.

To the Islesman the dial face of the year is not artificially divided, as in cities, by parliamentary session and recess, college terms, vacations short and long, by the rising and sitting of courts of justice; nor yet, as in more fortunate soils, by imperceptible gradations of coloured light—the green flowery year deepening into the sunset of the October hollyhock; the slow reddening of burdened orchards; the slow yellowing of wheaten plains. Not by any of these, but by the higher and more affecting element of animal life, with its passions and instincts, its gladness and suffering; existence like our own, although in a lower key, and untouched by solemn issues; the same music and wail, although struck on rude and uncertain chords.

To the Islesman the year rises into interest when the hills, yet wet with melted snow, are pathetic with newly-yeaned lambs, and it completes itself through the successive steps of weaning, fleecing, sorting, fattening, sale, final departure, and cash in pocket.

Alexander Smith (1830–67)
A Summer in Skye

Loch Coruisk

Picking your steps carefully over huge boulder and slippery stone, you come upon the most savage scene of desolation in Britain. Conceive a large lake filled with dark green water, girt with torn and shattered precipices; the bases of which are strewn with ruin since an earthquake passed that way, and whose summits jag the sky with grisly splinter and peak. There is no motion here save the white vapour streaming from the abyss. The utter silence weighs like a burden upon you; you feel an intruder in the place. The hills seem to possess some secret; to brood over some unutterable idea which you can never know. You cannot feel comfortable at Loch Coruisk, and the discomfort arises in a great degree from the feeling that you are outside everything—that the thunder-splitten peaks have a life with which you cannot intermeddle. The dumb monsters sadden and perplex. Standing there, you are impressed with the idea that the mountains are silent because they are listening so intently. And the mountains *are* listening, else why do they echo our voices in such a wonderful way? Shout here like an Achilles in the trenches. Listen! The hill opposite takes up your words, and repeats them one after another, and curiously tries them over with the gravity of a raven. Immediately after, you hear a multitude of skyey voices.

'Methinks that there are spirits among the peaks.' How strangely the clear strong tones are repeated by the granite precipices! Who could conceive that Horror had so sweet a voice! Fainter and more musical they grow; fainter, sweeter, and more remote, until at last they come on your ear as if from the blank of the sky itself. M'Ian fired his gun, and it reverberated in a whole battle of Waterloo. We kept the hills busy with shouts and the firing of guns, and then M'Ian led us to a convenient place for lunching. As we trudge along something lifts itself off a rock—'tis an eagle. See how grandly the noble creature soars away. What sweep of wings! What a lord of the air! And if you cast up your eyes you will see his brother hanging like a speck beneath the sun. Under M'Ian's guidance, we reached the lunching-place, unpacked our basket, devoured our fare, and then lighted our pipes and smoked—in the strangest presence. Thereafter we bundled up our things, shouldered our guns, and marched in the track of ancient earthquake towards our boat. Embarked once again and sailing between the rocky portals of Loch Scavaig, I said, 'I would not spend a day in that solitude for the world. I should go mad before evening.'

Alexander Smith
Ibid

Highland Portrait

Castles draw in their horns. The stones are streaming
with fine Highland rain. A woman's struggling
against the sour wet wind in a black skirt.
Mist on the mountains. Waterfalls are pouring
their tons of water with a hollow roaring.
The phantom chieftains pass the heavy port.

Fences straggle westwards. Absurd cattle
lift their shaggy heads through humming water.
A duck dives coolly into stylish seas.
Hotels are sleeping in their winter colours.
The oilskinned sailors wear their gleaming yellows.
Glencoes are wailing in the hollow trees.

Country of céilidhs and the delicate manners,
obstinate dowagers of emerald honours,
the rain has worn your metaphors away.
Only poor rays of similes are shining
from brooches and from buckles. The complaining
barren rocks and ravens fill the day.

Nothing to say except a world has ended.
The waters of Polldubh, direct and splendid,
will hump unsteady men to a boiling death.
Yet from the shaking bridge of fascination
we see in these the antisept in passion
whose surgeon's reason is a kind of birth.

Iain Crichton Smith (b. 1928)

A Shepherd at Sea

Next morning I went on board the sloop, and about seven o'clock a.m., we heaved anchor and got under way, but as the small breeze that was blowing was straight ahead of the vessel, we beat up the whole day without getting out of the loch, sometimes among the Summer Isles, and sometimes hard off the shore opposite them, to the south, and at the close of the day we found ourselves immediately off a rocky point betwixt the channel and the broad loch. As the sea was heavy in the mouth of the bay, the vessel wrought incessantly during the whole night. I became very uneasy, but knowing nothing of the nature of the sea fever, I thought I was attacked by the influenza. . . . As soon as we got clear of the Summer Isles, the tide then turning to the north, we took a long stretch in the same direction, passed the Summer Isles, doubled the point of Coygarch, and the day being fair and clear, got an excellent view of the mountains of that country. They had a verdant appearance, but a passenger assured me that the fine weather made them appear so, for that they were nevertheless mostly covered with a mossy surface.

Still holding in the same direction, and having an excellent spy-glass on board, we got a view of the shores of Loch Eynard; and passing the Rhu of Assynt, although then at a considerable distance out on the channel, a prodigious range of the rugged mountains on Lord Reay's country presented itself to view, forming the most striking and perforated outline I had yet seen. I was afterwards convinced that the extraordinary appearance which they exhibited had been occasioned in part by some small skiffs of mist which had been hovering about their summits, and which I had taken for the horizon beyond them, these causing them to appear as if bored through in many places.

Our skipper steered thus far to the north in hopes that the breeze would drop in the north-east before evening. In this, however, he was disappointed, and the tide turning to the south, he tacked about, steering to the south-west, or a little to the west, and a little before sunset the breeze sunk entirely, and there was not a breath. My patience now took its leave of me for some time altogether. Although I was never actually sick, yet I found myself growing squeamish and uneasy, forsaken by the breeze in the very midst of a broad channel, and, for anything that I knew, condemned to hobble on that unstable element for a week, or perhaps much longer. . . .

My chagrin was somewhat diverted near the fall of evening by contemplating the extensive prospect. We were becalmed exactly in the middle of the channel which separates Lewis from the mainland, and the evening being remarkably fine and clear we could see distinctly the Isle of Skye, the Shant Islands, the Lewis, and all that range of mountains in Ross-shire and Sutherland, stretching from Torridon to Cape Wrath. By reason of their distance they now appeared low. The sea, though in its natural perturbed state, being unruffled by the smallest breeze appeared an ocean of heaving crystal, of different colours in different directions, presenting alternately spots of the deepest green, topaz, and purple; for which I could not in the least account by any appearance in the sky, which was all of one colour.

Such a scene, so entirely new to me, could not fail of attracting my attention, which it did to such a degree that I remained on deck all night. The light of the moon at length prevailed. She hovered low above the Shant Isles, and shed a stream of light on the glassy surface of the sea, in the form of a tall crescent, of such a lustre that it dazzled the sight. . . . Early in the morning, all being quiet, I had wrapped myself in my shepherd's plaid, and was stretched among some cables on deck, busied in perusing Shakespeare's monstrous tragedy of *Titus Andronicus*, and just when my feelings were wrought to the highest pitch of horror, I was alarmed by an uncommon noise, as of something bursting, and which I apprehended was straight over me, when starting up with great emotion, I was almost blinded by a shower of brine. But how was I petrified with amazement at seeing a huge monster, in size like a horse, sinking into the sea by the side of the vessel, something after the manner of a rope tumbler, and so near me that I could have struck him with a spear. I bawled out to the crew to be upon the alert, for that here was a monstrous whale going to coup the ship, and seizing the boat-hook was going, as I thought, to maul him most terribly. He had rather got out of my reach, and one of the crew took it from me for fear I should lose it, assuring me that I could not pierce him although it was sharp, which it was not.

After the sun rose, the sails began to fill, and we moved on almost imperceptibly towards Stornoway. The whale kept by the vessel the whole morning, sometimes on one side, sometimes on the other. Being always immoderately addicted to fishing, I was in the highest degree interested. I was also impatient at such a huge fish being so near me. He was exactly the length of a vessel, a sloop, if I mistake not, about seventy or eighty tons. I once called to one of the sailors to come and see how he rubbed sides with the ship. 'Eh', said he, 'he be wanting one of us to breakfast with him!' . . .

We at length entered the harbour of Stornoway, and about seven o'clock in the evening cast anchor within a very short space of the houses, having been exactly sixty hours on the passage, a distance of scarcely so many miles.

James Hogg (1770–1835)
A Tour in the Highlands in 1803

Midnight, Lochinver

Wine-coloured, Homer said, wine-dark . . .
The seaweed on the stony beach,
Flushed darker with that wine, was kilts
And beasts and carpets . . . A startled heron
Tucked in its cloud two yellow stilts.

And eiderducks were five, no, two—
No, six. A lounging fishbox raised
Its broad nose to the moon. With groans
And shouts the steep burn drowned itself;
And sighs were soft among the stones.

All quiet, all dark: excepting where
A cone of light stood on the pier
And in the circle of its scope
A hot winch huffed and puffed and gnashed
Its iron fangs and swallowed rope.

The nursing tide moved gently in.
Familiar archipelagoes
Heard her advancing, heard her speak
Things clear, though hard to understand
Whether in Gaelic or in Greek.

Norman MacCaig (b. 1910)

Orkney

Farmers and crofters were poor a generation ago, but their poverty was not like urban poverty. They had as little money as the poor of Glasgow; their wealth was in their few acres and animals and children. There was always meat and drink in a farmhouse—the bere bannocks and butter, the dried cuithes, the white cheese, and home-brewed ale—and towards strangers a hospitality almost boundless.

The fishermen sold their haddocks along the street in the nineteen-thirties at threepence a pound. If anything, they were even poorer, living in their little houses above the harbour water, with nothing between them and hunger, between them and drowning, but a yawl.

Nowadays the people are much better off. The farms have been mechanized; land which formerly it was impossible to cultivate has been brought under the plough all over Orkney. A first glance will show how fertile the soils are— a chequer-work of pasture and cultivation from the shore half-way up the hills. The fishermen have bigger boats; they can fish in moderately deep water. They have their own co-operative and so get a secure price for their cod and lobsters and scallops. The life and prosperity of fishermen has always been more uncertain than the farmers'; probably it must be that way.

George Mackay Brown (b. 1921)
An Orkney Tapestry

The Shetland Islands

Superficially even, the Shetlands are quite unlike Scotland, and unless the visitor has been prepared in advance, he or she may find it difficult to account for the sense of something very different—the sense of something wanting. It may take them a little time to realise that what is affecting them is the total absence of trees and of running water. But one quickly gets accustomed to that, and appreciates that, even if trees and singing streams could be introduced, they would be no improvement; they would simply make the Shetlands like other places we know, whereas, without them, the Shetlands are complete in themselves, and the absence of these usual features of the countryside does not involve any deficiency or monotony. There is no less variety of form and colour; just as we find it difficult in other connections to imagine how we could get on without certain things we are accustomed to, so here it surprises one to discover how easily even the presence of trees and rivers can be dispensed with and how, instead of a sense of loss, we soon realize that their absence throws into relief features we seldom see or under-prize because of them—the infinite beauties of the bare land and the shapes and colours of the rocks which first of all impress one with a sense of sameness and next delight one with a revelation of the endless resource of Nature albeit in subtler and less showy or sensational forms than we are accustomed to appreciate in regions of more profuse development. It is in fact the treasures and rich lessons of a certain asceticism the Shetlands provide, and these offset in an invaluable way our normal indulgences in scenic display. But the spirit of the Shetlands is not easily or speedily apprehended; one must accustom oneself patiently to a different aspect of the world, a different rhythm of life, before one can fully understand how its variations from what we have been used to are counter-balanced by its own essential qualities. The lack of ostentatious appearances, the seeming bareness and reserve, make the Shetlands insusceptible of being readily or quickly understood; one must steep oneself in them, let them grow upon one, to savour them properly. It is a splendid discipline.

Hugh MacDiarmid (1892–1978)
The Uncanny Scot

HISTORY

Columba Comes to Scotland

Columba was a native of Ireland, and connected by birth with the princes of the land. Ireland was at that time a land of gospel light, while the western and northern parts of Scotland were still immersed in the darkness of heathenism. Columba . . . landed on the island of Iona in the year of our Lord 563, having made the passage in a wicker boat covered with hides. The Druids who occupied the island endeavoured to prevent his settling there, and the savage nations on the adjoining shores incommoded him with their hostility, and on several occasions endangered his life by their attacks. Yet by his perseverance and zeal he surmounted all opposition, procured from the king a gift of the island, and established there a monastery of which he was abbot. He was unwearied in his labours to disseminate a knowledge of the Scriptures throughout the Highlands and islands of Scotland, and such was the reverence paid to him that though not a bishop, but merely a presbyter and monk, the entire province with its bishops was subject to him and his successors. The Pictish monarch was so impressed with a sense of his wisdom and worth that he held him in the highest honour, and the neighbouring chiefs and princes sought his counsel and availed themselves of his judgment in settling their disputes.

When Columba landed on Iona he was attended by twelve followers whom he had formed into a religious body of which he was the head. To these, as occasion required, others were from time to time added, so that the original number was always kept up. Their institution was called a monastery and the superior an abbot, but the system had little in common with the monastic institutions of later times. The name by which those who submitted to the rule were known was that of Culdees, probably from the Latin *cultores Dei*—worshippers of God. . . . On entering the order certain vows were taken by the members, but they were not those which were usually imposed by monastic orders, for of these, which are three—celibacy, poverty and obedience—the Culdees were bound to none except the third. To poverty they did not bind themselves: on the contrary, they seem to have laboured diligently to procure for themselves and those dependent on them the comforts of life. Marriage also was allowed them, and most of them seem to have entered into that state. True, their wives were not permitted to reside with them at the institution, but they had a residence assigned to them in an adjacent locality. Near Iona there is an island which still bears the name of 'Eilen nam ban', women's island, where their husbands seem to have resided with them, except when duty required their presence in the school or sanctuary. . . .

In these respects and in others the Culdees departed from the established rules of the Romish church, and consequently were deemed heretical. The consequence was that as the power of the latter advanced that of the communities of the Culdees were suppressed and the members dispersed. . . .

Iona, from its position in the Western seas, was exposed to the assaults of the Norwegian and Danish rovers by whom these seas were infested, and by them it was repeatedly pillaged, its dwellings burned, and its peaceful inhabitants put to the sword. These unfavourable circumstances led to its gradual decline, which was expedited by the subversion of the Culdees throughout Scotland. Under the reign of Popery the island became the seat of a nunnery, the ruins of which are still seen. At the Reformation, the nuns were allowed to remain, living in community, when the abbey was dismantled.

Iona is now chiefly resorted to by travellers on account of the numerous ecclesiastical and sepulchral remains which are found upon it.

Thomas Bullfinch (1796–1861)
Bullfinch's Mythology

The Death of Columba

As the happy hour of his departure gradually approached, the saint became silent. Then as soon as the bell tolled out midnight, he rose hastily and went to the church; and running more quickly than the rest, he entered it alone, and knelt down in prayer beside the altar. At the same time his attendant, Diormit, who more slowly followed him, saw from a distance that the whole interior of the church was filled with a heavenly light in the direction of the saint. And as he drew near the door, the same light he had seen, and which was also seen by a few more of the brethren standing at a distance, quickly disappeared. Diormit therefore, entering the church, cried out in a mournful voice, 'Where art thou, father?' And feeling his way in the darkness, as the brethren had not yet brought in the lights, he found the saint lying before the altar; and raising him up a little, he sat down beside him, and laid his holy head on his bosom. Meanwhile the rest of the monks ran in hastily in a body with their lights, and beholding their dying father, burst into lamentations. And the saint, as we have been told by some who were present, even before his soul departed, opened wide his eyes and looked round him from side to side, with a countenance full of wonderful joy and gladness, no doubt seeing the holy angels coming to meet him. Diormit then raised the holy right hand of the saint, that he might bless his assembled monks. And the venerable father himself moved his hand at the same time, as well as he was able—that as he could not in words, while his soul was departing, he might at least, by the motion of his hand, be seen to bless his brethren. And having given them holy benediction in this way, he immediately breathed his last. After his soul had left the tabernacle of the body, his face still continued ruddy, and brightened in a wonderful way by his vision of the angels, and that to such a degree that he had the appearance, not so much of one dead, as of one in a quiet slumber.

Adamnan (*c.* 624–704)
Life of St Columba

Cantus

The earliest extant piece of Scottish verse, quoted in 'The Orygynale Cronykil' of Andrew of Wyntoun, completed about 1420, laments the death of Alexander III, who was thrown from his horse at Kinghorn in 1286; an event which gave rise to Scotland's Wars of Independence.

When Alexander our king was deid,
  That Scotland lede in lauche and le,   [law and peace
Away was sons of alle and brede,   [abundance
  Of wyne and wax, of gamyn and gle.
Our gold was changit into leid.   [lead
  Crist, borne into virgynyte,
Succoure Scotland and remeid,
  That stade is in perplexitie.

Andrew Wyntoun (1350?–1425?)
Chronykil

Bannockburn

After the death of Alexander III in 1286, there followed the long attempt by Edward I, 'the hammer of the Scots', to make Scotland subservient to England. It was his son Edward II who on 24th June 1314, confronted with a Scots army under Robert the Bruce, charged an unbroken phalanx of Scots pikemen and suffered defeat at Bannockburn, near Stirling, thus removing for the time being the threat of English domination.

John Barbour, archdeacon of Aberdeen, probably composed his best-known poem, from which the following extract is taken, in 1375. His language is archaic and, except for a few passages like the famous address to Freedom, his poetic manner apt to be settled jog-trot. Yet when the action excites his imagination, the lines do not lack vigour, and he suggests vividly the sense of chaos, terror and triumph which must have prevailed at Bannockburn in the closing moments of the battle.

There was the battle stricken weil;
So great dinning there was of dynts   [striking . . . blows
As wapnys upon armour stints,   [weapons were stopped by armour
And of spears so great bristing,   [breaking
With sic thrawing and sic thristing,   [such throwing and thrusting
Sic girning, granyng, and so great   [grimacing, groaning
A noise, as they can other beat,
And cryit ensenyeis on everilk side,   [battle cries . . . every side
Gifand and takand woundis wide,   [giving
That it was hideous for til hear   [for to
All four the battles, wicht that were   [companies, strong
Fechtand intil ae front wholly.   [fighting together on one front

Almichty God! Full douchtely   [doughtily
Sir Edward the Bruce and his men   [Robert's brother, later king of Ireland
Amang their faes contenyt them then,   [demeaned themselves
Fechtand into sa good covyne   [counsel
So hardy, worthy, and so fine,
That their avaward rushit was   [vanguard
And, maugre theiris, left the place,   [in spite of them
And to their great rout to warrand   [main army for safety
They went, that then had upon hand
So great not, that they were effrayit,   [so much to do . . . frightened
For Scottish men them had assayit,   [attacked
That then were in ane schiltrom all.   [one serried mass
Wha happnit in that ficht to fall
I trow again he suld not rise.
There, men micht see on many wise   [in many ways
Hardiment eschevit douchtely.   [brave deeds valiantly achieved
And mony that wicht were and hardy   [strong
Doun under feet lyand all deid,
Whar all the field of blood was red.
Armour and quyntis that they bare   [armourial signs
With blood was so defoulit there,
That they micht nocht discryvit be.   [recognized

Ah! Michty God! wha then micht see
The Steward Walter and his rout,   [company
And the good Douglas that was stout
Fechtand into the stalwart stour   [vigorous commotion
He suld say that til all honour
They were worthy, that in that ficht
Sa fast pressit their faes' micht
That they them rushit whar they yeid.   [went
There micht men see full mony a steed
Fleand on stray, that lord had nane.   [running riderless

Ah! lord! wha then good tent had tane   [who then had paid attention
To the good Earl of Murreff,   [Moray
And his, that swa great routis gaf,   [gave such great blows
And foucht so fast in that battale,
Tholand sic pain and sic travail   [enduring such pain and hardship
That where they come they made them gait!   [cut their own passage
Then men micht hear ensenyeis cry   [the battle cry
And Scottish men cry hardely,
On them! On them! On them! They fail . . .

> John Barbour (1316–95)
> *The Bruce*

Bannockburn

Unflinching foot 'gainst foot was set,
Unceasing blow by blow was met;
  The groans of those who fell
Were drown'd amid the shriller clang
That from the blades and harness rang,
  And in the battle-yell.
Yet fast they fell, unheard, forgot,
Both Southern fierce and hardy Scot;
And O! amidst that waste of life,
What various motives fired the strife!
The aspiring Noble bled for fame,
The Patriot for his country's claim;
This Knight his youthful strength to prove,
And that to win his lady's love;
Some fought from ruffian thirst of blood,
From habit some, or hardihood.
But ruffian stern, and soldier good,
  The noble and the slave,
From various cause the same wild road,
On the same bloody morning, trode,
  To that dark inn, the Grave!

> Sir Walter Scott (1771–1832)
> *The Lord of the Isles*

The March to Bannockburn

Writing to George Thomson, the editor of 'A Select Collection of Original Scottish Airs', for which Burns wrote many of his finest songs and Haydn, Beethoven and Weber, amongst others less distinguished, provided accompaniments to suit the tastes of Edinburgh's then recently-built New Town drawing-rooms, the poet declared:

You know that my pretensions to musical taste, are merely a few of Nature's instincts, untaught and untutored by Art. —For this reason, many musical compositions, particularly where much of the merit lies in Counterpoint, however they may transport and ravish the ears of you, Connoisseurs, affect my simple lug no otherwise than merely as melodious Din—On the other hand, by way of amends, I am delighted with many little melodies, which the learned Musician despises as silly and insipid—I do not know whether the old air, 'Hey tutti taitie,' may rank among this number; but well I know that, with Fraser's Hautboy, it has often filled my eyes with tears— There is a tradition, which I have met with in many places of Scotland, that it was Robert Bruce's March at the battle of Bannock-burn.—This thought, in my yesternight's evening walk, warmed me to a pitch of enthusiasm on the theme of Liberty and Independence, which I threw into a kind of Scots Ode, fitted to the Air, that one might suppose to be the gallant Royal Scot's address to his heroic followers on that eventful morning.

Robert Bruce's March to Bannockburn—
To its ain tune—

Scots, wha hae wi' Wallace bled,
Scots, wham Bruce has aften led,
Welcome to your gory bed,—
    Or to victorie.—

Now's the day, and now's the hour;
See the front o' battle lower;
See approach proud Edward's power,
    Chains and slaverie.—

Wha will be a traitor-knave?
Wha can fill a coward's grave?
Wha sae base as be a Slave?
    —Let him turn and flie:—

Wha for Scotland's king and law,
Freedom's sword will strongly draw,
Free-man stand, or free-man fa',
    Let him follow me.—

By Oppression's woes and pains!
By your Sons in servile chains!
We will drain our dearest veins,
But they *shall* be free!

Lay the proud Usurpers low!
Tyrants fall in every foe!
Liberty's in every blow!
Let us do—or die! ! !

So may God ever defend the cause of Truth and Liberty, as he did that day!—Amen!

Robert Burns (1759–96)
Letter to George Thomson, dated about 30 August 1793

The Declaration of Arbroath

Six years after Bannockburn, and during a two-year truce with the English, the Scottish nobles, assembled at Arbroath, sent a declaration of Scotland's national freedom to Pope John XXII in Avignon. The original Latin text is believed to have been the work of Bernard de Linton, Abbot of Arbroath and Chancellor of Scotland.

Most Holy Father and Lord, we know and from the chronicles and books of the ancients we find that among other famous nations our own, the Scots, has been graced with widespread renown. They journeyed from Greater Scythia by way of the Tyrrhenian Sea and the Pillars of Hercules, and dwelt for a long course of time in Spain among the most savage tribes, but nowhere could they be subdued by any race, however barbarous. Thence they came, twelve hundred years after the people of Israel crossed the Red Sea, to their home in the west where they still live today. The Britons they first drove out, the Picts they utterly destroyed, and, even though very often assailed by the Norwegians, the Danes and the English, they took possession of that home with many victories and untold efforts; and, as the historians of old time bear witness, they have held it free of all bondage ever since. In their kingdom there have reigned one hundred and thirteen of their own royal stock, the line unbroken by a single foreigner.

The high qualities and deserts of these people, were they not otherwise manifest, gain glory enough from this: that the King of kings and Lord of lords, our Lord Jesus Christ, after His Passion and Resurrection, called them, even though settled in the uttermost parts of the earth, almost the first to His most holy faith. Nor would He have them confirmed in that faith by merely anyone but by the first of His Apostles by calling—though second or third in rank—the most gentle Saint Andrew, the blessed Peter's brother, and desired him to keep them under his protection as their patron for ever.

The Most Holy Fathers your predecessors gave careful heed to these things and bestowed many favours and numerous privileges on this same kingdom and people, as being the special charge of the Blessed Peter's brother. Thus our nation under their protection did indeed live in freedom and peace up to the time when that mighty prince the King of the English, Edward, the father of the one who reigns today, when our kingdom had no head and our people harboured no malice or treachery and were then un-used to wars or invasions, came in the guise of a friend and ally to harass them as an enemy. The deeds of cruelty, massacre, violence, pillage, arson, imprisoning prelates, burning down monasteries, robbing and killing monks and nuns, and yet other outrages without number which he committed against our people, sparing neither age nor sex, religion nor rank, no one could describe nor fully imagine unless he had seen them with his own eyes.

But from these countless evils we have been set free, by the help of Him who though He afflicts yet heals and restores, by our most tireless Prince, King and Lord, the Lord Robert. He, that his people and his heritage might be delivered out of the hands of our enemies, met toil and fatigue, hunger and peril, like another Maccabaeus or Joshua, and bore them cheer-fully. Him, too, divine providence, his right of succession according to our laws and customs which we shall maintain to the death, and the due consent and assent of us all have made our Prince and King. To him, as to the man by whom salvation has been wrought unto our people, we are bound both by law and by his merits that our freedom may be still maintained, and by him, come what may, we mean to stand.

Yet if he should give up what he has begun, and agree to make us or our kingdom subject to the King of England or the English, we should exert ourselves at once to drive him out as our enemy and a subverter of his own rights and ours, and make some other man who was well able to defend us our King; for, as long as but a hundred of us remain alive, never will we on any conditions be brought under English rule. It is in truth not for glory, nor riches, nor honours that we are fighting, but for freedom—for that alone, which no honest man gives up but with his life itself.

Therefore it is, Reverend Father and Lord, that we beseech your Holiness with our most earnest prayers and suppliant hearts, inasmuch as you will in your sincerity and goodness consider all this, that, since with Him Whose vice-regent on earth you are there is neither weighing nor distinction of Jew and Greek, Scotsman or Englishman, you will look with the eyes of a father on the troubles and privations brought by the English upon us and upon the Church of God. May it please you to admonish and exhort the King of the English, who ought to be satisfied with what belongs to him since England used once to be enough for seven kings or more, to leave us Scots in peace, who live in this poor little Scotland, beyond which there is no dwelling-place at all, and covet nothing but our own. We are sincerely willing to do anything for him, having regard to our condition, that we can, to win peace for ourselves.

This truly concerns you, Holy Father, since you see the savagery of the heathen raging against the Christians, as the sins of Christians have indeed deserved, and the frontiers of Christendom being pressed inward every day; and how much it will tarnish your Holiness's memory if (which God forbid) the Church suffers eclipse or scandal in any branch of it during your time, you must perceive. Then rouse the Christian princes who for false reasons pretend that they cannot go to the help of the Holy Land because of wars they have on hand with their neighbours. The real reason that prevents them is that in making war on their smaller neighbours they find quicker profit and weaker resistance. But how cheerfully our Lord the King and we too would go there if the King of the English would leave us in peace, He from Whom nothing is hidden well knows; and we profess and declare it to you as the Vicar of Christ and to all Christendom.

But if your Holiness puts too much faith in the tales the English tell and will not give sincere belief to all this, nor refrain from favouring them to our prejudice, then the slaughter of bodies, the perdition of souls, and all the other misfortunes that will follow, inflicted by them on us and by us on them, will, we believe, be surely laid by the Most High to your charge.

To conclude, we are and shall ever be, as far as any duty calls us, ready to do your will in all things, as obedient sons to you as His Vicar; and to Him as the Supreme King and Judge, we commit the maintenance of our cause, casting our cares upon Him and firmly trusting that He will inspire us with courage and bring our enemies to nought.

May the Most High preserve you to His Holy Church in holiness and health and grant you length of days.

Given at the monastery of Arbroath in Scotland on the sixth day of the month of April in the year of grace thirteen hundred and twenty and the fifteenth year of the reign of our King aforesaid.

from *The Declaration of Arbroath*

Queen Margaret Comes to Scotland

So Edgar Atheling, seeing that everywhere things went not smoothly with the English, went on board ship with his mother and sisters, and tried to get back to the land where he was born. But the Sovereign Ruler, who ruled the winds and waves, troubled the sea, and the billows thereof were upheaved by the breath of the gale; so, while the storm was raging, they all, losing all hope of life, commended themselves to God, and left the vessel to the guidance of the waves. At length, tossed on the countless dangers of the deep, they were forced to bring up in Scotland. So that holy family brought up in a certain spot which was thenceforth called St Margaret's Bay by the inhabitants. While then the aforesaid family tarried in that bay, and were all awaiting in fear the upshot of the matter, news of their arrival was brought to King Malcolm, who at that time was, with his men, staying not far from that spot; so he sent off messengers to the ship to inquire into the truth of the matter. When the messengers came there, they were astonished at the unusual size of the ship, and hurried back to the King as fast as they could, to state what they had seen. On hearing these things the King sent off thither, from among his highest lords, a larger embassy of men more experienced than the former. So these, being welcomed as ambassadors from the King's majesty, carefully noted, not without admiration, the lordliness of the men, the beauty of the women, and the good-breeding of the whole family; and they had pleasant talk thereon among themselves. To be brief—the ambassadors chosen for this duty plied them with sweet words and dulcet eloquence, as to how the thing began, went on, and ended; while they, on the other hand, humbly and eloquently unfolded to them in simple words, the cause and manner of their arrival. So the ambassadors returned. When they had informed the King of the stateliness of the older men, and the good sense of the younger, the ripe womanhood of the matrons and the loveliness of the young girls, one of them went on to say, 'We saw a lady there—whom, by the by, from the matchless beauty of her person, and the ready flow of her pleasant eloquence, teeming, moreover, as she did with all other qualities, I declare to thee, O King, that I suspect, in my opinion, to be mistress of that family—whose admirable loveliness and gentleness one must admire, as I deem, rather than describe.' The King, hearing they were English and were there present, went in person to see them and talk with them . . .

The King, therefore, when he had seen Margaret and learnt she was begotten of royal, and even imperial, seed, sought to have her to wife and got her: for Edgar Atheling gave her away to him, rather through the wish of his friends than his own—nay, by God's behest. For as Hester of old was, through God's providence, for the salvation of her fellow-countrymen, joined in wedlock to King Ashasuerus, even so was this princess joined to the most illustrious King Malcolm. The wedding took place in the year 1070, and was held with great magnificence, not far from the bay where she brought up, at a place called Dunfermline, which was then the King's town.

John of Fordun (d. 1384)
Scotichronicon, translated by W. F. Skene

Before Flodden

Flodden, near the village of Branxton, Northumberland, was on September 9th, 1513 the scene of a battle that proved to be possibly the worst single disaster ever to befall Scotland. James IV, urged on by France and despite the advice of his own nobles, advanced over the Border with a great army on August 22nd.

But he wasted so much time amongst the Border castles, in particular Ford,
where he is supposed to have conducted an affair with the lady of the castle,
that the Earl of Surrey had time to bring up to Wooler an army which matched
in size the Scots army. Surrey outmatched James in generalship, and the king
died fighting, his own corps completely surrounded by the English. Not one
distinguished family in Scotland is said to have escaped losing some relative on
Flodden Field.

Before he set out on this venture, James, while worshipping at St Michael's,
Linlithgow, was visited by a warning spectre. The story is told by Robert
Lindsay of Pitscottie. It is quite possible that his young kinsman, Sir David
Lindsay of the Mount, in Fife, the future author of 'Ane Satire of the Three
Estatis', stage-managed the whole business.

At this time the king came to Lithgow, where he was at the counsall verrie
sad and dollorous, makand his prayers to God, to sen him ane guid success
in his voyage. And there cam ane man clad in ane blew gowne, belted about
him with ane roll of lining, and ane pair of brottikines on his feet, and all
other things conforme thereto. But he had nothing on his head, but side hair
to his shoulders and bald before. He seemed to be ane man of fifty years, and
cam fast forwards, crying among the lords, and specially for the king, saying
that he desired to speak with him, whill at the last he cam to the desk where
the king was at his prayers. But when he saw the king he gave no due
reverence nor salutation, but leaned him doun, gruflings upon the desk, and
said, 'Sir King, my mother has sent me to thee, desiring thee not to go where
thou art purposed, whilk if thou do, thou shall not fair weill in thy journey,
nor none that is with thee. Farder, scho forbade thee not to mell [mix] nor
use the counsell of women, whilk if thou do thou will be confoundit and
brought to shame.'

Be this man had spoken thir words to the king, the evensong was near
done, and the king paused on thir words, studying to give him ane answer.
But in the meantime, before the king's eyes, and in presence of the whole
lords that were about him for the time, this man evanisched away, and
could be no more seen. I heard Sir David Lindsay, lyon-herald, and John
Inglis, the marchell, who were at that time young men and special servants
to the king's grace, thought to have taken this man, but they could not, that
they might have speired [asked] further tidings at him, but they could not
touch him. But all their uncouth novells [news] and counsall could not stay
the king from his purpose and wicked interpryse, but hasted him fast to
Edinburgh to mak him ready, and to mak provision for himself and his
army against the said day appointed.

Robert Lindsay of Pitscottie (1500?–1565?)
The Chronicles of Scotland

Flodden

By this though deep the evening fell,
Still rose the battle's deadly swell,
For still the Scots, around their King,
Unbroken, fought in desperate ring,
Where's now their victor vaward wing,
   Where Huntly and where Home?—
O, for a blast of that dread horn,
On Fontarabian echoes borne,
   That to King Charles did come,
When Rowland brave, and Olivier,
And every Paladin and peer,
   On Roncesvalles died!
Such blast might warn them, not in vain,
To quit the plunder of the slain,
And turn the doubtful day again,
   While yet on Flodden side,
Afar, the Royal Standard flies,
And round it toils, and bleeds, and dies,
   Our Caledonian pride!
In vain the wish—for far away,
While spoil and havoc mark their way,
Near Sybil's Cross the plunderers stray.
'O, Lady,' cried the Monk, 'away!'
   And plac'd her on her steed,
And led her to the chapel fair,
   Of Tilmouth upon Tweed.
There all the night they spent in prayer,
And at the dawn of morning, there
She met her kinsman, Lord Fitz-Clare.

But as they left the dark'ning heath,
More desperate grew the strife of death.
The English shafts in volleys hail'd,
In headlong charge their horse assail'd;
Front, flank, and rear, the squadrons sweep
To break the Scottish circle deep,
   That fought around their King.
But yet, though thick the shafts as snow,
Though charging knights like whirlwinds go,
Though bill-men ply the ghastly blow,
   Unbroken was the ring;
The stubborn spear-men still made good
Their dark impenetrable wood,
Each stepping where his comrade stood,

The instant that he fell.
No thought was there of dastard flight;
Link'd in the serried phalanx tight,
Groom fought like noble, squire like knight,
    As fearlessly and well;
Till utter darkness closed her wing
O'er their thin host and wounded King.
Then skilful Surrey's sage commands
Led back from strife his shatter'd bands;
    And from the charge they drew,
As mountain-waves, from wasted lands,
    Sweep back to ocean blue.
Then did their loss his foemen know;
Their King, their Lords, their mightiest low,
They melted from the field as snow,
When streams are swoln and south winds blow,
    Dissolves in silent dew.
Tweed's echoes heard the ceaseless plash,
    While many a broken band,
Disorder'd, through her currents dash,
    To gain the Scottish land;
To town and tower, to town and dale,
To tell red Flodden's dismal tale,
And raise the universal wail.
Tradition, legend, tune, and song
Shall many an age that wail prolong:
Still from the sire the son shall hear
Of the stern strife, the carnage drear,
    Of Flodden's fatal field,
Where shiver'd was fair Scotland's spear,
    And broken was her shield!

Sir Walter Scott (1771–1832)
Marmion

A Lament for Flodden

Alas, where bene that richt redoubit Roy,   [king
That potent prince gentle King James the Ferde?   [fourth
I pray to Christ his soul for to convoy;
Ane greater noble rang not into erde.   [earth
O, Atropos! warye we may thy weird,   [we may curse thy fate
Lor he was mirrour of humility,
Fode sterne and lamp of liberality.

During his time so justice did prevail,
The savage Isles tremblit for terrour;
Eskdale, Ewesdale, Liddisdale and Annerdale
Durst nocht rebel, douting his dintis dour;   [because of his
And of his lordis had sic perfyte favour: determined blows
So, for to show that he aferit no fone,   [that he was afraid of no foes
Out through his realm he wald ride him alone.

And of his court, through Europe sprang the fame,
Of lusty lords and lovesome ladys ying,   [young
Triumphand tourneys, justing and knychtly game,
With all pastime according for ane king.
He was the glory of princely governing
Whilk through the ardent luve he had to France   [which
Agane England did move his ordinance.

Of Flodden field the ruin to revolve,   [go over again
Or that most dolent day for to deplore
I nil, for dreid that dolour you dissolve,   [I won't
Shaw how that prince in his triumphant glore
Destroyit was; what needeth process more?
Nocht by the virtue of Inglis ordinance,
But by his awin wilful misgoverance.

Allace! that day had he been counselabyll,
He had obtainit laude, glore and victory.
Whose piteous process, bene so lamentabyll
I nil at length it put in memorie.
I never read, in tragedy nor story,
At one journey so mony nobills slain
For the defence and luve of their soverane.

Sir David Lindsay of the Mount (1490–1555)
from *The Testament of the Papyngo*

The Flowers of the Forest

I've heard them lilting at our yowe-milking—
     Lasses a-lilting before dawn of day;
But now they are moaning on ilka green loaning—
     The Flowers of the Forest are a' wede away.

At buchts in the morning, nae blythe lads are scorning;   [sheep-folds
     Lasses are lonely and dowie and wae;—

Nac daffin', nac gabbin'—but sighing and sabbing   [joking ... talking
    Ilk ane lifts her leglin and hies her away.   [milk-pail

In hairst, at the shearing, nae youths now are jeering—   [harvest
    Bandsters are runkled and lyart or grey;   [binders ... wrinkled
At fair or at preaching, nae wooing, nae fleeching—   [flattering
    The Flowers of the Forest are a' wede away.   [faded

At e'en, in the gloaming, nae swankies are roaming,   [smart fellows
    'Bout stacks with the lasses at bogle to play;
But ilk maid sits drearie, lamenting her dearie—
    The Flowers of the Forest are a' wede away.

Dool and wae for the order sent our lads to the Border!
    The English, for ance, by guile wan the day;—
The Flowers of the Forest, that faucht aye the foremost—
    The prime of our land—are cauld in the clay.

We'll hear nae mair lilting at the yowe-milking;
    Women and bairns are heartless and wae,
Sighing and moaning on ilka green loaning—
    The Flowers of the Forest are a' wede away.

                                    Jean Elliot (1727–1805)

Sir Robert Rome-Raker

Sir David Lindsay's morality play, 'Ane Satire of the Three Estates', was first performed in the banqueting hall of Linlithgow Palace in 1540 before James V and his Queen. It sets out vividly the abuses against ordinary people which fed the grievances upon which the Reformation took root in Scotland, as it had earlier done in Germany and England. Adapted by Robert Kemp, the play was revived in the production by Sir Tyrone Guthrie at the Edinburgh Festival in 1949; so successfully that it was repeated on several later occasions. There has also been a revival of it by the students of Glasgow University.

*   In this extract, the Pardoner makes his entrance just as the Poor Man has been explaining to Diligence how the vicar has removed his last cow for payment of Church dues.*

Bona dies, bona dies!
Devout people, gude day I say you,
Now tarry a little while I pray you
    Till I be with you known!
Wat ye weel how I am namit?

Ane noble man and undefamit,
  If all the sooth were shown.   [if everything was known
I am Sir Robert Rome-raker,
Ane perfyte public pardoner
  Admittit by the Pape.
Sirs, I sall show you, for my wage,
My pardons and my pilgrimage,
  Which ye sall see and graip.   [reach for
I give to the devil with gude intent
This woeful wicked New Testament
  With them that it translatit.
Sen laymen knew the verity   [since laymen knew the truth
Pardoners gets no charity
  Without that they debate it. ...
Deil fell the brain that has it wrocht
Sae fall them that the Buik hame brocht,
  Als I pray to the Rood
That Martin Luther, that false loon,
Black Bullinger and Melancthon
  Had been smoored in their cude.   [smothered ... cradle
By Him that bure the crown of thorn
I wad Sanct Paul had never been born,
  Also I wad his buiks
Were never read into the Kirk,
But amang friars into the mirk,
  Or riven amang the rooks!
(*He lays down his wares on a board*)
My patent pardons you may see
Come frae the Khan of Tartary
  Weel seald with oyster shells.
Though ye have nae contrition
Ye sall have full remission
  With help of books and bells.
Here is ane relic, lang and braid,
Of Finn MacColl the richt chaft blade   [the right jawbone of Fingal, the
  With teeth and all together.   mythical Ossianic hero
Of Colin's cow here is ane horne
For eating of Mackonnal's corne
  Was slain into Balquidder.
Here is ane cord baith great and lang
That hangit John the Armistrang,   [Border freebooter put down
  Of due hemp saft and sound.   by James V
Gude haly people, I stand for'd
Wha ever beis hangit with this cord
  Needs never to be dround.
The culum of Sanct Bridis' cow   [backside

The gruntle of Sanct Anthony's sow,   [snout
   Whilk buir this haly bell: [carried
Wha ever he be hears this bell clink,
Give me ane ducat for til drink,   [to
   He sall never gang to Hell,
Without he be of Belial born.   [unless born of the Devil
Maisters, trow ye that this be scorn?
   Cum, win this pardon, cum.
Wha luves thair wives nocht with their hart,
I have power for them til part.
   Methink yow deif and dumb!
Hes nanc of yow curst wickit wives
That halds yow into sturt and stryfs?
   Cum, tak my dispensatioun:
Of that cummer I sall mak yow quyte   [woman ... quit
howbeit yourselves be in the wyte,   [bc to blame
   And mak ane false narratioun.
Cum, win the pardon. Now let see,
For meal, for malt, or for monie,
   For cok, hen, goose or gryse.   [young pig
Of relicts heir I haif anc hunder.
Why cum ye nocht? This is great wonder:
   I trow ye be nocht wyse.   [judge

Sir David Lindsay of the Mount (1490–1555)
Ane Satyre of the Three Estates

The Death of James V

... The king passed out of Hallirudhouse to Falkland, and thair became so
heavie and dolorous that he neither ate nor drank that had guid digestioun,
and so became so vehement seik that no man had hope of his lyff. Then he
sent for certain of his lords, both spiritual and temporal, to have thair
counsall. But or they cam, he was very near strangled to thc death by
extreme melancholie. Be this, the post cam out of Linlithgow schowing the
king guid tidings, that the queen was deliverit. The king inquired whidder
it was a man or woman. The messenger said it was ane fair dochter. He
answeired and said, 'Fairweill, it cam with ane lass and it will pass with ane
lass'; and so he commendit himself to the Almightie God, and spak little
from thenforth, but turned his back to his lords and his face to the wall.

At this time Sir David Beaton, Cardinal of Scotland, standing in presence
of the king, seeing him begin to fail of his strength and natural speech, held
ane throughe of papir to his grace, and caused him to subscribe the same,
whairin the Cardinal writ what he pleased for his awin particular weil;

7

thinkand to have had the auctorite and preheminence in the government of the countrie. Bot we may knaw hereby that the king's legacie was verie schort; for in this meantime he depairted. As I have shown you, he turned upon his back, and lookit and beheld all his lords round about, and gave ane little lauchter, syne kissed his hand and gave it til all his lords about him, and thairefter held up his hands to God, and yeildit the spirit.

Robert Lindsay of Pitscottie (1500?–65?)
The Chronicles of Scotland

Towards the Union

In 1547 James V had been five years dead, Mary Queen of Scots was a child in France, and the kingdom was in an unhappy state. A London Scot about whom virtually nothing else is known chose that moment to urge the Scots to abandon their sense of nationality and allow themselves be submerged into the more numerically powerful race.

I perceive that love to my country and nation hath made me unawares to have wandered furder than at the first I proposed: wherefore I will make an end, if first I shall repeat that I have already proved unto you, that these two realms were first a monarchy under Brutus, and so left by his order to his sons, by the superiority which was in his ancestors proved by the homages and other things afore alleged, the claim whereof did yet never cease, as also specially by force of your own late Act of Parliament, whereby he ought of right to marry our Princess, the inheritrice of the Crown of Scotland: by occasion whereof we shall be received, not into servitude, but into the same fellowship with Englishmen, the names of both subjects and realms ceasing, and to be changed into the name of Britain and Britons, as it was first, and yet still ought to be.

And how necessary that same form of the governance of one monarch or king is, you see to be more clear than the sun, and the same to be a ready and easy meane, how both to appease all discord, which otherwise will never stint, and also to establish us in everlasting peace, quiet and tranquility: unto which effects there is verily none other mean. And the thing itself (though I should hold my peace) doth sufficiently speak and avouch the same to be a way unto both realms most honourable, because not only the Empire shall by that occasion be the more large and strong in itself, and the King the more puissant and famous: profitable, for that discord shall cease, and concord come in place, and thereby the people and commonweal flourish and prosper: and godly, for that we shall agree all in one, and the same the true and Christian religion.

James Harryson
An Exhortation to the Scots

Scots and English

Across the Border, an anonymous author was stung to reply to James Harryson, the London Scot. 'The Complaint of Scotland' expresses in rugged Scots the point of view of the party expected to submit to the swallowing process in Harryson's proposals. Even to-day, more than two hundred and fifty years after the completion of incorporating union, some echo of the complainer's viewpoint is to be heard on both Scots and English tongues on occasion.

In the days of Moses, the Jews durst nocht have familiarity with the Samaritans, nor with the Philistans, nor the Romans with the Africans, nor the Greeks with the Persians, by raisoun that ilk [each] ane repute others to be of ane barbour nature; for every natioun reputis other natiouns to be barbarians, when ther twa naturis and complexiouns are contrar till otheris; and there is nocht twa natiouns under the firmament that are mair contrar and different fra otheris nor is Inglis men and Scottish men, houbeit that thay be within ane isle, and nichtbours, and of ane language. For Inglis men are subtil, and Scottish men are facile. Inglis men are ambitious in prosperity, and Scottish men are humane in prosperity. Inglis men are humble when they are subjeckit by force and violence, and Scottish men are merciful when they get victory. And to concludc, it is unpossible that Scottish men and English men can remain in concord under ane monarchy or ane prince, because ther natures and conditionus are as indefferent as is the nature of scheip and wolvis ... I trow [am sure] it is as unpossible to gar [make] Inglis men and Scottish men remain in gude accord under ane prince, as it is unpossible that twa Suns and twa Munis can be at one time togidder in the lift [sky], by reasoun of the grit difference that is betwix ther natures and conditiouns. Wharfore, as I haiff before rehearsit, there suld be na familiarity betwix Inglis men and Scottish men because of the grit difference that is betwix ther twa natures ...

> Anonymous
> *The Complaint of Scotland*

Confrontation and Reformation

The Protestant nobles were at the head of their numerous followers; the Queen chiefly relied upon a small but select body of French troops. The war was not very violently carried on, for the side of the Reformers became every day stronger ... At the same time, although the Lords found it easy to bring together large bodies of men, yet they had not the money or means necessary to keep them together for a long time, while the French veteran soldiers were always ready to take advantage when Reformed leaders were obliged to diminish their forces. Their difficulties became greater when the Queen Regent showed her design to fortify strongly the town of Leith and the adjacent island of Inchkeith, and place her French soldiers in garrison there; so that, being in possession of that seaport, she might at all times, when she saw occasion, introduce an additional number of foreigners.

Unskilled in the art of conducting sieges, and totally without money, the Lords of the Congregation had recourse to the assistance of England: and for the first time an English fleet and army approached the territories of Scotland by sea and land, not with the purpose of invasion, as used to be the case of old, but to assist the nation in its resistance to the arms of France and the religion of Rome.

The English army was soon joined by the Scottish Lords of the Congregation, and advancing to Leith, laid siege to the town, which was most valorously defended by the French soldiers ... They were, however, blockaded by the English fleet, so that no provisions could be received by sea; and on land being surrounded by a considerable army, provisions became so scarce that they were obliged to feed upon horse-flesh.

In the meantime, their mistress, the Queen Regent, had retired into the castle of Edinburgh, where grief, fatigue and disappointed expectations, threw her into an illness, of which she died on 10th of June 1560. The French troops in Leith being now reduced to extremity, Francis and Mary determined upon making peace in Scotland at the expense of the most important concessions to the Reformed party. They agreed that, instead of naming a new Regent, the administration of affairs should be conferred upon a council of government chosen by Parliament ... And they left the subject of religion to be disposed of as the Parliament should determine, which was, in fact, giving the full power to the Reformed party. All foreign troops, on both sides, were to be withdrawn accordingly ...

The Parliament of Scotland being assembled, it was soon seen that the Reformers possessed the power and inclination to direct all its resolutions upon the subject of religion. They condemned unanimously the whole fabric of Popery, and adopted, instead of the doctrines of the Church of Rome, the tenets contained in a confession, or avowal of faith, drawn up by the most popular of the Protestant divines. Thus the whole religious constitution of the Church was at once altered.

There was one particular in which the Scottish Reformers greatly differed from those of England. The English monarch, who abolished the power of the Pope, had established that of the crown as the visible Head of the Church of England ... On the contrary, the Reformed ministers of Scotland renounced the authority of any interference of the civil magistrate, whether subject or sovereign, in the affairs of the Church, declaring it should be under the exclusive direction of a court of delegates chosen from its own numbers, assisted by a certain number of the laity, forming what is called a General Assembly of the Church. The Scottish Reformers disclaimed also the division of the clergy into the various ranks of bishops, deans, prebendaries, and other classes of the clerical order ...

The laity of Scotland, and particularly the great nobility, saw with pleasure the readiness of the ministers to resign all those pretensions to worldly rank and consequence, which had been insisted upon by the Roman Catholic clergy, and made their self-denying abjuration of titles and worldly business a reason for limiting the subsistence which they were to derive from the funds of the Church, to the smallest possible sum of annual stipend, whilst they appropriated the rest to themselves without scruple.

It remained to dispose of the wealth lately enjoyed by the Catholic clergy, who were supposed to be possessed of half of the revenue of Scotland, so far as it arose from land. Knox and the other Reformed clergy had formed a plan for the decent maintenance of a National Church out of these extensive funds, and proposed, that what might be deemed more than sufficient for this purpose should be expended upon hospitals, schools, universities, and places of education. But the Lords, who had seized the revenues of the Church, were determined not to part with the spoil they had obtained; and those whom the preachers had found most active in destroying Popery were wonderfully cold when it was proposed to them to surrender the lands they had seized upon for their own use. The plan of John Knox was, they said, a 'devout imagination', a visionary scheme which showed the goodness of the preacher's intentions, but which it was impossible to carry into practice. In short, they retained by force the greater part of the Church revenues for their own advantage.

Sir Walter Scott (1771–1832)
Tales of a Grandfather

John Knox Faces His Sovereign

John Knox was probably the son of a Haddington farmer. Knox attended Glasgow University, and possibly also that of St Andrews where, as a Catholic priest, he acted for some years as notary of the diocese of St Andrews. In 1546 he attended George Wishart on his last mission, and after Wishart's execution found refuge in the Castle of St Andrews when the Protestants seized it following the murder of Cardinal Beaton. When the Castle surrendered, Knox was sent to the French galleys, from which he was released after just over a year and a half. He then became a preacher in England licensed to preach the reformed faith. When Mary Tudor came to the throne Knox took himself off to Geneva, returning to England to marry in 1555. But apart from occasional visits to Scotland, he remained abroad until 1559, when he returned and was at once outlawed. The death of the Queen Regent, however, led to the triumph of the Protestant party and by 1560 the Reformation was established.

The following year the young Queen Mary arrived at Leith, and she and Knox were soon at enmity. Knox married again in 1563, this time a girl of seventeen, but survived to preach at James VI's coronation at Stirling, and to die in his bed at his home in Edinburgh in 1572.

His 'Historie of the Reformation in Scotland', written at the request of the Protestants but not published during his lifetime, voices, it has been said, 'the prejudices of a party in the language of a fanatic.' Yet its power and vividness make it indubitably a work of literature, albeit a somewhat disagreeable one.

The book referred to in Knox's description of one of his verbal encounters with the Queen is 'A First Blast of the Trumpet Against the Monstrous Regiment of Women', which had appeared in 1560.

Ye think (quoth sche) that I have no just Authority?

Pleis your Majesty (said he) that learned Men in all Ages have had thair Judgements frie, and most comounly disagreeing from the comoun Judgement of the Warld; such also have they publisched, both with Pen and Toung, notwithstanding thay thaimeselves have lived in the comoun society with uthers, and have borne patiently with the Errours and Imperfectiounes, whilk [which] they could not amend. Plato the Philosopher wrait his Buik of the Comounwealthe, in the whilk [which] he damnethe mony Things that then were manteyned in the Warld, and requyred mony things to have been reformed; and yit nowithstanding he lived under sic [such] Policies, as then were universally receaved, without further trubling of ony Estate. Even so, Madam, am I content to do, in Upryghtnes of Hairt, and with a Testimony of a gude Conscience. I have communicat my Judgement to the Warld; if the Realme finds no Inconveniency in the Regiment [government] of a Woman, that quhilk [which] they approve sall [shall] I not further disallow, than within my awn Breist, bot sall be als [as] weill content to live under so lang as that ye defyll not your Hands with the Blude of the Saincts of God, that neyther I nor that Buik sall eyther hurt yow or your Authority; for in very deid, Madam, that Buik was written most especially against thet wicked Jesabell of England.

Bot (said sche) ye speik of Women in generall.

Most trew it is, Madam (said the uther) and yit it appeareth to me, that Wisdome suld persuade your Grace, never to rayse Truble for that, quhilk to this Day hes not trubled your Majesty, nether in Persone nor in Authority. . . . If I had intended to have trubled your Estate, becaus ye ar a Woman, I wald have chosen a Tyme more convenient for that Purpose, than I can do now, when your awn Presence is within the Realme.

Bot now, Madame, schortly to answer to the uther two Accusatiouns. I hartly prayse my God throw Jesus Christ, that Sathan the Enemy of Mankynd, and the Wicked of the Warld, have no uther Crymes to lay to my Charge, than sic [such] as the very Warld itself knaws to be most fals and vane. For in England I was resident onely the Space of fyve Yeirs. The Places wer Berwick, quhare [where] I abode two Yeirs, so long in Newcastle, and a Yeir in Londone. Now, Madame, if in ony of these Places, during the Tyme that I was thare, ony Man sall be able to prove that thare was eyther Battell, Seditioun or Mutiny, I sall confess that I myself was the Malefactour, and the Schedder of Blude. I eschame not [am not ashamed] farther to affirme, that God so blessed my waik [weak] Labours, that in Berwick quharein comonly thare used to be Slachter, be Ressouns [because] of Quarrells that used to aryse amongst the Souldiours thare was als [as] grit Quyetnes all the Tyme that I remained thare, as thare is this Day in Edinburghe.

And quhare they slander me of Magick, Necromancy, or of ony uther Airt forbidden of God, I have Witnesses (besyde my awn Conscience) all the Congregatiouns that ever hard [heard] me, quhat [what] I spak both against such Artes, and against those that use such Impiety. Bot seeing the Wicked of the Warld said, That my Maister the Lord Jesus was possessed with Beelzebub, I maun [must] patiently bear, albeit that I, a wretched Sinner, be unjustly accused of those, that never delyted in the Verity.

Bot yet, said sche, ye have teachit the Pepill to receave ane uther Religioun than their Princes can allow: And how can that Doctrine be of God, seeing that God commands Subjects to obey their Princes? . . . Think ye, quoth sche, that Subjects having power may resist thair Princes?

If thair Princes excede thair Bounds, quoth he, Madame, and do against that quharefore they suld be obeyed, it is no Doubt bot they may be resisted, even by Power [force]. For thare is nether gritter Honour nor gritter Obedience to be gevin to Kings and Princes than God has commandit to be gevin to Father and Mother: Bot so it is, that the Father may be stricken with a Phrensie, in the quhilk he wald slay his awn Children. Now, Madame, if the Children aryse, joyne thameselves togidder, apprehend the Father, tak the Sword and uther weapons from him; and finally bind his Hands and keep him in Prisoun till that his Frensie be overpast; think ye, Madame, that the Children do any Wrang? Or think ye, Madame, that God will be offendit with thame that have stayed [prevented] thair Father to comit Wickednes? It is even so, said he, Madame, with Princes, that wald murther the Children of God, that ar subjects unto thame. Thair blind Zeall is nathing bot a very mad Phrensie; and thairfore to tak the Sword from thame, to bind thair Hands, and to cast thame in Prisone, till that they be brocht to a more sober Mynd, is no Disobedience against Princes, bot just Obedience, becaus that it agreeth with the Will of God.

At these Words, the Quene stude as it wer amased [amazed] more than a Quarter of ane Hour; hir Countenance altered, so that Lord James began to entreat hir, and to demand, Quhat hes offended yow, Madam?

At lenth sche said, Weill then I perceave that my subjects sall obey you, and not me; and sall do what they list [like], and not quhat I command: And so maun [must] I be subject to thame, and not they to me.

God forbid, answered he, that ever I tak upoun me to command ony to obey me, or yit to sett Subjects at Liberty to do quhat pleases thame. Bot my Travell [effort] is that both Princes and subjects obey God: For it is he that subjects the Pepell under Princes, and causes Obedience to be gevin unto thame; yea, God craves of Kings, That they be, as it wer, Foster-fathers to his Kirk, and commands Quenis to be Nurisches [nurses] unto his Pepell. And this Subjectioun, Madame, unto God, and unto his troubled Kirk, is the grittest Dignity that Flesche can get upoun the Face of the Erthe, for it sall carry thame to everlasting Glory.

Yea, quoth sche, bot ye ar not the Kirk that I will nurische. I will defend the Kirk of Rome, for it is, I think, the trew Kirk of God.

Your will, quoth he, Madame is no Reason; nether doth your Thocht mak that Romane Harlott to be the trew and immaculate Spouse of Jesus Christ. And wonder not, Madame, that I call Rome ane Harlott; for that Kirk is altogidder polluted with all kynd of Spiritual Fornicatioun, alsweill [as well] Doctrin as in Maners. . . .

My Conscience, said sche, is not so.

Conscience, Madame, said he, requyres Knawlege; and I fear that rycht Knawlege ye have nane.

Bot, said sche, I have both heard and read.

So, Madame, said he, did the Jews who crucified Christ Jesus. . . .

John Knox (1513–72)
Historie of the Reformatioun in Scotland

Alas! Poor Queen

She was skilled in music and the dance
And the old arts of love
At the court of the poisoned rose
And the perfumed glove,
And gave her beautiful hand
To the pale Dauphin
A triple crown to win—
And she loved little dogs
   And parrots
  And red-legged partridges
And the golden fishes of the Duc de Guise
And a pigeon with a blue ruff
She had from Monsieur d'Elboeuf.

Master John Knox was no friend to her;
She spoke him soft and kind,
Her honeyed words were Satan's lure
The unwary soul to bind.
'Good sir, doth a lissome shape
And a comely face
Offend you God His Grace
Whose wisdom maketh these
Golden fishes of the Duc de Guise?

She rode through Liddesdale with a song;
'Ye streams sae wondrous strang,

Oh, mak' me a wrack as I come back
But spare me as I gang.'
While a hill-bird cried and cried
Like a spirit lost
By the grey storm-wind tost

Consider the way she had to go,
Think of the hungry snare,
The net she herself had woven,
Aware or unaware,
Of the dancing feet grown still,
The blinded eyes—
Queens should be cold and wise,
And she loved little things,
　　Parrots
　And red-legged partridges
And the golden fishes of the Duc de Guise
And the pigeon with the blue ruff
She had from Monsieur d'Elboeuf.

Marion Angus (1866–1946)

Queen Mary Resigns the Crown in Favour of Her Son

'We come, madam,' said the Lord Ruthven, 'to request your answer to the proposal of the Council.'

'Your final answer,' said Lord Lindesay; 'for with a refusal you must couple the certainty that you have precipitated your fate, and renounced the last opportunity of making peace with God, and ensuring your longer abode in the world.'

'My lords,' said Mary, with inexpressable grace and dignity, 'the evils we cannot resist we must submit to—I will subscribe these parchments with such liberty of choice as my condition permits me. Were I on yonder shore, with a fleet jennet and ten good loyal knights around me, I would subscribe my sentence of eternal condemnation as soon as the resignation of my throne. But here, in the castle of Lochleven, with deep water around me—and you, my lords, beside me—I have no freedom of choice—Give me the pen, Melville, and bear witness to what I do, and why I do it.'

'It is our hope your Grace will not suppose yourself compelled, by any apprehensions from us,' said the Lord Ruthven, 'to execute what must be your own voluntary deed.'

The Queen had already stooped towards the table, and placed the parchment before her, with the pen between her fingers, ready for the important act of signature. But when Lord Ruthven had done speaking, she looked up, stopped short, and threw down the pen. 'If,' she said, 'I am expected to declare I give away my crown of free will, or otherwise than because I am compelled to renounce it by the threat of worse evils to myself and my subjects, I will not put my name to such an untruth—not to gain full possession of England, France, and Scotland!—all once my own, in possession, or by right.'

'Beware, madam,' said Lindesay, and snatching hold of the Queen's arm, with his own gauntleted hand, he pressed it, in the rudeness of his passion, more closely perhaps, than he was himself aware of,—'beware how you contend with those who are the stronger, and have the mastery of your fate!'

He held his grasp on her arm, bending his eyes on her with a stern and intimidating look, till both Ruthven and Melville cried shame! and Douglas, who had hitherto remained in a state of apparent apathy, had made a stride from the door, as if to interfere. The rude Baron then quitted his hold, disguising the confusion which he really felt at having indulged his passion to such extent, under a sullen and contemptuous smile.

The Queen immediately began, with an expression of pain, to bare the arm which he had grasped, by drawing up the sleeve of her gown, and it appeared that his gripe had left the purple mark of his iron fingers upon her flesh— 'My lord,' she said, 'as a knight and gentleman, you might have spared my frail arm so severe a proof that you have the greater strength on your side, and are resolved to use it—But I thank you for it—it is the most decisive token of the terms on which this day's business is to rest.—I draw you to witness, both lords and ladies,' she said, showing the marks of the grasp on her arm, 'that I subscribe these instruments in obedience to the sign manual of my Lord of Lindesay, which you may see imprinted on mine arm.'

Lindesay would have spoken, but was restrained by his colleague Ruthven, who said to him, 'Peace, my lord. Let the Lady Mary of Scotland ascribe her signature to what she will, it is our business to procure it and carry it to the Council. Should there be debate hereafter on the manner in which it was adhibited, there will be time enough for it.'

Lindesay was silent accordingly, only muttering within his beard, 'I meant not to hurt her; but I think women's flesh be as tender as new-fallen snow.'

The Queen meanwhile subscribed the rolls of parchment with a hasty indifference, as if they had been matters of slight consequence, or of mere formality. When she had performed this painful task, she arose, and, having curtsied to the lords, was about to withdraw to her chamber. Ruthven and Sir Robert Melville made, the first a formal reverence, the second an obeisance in which his desire to acknowledge his sympathy was obviously checked by the fear of appearing in the eyes of his colleagues too partial to his former mistress. But Lindesay stood motionless, even when they were preparing to withdraw. At length, as if moved by a sudden impulse, he walked round the table which had hitherto been betwixt them and the Queen, kneeled on one knee, took her hand, kissed it, let it fall, and arose—'Lady,' he said, 'thou art a noble creature, even though thou hast abused God's choicest gifts. I pay that devotion to thy manliness of spirit, which I would not have paid to the power thou hast long undeservedly wielded—I kneel to Mary Stewart, not to the Queen.'

'The Queen and Mary Stewart pity thee alike, Lindesay,' said Mary—'alike they pity, and they forgive thee. An honoured soldier hadst thou been by a king's side—leagued with rebels, what art thou but a good blade in the hands of a ruffian?—Farewell, my Lord Ruthven, the smoother but the deeper traitor.—Farewell, Melville—Mayst thou find masters that can understand state policy better, and have the means to reward it more richly, than Mary Stewart—Farewell, George of Douglas—make your respected grand-dame comprehend that we would be alone for the remainder of the day—God wot, we have need to collect our thoughts.'

Sir Walter Scott (1771–1832)
The Abbot

The Last Letter

A few hours before she was to mount the scaffold at Fotheringay Castle, Mary Queen of Scots wrote her last letter, in French, to Henry III of France, younger brother of her first husband.

8 Feb. 1587

Royal brother, having by God's will, for my sins I think, thrown myself into the power of the Queen my cousin, at whose hands I have suffered much for almost twenty years, I have finally been condemned to death by her and her Estates. I have asked for my papers, which they have taken away, in order that I might make my will, but I have been unable to recover anything of use to me, or even get leave either to make my will freely or to have my body conveyed after my death, as I would wish, to your kingdom where I had the honour to be queen, your sister and old ally.

Tonight, after dinner, I have been advised of my sentence: I am to be executed like a criminal at eight in the morning. I have not had time to give you a full account of everything that has happened, but if you will listen to my doctor and my other unfortunate servants, you will learn the truth, and how, thanks be to God, I scorn death and vow that I meet it innocent of any crime, even if I were their subject. The Catholic faith and the assertion of my God-given right to the English crown are the two issues on which I am condemned, and yet I am not allowed to say that it is for the Catholic religion that I die, but for fear of interference with theirs. The proof of this is that they have taken away my chaplain, and, although he is in the building, I have not been able to get permission for him to come and hear my confession and give me the Last Sacrament, while they have been most insistent that I receive the consolation and instruction of their minister, brought here for that purpose. The bearer of this letter and his companions, most of them your subjects, will testify to my conduct at my last hour. It remains for me to beg your most Christian Majesty, my brother-in-law and old ally, who have always protested your love for me, to give proof now of your goodness on all these points: firstly by charity, in paying my unfortunate servants the wages due them—this is a burden on my conscience that only you can relieve; further, by having prayers offered to God for a queen who has borne the title Most Christian, and who dies a Catholic, stripped of all her possessions. As for my son, I commend him to you in so far as he deserves, for I cannot answer for him. I have taken the liberty of sending you two precious stones, talismans against illness, trusting that you will enjoy good health and a long and happy life. Accept them from your loving sister-in-law, who, as she dies, bears witness of her warm feeling for you. Again I commend my servants to you. Give instructions, if it please you, that for my soul's sake part of what you owe me should be paid, and that for the sake of Jesus Christ, to whom I shall pray for you tomorrow as I die, I be left enough to found a memorial mass and give the customary alms.

Wednesday, at two in the morning.

Your most loving and most true sister,

MARY R

To the Most Christian King, my brother and old ally.

The Execution of the Queen

The House of Fugger, merchant princes and bankers, operated from the town of Augsburg, lending money to Kings and Emperors. Count Philip Edward Fugger caused to be collected reports from agents all over Europe; and these reports, often vividly written, were subsequently published as 'The Fugger News-Letters', covering the period 1568–1605. The account of the execution of Mary Queen of Scots is described as being by Emanuel Tomascon, who was present at the event.

The gown in which the Queen was attired was of exquisite black velvet . . . In her hand she held a small cross of wood or of ivory with the picture of Christ thereon, and a book. On her neck hung a golden crucifix, and from her girdle a rosary.

Near her stood a Doctor of Theology, the Dean of Peterborough, who at the command of the gentleman spoke words of Christian comfort to her, exalting her to die as a Christian with a repentant heart. She at once interrupted him and begged him to keep his peace, for she was fully prepared for death. The Dean answered that he had been commanded to speak the truth to her. But she said for the second time: 'I will not listen to you, Mr Dean. You have naught to do with me. You disturb me.' Thereupon he was bidden to be silent by the gentleman.

The Earl of Kent said to her: 'Madam, I am grieved on your account to hear of this superstition from you and to see that which is in your hand.' She said it was seemly that she should hold the figure of Christ in her hand, thereby to think of Him. Thereupon he answered that she must have Christ in her heart, and further said that though she may demur in paying heed to the mercies vouchsafed to her by God-all-Highest, they would nevertheless plead for her with God Almighty, that He would forgive her sins and receive her into His Kingdom. Thereto the Queen made reply: 'Pray, then will I also Pray.' Then the aforesaid Doctor fell on his knees on the steps of the dais and read in an overloud voice a fervent and godly prayer for her, most suitable for such an occasion, also for the Queen of England and the welfare of the Kingdom. All those standing round repeated the prayer. But as long as it lasted the Queen was praying in Latin and fairly audibly, holding the crucifix in her hand.

When this prayer was now ended on both sides, the executioner knelt in front of the Queen. Him she forgave his deed, and also all those who lusted after her blood, or desired her death. She further forgave all and sundry and craved from God that He might also forgive her her trespasses. Thereafter she fell on her knees in ardent supplication and sought the remission of her sins. She said that she trusted to be saved through the death of Christ and His blood, and that she was ready to have her own blood spilt at His feet. Wherefore she held His picture and the crucifix in her hands. Further, she prayed for a happy, long and prosperous reign for the Queen of England, for the prosperity of the British Isles, for the afflicted Christian Church and the end of all misery. She also prayed for her son, the King of Scots, for his upright and honourable Government and of his conversion to the Catholic Faith. At the last she prayed that all the Saints in heaven might intercede for her on this day, and that God or His great goodness might avert great plagues from this Island, forgive her her sins and receive her soul into His heavenly hand.

Thereupon she stood up and prepared herself for death. She doffed her jewels and her gown, with the help of two women. When the executioner wished to assist her, she said to him that it was not her wont to be disrobed in the presence of such a crowd, nor with the help of such handmaidens. She herself took off her robe and pushed it down as far as the waist. The bodice of the underskirt was cut low and tied together at the back. She hastened to undo this.

Thereafter she kissed her ladies, commended them to God, and because one of them was weeping too loudly, she said to her: 'Have I not told you that you should not weep? Be comforted.' To her she gave her hand, and made her leave the dais. When she was thus prepared, she turned to her servitors, who were kneeling not far off, blessed them and made them all witnesses that she died a Catholic and begged them to pray for her. Afterwards she fell on her knees with great courage, did not change colour, and likewise gave no sign of fear. One of her tirewomen bound a kerchief before her eyes. As she knelt down she repeated the 70th Psalm: '*In te Domine Speravi.*' When she had said this to the end, she, full of courage, bent down with her body and laid her head on the block, exclaiming: '*In manuas tuas, Domine, commendo spiritum meum.*' Then one of the executioners held down her hands, and the other cut off her head with two strokes of the chopper. Thus ended her life.

The executioner took the head and showed it to the people, who cried: 'God spare our Queen of England!'

When the executioner held up the head, it fell in disarray so that it could be seen that her hair was quite grey and had been closely cropped.

Emanuel Tomascon
The Fugger News-Letters

The National Covenant

In times of trouble Scotsmen had long had the habit of forming 'bands'—alliances whose members undertook to pursue their particular object and defend one another against all except the King. The band of the Congregation in 1557 was the real foundation of the Reformed Church in Scotland. It was natural that eighty years later the Presybterian Scots who were opposing the plans of Charles I for a re-formed Kirk on Archbishop Laud's Anglican pattern should again draw up a band . . .

Its makers looked to the Bible. There they read of covenants between God and men—how the high priest Jehoiada 'made a covenant with the Lord and the King and the people, that they should be the Lord's people; between the King also and the people. And all the people of the land went into the house of Baal and brake it down; his altars and his images brake they in pieces thoroughly.' They remembered a document of 1581, the King's Confession, in which James VI and a number of his subjects had renounced the errors of 'papistrie'. They determined to make this the foundation of their new manifesto.

The National Covenant was presented to an impressive gathering of nobles, lairds, ministers and others in Greyfriars Kirk, Edinburgh, on February 28th 1638, after five days of preparation . . . It was very largely the work of an able young advocate, Archibald Johnston of Warriston, who was consumed with fervour for Presbyterianism but was also determined that, in what was really a public defiance of the King, all the forms of law should be properly observed . . .

The Covenant was quickly accepted in most parts of the country outside the north-east and the remoter Highlands and Islands. The Covenanters presented a front of quite extraordinary national solidity. The King and Government could do nothing effective to check them.

J. M. Reid (1901–70)
Kirk and Nation

The Solemn League and Covenant

The Glasgow Assembly of 1638, which resisted the attempts of the King's representative, the Marquis of Hamilton, to dissolve it when it decided that episcopacy was to be thrown out, did force Charles to send an army north. There followed the bloodless first Bishops' War, ending in the Pacification of Berwick. The second, a year later, resulted in the Covenanting Scots army pushing the King's troops down to Newcastle. By 1641, the Covenanters had achieved all that they ever hoped for. Unfortunately, the trouble between King Charles and his English Parliament led them to overreach themselves. The Scots tried to enforce their kind of religion not only on Scotland, but on future generations of English and Irish. They drew up a new 'bond', meant to be binding on the Parliaments for all time coming.

This was the Solemn League and Covenant, approved by the General Assembly and the Scots Estates in August 1643 and by the English Parliament a month later. There was a straightforward military alliance of the ordinary kind as well which bound the Scots to send an army of 20,000 to support the Parliamentarians on condition that England would bear the cost of it and that the English Fleet would protect the coasts of Scotland from invasion.

For the Scots this Solemn League and Covenant was an enormous mistake. It was a generous, idealistic mistake, no doubt. This small, poor country, already half-exhausted, though triumphant, was launching itself on a crusade from which it could not hope to gain anything except the advancement of true religion (as the Covenanters understood this) beyond its own borders, and some added security for its own Kirk at home. There was no idea of material conquest: the Scots did not dream that they might rule England and Ireland however successful their army might be: indeed, by insisting on uniformity, of religion, they were taking the risk that in some respects England might rule them. . . .

Their English allies' view of the Covenant was quite different. The Scots assumed that reformation in England 'according to the Word of God and the example of the best Reformed Churches' would produce something almost identical with the Scottish Kirk. But even the majority among the English Parliamentary leaders who called themselves Presbyterians were quite unwilling to accept a Church as independent of the State as the Scots Kirk claimed to be. The rebel Parliament was as determined to keep control

of organized religion as King Charles was. To nearly all its members and
their followers the Solemn League and Covenant was simply a means of
obtaining a new army which would allow them to win their war. Englishmen resented the demand that they should swear personally to follow the
Scots pattern in religion. The greatest soldier among them, Oliver Cromwell,
was to call the treaty 'a covenant made with death and an agreement with
hell'. Their greatest poet, John Milton, was to find that: 'New presbyter
is but old priest writ large.'

J. M. Reid
Ibid

Prelude to the Martyrs

*The capture of King Charles by the Scots, and their surrendering of him, on
promises of safe conduct, to the English; the defeat at Preston of a Scots force
hastily raised under Argyll to rescue him, and their proclamation of Charles II,
forcing Cromwell to engage their forces at Dunbar, set in motion circumstances
which were to bring men out to moorland conventicles to worship clandestinely
according to their conscience. 'I beseech you, in the bowels of Christ, think it
possible you may be mistaken', Cromwell had said to the Covenanting leaders.
With their defeat at Dunbar, the Scots lost everything the National Covenant
had brought them. Charles II's unwillingness to interpret his obligations, as the
Scots understood them, to maintain the Covenanting religion led to a fresh
uprising of hunted Covenanters and Cameronians. They neither gave tolerance
nor received it, and until what Burns called the 'glorious Revolution' of 1688,
which drove James II and VII off the throne and brought William and Mary to
power, the Presbyterian Kirk was in effect disbanded. The settlement of 1690
at last ended the confrontation which gave rise to such passionate paraphrases
of protest as metrical Psalm 124.*

Now Israel may say, and that truly,
If that the Lord had not our cause maintain'd;
If that the Lord had not our right sustain'd,
When cruel men against us furiously
Rose up in wrath, to make of us their prey;

Then certainly they had devour'd us all,
And swallow'd quick, for ought that we could deem;
Such was their rage, as we might well esteem.
And as fierce floods before them all things drown,
So had they brought our soul to death quite down.

The raging streams with their proud swelling waves,
Had then our soul o'erwhelmed in the deep.

But bless'd be God, who doth us safely keep,
And hath not giv'n us for a living prey
Unto their teeth, and bloody cruelty.

Ev'n as a bird out of the fowler's snare
Escapes away, so is our soul set free:
Broke are their nets, and thus escaped we.
Therefore our help is in the Lord's great name,
Who heav'n and earth by His great pow'r did frame.

Metrical Version of Psalm 124 by W. Whittingham from the *Scottish Psalter* (1650).

The Battle of Killiecrankie

John Graham of Claverhouse, later Viscount Dundee (c. 1649–89), a relative of the great Marquis of Montrose, distinguished himself against the Covenanters, particularly in the South-west. In 1688, he was second in command of the army which had been ordered into England to aid the falling dynasty of the Stuarts. After James II's flight, Dundee returned to Scotland and, with a price of £20,000 on his head, assumed leadership of the Stuart interest. Pursued by a force of 4,000 led by General Hugh Mackay, Dundee gave battle on 17th July, 1689, at the Pass of Killiecrankie, in Perthshire, and won the day. However, a bullet entered his body beneath the breast-plate, and he was carried, dying, to the Castle of Blair. W. E. Aytoun, a lawyer by training, became a contributor to Blackwood's Magazine. He is best remembered for his prose piece 'The Glenmutchkin Railway' and for 'The Bon Gaultier Ballads'.

Soon we heard a challenge-trumpet
   Sounding in the Pass below,
And the distant tramp of horses,
   And the voices of the foe:
Down we crouched amid the bracken,
   Till the Lowland ranks drew near,
Panting like the hounds in summer,
   When they scent the stately deer,
From the dark defile emerging,
   Next we saw the squadrons come,
Leslie's foot and Leven's troopers
   Marching to the tuck of drum;
Through the scattered wood of birches,
   O'er the broken ground and heath,
Wound the long battalion slowly,
   Till they gained the plain beneath;

8

Then we bounded from our covert.—
  Judge how looked the Saxons then,
When they saw the rugged mountain
  Start to life with armed men!
Like a tempest down the ridges
  Swept the hurricane of steel,
Rose the slogan of Macdonald—
  Flashed the broadsword of Lochiel!
Vainly sped the withering volley
  'Mongst the foremost of our band—
On we poured until we met them,
  Foot to foot, and hand to hand.
Horse and man went down like drift-wood
  When the floods are black at Yule,
And their carcasses are whirling
  In the Garry's deepest pool.
Horse and man went down before us—
  Living foe there tarried none
On the field at Killiecrankie,
  When the stubborn fight was done!

And the evening star was shining
  On Schehallion's distant head,
When we wiped our bloody broadswords,
  And returned to count the dead.
There we found him gashed and gory,
  Stretched upon the cumbered plain,
As he told us where to seek him,
  In the thickest of the slain.
And a smile was on his visage,
  For within his dying ear
Pealed the joyful note of triumph,
  And the clansmen's clamorous cheer:
So, amidst the battle's thunder,
  Shot, and steel, and scorching flame,
In the glory of his manhood
  Passed the spirit of the Graeme!

W. E. Aytoun (1813–65)
Lays of the Scottish Cavaliers

The Massacre of Glencoe

Gilbert Burnet, the son of an Edinburgh advocate, was a broad-minded and tolerant churchman, one-time Professor of Divinity at Glasgow University,

*and an adviser on church matters to William and Mary. He finished his career
as Bishop of Salisbury, and recorded his experiences at home and abroad in his
'History of My Own Time'.*

The Earl of Breadalbane, the most powerful man in Scotland after Argyll,
put up to King William a scheme for quieting the Highlands, the sympathies
of many of the clan chiefs being with the deposed James VII and II. The
Government was persuaded to allocate fifteen thousand pounds for the purpose of distributing among the clans, but the chieftans made such demands
that at last it was announced that an indemnity would be paid only to those
who swore oaths of allegiance to William by 31st December 1691. For those
who did not, there was to be a threat of military action.

All were so terrified that they came in; and even that Macdonald [of
Glencoe] went to the Governor of Fort William, on the last day of December,
and offered to take the oaths; but he, being only a military man, could not,
or would not, tender them, and Macdonald was forced to seek for some of
the legal magistrates to tender them to him. The snows were then fallen, so
four or five days passed before he could come to a magistrate: he took the
oaths in his presence, on the fourth or fifth of January, when, by the strictness of law, he could claim no benefit by it.

The matter was signified to the Council, and the person had a reprimand
for giving him the oaths when the day was past. This was kept up from the
king: and the Earl of Breadalbane came to Court to give an account of his
diligence, and to bring back the money, since he could not do the service
for which he had it. He informed against this Macdonald as the chief person
who had defeated that good design: and that he might both gratify his own
revenge, and render the king odious to all the Highlanders, he proposed that
orders should be sent for a military execution on those of Glencoe.

An instruction was drawn by the Secretary of State, Lord Stair, to be
both signed and countersigned by the king (that so he might bear no part
of the blame, but that it might lie wholly on the king), that such as had not
taken the oaths by the time limited should be shut out of the benefit of the
indemnity, and be received only upon mercy. But when it was found this
would not authorize what was intended, a second order was got to be signed
and countersigned, that if the Glencoe men could be separated from the
rest of the Highlanders, some example might be made of them, in order to
strike terror into the rest.

The king signed this order without any inquiry about it; for he was too
apt to sign papers in a hurry, without examining the importance of them.
This was one effect of his slowness in dispatching business; for, as he was
apt to suffer things to run on till there was a great heap of papers laid before
him, so then he signed them a little too precipitately. But all this while the
king knew nothing of Macdonald's offering to take the oaths within the
time, nor of his having taken them, soon after it was passed, when he came
to a proper magistrate.

As these orders were sent down, the Secretary of State [Stair] wrote many private letters to Levingston, who commanded in Scotland, giving him a strict charge and particular directions for the execution of them: and he ordered the passes in the valley to be kept, describing them so minutely, that the orders were certainly drawn by one who knew the country well. He gave also a positive direction that no prisoners should be taken, that so the execution might be as terrible as was possible. He pressed this upon Levingston with strains of vehemence that looked as if there was something more than ordinary in it: he indeed grounded it on his zeal for the king's service, adding, that such rebels and murderers should be made examples of.

Gilbert Burnet (1643–1715)
History of My Own Time

The Order Gets to the End of the Line

February 13th, 1692

To Captain Robert Campbell of Glenlyon
'For Their Majesties' Service'

Sir,
You are hereby ordered to fall upon the rebels, the M'Donalds, of Glencoe, and putt all to the sword under seventy. You are to have special care that the old fox and his sons doe on no account escape your hands. You are to secure all the avenues, that no man escape. This you are to put into execution att five o'clock in the morning precisely, and by that time, or very shortly after it, I'll strive to be att you with a larger party. If I doe not come to you att five, you are not to tarry for me, but to fall on. This is by the king's special command, for the good and safety of the country, that these miscreants be cutt off root and branch. See that this be putt in execution without feud or favour, else you may expect to be treated as not true to the king's government, nor a man fitt to carry a commission in the king's service. Expecting you will not faill in the fulfilling hereof as you love yourself, I subscribe these with my hand.

Robert Duncanson

The Massacre of Glencoe

'O tell me, Harper, wherefore flow
Thy wayward notes of wail and woe
Far down the desert of Glencoe,
        Where none may list their melody?

Say, harp'st thou to the mists that fly,
Or to the dun deer glancing by,
Or to the eagle that from high
    Screams chorus to thy minstrelsy?'—
'No, not to these, for they have rest,—
The mist-wreath has the mountain-crest,
The stag his lair, the erne her nest,
    Abode of lone security.
But those for whom I pour the lay,
Not wildwood deep, nor mountain gray,
Not this deep dell, that shrouds from day,
    Could screen from treach'rous cruelty.

'Their flag was furl'd, and mute their drum,
The very household dogs were dumb,
Unwont to bay at guests that come
    In guise of hospitality.
His blithest notes the piper plied,
Her gayest snood the maiden tied,
The dame her distaff flung aside,
    To tend her kindly housewifery.

'The hand that mingled in the meal,
At midnight drew the felon steel,
And gave the host's kind breast to feel
    Meed for his hospitality!
The friendly hearth which warm'd that hand,
At midnight arm'd it with the brand,
That bade destruction's flames expand
    Their red and fearful blazonry.

'Then woman's shriek was heard in vain,
Nor infancy's unpitied plain,
More than the warriors groan, could gain
    Respite from ruthless butchery!
The winter wind that whistled shrill,
The snows that night that cloaked the hill,
Though wild and pitiless, had still
    Far more than Southern clemency.

'Long have my harp's best notes been gone,
Few are its strings, and faint their tone,
They can but sound in desert lone
    Their grey-hair'd master's misery
Were each grey hair a minstrel string,
Each chord should imprecations fling,

Till startled Scotland loud should ring,
   "Revenge for blood and treachery!" '

                                   Sir Walter Scott (1771–1832)

Lord Belhaven Opposes the Union

*The failure of the Darien expedition, a widely-felt financial disaster believed
by the Scots to have been manipulated by the English Government, and the
threat of a separate choice of succession to Queen Anne after more than a hundred
years of the united crown, spurred the English and their Scottish allies to an
all-out effort to secure, not the federated union urged by nationalist politicians
like Fletcher of Saltoun, but full incorporating union. Daniel Defoe, in the guise
of 'Alexander Goldsmith', came up to Scotland to facilitate matters by secret
discussion and diplomacy, reporting back to Queen Anne's minister, Robert
Harley.*

*The Union of 1707 went through, bringing about the end of 'ane auld sang',
in Lord Seafield's cynical words. Once popular resentment at the way the business
had been managed subsided, Scots traders began to take advantage of the
new opportunities created. Scots initiative and the slow development of communications kept in being a kind of de facto independence alongside growing
prosperity for almost two more centuries. Then the power of decision-making
and financial control of native enterprises began to seep South; slowly at
first, a trickle between the world wars, and a rapid, emptying deluge after 1945.
Now one would be hard put to it to find a dozen major firms left in Scotland
which are still under Scottish control.*

*Lord Belhaven's rhetoric, old-fashioned though it may have seemed even in
1707, sounds the lament for our lost initiatives.*

My Lord Chancellor,
When I consider this Affair of an Union betwixt the Two Nations, as it is
express'd in the several Articles thereof, and now the Subject of our Delibera-
tion at this time; I find my Mind crowded with variety of very Melancholy
Thoughts, and I think it my Duty to disburden my self of some of them, by
laying them before, and exposing them to the serious Consideration of this
Honourable House.

   I think I see a Free and Independent Kingdom delivering up That, which
all the World hath been fighting for, since the days of Nimrod; yea, that
for which most of all the Empires, Kingdoms, States, Principalities and
Dukedoms of Europe, are at this very time engaged in the most Bloody
and Cruel Wars that ever were, to wit, A Power to Manage their own Affairs
by themselves, without the Assistance and Counsel of any other.

   I think I see a National Church, founded upon a Rock, secured by a
Claim of Right, hedged and fenced about by the strictest and pointedest
Legal Sanction that Sovereignty could contrive, voluntarily descending

into a Plain, upon an equal level with Jews, Papists, Socinians, Arminians, Anabaptists, and other Sectaries etc.

I think I see the Noble and Honourable Peerage of Scotland, whose Valiant Predecessors led Armies against their Enemies upon their own proper Charges and Expenses, now divested of their Followers and Vassalages, and put upon such an Equal Foot with their Vassals, that I think I see a petty English Exciseman receive more Hommage and Respect, than what was paid formerly to their *quondam Maccallanmores.*

I think I see the present Peers of Scotland, whose Noble Ancestors conquered Provinces, over-run Countries, reduc'd and subjected Towns and fortify'd Places, exacted Tribute through the greatest part of England, now walking in the Court of Requests like so many English Attornies, laying aside their Walking Swords when in Company with the English Peers, lest their Self-defence should be found Murder.

I think I see the Honorable Estate of Barons, the bold Asserters of the Nation's Rights and Liberties in the worst of Times, now setting a Watch upon their Lips and a Guard upon their Tongues, lest they be found guilty of *Scandalum Magnatum.*

I think I see the Royal State of Burrows [burghs] walking their desolate Streets, hanging down their Heads under Disappointments; wormed out of all the Branches of their old Trade, uncertain what hand to turn to, necessiate to become Prentices to their unkind Neighbours; and yet after all finding their Trade so fortified by Companies, and secured by Prescriptions, that they despair of any success therein . . .

I think I see the Honest Industrious Tradesman loaded with new Taxes, and Impositions, disappointed of the Equivalents, drinking Water in place of Ale, eating his fat-less Potage, Petitioning for Encouragement for his Manufacturies, and Answered by counter Petitions . .

I think I see the Incureable Difficulties of the Landedmen, fettered under the Golden Chain of Equivalents, their pretty Daughters Petitioning for want of Husbands, and their Sons for want of Imployments.

I think I see our Mariners, delivering up their ships to their Dutch Partners; and what through Presses and Necessity, earning their bread as underlings in the Royal English Navy.

But above all, My Lord, I think I see our Ancient Mother CALEDONIA, like Caesar sitting in the midst of our Senate, Rufully looking round about her, Covering Herself with her Royal Garment, attending the Fatal Blow, and breathing out her last with a *Et tu quoque mi fili.*

Are not these, My Lord, very afflicting Thoughts? And yet they are but the least part Suggested to me by these Dishonourable Articles; should not the Consideration of these things vivifie these dry Bones of ours? Should not the memory of our Noble Predecessors Valour and Constancie, rouse up our drouping Spirits? Are our Noble Predecessors Souls got so far into the English Cabbage-Stock and Colliflowers, that we should shew the least Inclination that way? Are our Eyes so Blinded? Are our Ears so Deafned? Are our Hearts so Hardned? Are our Tongues so Faltered? Are our Hands so Fettered, that in this day, I say, My Lord, That in this our day, that we should not mind the things that concern the very Being and Well-being of our Ancient Kingdom, before the day be hid from our Eyes.

No, My Lord, GOD forbid, Man's Extremity is GOD's Opportunity. He is a present Help in time of need; and a Deliverer, and that right early. Some unforeseen Providence will fall out, that may cast the Ballance; some Joseph or other will say, Why do ye strive together, since you are brethren? None can Destroy Scotland, save Scotland's self; hold your Hands from the Pen, you are Secure.

Daniel Defoe (1660?–1731)
History of the Union

The Consequence of the Union

But the hands were not held from the pen. When it was all over, Defoe who, in Agnes Mure Mackenzie's words was 'fundamentally decent', spy or not, had this to say.

If nothing else were the consequence of the Union, this must be allowed that they [the Scots] are thereby disarmed from the power of doing themselves right against us, in a parliamentary manner, which strongly implies that they are more particularly in the parliamentary justice that remains, and that we ought to esteem everything that touches the honour of Scotland nationally as equally affecting all Britain. Nay, we should be nicer in an affront to the nation and nobility of Scotland, by how much the more frankly they have by the Union given themselves, as it were, into our hands.

Daniel Defoe
The Scots Union and Nation Vindicated

Bailie Nicol Jarvie Upholds the Union

When the cloth was removed, Mr Jarvie compounded with his own hands a very small bowl of brandy-punch, the first of which I had ever the fortune to see.

'The limes,' he assured us, 'were from his own little farm yonder-awa' (indicating the West Indies with a knowing shrug of his shoulders), 'and he had learned the art of composing the liquor from auld Captain Coffinkey, who acquired it,' he added in a whisper, 'as maist folk thought, among the Buccaneers. But it's excellent liquor,' said he, helping us round; 'and good ware has aften come frae a wicked market. And as for Captain Coffinkey, he was a decent man when I kent him, only he used to swear awfully.—But he's dead, and gaen to his account, and I trust he's accepted—I trust he's accepted.'

We found the liquor exceedingly palatable, and it led to a long conversation between Owen and our host, on the opening which the Union afforded to trade between Glasgow and the British colonies in America and the West Indies, and on the facilities which Glasgow possessed of making up *sortable* cargoes for that market Mr Jarvie answered some objection which Owen made on the difficulty of sorting a cargo for America, without buying from England, with vehemence and volubility.

'Na, na, sir, we stand on our ain bottom—we pickle in our ain pock-neuk. —We hae our Stirling serges, Musselburgh stuffs, Aberdeen hose, Edinburgh shalloons, and the like, for our woollen or worsted goods—and we hae linens of a' kinds better and cheaper than you hae in Lunnon itsel'— and we can buy your north o' England wares, as Manchester wares, Sheffield wares, and Newcastle earthenware, as cheap as you can at Liverpool— and we are making a fair spell at cottons and muslins.—Na, na! let every herring hing by its ain head, and every sheep by its ain shank, and ye'll find, sir, us Glasgow folk no sae far ahint but what we may follow.'

Sir Walter Scott (1771–1832)
Rob Roy

Prince Charles Edward Stuart is Encouraged to Come to Scotland

After the abortive visit to the Highlands by the Old Chevalier, King James, in 1715, and the defeat of his hopes at the skirmish of Sheriffmuir, Jacobite negotiations in Scotland continued. David, Lord Elcho, the eldest son of the 4th Earl of Wemyss, made his way to the Court of the Old Pretender at Rome in 1740, then back in Scotland worked with John Murray of Broughton, James's agent and later Prince Charles's Secretary. Murray, who had a vested interest in persuading the Prince to come to Scotland, turned King's evidence after being imprisoned in the Tower, and received a pardon and a pension of £200 per annum. Elcho, an altogether more admirable character, fought for the Prince, but later supported Lord George Murray, who, at Derby, opposed successfully the Prince's wish to march on London. Elcho, who endured self imposed banishment and so saved his life, died in Paris in 1787, disillusioned with the man for whom he had wrecked his own life, speeding Charles from the field of Culloden with the words: 'There you go for a damned Italian coward.'

He left in manuscript a personal 'Journal', but also a shrewd and fairly detached narrative, 'A Short Account of the Affairs of Scotland in the Years 1744, 1745, 1746.'

In the month of August 1744, Mr Murray of Broughton (who was the Chevalier's agent in Scotland) went to Paris, where he saw the Prince, and informed him that if he could prevail upon the French to give him 6,000 men and 30,000 lewis d'ors and ten thousand Stand of arms, that he was charged to tell him he would be joined upon his landing by a great number of his friends, but if he could not obtain these succours it was impossible for them to do anything for him.

Mr Murray returned from France in October 1744, and gave out, in all the meetings he had with the Prince's friends, that the Prince told him he would certainly be in Scotland next Summer whether the King of France assisted him or not. Most of the gentlemen of that party look'd upon it as a mad project, and were utterly against it. Mr Murray, and some others who were in desperate circumstances, certainly encouraged the Prince underhand; others, such as the Duke of Perth, out of zeal, There were likewise some gentlemen, who were against his coming, used in their conversations to say that they would do all they could to prevent his coming, but if he did come and persisted in staying, they believed they could not hinder themselves from joining his fortune.

Mr Murray, in the beginning of the year 1745, sent over Young Glengarry to the Prince with a State of his Affairs in Scotland, in which it is believed he represented everybody that had ever spoke warmly of the Stuart family as people that would certainly join him if he came.

Lord Elcho (1721–87)
A Short Account of the Affairs of Scotland in the Years 1744–6

The Prince Arrives

On 25th July 1745, the armed brig 'Doutelle' landed the Prince with a few friends in Loch nan Uamh, between Moidart and Arisaig.

Everybody was vastly alarmed at this news, and were determined when he came to endeavour all in their power to prevail upon him to go back; and the gentlemen of the party then at Edinburgh sent Mr Murray to the Highlands to let the Prince know their sentiments; but upon his not coming all the month of June, Mr Murray returned to the Lowlands . . .

The frigate in which the Prince was . . . about the middle of July made the isles of Barra. Mr Macdonald was sent ashoar upon South Uist, where he met Mr Macdonald of Buisdale, brother to Clanronald, who told him he came from Sir Alexander Macdonald and Macleod to beg that if the Prince was in that ship, he might go back to France, for that it was a bad project he came upon, and could never be attended with success.

The Prince came and lay ashoar that night upon South Uist, and held a Council with the gentlemen that came along with him what was to be done;

they were all for going back again to France, except Sir Thomas Sheridan. Even the Prince himself seemed for it, but Sir Thomas, as he had always a great deal to say with the Prince, persuaded him to remain. So they embark'd aboard ye ship and steer'd the mainland, and made the bay of Lochnanuagh in Arisaig, and landed at a place call'd Borodale.

Lord Elcho
Ibid

Prince Charles and Lochiel

John Home, born at Leith, became a minister after fighting on the Hanoverian side in the Forty-five, being captured at the Battle of Falkirk, and becoming a Jacobite prisoner in Doune Castle. His ministry at Athelstaneford, East Lothian, came to an end because of the Church of Scotland's attitude to his successful tragedy of 'Douglas'. Home became private secretary to Lord Bute, tutor to the Prince of Wales, and on the latter's accession as George III, the writer was given a pension of £300. His 'History of the Rebellion' came out in 1802.

It is impossible to imagine an abode more suitable to the circumstances and designs of Charles than Borodale, which is one of the most remote and inaccessible places in the Highlands of Scotland, surrounded on every side by the territories of those chiefs, who, in former times had fought the battles of the family of Stuart.

He was no sooner arrived at Borodale, than Charles and he retired by themselves. The conversation began on the part of Charles, with bitter complaints of the treatment he had received from the ministers of France, who had so long amused him with vain hopes, and deceived him with false promises; their coldness on his cause, he said, but ill agreed with the opinion he had of his own pretensions, and with that impatience to assert them, with which the promises of his father's brave and faithful subjects had inflamed his mind. Lochiel acknowledged the engagements of the chiefs, but observed that they were no way binding, as he had come over without the stipulated aid; and therefore, as there was not the least prospect of success, he advised his Royal Highness to return to France, and to reserve himself and his faithful friends for a more favourable opportunity. Charles refused to follow Lochiel's advice, affirming that a more favourable opportunity than the present would never come: that almost all the British troops were abroad, and kept at bay by Marshal Saxe, with a superior army: that in Scotland there were only a few new raised regiments, that had never seen service, and could not stand before the Highlanders: that the very first advantage gained over the troops would encourage his father's friends at home to declare themselves: that his friends abroad would not fail to give their assistance: that he only wanted the Highlanders to begin the war.

Lochiel still resisted, entreating Charles to be more temperate, and consent to remain concealed where he was, till he (Lochiel) and his other friends should meet together, and concept what was best to be done. Charles, whose mind was wound up to the utmost pitch of impatience, paid no regard to this proposal, but answered, that he was determined to put all to the hazard. 'In a few days,' said he, 'with the few friends that I have, I will errect the royal standard, and proclaim to the people of Britain, that Charles Stuart is come over to claim the crown of his ancestors; to win it, or to perish in the attempt; Lochiel, who, my father has often told me, was our firmest friend, may stay at home, and learn from the newspapers the fate of his prince.' 'No,' said Lochiel, 'I'll share the fate of my prince; and so shall every man over whom nature or fortune hath given me any power.' Such was the singular conversation, on the result of which depended peace or war. For it is a point agreed among the Highlanders, that if Lochiel had persisted in his refusal to take arms, the other chiefs would not have joined the standard without him, and the spark of rebellion must have instantly expired.

John Home (1722–1808)
History of the Rebellion of 1745

Prince Charles Reports to His Father

Sir,

Since my landing everything has succeeded to my wishes. It has pleased God to prosper me hitherto even beyond my expectations. I have got together 1,300 men, and am promised more brave, determined men who are resolved to die or conquer with me. The enemy marched a body of regular troops to attack me; but when they came near they chang'd their mind, and, by taking a different rout, and making forced marches, have escaped to the north, to the great disappointment of my Highlanders. But I am not at all sorry for it. I shall have the greater glory in beating them when they are more numerous and supported by their dragoons.

I have occasion every day to reflect on your Majesty's last words to me— That I should find power, if tempered with justice and clemency, an easy thing to myself and not greivous to those under me. 'Tis owing to the observance of this rule, and to my conformity to the customs of the people, that I have got their hearts to a degree not to be easily conceived by those who do not see it. One who observes the discipline I have established would take my little army to be a body of pick'd veterans, and to see the love and harmony that reigns amongst us he could be apt to look upon it as a large well-ordered family in which every one loves another better than himself.

I keep my health better in these wild mountains than I used to do in the Campagnie Felice, and sleep sounder lying on the ground than I used to do in the palaces at Rome. . . .
Perth, 10th September, 1745.

The Lyon in Mourning
edited by Bishop Robert Forbes (1708–75)

The Prince in Edinburgh

At first things went well. The Prince's army entered and occupied Edinburgh, though without being able to capture the Castle, and Sir John Cope was defeated at the Battle of Prestonpans.

The Prince got the news of Edinburgh's being taken the next morning, 17 of September. . . . When the Army came near the town it was met by vast multitudes of people, who, by their repeated shouts and huzzas, expressed a great deal of joy to see the Prince. When they came into the suburbs, the crowd was prodigious, and all wishing the Prince prosperity; in short, nobody doubted but that he would be joined by 10,000 men at Edinburgh if he could arm them . . .

The Prince continued on horseback always followed by the crowd, who were happy if they could touch his boots or his horse furniture. In the steepest part of the park going down to the Abbey, he was obliged to alight and walk, but the mob, out of curiosity, and some out of fondness to touch him or kiss his hand, were like to throw him down; so, as soon as he was down the hill, he mounted his horse and rode through St Ann's yards into Holyrood House amidst the cries of 60,000 people, who filled the air with their acclamations of joy. . . . The crowd continued all that night in the outward court of the Abbey, and huzza'd every time the Prince appeared at the window . . .

Not one of the mob who were so fond of seeing him ever asked to enlist in his service, and when he marched to fight Cope, he had not one of them in his army . . .

At night there came a great many ladies of fashion, to kiss his hand, but his behaviour to them was very cool: he had not been much used to women's company, and was always embarassed while he was with them. . . .

The Prince lived in Edinburgh from the 22 of September to the 31 of October, with great splendour and magnificence; had every morning a numerous Court of his officers. After he had held a Council, he dined with his principal officers in public, where there was always a crowd of all sorts of people to see him dine. After dinner, he rode out attended by his life guards, and reviewed his army, where there was always a great number of spectators in coaches and on horseback. After the review, he came to the Abbey, where he received the ladies of fashion that came to his drawing-room. Then he supped in public, and generally there was music at supper, and a ball afterwards.

Lord Elcho
A Short Account of the Affairs of Scotland in the Years 1744–46

The March Into England

The road between Preston and Wigan was crouded with people standing at their doors to see the army go by, and they generally all that day's march profess'd to wish the Prince's army success; but if arms was offer'd to them and they were desired to go along with the army, they all declined, and said they did not understand fighting. The 29th, when the Prince arrived with his army at Manchester, the mob huzza'd him to his lodgings, the town was mostly illuminated, and the bells rung. . . .

After all these proceedings, it was natural enough to imagine that there would be a great joining, but everybody was astonished to find that all that was to join was about 200 common fellows who, it seems, had no subsistance, for they used to say by way of showing their military inclination, that they had for some time been resolved to enlist with whichever of the two armies came first to town. . . . The Prince was so far deceived with these proceedings at Manchester . . . that he thought himself sure of success, and his conversation that night at table was, in what manner he should enter London, on horseback or on foot, and in what dress. . . .

The principal officers of the army, who thought otherwise upon these topicks, met at Manchester, and were of opinion that now they had marched far enough into England, and as they had received not the least encouragement from any person of distinction, the French not having landed, and only joined by 200 vagabonds, they had done their part; and as they did not pretend to put a King upon the throne of England without their consent, that it was time to represent to the Prince to go back to Scotland. But after talking a great deal about it, it was determin'd to march to Derby, that so neither the French nor the English might have it to say, the army had not marched far enough into England to give the one encouragement to land and the other to join.

Lord Elcho
Ibid

The Decision at Derby

At Derby, Lord George Murray and the Prince had a disagreement as to whether to advance upon London, or return to Scotland. Lord George, more realistic in a military sense than the Prince, seems to have realized that even if London had been taken, it could not have been held by the Highland army.

Lord George concluded by saying that the Scots army had done their part; that they came into England at the Prince's request to join his English friends, and to give them courage by their appearance to take arms and declare for him publickly as they had done, or join the French if they landed; but as none of these things had happened, that certainly 4,500 Scots had never thought of putting a King upon the English Throne by themselves. So he said his opinion was that they should go back and join their friends in Scotland, and live and die with them. . . .

After Lord George had spoke, he desired all the rest of the gentlemen present to speak their sentiments, and they all agreed with Lord George except two, who were for going to Wales to see if the Welsh would join . . . The Prince heard all these arguments with the greatest impatience, fell into a passion, and gave most of the gentlemen that had spoke very abusive language, and said that they had a mind to betray him. The case was that he knew nothing about the country nor had the smallest idea of the force that was against him, nor where they were situated. His Irish favourites, to pay court to him, always represented the whole nation as his friends. . . . He continued all that day positive he would march to London; the Irish in the army were always for what he was for . . . the Scots were all against it. So that night the Prince sent for them and told them he consented to go to Scotland. And at the same time he told them that for the future he would have no more Councils, for he would neither ask nor take their advice; that he was accountable to nobody for his actions but to his father.

Lord Elcho
Ibid

Culloden

Although the Highland army defeated General Hawley at the Battle of Falkirk, the Duke of Cumberland was by now in strenuous pursuit. The Battle of Culloden took place in bitter cold on 16th April 1746.

About two hours after the Prince's arrival at Culloden, a party of horse that had been left to observe the Duke of Cumberland's motions, brought word that there was a party of his horse within two miles. . . . They [the

Highland officers] endeavoured to get the men together as fast as possible, but as they were dispersed all over the country as far as Inverness, there was near two thousand of them that was not at the battle; so all the Prince assembled was about five thousand men, which he march'd up the hill from Culloden. . . . It was a dark, misty, rainy day, and the wind blew in the face of the Prince's army. There was no manner of Council held upon the field. . . .

On Wednesday, the 16 of April, 1746, about half an hour after eleven, the Duke of Cumberland's army appeared two miles off, straight in front of the Prince's. . . . The Duke's army continued always advancing and keeping a continued fire both of cannon and muskettery, which killed a vast number of the Prince's people. At last, when they were very near, the word of command to advance was given, and all the line moved forward; but in the advancing, the whole left wing of the Prince's army gave way, and run away without firing their musketts; the centre joined the right, and in a sort of mob, without any order or distinction of Corps, mixt together, rush'd in and attack't the Duke's left wing, and broke the regiments opposite to them in the first line; but the second line, marching up, beat them off, and obliged them to turn their backs, and run away. . . .

The Prince who, at the beginning of the action was behind the Irish piquetts guarded by sixteen of Fitzjames's horse, turn'd about his horse and went off as soon as the left wing gave way, and never offer'd to rally any of the broken Corps; but indeed, it would have been to no purpose, for none of the Highlanders who escaped ever stopped until they got home to their own houses.

Lord Elcho
Ibid

Culloden: The Prince's Behaviour

John Cameron, Presbyterian preacher and Chaplain at Fort William, gave a somewhat different account to Robert Forbes, Bishop of Ross and Caithness, compiler of 'The Lyon in Mourning'.

The Prince was in the heat of the action, had one of his grooms killed close by him, the horse he rode on killed by a musket ball which struck him within an inch of the Prince's leg. Some of the Camerons on the right gave way, being flanked, as they expected, from the park wall, which the Argyll-shire men had broke down. Lochiel endeavoured to rally them, but could not. . . .

Major Kennedy . . . after the Highlanders were broke and the French engaged . . . went to the Prince and told him they could not hold it long . . . and begged he would retire. In this request he was joined by others.

The Prince complied with great reluctance, retired in good order and in
no hurry.

The Lyon in Mourning

Culloden: *An Artist's Impression*

*The most vivid account of what happened on Culloden field to end forever
Jacobite hopes, give victory to the unattractive but efficient William Augustus,
Duke of Cumberland (1721–65), and turn the defeated Prince into a song-
writer's symbol for lost opportunity, comes from the Orcadian engraver Sir
Robert Strange, who fought with the Jacobite army, yet lived to be knighted and
to become an acknowledged master of his craft in London and on the Continent.*

The right of our army, commanded by Lord George Murray, had made a
furious attack, cut their way through Barrel's and Munro's regiments, and
had taken possession of two pieces of cannon; but a reinforcement of
Wolfe's regiment, etc. coming up from the Duke's second line, our right
flank was obliged to give way, being at the same time flanked with some
pieces of artillery, which did great execution. Towards the left the attack had
been less vigorous than on the right, and of course had made little impression
on the Duke's army; nor was it indeed general, for the centre, which had
been much galled by the enemy's artillery, almost instantly quitted the field.
The scene of confusion was now great; nor can the imagination figure it.
The men in general were betaking themselves precipitately to flight; nor
was there any possibility of their being rallied. Horror and dismay were
painted in every countenance. It was now time to provide for the Prince's
safety; his person had been abundantly exposed. He was got off the field and
very narrowly escaped falling in with a body of horse which, having been
detached from the Duke's left, were advancing with incredibile rapidity,
picking up the stragglers, and, as they gave no quarter, were levelling them
with the ground. The greater number of the army were already out of danger,
the flight having been so precipitate. We got upon a rising ground, where we
turned round and made a general halt, The scene was, indeed, tremendous.
Never was so total a rout—a more thorough discomfiture of an army. The
adjacent country was in a manner covered with its ruins. The whole was
over in about twenty-five minutes. The Duke's artillery kept still playing,
though not a soul upon the field. His army was kept together, all but the
horse. The great pursuit was upon the road towards Inverness. Of towards
six thousand men, which the Prince's army at this period consisted of, about
one thousand were asleep in Culloden parks, who knew nothing of the
action till awakened by the noise of the cannon. These in general endeavoured to save themselves by taking the road towards Inverness; and
most of them fell a sacrifice to the victors, for this road was in general

strewed with dead bodies. The Prince at this moment had his cheeks
bedewed with tears; what must not his feelings have suffered!

Sir Robert Strange (1721–92)
Memoirs

The Tears of Scotland

Mourn, hapless Caledonia, mourn
Thy banish'd peace, thy laurels torn!
Thy sons, for valour long renown'd,
Lie slaughter'd on their native ground;
Thy hospitable roofs no more
Invite the stranger to the door;
In smoky ruins sunk they lie,
The monuments of cruelty.

The wretched owner sees afar
His all become the prey of war;
Bethinks him of his babes and wife,
Then smites his breast and curses life.
Thy swains are famish'd on the rocks
Where once they fed their wanton flocks;
Thy ravish'd virgins shriek in vain;
Thy infants perish on the plain.

What boots it then, in ev'ry clime,
Through the wide-spreading waste of time,
Thy martial glory, crown'd with praise,
Still shone with indiminish'd blaze?
Thy tow'ring spirit now is broke,
Thy neck is bended to the yoke:
What foreign arms could never quell,
By civil rage and rancour fell.

The rural pipe and merry lay
No more shall cheer the happy day;
No social scenes of gay delight
Beguile the dreary winter night;
No strains but those of sorrow flow,
And nought be heard but sounds of woe,
While the pale phantoms of the slain
Glide nightly o'er the silent plain.

O baneful cause, O fatal morn,
Accurs'd to ages yet unborn!
The sons against their fathers stood,
The parents shed his children's blood.
Yet, when the rage of battle ceas'd,
The victor's soul was not appeas'd;
The naked and forlorn must feel
Devouring flames, and murd'ring steel!

The pious mother, doom'd to death,
Forsaken, wanders o'er the heath;
The bleak wind whistles round her head,
Her helpless orphans cry for bread;
Bereft of shelter, food, and friend,
She views the shades of night descend;
And, stretch'd beneath th' inclement skies,
Weeps o'er her tender babes, and dies.

While the warm blood bedews my veins,
And unimpair'd remembrance reigns,
Resentment of my country's fate
Within my filial breast shall beat;
And, spite of her insulting foe,
My sympathising verse shall flow:
'Mourn, hapless Caledonia, mourn
Thy banish'd peace, thy laurels torn!'

Tobias Smollett (1721–71)

Back to France

After weeks of wandering through the Highlands with a price on his head, cared for and fed by faithful Highlanders, arrangements were finally made for the Prince to leave Scotland for the last time. In 1750, the Prince daringly appeared in London, where a stay of five days finally convinced him that the cause of the Stuarts was hopeless.

On the 30th August the Prince met Lochiel by Loch Ericht, on the south-eastern slope of Ben Alder, a great hill that rises to more than 3,700 feet about twenty-five miles east of Fort William. It was a joyful occasion, for the Prince's mood was gay and Lochiel or those with him had prepared what must have seemed, after lean days in the heather, a state banquet. There was mutton and 'an anker of whisky of twenty Scots pints', well-cured beef sausages, butter and cheese and a bacon-ham. The hut in which they ate was small and smoky, but the Prince's appetite was good. He took a hearty dram when he went in, and called for a good many more to drink the health of so many friends. He was given a silver spoon, and ate heartily from a large sauce-pan of minced collops. 'Now, gentlemen, I live like a prince,' he said. He asked Lochiel, a little enviously, if he had been accustomed to living so richly, and Lochiel, still lame from his wounds, admitted that Cluny had looked after him very well.

Cluny himself—Ewen MacPherson, chief of the clan—had gone to Achnacarry to look for the Prince, but returned on the 1st September, and after two or three days they moved a couple of miles higher up the hill to 'a romantic comical habitation' known as Cluny's Cage. The site of this is uncertain. The Ordnance Survey marks it confidently, but it may well have been on a higher slope. It was concealed by a grove of holly, it afforded wide views, and was constructed, against the steepness of the ground, on two floors, and was roofed with turf. Against a great slab of grey rock behind it the smoke from its chimney was invisible, and with a fire to warm them six or seven people could find room to play cards and cook another meal.

There, for a week, the Prince lived in such comfort as he had not known for a long time; having for company and attendance Lochiel, Cluny, Lochgarry, and Dr Cameron; Allan Cameron, who was Lochiel's chief servant, and four of Cluny's servants' Cluny's brother-in-law, MacPherson of Breakachie, was sent to find Colonel John Roy Stewart, a friend of the Prince's, and enquire about shipping. Before he returned they heard there were French ships in Loch nan Uamh, and at one o'clock in the morning of the 13th set off on a last journey, and spent the next day in a hut lower down the hill. There they were joined by Breakachie and John Roy, who had not been told of the Prince's presence. Charles, in holiday spirits, lay down completely hidden in a plaid, and surprised John Roy by suddenly peeping out: the Colonel fainted and fell into a puddle at the door.

They marched north, between Ben Alder and Loch Ericht, then west through the Ben Alder Forest and past the south end of Loch Laggan towards Glen Roy. They moved by night, lay hidden and rested by day. They crossed Glen Roy, and the river Lochy by moonlight in a crazily leaking boat, and came to Achnacarry. Another day there, and by night along Loch Arkaig. Cluny and Dr Cameron had gone ahead to provide food, and a cow was killed and bannocks baked for a last meal before the Prince's march to Borrodale.

It was the 19th September when, in the very place where he had landed fourteen months before, the Prince and Lochiel with many followers went aboard the ship L'Heureux, which before midnight weighed anchor and set sail for France.

But Cluny remained in Scotland. He was, said the Prince, 'the only person in whom he could repose the greatest confidence', and his task now was to make preparation for Charles's return. So Cluny went back to his cage, and for eight years waited, without reward, for the Prince to come into his own again.

Eric Linklater (b. 1899)
The Prince in the Heather

Will Ye No Come Back Again?

Bonnie Charlie's now awa,
   Safely owre the friendly main;
Mony a heart will break in twa,
   Should he ne'er come back again.

         Will ye no come back again?
         Will ye no come back again?
         Better lo'ed ye canna be,
         Will ye no come back again?

Ye trusted in your Hieland men,
   They trusted you, dear Charlie;
They kent you hiding in the glen,
   Your cleadin' was but barely.

English bribes were a' in vain,
   An' e'en though puirer we may be;
Siller canna buy the heart
   That beats aye for thine and thee.

We watched thee in the gloaming hour,
   We watched thee in the morning grey;
Tho' thirty thousand pounds they'd gie,
   Oh there is nane that wad betray!

Sweet's the laverock's note and lang,
   Lilting wildly up the glen;
But aye to me he sings ae sang,
   Will ye no come back again?

Lady Nairne (1766–1845)

Waverley Attends a Jacobite Trial

It was the third sitting of the Court, and there were two men at the bar. The Verdict of Guilty was already pronounced. Edward just glanced at the bar during a momentous pause which ensued. There was no mistaking the stately and noble features of Fergus MacIvor, although his dress was squalid and his countenance tinged with a sickly yellow hue of long and close imprisonment. By his side was Evan Maccombish. Edward felt sick and dizzy as he gazed on them; but he was recalled to himself as the Clerk of the Arraigns pronounced the solemn words: 'Fergus MacIvor of Glennaquoich, otherwise called Vich Ian Vohr, and Evan MacIvor in the Dhu of Tarrascleugh, otherwise called Evan Dhu, otherwise called Evan MacCombich or Evan Dhu MacCombish—you and each of you stand attainted of high treason. What have you to say for yourselves why the Court should not pronounce judgement against you, that you die according to the law?'

Fergus, as the presiding Judge was putting on the fatal cap of judgement, placed his own bonnet upon his head, regarded him with a steadfast and stern look, and replied in a firm voice, 'I cannot let this numerous audience suppose that to such an appeal I have no answer to make. But what I have to say, you would not bear to hear, for my defence would be your condemnation. Proceed, then, in the name of God, to do what is permitted to you. Yesterday, and the day before, you have condemned loyal and honourable blood to be poured forth like water. Spare not mine. Were there of all my ancestors in my veins, I would have peril'd it in this quarrel.' He resumed his seat, and refused again to rise.

Evan MacCombich looked at him with great earnestness, and, rising up, seemed anxious to speak; but the confusion of the court, and the perplexity arising from thinking in a language different from that in which he was to express himself, kept him silent. There was a murmur of compassion among the spectators, from an idea that the poor fellow intended to plead the influence of his superiors as an excuse for his crime. The Judge commanded silence, and encouraged Even to proceed.

'I was only ganging to say, my Lord,' said Evan, in what he meant to be in an insinuating manner, 'that if your excellent honour, and the honourable Court, would let Vich Ian Vohr go free just this once, and let him gae back to France, and no to trouble King George's government again, that ony six o' the very best of his clan will be willing to be justified in his stead; and if you'll just let me gae down to Glennaquoich, I'll fetch them up to ye masel', to head or hang, and you may begin wi' me the very first man.'

Not withstanding the solemnity of the occasion, a sort of laugh was heard in the Court at the extraordinary nature of the proposal. The Judge checked this indecency, and Evan, looking sternly around, when the murmur abated, 'If the Saxon gentlemen are laughing,' he said, 'because a poor man, such as me, thinks my life, or the life of six of my degree, is worth that of Vich Ian Vohr, it's like enough they may be very right; but if they laugh because they think I would not keep my word, and come back to redeem him, I can tell them they ken neither the heart of a Highlandman nor the honour of a gentlemen.'

There was no further inclination or laugh among the audience, and a dead silence ensued.

The Judge then pronounced upon both prisoners the sentence of the law of high treason, with all its horrible accompaniments. The execution was appointed for the ensuing day. 'For you, Fergus MacIvor,' continued the Judge, 'I can hold out no hope of mercy. You must prepare against to-morrow for your last sufferings here, and your great audit hereafter.'

'I desire nothing else, my lord,' answered Fergus, in the same manly and firm tone.

The hard eyes of Evan, which had been perpetually bent on his Chief, were moistened with a tear. 'For you, poor ignorant man,' continued the Judge, 'who, following the ideas in which you have been educated, have this day given us a striking example how the loyalty due to the King and state alone, is, from your unhappy ideas of clanship, transferred to some ambitious individual, who ends by making you the tool of his crimes—for you, I'd say, I feel so much compassion, that if you can make up your mind to petition for grace, I will endeavour to procure it for you. Otherwise—'

'Grace me no grace,' said Evans; 'Since you are to shed Vich Ian Vohr's blood, the only favour I would accept from you is—to bid them loose my hands and gie me my claymore, and bind you just a minute sitting where you are!'

'Remove the prisoners', said the Judge; 'His blood be upon his own head!'

Sir Walter Scott (1771–1832)
Waverley

Hame, Hame, Hame

Hame, hame, hame, O hame fain wad I be—
O hame, hame, hame, to my ain countree!

When the flower is i' the bud and the leaf is in the tree,
The larks shall sing me hame in my own countree;
Hame, hame, hame, O hame fain wad I be—
O hame, hame, hame, to my own countree!

The green leaf o' loyaltie's beginning for to fa',
The bonnie White Rose it is withering an' a';
But I'll water 't wi' the blude of usurping tyrannie,
An' green it will graw in my ain countree.

O, there's nocht now frae ruin my country can save,
But the keys o' kind heaven, to open the grave;
That a' the noble martyrs wha died for loyaltie
May rise again an' fight for their ain countree.

The great now are gane, a' wha ventured to save,
The new grass is springing on the tap o' their grave;
But the sun through the mirk blinks blythe in my e'e,
'I'll shine on ye yet in your ain countree.'

Hame, hame, hame, O hame fain wad I be—
O hame, hame, hame, to my ain countree!

                                   Allan Cunningham (1784–1842)

The End of Two Jacobite Lords

Arthur, 6th Lord Balmerino (1688–1746), joined the supporters of James Edward, the Old Pretender, after the Battle of Sheriffmuir in November 1715, then lived abroad until his father secured a pardon for him in 1733. Balmerino fought at Derby, was captured at Culloden, and was tried for treason in London. Unlike that of octogenarian Simon Fraser, Lord Lovat, who separately shared the fate of the Jacobite lords on Tower Hill, Balmerino's loyalty to the Jacobite cause was untainted by any suggestion of double-dealing. Unlike Lord Kilmarnock, for him there was to be no ignominious change of heart.

On 21st August 1746, Horace Walpole sat down in Windsor to write to his friend Horace Mann, Minister at the Court of Tuscany.

I came from the town . . . the day after the execution of the rebel lords: I was not at it, but had two persons come to me directly who were at the next house to the scaffold: and I saw another who was upon it, so that you may depend upon my accounts.

Just before they came out of the Tower, Lord Balmerino drank a bumper to King James's health. As the clock struck ten, they came forth on foot, Lord Kilmarnock all in black, his hair unpowdered in a bag [wig], supported by Foster, the great Presbyterian, and Mr Home, a young clergyman, his friend. Lord Balmerino followed, alone, in a blue coat, turned up with red (his rebellious regimentals), a flannel waistcoat, and his shroud beneath; their hearses following. They were conducted to a house near the scaffold: the room forwards had benches for spectators, in the second Lord Kilmarnock was put, and in the third backwards Lord Balmerino: all three chambers hung with black. Here they parted! Balmerino embraced the other and said, 'My lord, I wish I could suffer for both!' He had scarce left him, before he desired again to see him, and then asked him, 'My Lord Kilmarnock, do you know anything of the resolution taken in our army, the day before the battle of Culloden, to put the English prisoners to death?' He replied, 'My Lord, I was not present; but since I came hither, I have had all the reason in the world to believe that there was such order taken; and I hear the Duke has the pocket-book with the order.' Balmerino answered, 'It was a lie raised to excuse their barbarity to us.'

Take notice, that the Duke's [Cumberland's] charging this on Lord Kilmarnock (certainly on misinformation) decided this unhappy man's fate! The most now pretended is, that it would have come to Lord Kilmarnock's turn to have given the word for the slaughter, as lieutenant-general, with the patent for which he was immediately drawn into the Rebellion, after having been staggered by his wife, his mother, his own poverty, and the defeat of Cope. He remained an hour and a half in the house, and shed tears. At last he came to the scaffold, certainly much terrified, but with a resolution that prevented his behaving in the least meanly or unlike a gentleman. He took no notice of the crowd, only to desire that the baize might be lifted up from the rails, that the mob might see the spectacle.

He stood and prayed for some time with Foster, who wept over him, exhorted and encouraged him. He delivered a long speech to the Sheriff, and with a noble manliness stuck to the recantation he had made at his trial; declaring he wished that all who embarked in the same cause might meet the same fate. He then took off his bag, coat and waistcoat, with great composure, and after some trouble put on a napkin-cap, and then several times tried the block; the executioner, who was in white, with a white apron, out of tenderness concealing the axe behind himself. At last the Earl knelt down, with a visible unwillingness to depart, and after five minutes dropped his handkerchief, the signal, and his head was cut off at once, only hanging by a bit of skin, and was received in a scarlet cloth by four of the undertaker's men kneeling, who wrapped it up and put it into the coffin with the body; orders having been given not to expose the heads, as used to be the custom.

The scaffold was immediately new-strewed with sawdust, the block new-covered, the executioner new-dressed, and a new axe brought. Then came old Balmerino, treading with the air of a general. As soon as he mounted the scaffold, he read the inscription on his coffin, as he did again afterwards: he then surveyed the spectators, who were in amazing numbers, even upon masts of ships in the river; and pulling out his spectacles read a treasonable speech, which he delivered to the Sheriff, and said the young Pretender was so sweet a Prince, that flesh and blood could not resist following him; and lying down to try the block, he said, 'If I had a thousand lives, I would lay them all down here in the same cause.' He said, if he had not taken the sacrament the day before, he would have knocked down Williamson, the Lieutenant of the Tower, for his ill usage of him. He took the axe and felt it, and asked the headsman how many blows he had given Lord Kilmarnock; and gave him three guineas. Two clergymen, who attended him, coming up, he said, 'No gentlemen, I believe you have already done me all the service you can.' Then he went to the corner of the scaffold, and called very loud for the warder, to give him his perriwig, which he took off, and put on a night-cap of Scotch plaid, and then pulled off his coat and waistcoat and lay down; but being told he was on the wrong side, vaulted round, and immediately gave the sign by tossing up his arm, as if he were giving the signal for battle. He received three blows, but the first certainly took away all sensation. He was not a quarter of an hour on the scaffold; Lord Kilmarnock above half a one. Balmerino certainly died with the intrepidity of a hero, but with the insensibility of one too. As he walked from his prison to execution, seeing every window and top of house filled with spectators, he cried out, 'Look, look, how they are all piled up like rotten oranges!'

Horace Walpole (1717–97)
Letters

Culloden and After

You understand it? How they returned from Culloden
over the soggy moors aslant, each cap
at the low ebb no new full tide could pardon:
how they stood silent at the end of the rope
unwound from battle: and to the envelope
of a bedded room came home, polite and sudden.

And how, much later, bards from Tiree and Mull
would write of exile in the hard town
where mills belched English, anger of new school:
how they remembered where the sad and brown
landscapes were dear and distant as the crown
that fuddled Charles might study in his ale.

There was a sleep. Long fences leaned across
the vacant croft. The silly cows were heard
mooing their sorrow and their Gaelic loss.
The pleasing thrush would branch upon a sword.
A mind withdrew against its dreamed hoard
as whelks withdraw or crabs their delicate claws.

And nothing to be heard but songs indeed
while wandering Charles would on his olives feed
and from his Minch of sherries mumble laws.

Iain Crichton Smith (b. 1928)

The First Steamship

It is said that a Spaniard constructed the first steamship in 1543, but that although she was able to move herself, she was both too expensive and too unsafe to be of any practical use. In 1787 Patrick Millar of Dalswinton, the Dumfriesshire laird, from whom Burns rented Ellisland, decided that the steam-engine which James Watt of Greenock had invented in 1769 could be applied to work a paddle-wheel. He accordingly called in a young engineer, William Symington of Leadhills (1763–1831), and together they produced a vessel which sailed on Dalswinton Loch with Burns as one of the passengers. Symington went on to produce the world's first really practical steamboat, the 'Charlotte Dundas', in 1802, though the first passenger steamer in the world was Henry Bell's (1767–1830) 'Comet'.

On October 14th 1788 a boat was put in motion by a steam-engine, upon Mr Millar of Dalswinton's piece of water at that place. That gentleman's improvements in naval affairs are well known to the public. For some time past his attention has been turned to the application of the steam engine to the purposes of navigation. He has now accomplished, and evidently shewn to the world, the practicability of this, by executing it upon a small scale. A vessell, twenty-five feet long and seven broad, was, on the above date, driven with two wheels by a small engine. It answered Mr Millar's expectations fully, and afforded great pleasure to the spectators. The success of this experiment is no small accession to the public. Its utility in canals, and all inland navigation, points it out to be of the greatest advantage, not only to this island, but to many other nations of the world.

The Scots Magazine, November 1788

The Sutherland Clearances

During the first half of the nineteenth century, the proprietors of many of the large Highland estates decided, under adverse economic pressures, to introduce sheep-runs on a profitable scale. To do this they had to dispose of the crofters who occupied the land. However economically justified in the interests both of the landlords and the majority of the crofters their policy may have been, the physical eviction of these unfortunate, bewildered and justly resentful people, was conducted without consideration of health or future welfare. The worst atrocities were perpetrated in the county of Sutherland, staining for ever an ancient family name. While it is probably true that the Highlands could not have continued to support the population of 1814 in the face of rising standards of living, the shock of the Clearances—and of the exoneration of their most infamous instrument, Patrick Sellar, by a Court with a packed jury—coming just over half a century after Culloden and its aftermath, dealt a psychological

blow to the Highlanders' pride of self-sufficiency from which, some might say,
they have never wholly recovered. The Cromarty-born geologist and writer,
Hugh Miller, sets the scene in an account subsequently collected into Alexander
Mackenzie's 'A History of the Highland Clearances'.

A disasterous change . . . took place, in the providence of God, in the noble
family of Sutherland, and which . . . may be regarded as pregnant with the
disasters which afterwards befell the county.

The marriage of the young countess into a noble English family was
fraught with further disaster to the county. There are many Englishmen
quite intelligent enough to perceive the difference between a smoky cottage
of turf, and a whitewashed cottage of stone, whose judgments of their
respective inhabitants would be of but little value. Sutherland, as a county
of men, stood higher at this period than perhaps any other district in the
British Empire; but . . . it by no means stood high as a county of farms and
cottages. The marriage of the countess brought a new set of eyes upon it—
eyes accustomed to quite a different face of things. It seemed a wild, rude
county, where all was wrong, and all had to be set to right—a sort of Russia
on a small scale, that had just got another Peter the Great to civilize it—or a
sort of barbarous Egypt, with an energetic Ali Pasha at its head. Even the
vast wealth and great liberality of the Stafford family militated against this
hapless county! It enabled them to treat it as a mere subject of an interesting
experiment, in which gain to themselves was really no object—nearly as little
so, as if they had resolved on dissecting a dog alive for the benefit of science.
It was a still farther disadvantage, that they had to carry on their experiment
by the hands, and to watch its first effects with the eyes, of others. The
agonies of the dog might have had their softening influence on a dissecter who
held the knife himself; but there could be no such influence exerted over
him, did he merely issue orders to his footman that the dissection should be
completed, remaining, meanwhile, out of sight and out of hearing.

The plan of improvement sketched out by his English family was a plan
exceedingly easy of conception. Here is a vast tract of land, furnished with
two distinct sources of wealth. Its shores may be made the seats of extensive
fisheries, and the whole of its interior parcelled out into productive sheep
farms. All is waste in its present state; it has no fisheries, and two-thirds of its
internal produce is consumed by the inhabitants. It had contributed for the
use of the community and the landlord, its large herds of black cattle;
but the English family saw . . . that for every pound of beef which it produced,
it could be made to produce two pounds of mutton, and perhaps a pound of
fish in addition. And it was resolved, therefore, that the inhabitants of the
central districts, who, as they were mere Celts, could not be transformed, it
was held, into store farmers, should be marched down to the sea-side, there to
convert themselves into fishermen, on the shortest possible notice, and that a
few farmers of capital, of the industrious Lowland race, should be invited
to occupy the new sub-divisions of the interior.

And, pray, what objections can be urged against so liberal and large-minded a scheme? The poor inhabitants of the interior had very serious objections to urge against it. Their humble dwellings were of their own rearing; it was they themselves who had broken in their little fields from waste; from time immemorial, far beyond the reach of history, had they possessed their mountain holding—they had defended them so well of old that the soil was still virgin ground, in which the invader had found only a grave.

Hugh Miller (1802–56)

Highland Eviction

In March 1814, a large proportion of the Highlanders of the parishes of Farr and Kildonan, in Sutherland, were given until May to quit their farms. Most of them had nowhere to go, and so were summarily ejected. Thus the business of destruction began, continuing throughout the Highlands for more than a generation.

The work of devastation was begun by setting fire to the houses of the small tenants in extensive districts—Farr, Rogart, Golspie, and the whole parish of Kildonan. I was an eye-witness of the scene. The calamity came on the people quite unexpectedly. Strong parties for each district, furnished with faggots and other combustibles, rushed on the dwellings of the devoted people, and immediately commenced setting fire to them, proceeding in their work with the greatest rapidity, till about three hundred houses were in flames. Little or no time was given for the removal of persons or property—the consternation and confusion were extreme—the people stirring to remove the sick and helpless before the fire should reach them—next struggling to save the most valuable of their effects—the cries of the women and children—the roaring of the affrighted cattle, hunted by the dog of the shepherds amid the smoke and the fire—altogether composed a scene that completely baffled description. A dense cloud of smoke enveloped the whole country by day, and even extended far on the sea, At night, an awfully grand but terrific scene presented itself—all the houses in an extensive district in flames at once. I myself ascended a height about eleven o'clock in the evening, and counted two hundred and fifty blazing houses, many of the owners of which were my relations, and all of whom I personally knew, but whose present condition I could not tell. The conflagration lasted six days, till the whole of the dwellings were reduced to ashes or smoking ruins. During one of these days, a boat lost her way in the dense smoke as she approached the shore, but at night she was enabled to reach a landing-place by the light of the flames.

Donald McLeod (1831–1916)
Gloomy Memories

An English Comment on the Clearances

There is at this time a considerable ferment in the country concerning the management of the Marquis of Stafford's Estates: they comprize nearly two-fifths of the County of Sutherland, and the process of converting them into extensive sheep-farms is being carried on. A political economist has no hesitation concerning the fitness of the end in view, and little scruple as to the means. Leave these bleak regions, he says, for cattle to breed in, and let men remove to situations where they can exert themselves and thrive. The traveller who looks only at the outside of things, might easily assent to this reasoning. I have never—not even in Galicia—seen any human habitations so bad as the highland *black-houses*; by that name the people of the country call them, in distinction from such as are built with stone and lime. The worst of these *black-houses* are the *bothies*—made of very large turfs, from four to six feet long fastened with wooden pins to a rude wooden frame. The Irish cabin, I suppose, must be such a heap of peat with or without stones, according to the facility of collecting them, or the humour of the maker. But these men-sties are not inhabited, as in Ireland, by a race of ignorant and ferocious barbarians, who can never be civilized until they are regenerated— till the very nature is changed. Here you have a quiet, thoughtful, contented, religious people, susceptible of improvement, and willing to be improved. To transplant these people from their native mountain glens to the sea coast, and require them to become some cultivators, others fishermen, occupations to which they have never been accustomed—to expect a sudden and total change of habits in the existing generation, instead of gradually producing it in their children; to expel them by the process of law from their black-houses, and if they demur in obeying the ejectment, to oust them by setting fire to these combustible tenements—this surely is as little defensible on the score of policy as of morals.

Robert Southey (1774–1843)
Journal of a Tour in Scotland 1819

Emigration

By the time of the conflagration McLeod recollected, it was not merely to the 'sea-side' that the Highlanders were being pushed, but over the seas. Some sailed in conditions of intolerable squalor; others were able to afford a more comfortable passage. Even through the restrained reporting of a local newspaper, dealing with one sailing out of hundreds, the magnitude of the human loss to Scotland becomes plain.

A large body of emigrants sailed from Tobermory, on the 27th September, for New South Wales. The vessel was the 'Brilliant', and its size and splendid fittings were greatly admired. The people to be conveyed by this vessel are decidedly the most valuable that have ever left the shores of great Britain. They arc of excellent moral character, and, from their knowledge of agriculture, and management of sheep and cattle, must prove a most valuable acquisition to a colony like New South Wales. The Rev. Mr Macpherson, of Tobermory, preached a farewell sermon before the party sailed. The total number of emigrants was 322, made up as follows:—From Ardnamurchan and Strontian, 105; from Coll and Tiree, 104; from Mull and Iona, 56; from Morven, 25; and from Dunoon, 28. There were two teachers and two surgeons. A visitor from New South Wales presented as many of the party as he met with letters of introduction, and expressed himself highly gratified with the prospect of having so valuable an addition to the colony. A Government agent superintended the embarkation.

The *Inverness Courier* for 11th October, 1837

Lochaber No More

David Balfour, who is crossing from Mull to the mainland, passes an emigrant ship bound for America.

The passage was a very slow affair. There was no wind, and as the boat was wretchedly equipped, we could pull but two oars on one side, and one on the other. The men gave way, however, with a good will, the passengers taking spells to help them, and the whole company giving the time in Gaelic boat-songs. And what with the songs, and the sea air, and the good-nature and the spirit of all concerned, and the bright weather, the passage was a pretty thing to have seen.

But there was one melancholy part. In the mouth of Loch Aline we found a great sea-going ship at anchor; and this I supposed at first to be one of the King's cruisers which were kept along that coast, both summer and winter, to prevent communication with the French. As we got a little nearer, it became plain she was a ship of merchandise; 'nd what so more puzzled me, not only her decks, but the sea-beach also, were quite black with people, and skiffs were continually plying to and fro between them. Yet nearer, and there began to come to our ears a great sound of mourning, the people on board and those on the shore crying and lamenting one to another so as to pierce the heart.

Then I understood this was an emigrant ship bound for the American colonies.

We put the ferry-boat alongside, and the exiles leaned over the bulwarks, weeping and reaching out their hands to my fellow-passengers, among whom they counted some dear friends. How long this might have gone on I do not know, for they seemed to have no sense of time; but at last the captain of the ship, who seemed near beside himself (and no great wonder) in the midst of this crying and confusion, came to the side and begged us to depart.

Thereupon Neil sheered off; and the chief singer in our boat struck into a melancholy air, which was presently taken up both by the emigrants and their friends upon the beach, so that it sounded from all sides like a lament for the dying. I saw the tears run down the cheeks of the men and women in the boat, even as they bent at the oars; and the circumstances and the music of the song (which was called 'Lochaber No More') were highly affecting even to myself.

R. L. Stevenson (1850–94)
Kidnapped

Canadian Boat Song

Listen to me, as when ye heard our father
    Sing long ago the song of other shores—
Listen to me, and then in chorus gather
    All your deep voices as ye pull your oars:
Fair these broad meads—these hoary woods are grand;
But we are exiles from our fathers' land.

From the lone shieling of the misty island
    Mountains divide us, and the waste of seas—
Yet still the blood is strong, the heart is Highland,
    And we in dreams behold the Hebridies.

We ne'er shall tread the fancy-haunted valley,
    Where 'tween the dark hills creeps the small clear stream,
In arms around the patriarch banner rally,
    Nor see the moon on royal tombstones gleam.

When the bold kindred, in the time long-vanish'd,
    Conquer'd the soil and fortified the keep,
No seer foretold the children would be banish'd
    That a degenerate lord might boast his sheep.

Come foreign rage—let Discord burst in slaughter!
    O then for clansmen true, and stern claymore—
The hearts that would have given their blood like water
    Beat heavily beyond the Atlantic roar.
Fair these broad meads—these hoary woods are grand;
But we are exiles from our fathers' land.

Anonymous

A Highland Home

During the second half of the nineteenth century, an increasing number of Highland houses and Highland estates were bought by absentee landlords. Sporting interests and the building of houses for use as holiday homes became factors in the economy. Some Highlanders who had made money in business acquired estates from the dispossessed owners of the 'old order'.

Lochaline House was one such home. First built in 1825, refurbished about 1855, it was enlarged in the 1870s, then dismantled in 1899 and set on fire in 1910 because the then owner had built a more elaborate 'schloss' at the head of the loch.

Agnes King, from whose diary this remembrance of the house in the late 1850s is taken, was probably born about 1844, and apparently wrote her journal in 1902, shortly after the coronation of Edward VII, when she must have been about sixty.

Lochaline House stands about a quarter of a mile up from the shore of the Sound of Mull, and facing the mountains of Mull; Benmore with its double peaks being a beautiful object. The house consists of a large centre block with wings in each side, large and commodious—built for comfort more than appearance, though it looks handsome from the Sound. In front of it is a large lawn with a belting of trees all around, and a wood behind with the hills rising beyond. A pathway skirts the lawn under the trees, and the view from this path up and down the Sound of Mull is most extensive and exquisite. Oban is seen on the one side and Ardnamurchan on the other [sic], with the green isles, Aros, Duart and Ardtornish Castles.

Near the house and reached by the same path is the flower garden, made in an old quarry, a sheltered and sunny situation. Did ever such profusion of flowers grow anywhere else? The sweet scents filled the air, and the blaze of flowers was so unexpected that all were struck by it—you came upon the garden suddenly. The large garden with quantities of fruit and vegetables was some distance from the house. Flowers were in it also—such roses, rocket phloxes and every sweet smelling thing, balm, southernwood, lavendar—and immense hydrangeas and fuschias. I never see the same lovely old white low-growing Provence rose now, that used to flourish there.

I think the family occupied the house for one summer before it was quite finished, going back to Tobermory for the winter before moving the household permanently into it. But alas! before the next summer came my grandmother was dead. . .

Grandfather's sister, Mrs Campbell, kept house for him until my mother was seventeen, when she took the head of it on her return from school in Edinburgh. And well she filled the difficult post, for it was no ordinary household she was called upon to manage. Hospitality was the rule of the house, and there was scarcely a day but what some strangers unexpectedly came. In these days neither by road nor water was there regular communication with the south, as there is now in that district, and so people travelled very much in their own sailing boats from place to place. Indeed there was no house of any pretentions without its boat-house. It was as necessary as stables, and more so.

The cooking of a Highland kitchen was a continual process, like that on a passenger steamer on a long journey. Different classes had to be served at different periods of the day, from early morn till night. Dairymaids, and all sorts of maids, with shepherds, farm servants, and herd-lads, often strangers also, were fed in the large hall adjoining the kitchen. Upstairs in the dining room the family, and visitors in the house, were always a goodly number, while often a boat load of people were landed for the night, from stress of weather or other cause.

Ducks, hens, geese, and turkeys, all supplied from the home farm—in such quantities as would terrify the modern cook and landlady if required to order them daily from the market, and sheep and lambs from the hills, with a bullock now and then, game from the moors and fish from the rivers and sea, made a plentiful supply for all. So abundant was the supply of salmon there at that time that servants when engaged, stipulated not to have it served more than so many days a week.

Much forethought was also required in the ordering of such a household. When one thinks of the comfort and plenty which reigned in that home one can scarcely believe that there were no shops or markets to draw upon. Twice a year stores were ordered from Glasgow, and the store-room filled, and what a business was that! Medicines too were ordered at the same time, kept locked up in the 'Medicine Press', from which the whole community were supplied with physic.

Agnes King (b.c. 1844)
*Little Sketch of Those who are gone,
and Scenes of Long ago,* quoted in
Philip Gaskell's *Morvern
Transformed*

PEOPLE

Columba: A Seventh-Century Portrait

Saint Columba (521–97), or Columcille, was a member of the reigning family of Ireland, and closely related to that of Dalriada (Argyll). In 563, he and twelve disciples sailed to Iona, where he built a church and a monastery. From there he converted the Picts of northern Scotland. Abbot Adamnan of Iona about 679 completed the life of the Saint begun perhaps twenty years before by Abbot Cuminius.

Saint Columba was born of noble parentage ... In the forty-second year of his age, desiring to make a pilgrimage from Ireland to Britain, he sailed forth. And he, who even from boyhood had been devoted to the school of Christ and the study of wisdom, preserving by the gift of God integrity of body and purity of soul, showed that although placed upon earth he was fitted for a heavenly life. For he was angelic of aspect, clean in speech, holy in deed, of excellent disposition, great in counsel, for thirty-four years trained as an Island-soldier (of Christ). He could not pass the space even of a single hour without applying himself either to prayer, or reading, or writing, or to some manual labour. By day and by night he was so occupied, without any intermission, in unwearied exercises of fasts and vigils that the burden of anyone of these particular labours might seem to be beyond human endurance. And, amid all, dear to all, ever showing a pleasant, holy countenance, he was gladdened in his inmost heart by the joy of the Holy Spirit.

Adamnan (c. 624–704)
Life of Columba.

Columba on Iona

So Colmcille went journeying, through pass and through hill-mounth,
on moor-path and ben-crag, by waterfall and loch-round,
in wheel-cart and long-boat, on stream-race and sea-sound,—
filling out the measure of the days of the Saviour,
carrying His leaven to the griddle of Gaeldom.

They would say in Iona, the Gaels of Dál Riada,
'He's walking again, the great-grandson of Niall;
he's tall as a spruce; he is sunny as summer;
he is fair and unspotted as the eggs of the puffin;
he has anger and kindness in his fine hands like wingbones,
and mercy in his nostril, and judgment in his lips' mould.'

And over he would come, with the Johnswort yellow in his girdle,
(hard heels a-slapping in his sandals with the spirit of his walking
and blessings spraying out as road-pools from the cartwheels' hurtle)
ramming them with eyes to find out of what craft to be talking,
and talking (through the gossiping, the parley of crops and of seasons—
of hauls of red herring,—the crotchets of sheep, and fleeces)
of one last cropping, one parting of fish on a shingle.
As Christ talked; and men felt the world and the next world mingle.

Robert Farren (b. 1909)
The First Exile

Columba: A Twentieth-Century Portrait

Altogether he was a remarkable man. Tall, well-featured with long hair
falling to each shoulder from the temples (for the early Celtic priests shaved
the front of their heads), he had a commanding presence, and was, in fact,
full of a restless energy, passionate and impetuous. He had that quality of
voice which does not appear to be raised when speaking to those at hand and
which yet can be heard clearly at a distance. A statesman, an organizer, he
was almost continuously on the move, over land, by sea, daring any peril,
unsparing of himself, teaching, converting, founding, succeeding.

He succeeded very well indeed—so well that his own folk, the Gaels or
Scots (Ireland is called Scotai in the old records), who landed, as he landed,
on the Argyllshire part of Scotland, managed in time to give their kings to
Scotland, their tongue, and their particular methods of Church government. All that was distinctive of the ancient Pictish Scotland, strong enough
in its time to repel the Romans, faded away before this Columban energy
and statesmanship, leaving scarcely a trace behind. It is the great mystery
in Scottish history, that to this day scholars debate the identity of the Picts,
what tongue they spoke and how they were governed in church and state.
Statesmanship that is successful has doubtless its own reward, even if suspicion of doubtful dealings be not inevitably aroused. In any case, I was
inclined to be one of those who felt no great urge to pay further tribute to
Columba and Iona; who in fact would rather learn somewhat more of our
real forbears, the Picts, and give his proper place to that Ninian who was a
missionary in Scotland one hundred and fifty years before Columba arrived...

In a word, I was prepared to be prejudiced to the hilt against Columba. But, unfortunately, Iona is the last place in the world to help a prejudice. If one doesn't forget it, at least one cannot be bothered with it for the moment, not in the rain, in the soft air . . .

For one can also see that other half of Columba's character, the affectionate part, full of warmth and understanding . . . It had the nobility from which, perhaps, all his restless energy received direction. Tolerance, temperance, kindness, simplicity obedience, forgiveness—we know the rules that governed their lives; but, above all, from their religion they got the conception of charity of love. It is the ancient goodness of the human heart, the primordial goodness. And a religion that enshrines it will always persist. Those who have this goodness in them are aware of life in the same way as they are aware of light. Truly, life itself in an inner light.

And, at its best, it is a universal light. Columba loved the birds, and the white horse that carried the farm produce bore Columba a special affection. Indeed, as Adamnan relates . . . the white horse wept on taking leave of its dying master. Which may be an exaggeration of the truth; but still of the truth. And that wise and scholarly men of his age believed it to be the simple truth shows at least what they wanted to believe. Which is the essence of the matter. Beyond miracle and morality and theology, they desired this goodness. And kings and priests and murderers and perverts of all kinds went to Columba in Iona to find again the peace of that goodness.

Neil M. Gunn (1891–1973)
Off in a Boat

The Murder of St Magnus

During the reign of Malcolm II and shortly before Duncan came to the Scottish throne, to be murdered and followed by Macbeth, Orkney, Shetland, the Western Isles and the Isle of Man were in the hands of the Norsemen. 'The Orkneyinga Saga', though actually composed in Iceland, recalls how, in 1106, when Earl Hakon was ruler in Orkney, his kinsman Earl Magnus quite properly claimed a share of the realm. Magnus, restrospectively to his anonymous 'biographer' at any rate, was possessed of all the Christian virtues, while Hakon was a Norse man-of-action.

The kinsmen Magnus and Hakon kept watch and ward over the land . . . just so long as they were on good terms . . . But when the kinsmen had ruled the land for a time, it came about, as often happens, and always may, that a number of mischief-mongers contrived to break up their good fellowship. Then malcontents gathered more about Hakon, for he was very jealous of the popularity and lordliness of his kinsman Magnus.

Two men of Earl Hakon's following are specially named as being by far the worst of the busy-bodies between the kinsmen—Sigurd and Sighvat Socks. So strong did the slander grow upon the tongues of evil men that the kinsmen mustered forces and each Earl went to meet the other with a large company . . . This meeting was in Lent, a little before Palm Sunday. And since their many well-wishers took it in hand to avert a breach between them and would stand by neither to the detriment of the other, they bound themselves to a settlement with oaths and by the right hand of fellowship.

And after some time had passed, Earl Hakon with false heart and fair words, called a meeting on a day appointed between himself and the blessed Earl Magnus, to settle it that nothing should disturb or nullify their fellowship and the established peace just made between them. This meeting for an established peace and final settlement between them was to be in Egilsay in Easter week the next spring.

This proposal pleased Earl Magnus, being as he was a very whole-hearted man, without any suspicions, deceit, or greed of gain. And each was to have two ships and an equal number of men. They both swore to keep the terms of peace that the wisest men from both parties had thought fit to lay down between them.

Now when Eastertide was past, each made ready for this meeting. Earl Magnus summoned to him all those men in his realm whom he thought most eager for peace and most likely to do their best for both kinsmen. He had two ships and exactly the agreed number of men. And when he was ready for sea, he sailed for Egilsay.

And as they were rowing in calm and smooth water, there rose a wave under the ship that the Earl was steering, and it broke under the ship just where the Earl sat. The Earl's men were filled with amazement at this occurence, that a wave should break in a calm sea where no man had known of it to have broken before, and in deep water too.

Then said the Earl: ' 'Tis no wonder you are surprised at this miracle or portent that was never seen before. Now my mind tells me that this is my death-omen. It may be, that will come to pass what was foretold of Earl Hakon, that the son of Earl Paul would commit the foulest of crimes. To my mind we should do well to assume that my kinsman Hakon does not mean to play fair with us at this meeting.'

The Earl's men grew heavy of heart at these words, when he spoke of his short hope of life. And they bade him take heed for his life, and not go further trusting in Hakon.

Earl Magnus answers: 'Our voyage shall still go on, and may God's will be done therein.' . . .

Earl Magnus with his band of men arrived first in Egilsay. And when they espied Earl Hakon coming, they saw that he had eight warships; then he knew for certain that there was foul play afoot. Earl Magnus went up inland over the isle with his men, and betook himself to the church to pray, and was there that night. Now his men offered to stand on guard for him. The Earl answers: 'I will not put your lives in peril for my sake. And if there be no peace between us kinsmen, then be it as God wills.' . . . Now since he knew

already the hours of his life—whether by second sight or from divine knowledge—he would not flee nor shirk meeting his enemies. He did not go into the
church for any other reason than that he wished to save his life. There he
prayed earnestly to God and commended himself into His hand, and had a
Mass sung for him and took the sacrament.

Early next morning he left the church and two others with him, and went
down by another way to the shore to a hiding place, and prayed again to God.

Hakon and his men came ashore in the morning, and ran first to the church
and ransacked it, and did not find the Earl. They then sought him throughout
the rest of the island. When Earl Magnus saw this, he called out to them and
told them where he was: he bade them seek nowhere else for him. And then
Hakon spied him, he and his men leapt down to him with yelling and clatter
of arms.

Earl Magnus was on his knees at his prayers when they reached him.
And when he had finished his prayers and crossed himself, with steadfast
heart he said to Earl Hakon: 'Thou didst not well, kinsman, to go back on
thine oaths, and it is much to be hoped that thou dost this more through
the malice of others than of thine own. Now I will offer thee three choices,
of which thou shalt make one, rather than break thine oaths and have me
put to death innocent.'

Hakon's men asked what were his offers.

'The first,' said the Earl, 'is that I would go south to Rome, or out to the
Holy Land and visit holy places, and take abroad two ships fully equipped
and well-manned, and seek betterment for both our souls. This I would
swear, never to come back again to the Orkneys while I live.'

Hakon and his men at once refused this.

Then said Earl Magnus: 'Now since my life is in your hands, and since
I have been in many things a sinner before Almighty God and must needs
do penance for that, and since to my thinking it is unseemly that thou kill me,
send me up into Scotland to some of our common friends and kinsmen, and
let me be there kept under watch and ward, and two men with me to bear
me company. See thou to it that I may not escape from my imprisonment
except by thy will.'

They at once refused this, and gave many reasons why it could not possibly
be.

Magnus said: 'But there is still one choice I must offer thee. And God
knows that I am looking more to your souls than to my life; and it better
befits thee than to take my life. Maim my body as thou likest, or pluck out
my eyes, and put me in a darksome dungeon.'

Then said Earl Hakon: 'I accept this settlement and ask nothing further.'

Then the chiefs started up and said to Earl Hakon: 'We will kill one of the
two of you now; and never from this day forth shall both of you rule the
land.'

Then answers Hakon: 'If you are going to be so particular in this matter,
rather kill him, for I will rather rule realm and lands than die so suddenly.'
So says Holbodi, a trustworthy bondi from the Hebridies, concerning their

conversation. He was one of the two men with Earl Magnus when they made him captive.

The worthy Magnus was as blithe as if he had been bidden to a feast. Not a word did he utter of hate or anger. And after this conversation, he fell to praying, and hid his face in his hands, letting fall many tears before Almighty God.

When Saint Magnus the Earl was doomed to death, Hakon bade Ofeig his standard-bearer kill the Earl, but he refused very indignantly. Then he compelled Lifolf his cook to kill Magnus, but he began to sob aloud.

Earl Magnus said to him: 'Thou shalt not weep for this, for there is fame in the doing of such deeds. Be stedfast of heart, for thou shalt have my clothes as is the custom and law of men of old. And thou shalt have no fear, for thou dost this against thy will, and he who forces thy hand is a greater sinner than thou.'

Now when the Earl had spoken thus, he took off his kirtle and gave it to Lifolf. After this he asked his leave to pray, and it was given him.

He fell upon the earth and commended himself to God, offering himself as a sacrifice. Not only did he pray for himself and his friends, but also for his enemies and murderers, and forgave from the bottom of his heart those who had done him evil; and confessed his own sins to God and prayed that they be washed from him by the shedding of his blood, and commended his soul into God's hands, and besought God's angels to meet his spirit and carry it to the rest of Paradise . . . Then when the friend of God was led to slaughter, he said to Lifolf: 'Stand thou before me, and hew on my head a great wound, for it is not seemly to behead chiefs like thieves. Take good heart, poor wretch, for I have prayed to God for thee, that he be merciful unto thee.'

After that he crossed himself, and bowed himself to the stroke; and he was struck in the middle of the head with a single blow, and so passed from the world to God.

The Orkneyinga Saga, translated by A. B. Taylor

Lament for Wallace

Sir William Wallace (c. 1270–1305), the national hero of Scotland, is believed to have been born in Elderslie, Renfrewshire. He rallied the Scots against the occupation forces of England's Edward I. After the Scots victory at Stirling, Wallace became Guardian of Scotland. His army, however, was defeated at the Battle of Falkirk. Eight years later Wallace was betrayed to the English by Sir John Menteith; taken, fettered, to London; given a sham trial and cruelly butchered the same day.

For many of the details of his early life we are dependent on Henry the Minstrel, 'Blind Harry', who, though writing two hundred years later, claimed as his authority a lost contemporary Latin work by John Blair.

Alas, Scotland, to whom sall thou complain!
Alas, fra pain wha sall thee now restrain!
Alas, they help is fastlie brocht to ground,   [falsely
Thy best chyftane in braith bands is bound;   [violent
Alas, thou has now lost they guide of licht!
Alas, wha sall defend thee in thy richt?
Alas, thy pain approachis wonder near,
With sorrow soon thou mon bene set in fear!   [must be
Thy gracious guide, thy greatest governoure,
Alas, owre near is cumyn his fatal hour!
Alas, wha sall thee beit now off thy baill?   [cure thee of thy woe
Alas, when sall of harmis thou be haill?
Wha sall thee defend? Wha sall thee now mak free?
Alas, in war wha sall thy helper be?
Wha sall thee help? Wha sall thee now radem?   [redeem
Alas, wha sall the Saxons fra thee flem?   [drive off
I can no mair but beseik God of grace
Thee to restore in haste to rychtwysnace;   [wisdom
Sen guid Wallace may succour thee no mair
The loss of him encressit meikle care.   [increases much care

Henry the Minstrel (*c.* 1480–92)
The Actis and Deidis of the Illustre and Vailyeant Campioun Schir William
Wallace, Knicht of Ellerslie.

King Robert the Bruce

Robert the Bruce, who continued and completed the task of liberating Scotland
from the yoke of the English kings, had as his principle chronicler John Barbour,
Archdeacon of Aberdeen. His poem 'The Brus' was produced in 1376. Bruce
and Douglas—Sir James Douglas, who died fighting the Moors at Tebas de
Ardales on 25th March 1330, carrying the enbalmed heart of the great King—
were Barbour's heroes, and accordingly he minimized the King's shortcomings
and over-emphasized his virtues. Nevertheless, Bruce's most scholarly biographer
of our own day does give a firm portrait of King Robert I.

The king's sense of humour comes out even in dry official documents, but
is best remembered in his reply to the nobles who rebuked him for risking
his life in the encounter with Sir Henry de Bohun at Bannockburn. His
immense courage is attested by the whole of his career. Patience, on the
other hand, he was forced to learn, yet once learned it became his most
dominant characteristic. Men trusted his word and his judgements, so that

decisions and laws made by him were respected and, in after years, invented in order to be respected. In a period when there were virtually no professionals, generalship was not of a high order. But modern military experts agree that Bruce's handling of Bannockburn was masterly. The secret of his success here lay in the fact that behind his tactical brilliance and superlative gifts of leadership Bruce had an exceptionally good grasp of strategy: he always knew what should take priority. Directly or indirectly, Barbour's portrait gives us these qualities. His terms of reference forbade him to write of short-comings, such as the evident rashness and hot-headedness of Bruce's earlier years. Barbour hardly brings out Bruce's ambition, yet it cannot be doubted that from young manhood Bruce was determined to play a leading part. The truth about his submission to Edward I in 1301–2 has now been established in sufficient detail to disprove all the old charges of treachery and double-dealing, yet the fact remains that Bruce did change sides two years in advance of his colleagues. Barbour also fails to mention, presumably because word and concept were alike lacking in his time, one of Bruce's greatest gifts, the imaginative quality of his mind which allowed him to be revolutionary in more than just the political sense.

Finally, we must return to Robert Bruce's kingliness. It was suggested earlier that the key to much of his conduct may be sought in the background, at once aristocratic and royal, in which his grandfather was brought up and lived out his long career. There is an unmistakable assurance about the manner in which Bruce assumed kingship even though he reached the throne by a revolutionary coup. Even his flight in the heather did not snuff out his claims to royalty, though the news of it inspired mocking ballads in England and became common gossip as far away as Italy. The *regia dignitas* of Scotland was never in safer hands than those of King Robert I. Barbour convincingly makes the magnates gathered at his deathbed mourn their lord as a great exponent of kingship and kingliness: 'for better governour than he mycht in na cuntre fundyn be.'

G. W. S. Barrow (b. 1924)
Robert Bruce

Robert the Bruce Stricken with Leprosy

'My life is done, yet all remains,
    The breath has vanished, the image not,
The furious shapes once forged in heat
    Live on, though now no longer hot.

'Steadily the shining swords
    In order rise, in order fall,
In order on the beaten field
    The faithful trumpets call.

'The women weeping for the dead
  Now are not sad but dutiful,
The dead men stiffening in their place
  Proclaim the ancient rule.

'Great Wallace's body hewn in four,
  So altered, stays as it must be.
O Douglas, do not leave me now.
  For by your side I see

'My dagger sheathed in Comyn's heart,
  And nothing there to praise or blame,
Nothing but order which must be
  Itself and still the same.

'But that Christ hung upon the Cross,
  Comyn would rot until Time's end
And bury my sin in boundless dust,
  For there is no amend

'In order; yet in order run
  All things by unreturning ways.
If Christ live not, nothing is there
  For sorrow or for praise.'

So the King spoke to Douglas once
  A little time before his death,
Having outfaced three English kings
  And kept a people's faith.

Edwin Muir (1887–1959)

King James IV

The writer of this portrait of the talented but impetuous king who fell at Flodden was the Spanish Ambassador at the Scottish Court. The report from which it comes is dated 25th July 1498.

The king is twenty-five years and some months old. He is of noble stature, neither tall nor short, and as handsome in complexion and shape as a man can be. His address is very agreeable. He speaks the following foreign languages: Latin, very well; French, German, Flemish, Italian, and Spanish . . . He likes very much to receive Spanish letters. His own Scotch language is as different from English as Aragonese from Castilian. The king speaks, besides, the language of the savages who live in some parts of Scotland and on the islands. It is as different from Scotch as Biscayan is from Castilian. His knowledge of language is wonderful. He is a good historian. He has read many Latin and French histories, and profited by them, as he has a very good memory. He is well read in the Bible and in some other devout books. He never cuts his hair or his beard. It becomes him very well.

He fears God, and observes all the precepts of the Church. He does not eat meat on Wednesdays and Fridays. He would not ride on Sundays for any consideration, not even to mass. He says all his prayers. Before transacting any business he hears two masses. After mass he has a cantata sung, during which he sometimes despatches very urgent business. He gives alms liberally, but is a severe judge, especially in the case of murderers. He has a great predilection for priests and receives advice from them, especially from the Friars Observant, with whom he confesses. Rarely, even in joking, a word escapes him that is not the truth. He prides himself much upon it, and says it does not seem to him well for kings to swear their treaties as they do now. The oath of a king should be his royal word, as was the case in bygone ages. He is neither prodigal nor avaricious, but liberal when occasion requires. He is courageous, even more so than a king should be. I am a good witness of it. I have seen him often undertake most dangerous things in the last wars. I sometimes clung to his skirts and succeeded in keeping him back. On such occasions he does not take the least care of himself. He is not a good captain, because he begins to fight before he has given his orders. He said to me that his subjects serve him with their persons and goods, in just and unjust quarrels, exactly as he likes, and that, therefore, he does not think it right to begin any warlike undertaking without being himself the first in danger. His deeds are as his words. For this reason, and because he is a very humane prince, he is much loved.

Don Pedro de Ayala
from Bergenroth's *Simancas Papers*

The Gudeman of Ballangeigh

James V (1512–42) used frequently to traverse the vicinity of his several palaces, in various disguises, in search of adventures. The two comic songs, entitled 'The Gaberlunzie Man', and 'We'll gang na mair a-roving' are said to have been founded upon the success of his amours, when travelling in the disguise of a beggar. An adventure he had at the village of Cramond, four miles from Edinburgh, is said to have nearly cost him his life.

While, one evening, visiting a pretty girl, of the lower rank, who resided in that village, to whom he had rendered his addresses acceptable, while returning home, he was beset by four or five persons. Naturally gallant, and an admirable master of his weapon, the king took post on the high and narrow bridge, over the Almond river, and defended himself bravely with his sword. A peasant who was threshing in a neighbouring barn, came out upon the noise, and whether moved by compassion, or by natural gallantry, took the weaker side, and laid about him with his flail so effectually as to disperse the assailants well threshed, even according to the letter. He then conducted the king into his barn, where his guest requested a basin and towel, to remove the stains of the broil. This being procured with difficulty, James employed himself in learning what was the summit of his deliverer's earthly wishes, and found that they were bounded by the desire of possessing, in perpetuity, the farm of Braehead, upon which he laboured as a bondsman. The lands chanced to belong to the crown, and James directed him to come to the palace of Holyrood, and enquire for the gudeman of Ballangeigh.

The poor man came as appointed, and, as the king had given orders for his admission, he was soon brought into the royal presence. James, still dressed in his travelling attire, received him as the gudeman of Ballangeigh, conducted him from one apartment to another, by way of shewing him the palace, and then asked him if he would like to see the king. John Howison, for such was his name, said, that nothing would give him so much pleasure, if he was only brought into the king's hall, without giving offence. The gudeman of Ballangeigh, of course, undertook that the king would not be angry. 'But,' said John, 'how am I to know his grace from the nobles who will be all about him?' 'Easily', replied the king, 'all the others will be bareheaded— the king alone will wear his bonnet.' On John being introduced into the great hall, which was filled by the nobility and officers of the crown, he was somewhat frightened, and drew near to his attendant but was unable to distinguish the king. 'I told you that you would know him by his wearing his hat,' said his conductor. 'Then,' said John, after he had looked round the room, 'it must be either you or me, for all but us are bareheaded.'

The king laughed at John's fancy, and, that the good yeoman might have mirth also, he made him a present of the farm of Braehead, which he had wished so much to possess, on condition, that he and his successors should be ready to present a ewer and basin, for the king to wash his hands, when his majesty should come to Holyrood palace, or should pass the bridge of Cramond. Accordingly, in the year 1822, when Geo. IV came to Scotland, a descendant of John Howison, who still possesses the estate which was given to his ancestor, appeared at a solemn festival, and offered his majesty water from a silver ewer, that he might perform the service by which he held his land.

Anonymous
Annals of Edinburgh

Knox Preaches

The Reverend James Melville, nephew of the more famous Andrew Melville, was as staunch an opponent of James VI's attempts to impose Episcopacy on

Scotland as was his uncle. As a student in 1571, he heard John Knox (c. 1515–1572) preach at St Andrews.

Bot of all the benefits I had that year was the coming of that maist notable prophet and apostle of our nation, Mr John Knox to St Andrews ... I heard him teach there the prophecy of Daniel that simmer, and the winter following. I had my pen and my little book, and took away sic [such] things as I could comprehend. In the opening up of his text he was moderate the space of ane half hour; bot when enterit to application, he made ane so to grue [shudder[and tremble, that I could nocht hold a pen to write ... I saw him every day go hulie [slowly] and fear, with a furring of marten about his neck, a staff in the ane hand and guid godly Richart Ballanden, his servent, holding up the other oxter. The said Richart and another servent, lifted him up to the pulpit, where he behovit to lean on his first entry; bot or he had done with his sermon, he was so active and vigorous that he was like to ding that pulpit in blads [break the pulpit in pieces] and fly out of it!

James Melville (1556–1614)
Autobiography and Diary

The Death of Knox

This account is by Knox's secretary, whom James Melville called 'the guid godlie Richart Ballanden'.

Richart, sitting down before him said: 'Now Sir, the time that ye have long callit to God for, to wit, ane end of your battle, is cum; and seeing all natural power now fails, remember upon the comfortable promises which often times ye have schowin to us of our saviour, Jesus Christ; and that we may understand, and know that ye hear us, make us some sign; and so he lifted up his head and in contentment thereafter rendered up the spirit, and sleepit away without ony pane ...

On this manner departed this man of God, the licht of Scotland, the comfort of the kirk within the same, the mirror of godliness and patron and example to all true ministers, in purity of life, soundness of doctrine, and in bauldness in reproving of wickedness.

Richard Bannatyne (d. 1605)
Journal of the Transactions in Scotland 1570–73

The Knoxian Blight

It is easy to point out Knox's faults, and it is impossible to deny their seriousness. He had no sense of justice; what he praised in his friends he condemned in his enemies. He was not sagacious; his wild epistles to England and his treatment of the young Scottish Queen intensified the calamities which they were intended to avert. He was disingenuous, as all his writings prove. He was vindictive in his unrelenting pursuit of Mary Stuart, he was ruthless towards the Catholics, repeatedly clamouring for their extermination. Normally he was altogether without self-control; he could, however, assume it in an emergency. He was incapable of living in peace; he quarrelled in succession with almost all his friends, with Cranmer, the English at Frankfort, Calvin, Moray, Kirkcaldy, Lethington; he fought in his maturity with queens, and in his dotage with the nonentities of St Andrews.

His greatness lay in two qualities: the inexhaustible vehemence of his powers, and the constancy of his aim. The effect he had on men less unrelenting was like that of a wind, which blows with a steadfast violence, and by its persistence bends everything and keeps it bent. His will, like the mistral, had something in it unnatural and mechanical. It never relaxed, because it could not. It went on, as if independent of him, when his body was powerless, and he was lying on his deathbed; it lived in his last gesture, the hand stubbornly upraised as he gave up his spirit. It had goaded the Scottish nobles to revolt and Mary to shame and destruction: it had not given its possessor a respite for thirteen years. It was cruel and terrible, but it is perhaps the most heroic and astonishing spectacle in all Scottish history.

Edwin Muir (1887–1959)
John Knox

The Two Queens and the Diplomat

Sir James Melville of Halhill entered the service of Mary Queen of Scots as a page when he was fourteen. On her return to Scotland, Melville became a Privy Councillor, and was sent to England to find out what Queen Elizabeth really thought about the proposals for Mary's second marriage. Later, he was unsuccessful in his attempts to prevent the murder of David Rizzio, and also unsuccessfull in trying to persuade Mary against marrying Bothwell. Melville also gave advice to Mary's son, James VI and I, but after the Union of the Crowns in 1603, he retired to his estate in Fife, where he wrote his memoirs.

Then sche tok out the Quenis picture and kissit it; and I kissit hir hand, for the gret love I saw sche bure to the Quen. Sche schew me also a fair ruby, gret lyk a racket ball. Then I desyred that sche wald eyther send it as a token unto the Quen, or also my Lord of Lecester's picture. Sche said, gene [if] the Quen wald follow hir consaill, that sche wald get them baith with tym,

11

and all that sche had; bot suld send hir a dyamont for a token with me . . .

Hir hair was reder than yellow, curlit apparently of nature. Then sche entrit to dicern what kind of coulour of hair was reputed best; and inquyred whither the Quenis or hirs was best, and whilk [which] of them twa was fairest. I said, the fairnes of them baith was not ther worst faltes. Bot sche was ernest with me to declare whilk of them I thocht fairest. I said, sche was the fairest Queen in Scotland. Yet sche was ernest. I said, they wer baith the fairest ladyes of ther courtes, and that the Quen of England was whytter, bot our Quen was very lusome [lovely]. Sche inquyred whilk of them was of hyest stature. I said, our Quen. Then sche said, the Quen was over heych [too tall], and that hir self was nother over hich nor over laich [too small]. Then sche askit what kynd of exercyses sche used. I said, that I was dispatchit out of Scotland, that at the Quen was bot new com bak from the hyland hunting; and when sche had leaser [leisure] fra the affaires of hir contre, sche red [read] upon gud bukis, the histories of dyvers [various] contrees, and somtymes wald play upon lute and virginelis. Sche sperit [asked if] gene sche plaid weill. I said, raisonably for a Quen.

Sir James Melville (1535–1617)
Memoirs of My Own Life

Mary in English Hands

Following the defeat of her supporters at Langside on 13th May 1568, Mary rode to Sanquhar. On the 15th she reached Dundrennan, from where she wrote to Queen Elizabeth asking to be received. In the company of a small party she crossed the Solway on the afternoon of the 16th, landing at Workington. Next day she was taken to Cockermouth, and on the 18th to Carlisle Castle. There she was detained until July, when she was moved to Bolton to lessen the possibility of rescue by sea.

On 28th May, Mary received in her apartments at Carlisle Castle the warden, Lord Scrope, accompanied by the vice-chamberlain, Sir Francis Knollys. Knollys duly made his report to Cecil, Lord Burghley.

This ladie and prynces is a notable woman; she semethe to regard no ceremonious honor besyde the acknolegying of hyr estate regalle: she showeth a disposition to speak motche, to be bold, to be plesant, and to be very famylyare. She showeth a great desyer to be avenged of hyr enymyes, she showeth a redines to expone hyr selffe to all perylls in hope of victorie, she delytethe motche to hear of hardiness and valiancye, commendyng by name all approved hardye men of hyr countrye, althoe they be hyr enemyes, and she concealithe no cowardnes even in hyr frendes. The thynge that moste she thirstethe after is victorye, and it seemeth to be indifferent to have hyr enemies demynysshed eyther by the sword of hyr frendes, or by the liberall promyses and rewardes of hyr purse, or by devysyon and qwarylls raised amongst theym selffes: so that for victories sake payne and parylle [peril] semethe pleasant unto hyr: and in respect of victorie, welthe and all things semethe to hyr contemlptible and vyle. Nowe what is to be done with sotche a ladie and pryncesse, or whether sotche a pryncesse and ladie be to be norysshed in one's bosome? or whether it be good to halte and disembyll with sotche a ladye, I referr to your judgement.

Sir Francis Knollys

Mary, Queen of Scots

Whether she was a beauty by our standards or not, Mary Stuart was certainly rated a beauty by the standards of her own time: even the venomous Knox, never inclined to pay compliments to those with whose convictions he disagreed, described her as 'pleasing', and recorded that the people of Edinburgh called out 'Heaven bless that sweet face' as she passed on her way. Sir James Melville, an experienced man of the world who prided himself on his detachment, called her appearance 'very lovesome'. Ronsard paid her superb tributes: he wrote of her hands which he particularly admired and their long, ringless fingers, which he compared in a poetic phrase to five unequal branches; he wrote of the unadorned beauty of her throat, free of any necklace, her alabaster brow, her ivory bosom. When she was a young widow, he wrote of her pacing sadly but gracefully at Fontainebleau, her garments blowing about her as she walked, like the sails of a ship ruffled in the wind. The word goddess was the one which seemed to come most naturally to Brantôme in writing of her: she was *'une vraie Déesse'* of beauty and grace; he picked out her complexion for special praise, and described its famous pallor which rivalled and eclipsed the whiteness of her veil, when she was in mourning. Furthermore Mary had the additional charm of a peculiarly soft, sweet speaking voice: not only did Ronsard and Brantôme praise her *'voix très douce et très bonne'* in France but even the critical Knox admitted that the Scots were charmed by her pretty speech when she made her oration at the Tolbooth at the opening of Parliament, 'exclaiming *vox Dianae!* The voice of a goddess . . . was there ever orator spake so properly and so sweetly!' It was also a point on which even the most hostile English observers commented on her first arrival in that country, including Knollys and Cecil's own emissary White.

Her effect on the men around her was certainly that of a beautiful woman: the poet Châtelard fell violently, if slightly hysterically, in love with her; not only on the eve of his execution did he call her 'the most beautiful and the most cruel princess in the world', but on their journey back to Scotland he exclaimed that the galleys needed no lanterns to light their way 'since the eyes of this Queen suffice to light up the whole sea with their lovely fire'.

The Seigneur de Damville was also said to have been so enamoured of the young queen that he followed her to Scotland, leaving his young wife at home, and if we are to believe Brantôme, Mary's little brother-in-law Charles was so much in love with her that he used to gaze at her portrait with longing and desired to marry her himself after the untimely death of Francis. In Scotland Mary's beauty as well as her position was said to have captured not only the obsessional Arran, but the dashing Sir John Gordon and the youthful handsome George Douglas. Her first English jailer, Sir Francis Knollys, although unpromising material for female wiles, was considerably seduced by the charming personality of his captive; and although the later so-called *affair* with Lord Shrewsbury was undoubtedly the creation of his wife's malicious imagination, nevertheless the fact that the accusation could be taken so seriously by the English court shows that all her life Mary was considered a beautiful and desirable woman, whose physical attractions could never be totally left out of account. At the time of her illness at Jedburgh when she was twenty-three, the Venetian ambassador wrote of her being a princess who was 'personally the most beautiful in Europe'. There seems no reason to doubt that this was the general verdict of Europe during her lifetime, and that Mary Queen of Scots was a romantic figure to her own age, no less than to subsequent generations.

Antonia Fraser (b. 1933)
Mary, Queen of Scots

The Marquis of Montrose

James Graham, 1st Marquis of Montrose (1612–50), was one of the four nobles who supported the National Covenant which opposed the episcopal policies of Charles I. In 1641, however, he was won over by the King, fought a series of brilliant encounters on the King's behalf in Scotland, but after a defeat at Invercarron was betrayed by Macleod of Assynt, brought in humiliating circumstances to Edinburgh, and publicly hanged.

He was ane accomplished gentleman of many excellent partes, a bodie not tall, but comely and well composed in all his lineamentes; his complexion neerly whitte, with flaxin haire; of a ståyed, grave and solide looke, and yet his eyes sparkling and full of lyfe; of speeche slowe, but wittie and full of sence; a presence graitfull, courtly and so winneing upon the beholder, as it seemed to claime reverence without seweing [suing] for it; for he was so affable, so courteous, so bening [benign] as seemed verely to scorne ostentation and the keeping of state, and therefore he quicklie made a conquesse of the heartes of all his followeres, so as whan he list he could have lead them in a chaine to have followed him with charefullness in all his interpryses; and I am certanely persuaded that this his gratious, humane and courteous fredome of behaviour, being certanly acceptable before God as well as men, was it that wann him so much renoune and inabled him cheifly, in the love of his followers, to goe through so great interprysses, wheirin his equall had failed, altho they exceeded him farre in power, nor can any other reason be given for it but only this that followeth. . . .

Our nation . . . haveing never been conquered, but alwayes a free-born people, ar only won with courtesies, and the humble, myld, chearfull and affable behaviours of their superioures . . . [Montrose] did not seeme to affect state, nor to claime reverence, nor to keepe a distance with gentlemen that ware not his domestickes; but rather in a noble yet courteous way he seemed to slight those vanisheing smockes of greatness, affecting rather the reall possession of mens heartes than the frothie and outward showe of reverence; and therefor was all reverence thrust upon him, therefore all did loue [love] him; therefor all did honour him and reverence him, yea, haveing once acquired their heartes, they were readie not only to honour him but to quarrell with any that would not honour him and would not spare their fortunes, nor their dearest blood about their heartes, to the end he might be honoured; therefore they sawe that he tooke the right course to obtaine honour.

Patrick Gordon of Ruthven (d. 1660)
Britane's Distemper

Lines on the Execution of Charles I

Great, good, and just, could I but rate
My Grief, and thy too rigid fate,
I'd weep the world in such a strain
As it should deluge once again.
But since thy loud-tongued blood demands supplies
More from Briareus' hands than Argus' eyes,
I'll sing thy obsequies with trumpet sounds,
And write thine epitaph in blood and wounds.

James Graham, Marquis of Montrose
(1612–50)

A Covenanter is Caught and Examined

Of those who fought, clumsily and often ineptly, for the right to worship in the form their conscience dictated rather than according to the Episcopal form laid down by sovereign and state, none was more famous than Hugh Mackail, since

he became the prototype for Scott's Ephraim Macbriar in 'Old Mortality'.
Licensed to preach in 1661, when he was just twenty, Mackail lost no time in
denouncing Archbishop James Sharp (himself to be murdered on Magus Muir,
near St. Andrews, by a band of Covenanters led by Hackston of Rathillet) as a
'Judas in the Church'.

Mackail eluded the first attempt to arrest him, and fled abroad; but he was
back in Scotland in time to join the insurgents in the Pentland rising of November
1666. His health, weakened by wandering, forced him to drop out of the rain-
swept, wind-soaked Covenanting army's march at Colinton; but he was soon
after arrested near Liberton. Scott, quoted by Alexander Smellie, begins this
description of the examination of Mackail by means of the Boot.

'The executioner enclosed the leg and knee within the tight iron case, and
then, placing a wedge of the same metal between the knee and the edge of
the machine took a mallet in his hand, and stood waiting for further orders.
A surgeon placed himself by the other side of the prisoner's chair, bared the
prisoner's arm, and applied the thumb to the pulse in order to regulate the
torture according to the strength of the patient. When these preparations
were made, the President (the Earl of Rothes) glanced his eye round the
Council as if to collect their suffrages, and, judging from their mute signs,
gave a nod to the executioner, whose mallet instantly descended on the wedge,
and, forcing it between the knee and the iron boot, occasioned the most
exquisite pain, as was evident from the flush on the brow of the sufferer.'
It was not once that the awful wedge was driven down. Displeased that he
did not receive the information he wanted, Rothes kept demanding 'one
touch more'. Eleven times the mallet descended, until the poor limb was
shattered and shapeless. . . . Then they carried him, bleeding and spent, to
his dungeon.

Alexander Smellie (1857–1923)
Men of the Covenant

Death of a Covenanter

Brought to trial on 11th December 1666, Makail admitted to being 'one of that
afflicted party and persuasion called Presbyterians'; that he had been seen with
insurgents in Ayr, Ochiltree and Lanark; and that when captured he had a
sword in his hand. On 22nd December he was sentenced to be hanged at the
Mercat Cross of Edinburgh in four days' time. On the eve of his death, to
someone who asked after his injured leg he is said to have replied: 'Oh, the fear of
my neck makes me forget my leg!'

Whether one regards the Covenanters as martyrs in the cause of freedom of
conscience, or merely as hectically deluded insurgents, 'perverse and brave' in
Edwin Muir's words, many of them had what Edmund Gosse called 'the

Renaissance attitude towards death', as Mackail's last words, emulated less eloquently by many later Covenanters, testify.

Now I leave off to speak any more to creatures, and turn my speech to Thee, O Lord. Now I begin my intercourse with God, which shall never be broken off. Farewell, father and mother, friends and relations! Farewell, the world and all delights! Farewell, meat and drink! Farewell, sun, moon and stars! Welcome, God and Father! Welcome, sweet Jesus, the mediator of the new Covenant! Welcome, blessed spirit of Grace, God of all consolation! Welcome, glory! Welcome, eternal life! Welcome, death!

Hugh Mackail

Blows the Wind Today

Blows the wind today, and the sun and the rain are flying,
    Blows the wind on the moors today and now,
Where about the graves of the martyrs the whaups are crying,
    My heart remembers how!

Grey recumbent tombs of the dead in desert places,
    Standing stones on the vacant wine-red moor,
Hills of sheep, and the homes of the silent vanished races,
    And winds, austere and pure:

Be it granted me to behold you again in dying,
    Hills of home! and to hear again the call;
Hear about the graves of the martyrs the peewees crying,
    And hear no more at all.

Robert Louis Stevenson (1850–94)

Andrew Fletcher of Saltoun

Andrew Fletcher of Saltoun (1655–1716) was brought up by the historian Gilbert Burnet, later Bishop of Gloucester. Fletcher first sat in the Scottish Parliament in 1618, but put up so much opposition to the succession of the Catholic Duke of York (later briefly James VII and II) that he had to flee to Holland. Involvement with the Monmouth affair then forced him to flee to Spain, and from there he went to Hungary where he fought against the Turks, before returning to Scotland after the abdication of James VII and II in 1688.

As leader of the nationalist party on his return to Parliament he opposed incorporating union with England, advocating instead federal union. Who, more than two and a half centuries later, aware of the steady Scottish emigration rate, the higher than United Kingdom average unemployment figure, and the now almost total erosion of the Scots power of economic decision-making, can lay his hand on his heart and assert with confidence that Fletcher was not possibly right? After the Union of 1707, he retired from public life in disgust.

This portrait of him is by a member of the Lockhart family of Carnwath. George Lockhart was a Jacobite member of the Scottish Parliament from 1702, and was killed in a duel.

He was blessed with a soul that hated and despised whatever was mean and unbecoming a gentleman, and was so steadfast to what he thought right that no hazard nor advantage, no, not the universal empire nor the gold of America, could tempt him to yield or desert it. And I may affirm that in all his life he never once pursued a measure with the prospect of any by-end to himself, nor further than he judged it for the common benefit and advantage of his country. He was master of the English, Latin, Greek, French and Italian languages, and well versed in history, the civil law and all kinds of learning; and as he was universally accomplished, he employed his talents for the good of mankind.

He was a strict and nice observer of all the points of honour, and his word sacred; as brave as his sword, and had some experience in the art of war, having in his younger days been some time a volunteer in both the land and sea service. In his travels he had studied, and came to understand, the respective interests of the several princes and states of Europe. In his private conversation affable to his friends (but could not endure to converse with those he thought enemies to their country), and free of all manner of vice. He had a penetrating, clear and lively apprehension, but so extremely wedded to his own opinions that there were few (and those too must be his beloved friends and of whom he had a good opinion) he could endure to reason against with . . .

He was no doubt an enemy to all monarchial governments, at least thought they wanted to be much reformed; but I do very well believe his aversion to the English and the Union was so great, in revenge to them he would have sided with the royal family. But as that was subject not fit to be entered upon with him, this is only a conjecture from some innuendoes I have heard him make . . .

To sum up all, he was a learned, gallant, honest, and every other way well-accomplished gentleman; and if ever a man proposes to serve and merit well of his country, let him place his courage, zeal and constancy as a pattern before him, and think himself sufficiently applauded and rewarded by obtaining the character of being like Andrew Fletcher of Saltoun.

George Lockhart (1673–1731)
Lockhart Papers

A Highland Chieftain

Fergus and Waverley met, the latter was struck with the peculiar grace and dignity of the Chieftain's figure. Above the middle size, and finely proportioned, the Highland Dress, which he wore in its simplest mode, set off his person to great advantage. He wore the trews, or close trowsers, made of tartan, chequed scarlet and white; In other particulars, his dress strictly resembled Evan's excepting that he had no weapon save a dirk, very richly mounted with silver. His page, as we have said, carried his claymore; and the fowling-piece, which he held in his hand, seemed only designed for sport. He had shot in the course of his walk some young wild-ducks, as, though *close-time* was then unknown, the broods of grouse were yet too young for the sportsman. His countenance was decidedly Scottish, with all the peculiarities of the Northern physiognomy, but yet had so little of its harshness and exaggeration, that it would have been pronounced in any country extremely handsome. The marshall air of the bonnet, with a single eagle's feather as a distinction, added much to the manly appearance of his head, which was besides ornamented with a far more natural and graceful cluster of close black curls than ever were exposed to sail in Bond Street.

An air of openness and affability increased the favourable impression derived from this handsome and dignified exterior. Yet a skilful physiognomist would have been less satisfied with the countenance on the second than on the first view. The eyebrow and upper lip bespoke something of the habit of peremptory command and decisive superiority. Even his courtesy, though open, frank, and unconstrained, seemed to indicate a sense of personal importance; and, upon any check or accidental excitation, a sudden though, transient lour of the eye, showed a hasty, haughty, and vindictive temper, not less to be dreaded because it seemed much under its owner's command. In short, the countenance of the Chieftain resembled a smiling summer's day, in which, notwithstanding, we are made sensible by certain, though slight signs, that it may thunder and lighten before the close of the evening.

Sir Walter Scott (1771–1832)
Waverley

A Lowlander Sees the Prince

Alexander Carlyle, nicknamed 'Jupiter' because of his stately appearance, was educated at the Universities of Edinburgh, Glasgow, and Leyden. He entered the church, becoming minister of Inveresk, near Edinburgh. A shrewd and cultured man, his manuscript autobiography, published fifty-five years after his death, is one of the liveliest accounts we have of the life of his times. Carlyle saw Prince Charles soon after the Jacobite victory at Prestonpans.

I remained at home all this week, about the end of which my friend William Seller came from Edinburgh to see me, and pressed me much to come to Edinburgh and stay with him at his father's house. . . . As Prince Charles had issued a proclamation allowing all the Volunteers of Edinburgh three weeks, during which they might pay their court to him at the Abbey, and receive a free pardon, I went twice down to the Abbey Court with my friend about twelve o'clock, to wait till the Prince should come out of the Palace and mount his horse to ride to the east side of Arthur Seat to visit his army. I had the good fortune to see him both days, one of which I was close by him when he walked through the guard. He was a good-looking man, of about five feet ten inches; his hair was dark red, and his eyes black. His features were regular, his visage long, much sunburnt and freckled, and his countenance thoughtful and melancholy. He mounted his horse and rode off through St Ann's Yards and the Duke's Walk to his army. There was no crowd after him—about three or four hundred each day. By that time curiosity had been satisfied.

In the house where I lived they were all Jacobites, and I heard much of their conversation. When young Seller and I retired from them at night, he agreed with me that they had less ground for being so sanguine and upish than they imagined. The court at the Abbey was dull and sombre—the Prince was melancholy; he seemed to have no confidence in anybody, not even in the ladies, who were much his friends; far less had he the spirit to venture to the High Church of Edinburgh and take the sacrament, as his great-uncle Charles II had done the Covenant, which would have secured him the low-country commons, as he already had the Highlanders by attachment. He was thought to have loitered too long at Edinburgh, and, without doubt, had he marched immediately to Newcastle, he might have distressed the city of London not a little. But besides that his army wanted clothing and necessaries, the victory at Preston put an end to his authority. He had not a mind fit for command at any time, far less to rule the Highland chiefs in prosperity.

Alexander Carlyle (1722–1805)
Autobiography

Prince Charles and Flora Macdonald

Prince Charles Edward, after the battle of Culloden, was conveyed to what is called the Long Island, where he lay for some time concealed. But intelligence having been obtained where he was, and a number of troops having come in quest of him, it became absolutely necessary for him to quit that country without delay. Miss Flora Macdonald, then a young lady animated by what she thought the sacred principle of loyalty, offered, with the magnanimity of a Heroine, to accompany him in an open boat to Sky, though the coast they were to quit was guarded by ships. He dressed himself in women's clothes, and passed as her supposed maid, by the name of Betty Bourke, an Irish girl. They got off undiscovered, though several shots were fired to bring them to, and landed at Mugstot, the seat of Sir Alexander Macdonald. Sir Alexander was then at Fort Augustus, with the Duke of Cumberland; but his lady was at home. Prince Charles took his post upon a hill near the house. Flora Macdonald waited on Lady Margaret, and acquainted her of the enterprise in which she was engaged. Her ladyship, whose active benevolence was ever seconded by superior talents, shewed a perfect presence of mind, and readiness of invention, and at once settled that Prince Charles should be conducted to old Rasay, who was himself concealed with some select friends. The plan was instantly communicated to Kingsburgh, who was dispatched to the hill to inform the Wanderer, and carry him refreshment. When Kingsburgh approached, he started up, and advanced, holding a large knotted stick, and in appearance ready to knock him down, till he said, 'I am Macdonald of Kingsburgh, come to serve your highness.' The Wanderer answered, 'It is well,' and was satisfied with the plan. Flora Macdonald dined with Lady Margaret, at whose table there sat an officer of the army, stationed here with a party of soldiers, to watch for Prince Charles in case of his flying to the isle of Sky. She afterwards often laughed in good humour with this gentleman, of her having so well deceived him.

After dinner, Flora Macdonald on horseback, and her supposed maid, and Kingsburgh, with a servant carrying some linen, all on foot, proceeded towards that gentleman's house. Upon the road was a small rivulet which they were obliged to cross. The Wanderer, forgetting his assumed sex, that his clothes might not be wet, held them up a great deal too high. Kingsburgh mentioned this to him, observing, it might make a discovery. He said he would be more careful for the future. He was as good as his word; for the next brook they crossed, he did not hold up his clothes at all, but let them float upon the water. He was very awkward in his female dress. His size was so large, and his strides so great, that some women whom they met reported that they had seen a very big woman, who looked like a man in women's clothes, and that perhaps it was (as they expressed themselves) the Prince, after whom so much search was making.

At Kingsburgh he met with a most cordial reception; seemed gay at supper, and after it indulged himself in a cheerful glass with his worthy host. As he had not had his clothes off for a long time, the comfort of a good bed was highly relished by him, and he slept soundly till next day at one o'clock.

The mistress of Corrichatachin told me, that in the forenoon she went into her father's room, who was also in bed, and suggested to him her apprehensions that a party of the military might come up, and that his guest and he had better not remain here too long. Her father said, 'Let the poor man repose himself after his fatigues; and as for me, I care not, though they take off this old grey head ten or eleven years sooner than I should die in the course of nature.' He then wrapped himself in the bed-clothes, and again fell fast asleep.

On the afternoon of that day, the Wanderer, still in the same dress, set out for Portree, with Flora MacDonald and a man servant. His shoes being very bad, Kingsburgh provided him with a new pair, and taking up the old ones, said, 'I will faithfully keep them till you are safely settled at St James's. I will then introduce myself by shaking them at you, to put you in mind of your night's entertainment and protection under my roof.'—He smiled, and said, 'Be as good as your word!'—Kingsburgh kept the shoes as long as he lived. After his death, a zealous Jacobite gentleman gave twenty guineas for them.

James Boswell (1740–95)
Journal of a Tour to the Hebrides

Prince Charles in Old Age

After the defeat at Culloden on 16th April 1746, Prince Charles finally embarked for France on 19th September, aboard the ship 'l'Heureux', at the same place, Loch Nan Uamh, where he had first landed on 25th July 1745. He spent his exile in France, from where he was eventually expelled; formed an association with Clementina Walkinshaw, whom he had met after the Battle of Falkirk; but in Rome, where he settled as Count Albany, made an unhappy marriage with Princess Louise of Stolberg, who became the mistress of the poet Alfieri. Music and the presence of Charlotte, his daughter by Clementina, who joined him in 1784, gave him some comfort in his final distracted years.

To the last, his heart was with Scotland. The following anecdote was related by his brother, Cardinal York, to Bishop Walker, the late Primus of the Episcopal Church of Scotland: Mr Greathead, a personal friend of Mr Fox, succeeded, when at Rome in 1782 or 1783, in obtaining an interview with Charles Edward; and, being alone with him for some time, studiously led the conversation to his enterprise in Scotland, and to the occurrences which succeeded the failure of that attempt. The Prince manifested some reluctance to enter upon these topics, appearing at the same time to undergo so much mental suffering, that his guest regretted the freedom he had used in calling up the remembrance of his misfortunes. At length, however, the Prince seemed to shake off the load which oppressed him; his eye brightened, his face assumed unwonted animation, and he entered upon the narrative of his Scottish campaigns with a distinct but somewhat vehement energy of manner—recounted his marches, his battles, his victories, his retreats, and his defeats—detailed his hairbreadth escapes in the Western Isles, the inviolable and devoted attachment of his Highland friends, and at length proceeded to allude to the terrible penalties with which the chiefs among them had been visited. But here the tide of emotion rose too high to allow him to go on—his voice faltered, his eyes became fixed, and he fell convulsed on the floor. The noise brought into his room his daughter, the Duchess of

Albany, who happened to be in an adjoining apartment, 'Sir,' she exclaimed, 'what is this? You have been speaking to my father about Scotland and the Highlanders! No one dares to mention those subjects in his presence!'

He died on the 30th of January 1788, in the arms of the Master of Nairn. The monument erected to him, his father, and brother, in St Peter's, by desire of George IV, was perhaps the most graceful tribute ever paid by royalty to misfortune—REGIO CINERI PIETAS REGIA.

W. E. Aytoun (1813–1865)
Note in *Lays of the Scottish Cavaliers and Other Poems*

A Jacobite Lord

Simon Fraser, Lord Lovat, the last peer to be condemned in these islands for treason, was executed at the age of eighty on Tower Hill for his part in the Jacobite rising of the '45. Although a cultured courtier when at the Palaces of Versailles, St Germain and Windsor, he was something of a mountain brigand when in his own Highland country, earning the nickname of 'Fox of the '45' because of his habitual dissembling.

He had all the atrocity of the oldest and most barbarous times. He began with the rape of his wife. He sent some of his banditti (for he had a set of retainers, trained, like those of the old Man of the Mountain, to obey him in all acts of violence) who set fire to Culloden House, the seat of President Forbes, who was his relation, and for whom he was at the same time professing the warmest attachment and regard. He had employed some of them to waylay and assassinate another relation, Sir Ludovic Grant, my father-in-law. In short, there was no outrageous villainy of which he was not capable; yet he joined to the savageness of the worst feudal times the smoothness as well as the cunning of the most civilised hypocrisy. He was indeed proverbially known as a flatterer. My uncle, Mr Rose of Kilravock, happened to be in Edinburgh when my Lord was passing through to the north, and called on his cousin, for such he was, to enquire after his health. Lord Lovat pressed him to be seated, but my uncle excused himself on the ground of his very short stay in town and having a great deal to do. On Lord Lovat's insisting, however, he took a seat, and at that instant a gentleman, whom the moment before Lovat had embraced as his friend and given a very favourable character, left the room. He had no sooner done so, than Lovat abused him in the most unmeasured terms and said he was one of the greatest scoundrels in the world. Another and another of the company went away with not much better characters from his Lordship. At last, after a pretty long stay, my uncle took his leave. 'My dear Hugh', said Lovat, 'you said you were in a hurry, but if my watch does not deceive me, you have stayed half an hour.'— 'That is true,' rejoined my uncle, 'but I took care you should have no audience to give my character to.'—'Ah!' said Lovat with perfect sang-froid. 'You are a wag, Hugh; you are a wag!'

When Lovat was in the Tower, a few days before his execution, Hogarth came to visit him with the intention of drawing a sketch of him, which he made and it was afterwards engraved and is a striking likeness. When the turnkey announced him, Lord Lovat was in the act of shaving. When Hogarth entered the room, Lovat hastened to embrace him, expressed himself delighted with his visit, and, kissing him from cheek to cheek, covered his face all over with the suds from his own. So little was his love of horseplay damped by his approaching death. All his behaviour indeed previously to and at his execution evinced the perfect possession of his mind and even of gaiety. His conscience slept; or did he find some salve for its upbraidings in the idea of the wildness of the time and his character of Chieftain, indignant of rivalry and opposition? After all his atrocities, he died like a hero.

Henry Mackenzie (1745–1831)
Anecdotes and Egotisms

James Boswell on Himself

James Boswell, the son of Lord Auchinleck, was admitted to the Scottish Bar in 1766, after spending a dissipated youth faithfully chronicled in a series of diaries and journals discovered in the twentieth century at Malahide Castle in Ireland, the seat of his great-grandson. His law career was unsuccessful, yet—a faithful recorder of the conversations of others—he not only persuaded Dr Samuel Johnson to visit the Hebrides in 1773, but in 1785 produced one of the most fascinating travel-books ever written 'A JOURNAL OF A TOUR IN THE HEBRIDES', and in 1791 followed it up with his 'LIFE OF SAMUEL JOHNSON', one of the two or three finest biographies in the English language.

Boswell is pleasant and gay,
For frolic by nature design'd;
He heedlessly rattles away
When the company is to his mind.
'This maxim', he says, 'you may see,
We never have corn without chaff',
So not a bent sixpence cares he,
Whether with him or at him you laugh.

James Boswell (1740–95)

Boswell and Johnson at Dunvegan

I was elated by the thought of having been able to entice such a man to this remote part of the world. A ludicrous, yet just image presented itself to my mind, which I expressed to the company. I compared myself to a dog who has got hold of a large piece of meat and runs away with it to a corner, where he may devour it in peace, without any fear of others taking it from him. 'In London, Reynolds, Beauclerk, and all of them, are contending who shall enjoy Dr Johnson's conversation. We are feasting upon it, undisturbed, at Dunvegan. . . .

After the ladies were gone from the table, we talked of the Highlanders not having sheets; and this led us to consider the advantage of wearing linen. —*Johnson*. 'All animal substances are less cleanly than vegetables. Wool, of which flannel is made, is an animal substance; flannel therefore is not so cleanly as linen. I remember I used to think tar dirty; but when I knew it only to be a preparation of the juice of the pine, I thought so no longer. It is not disagreeable to have the gum that oozes from a plum-tree upon your fingers, because it is regretable; but if you have any candle-grease, any tallow upon your fingers, you are uneasy till you rub it off—I have often thought, that, if I kept a seraglio, the ladies should all wear linen gowns—or cotton—I mean stuffs made of vegetable substances. I would have no silk; you cannot tell when it is clean: It will be very nasty before it is perceived to be so. Linen detects its own dirtiness.'

To hear the grave Dr Samuel Johnson, 'that majestick teacher of moral and religious wisdom,' while sitting solemn in an arm-chair in the Isle of Sky, talk, *ex cathedra*, of his keeping a seraglio, and acknowledge that the supposition had *often* been in his thoughts, struck me so forcibly with ludicrous contrast, that I could not but laugh immoderately. He was too proud to submit, even for a moment, to be the object of ridicule, and instantly retaliated with such keen sarcastick wit, and such a variety of degrading images, of every one of which I was the object, that, though I can bear such attacks as well as most men, I yet found myself so much the sport of all the company, that I would gladly expunge from my mind every trace of this severe retort.

James Boswell
A Journal of a Tour to the Hebrides

Boswell Visits The Dying Hume

Whether one regards James Boswell's account of his interview with the dying philosopher David Hume as one of the greatest of all journalistic scoops, or as a monumental piece of crass tastelessness, the characters of two of the most interesting of eighteenth-century Scots are vividly reflected through it.

On Sunday forenoon the 7 of July 1776, being too late for Church, I went to see Mr David Hume, who was returned from London and Bath, just a-dying. I found him alone, in a reclining posture in his drawing-room. He was lean, ghastly, and quite of an earthy appearance. He was drest in a suit of grey cloth with white metal buttons, and a kind of scratch wig. He was quite different from the plump figure which he used to present. He had before him Dr Campbell's *Philosophy of Rhetorick*. He seemed to be placid and even cheerful. He said he was just approaching to his end. I think these were his words. I know not how I contrived to get the subject of Immortality intro-duced. He said he never had entertained any belief in Religion since he began to read Locke and Clarke. I asked him if he was not religious when he was young. He said he was, and he used to read the *Whole Duty of Man*; that he made an abstract from the Catalogue of vices at the end of it, and examined himself by this, leaving out Murder and Theft and such vices as he had no chance of committing, having no inclination to commit them. This, he said, was a strange Work; for instance, to try if, notwithstanding his ex-celling his school-fellows, he had no pride of vanity. He smiled in ridicule of this as absurd and contrary to fixed principles and necessary consequences, not adverting that Religious discipline does not mean to extinguish, but to moderate, the passions; and certainly an excess of pride or vanity is dangerous and generally hurtful. He then said flatly that the Morality of every Religion was bad, and, I really thought, was not jocular when he said 'that when he heard a man was religious, he concluded he was a rascal, though he had known some instance of very good men being religious.' This was just an extravagant reverse of the common remark as to Infidels. I had a strong curiosity to be satisfied if he persisted in disbelieving a future state even when he had death before his eyes. I was persuaded from what he now said, and from his manner of saying it, that he did persist. I asked him if it was not possible that there might be a future state. He answered It was possible that a piece of coal put upon the fire would not burn; and he added that it was a most unreasonable fancy that he should exist for ever. That immortality, if it were at all, must be general; that a great proportion of the human race has hardly any intellectual qualities; that a great proportion dies in infancy before being possessed of reason; yet all these must be immortal; that a Porter who gets drunk by ten o'clock with gin must be immortal; that the trash of every age must be preserved, and that new Universes must be created to contain such infinite numbers. This appeared to me an unphilosophical objection, and I said, 'Mr Hume, you know Spirit does not take up space'. . . .

I asked him if the thought of Annihilation never gave him any uneasiness. He said not the least; no more than the thought that he had not been, as Lucretius observes. 'Well,' said I, 'Mr Hume, I hope to triumph over you when I meet you in a future state; and remember you are not to pretend you was joking with all this Infidelity.' 'No, No,' said he, 'But I shall have been so long there before you come that it will be nothing new.' In this style of good-humour and levity did I conduct the conversation. Perhaps it was wrong on so aweful a subject. But as nobody was present, I thought it could have no bad effect. I however felt a degree of horror, mixed with a sort of wild, strange, hurrying recollection of my excellent Mother's pious instructions, of Dr Johnson's noble lessons, and of my religious sentiments and affections during the course of my life. I was like a man in sudden danger eagerly seeking his defensive arms; and I could not but be assailed by momentary doubts while I had actually before me a man of such strong abilities and extensive inquiry dying in the persuasion of being annihilated. But I maintained my Faith. I told him that I believed the Christian Religion as I believed History. Said he: 'You do not believe it as you believe the Revolution.' 'Yes,' said I, 'but the difference is that I am not so much interested in the truth of the Revolution; otherwise I should have anxious doubts concerning it. A man who is in love has doubts of the affection of his Mistress, without cause.' . . .

He had once said to me on a forenoon, while the sun was shining bright, that he did not wish to be immortal. This was a most wonderful thought. The reason he gave was that he was very well in this state of being, and that the chances were very much against his being so well in another state; and he would rather not be more than be worse. I answered that it was reasonable to hope he would be better; that there would be a progressive improvement. I tried him at this Interview with that topick, saying that a future state was surely a pleasing idea. He said No, for that it was allways seen through a gloomy medium; there was always a Phlegethon or a Hell. 'But,' said I, 'would it not be agreeable to have hopes of seeing our friends again?' and I mentioned three Men lately deceased, for whom I knew he had a high value: Ambassadour Keith, Lord Alemoor, and Baron Muir. He owned it would be agreeable, but added that none of them entertained such a notion. I believe he said, such a foolish, or such an absurd, notion; for he was indecently and impolitely positive in incredulity. 'Yes,' said I, 'Lord Alemoor was a believer.' David acknowledged that *he* had *some* belief. I somehow or other brought Dr Johnson's name into our conversation. I had often heard him speak of that great Man in a very illiberal manner. He said upon this occasion, 'Johnson should be pleased with my *History*.' Nettled by Hume's frequent attacks upon my revered friend in former conversations, I told him now that Dr Johnson did not allow him much credit; for he said, 'Sir, the fellow is a Tory by chance.' I am sorry that I mentioned this at such a time. I was off my guard; for the truth is that Mr Hume's pleasantry was such that there was no solemnity in the scene; and Death for the time did not seem dismal. It surprised me to find him talking of different matters with a tranquillity of mind and a clearness of head which few men possess at any time.

Two particulars I remember: Smith's *Wealth of Nations*, which he recommended much, and Monboddo's *Origin of Language*, which he treated contemptuously. I said, 'If I were you, I should regret Annihilation. Had I written such an admirable History, I should be sorry to leave it.' He said, 'I shall leave that History, of which you are pleased to speak so favourably, as perfect as I can.' He said, too, that all the great abilities with which Men had ever been endowed were Relative to this World. He said he became a great friend to the Stuart Family as he advanced in studying for his History; and he hoped he had vindicated the two first of them so effectively that they would never again be attacked. Mr Lauder, his Surgeon, came in for a little, and Mr Mure, the Baron's son, for another small interval. He was, as far as I could judge, quite easy with both. He said he had no pain, but was wasting away. I left him with impressions which disturbed me for some time.

James Boswell
Journal

Alexander Carlyle Meets Tobias Smollett

It was also on one of those years (1753–6) that Smollett visited Scotland for the first time, after having left Glasgow immediately after his education was finished, and his engaging as a surgeon's mate on board a man-of-war, which gave him an opportunity of witnessing the siege of Carthagena, which he has so minutely described in his *Roderick Random*. He came out to Musselburgh and passed a day and a night with me, and went to church and heard me preach. I introduced him to Cardonnel the Commissioner, with whom he supped, and they were much pleased with each other. Smollett has reversed this in his *Humphrey Clinker*, where he makes the Commissioner his old acquaintance. He went next to Glasgow and that neighbourhood to visit his friends, and returned again to Edinburgh in October, when I had frequent meetings with him—one in particular, in a tavern, where there supped with him Commissioner Cardonnel, Mr Hepburn of Keith, John Home, and one or two more.

Smollett was a man of very agreeable conversation and of much genuine humour; and, though not a profound scholar, possessed a philosophical mind, and was capable of making the soundest observations on human life, and of discerning the excellence or seeing the ridicule of every character he met with. Fielding only excelled him in giving a dramatic story to his novels, but, in my opinion, was inferior to him in the true comic vein. He was one of the many very pleasant men with whom it was my good fortune to be intimately acquainted.

Alexander Carlyle (1722–1805)
Autobiography

Epitaph on John Murray

Ah, John, what changes since I saw thee last;
Thy fishing and thy shooting days are past,
Bagpipes and hautboys thous canst sound no more;
Thy nods, grimaces, winks and pranks arc o'cr.
Thy harmless, queerish, incoherent talk,
Thy wild vivacity, and trudging walk
Will soon be quite forgot. Thy joys on earth—
A snuff, a glass, riddles and noisy mirth—
Are vanished all. Yet blest, I hope, thou art,
For, in thy station, weel thou play'dst thy part.

*From his gravestone in the kirkyard of Kells,
Galloway*

James Watt as a Boy

Mr Watt Senior of Greenock was an upright, benevolent, intelligent man; his wife, Miss Muirhead, a fine-looking woman, with pleasing, graceful manners, a cultivated mind, an excellent understanding, and an equal, cheerful temper.

Their son James was a sickly, delicate child and received from his mother his first lessons in reading; his father taught him writing and arithmetic. When he was six years of age, a gentleman calling upon Mr Watt observed the child bending over a hearth stone with a piece of coloured chalk in his hand. 'Mrs Watt', said he, 'you ought to send that boy to a public school, and not allow him to trifle away his time at home'. 'Look how my child is occupied before you condemn him', replied the father; the gentleman then observed that the child had drawn mathematical lines and circles on the hearth, and was then marking in letters and figures, the result of some calculation he was carrying on; he put various questions to the boy, and was astonished and gratified with the mixture of intelligence, quickness and simplicity displayed in his answers. 'Forgive me, Mr Watt, this boy's education has not been neglected; he is no common child'.

His parents were indulgent, yet judicious in their kindness, and their child was docile, grateful, and affectionate. Owing to variable health, his attendance on public classes at Greenock was irregular. His parents were proud of his talents, and encouraged him to prosecute his studies at home. His father gave him a set of small carpenter's tools, and one of James' favourite amusements was to take his little toys to pieces, reconstruct them, and invent new playthings.

Sitting one evening with his aunt Mrs Muirhead at the tea table, she said, 'James Watt, I never saw such an idle boy; take a book or employ yourself usefully; for the last hour you have not spoken one word but taken off the lid of that kettle and put it on again, holding now a cup and now a silver spoon over the steam, watching how it rises from the spout, and catching and collecting the drops of hot water it falls into. Are you not ashamed of spending your time in this way?' It appears that when thus blamed for idleness, his active mind was employed in investigating the properties of steam; he was then fifteen, and once in conversation he informed me that before he was that age he had read twice with great attention S. Gravesande's *Elements of Natural Philosophy*, adding that it was the first book upon that subject put into his hands, and that he still thought it one of the best. When health permitted, his young, ardent mind was constantly occupied, not with one but with many pursuits. Every new acquisition in science, languages, or literature, seemed made without an effort. While under his father's roof, he went on with various chemical experiments, repeating them again and again until satisfied of their accuracy from his own observations. He had made for himself a small Electrical Machine, and sometimes startled his young friends by giving them sudden shocks from it. His early years were passed in Greenock; from the age of fourteen he was often in Glasgow with his uncle Mr Muirhead; and read and studied much on Chemistry and Anatomy. He took a deep interest in this latter subject, and in all connected with the medical art, and was once observed carrying off a child's head, that had died of some uncommon complaint, for the purpose of dissection. Under Mr Muirhead's roof he met with good society, and formed friendships with several intelligent and superior young men; they had frequent meetings to give or receive information. These gentlemen acknowledged and appreciated Mr Watt's superior abilities; his manners were so kind and unassuming, that no jealous feelings were ever excited.

His warm affections and stern integrity commanded their esteem and regard; yet they sometimes feared while they loved him, as he had no patience for folly, and could be sarcastic. . . . He enjoyed society in a small select circle; his talents for conversation were always remarkable; he seldom rose early, but accomplished more in a few hours' study than ordinary minds do in many days; he never was in a hurry, and always had leisure to give to his friends, to poetry, romance, and the publications of the day; he read indiscriminately almost every new book he could procure. On a friend's entreating him to be more select in his choice, he replied 'I have never yet read a book, or conversed with a companion, without gaining information, instruction or amusement'. He was alternately active, or apparently very indolent and was subject to occasional fits of abstraction. He had a quick perception of the beauties of nature, and delighted in exploring the wild glens of his native land, and tracing to their source the mountain torrents. Though modest and unpretending, yet, like other great men, he was conscious of his own high talents, and superior attainments, and proudly looked forward to their raising him to future fame and honour.

> Marion Campbell
> *Watt's cousin, dictated to her daughter, Jane Campbell,*
> *in 1798. From the original manuscript.*

Watt's Achievement

When James Watt (1736–1819) died Francis Jeffrey wrote an obituary of him in the 'Edinburgh Review'.

We have said that Mr Watt was the great *improver* of the steam-engine; but, in truth, as to all that is admirable in its structure, or vast in its utility, he should rather be described as its *inventor*. It was by his inventions that its action was so regulated, as to make it capable of being applied to the finest and most delicate manufactures, and its power so increased, as to set weight and solidarity at defiance. By his admirable contrivance, it has become a thing stupendous alike for its force and its flexibility,—for the prodigious power which it can exert, and the ease, and precision, and ductility, with which it can be varied, distributed, and applied. The trunk of an elephant, that can pick up a pin or rend an oak, is as nothing to it. It can engrave a seal, and crush masses of obdurate metal before it,—draw out, without breaking, a thread as fine as gossamer, and lift a ship of war like a bauble in the air. It can embroider muslin and forge anchors,—cut steel into ribbons, and impel loaded vessels against the fury of the winds and waves.

It would be difficult to estimate the value of the benefits which these inventions have conferred upon this country. There is no branch of industry that has not been indebted to them; and, in all the most material, they have not only widened most magnificently the field of its exertions, but multiplied a thousand-fold the amount of its productions. It is our improved steam-engine that has fought the battles of Europe, and exalted and sustained, through the late tremendous contest, the political greatness of our land. It is the same great power which now enables us to 'pay the interest of our debt, and to maintain the arduous struggle in which we are still engaged, [1819], with the skill and capital of countries less oppressed with taxation. But these are poor and narrow views of its importance. It has increased indefinitely the mass of human comforts and enjoyments, and rendered cheap and accessible, all over the world, the materials of wealth and prosperity. It has armed the feeble hand of man, in short, with a power to which no limits can be assigned; completed the dominion of mind over the most refractory qualities of matter; and laid a sure foundation for all those future miracles of mechanic power which are to aid and reward the labours of after generations. It is to the genius of one man, too, that all this is mainly owing; and certainly no man ever bestowed such a gift on his kind. The blessing is not only universal, but unbounded; and the fabled inventors of the plough and the loom, who were deified by the erring gratitude of their rude contemporaries, conferred less important benefits on mankind than the inventor of our present steam-engine. . . .

Independently of his great attainments in mechanics, Mr Watt was an extraordinary, and in many respects a wonderful man. Perhaps no individual in his age possessed so much and such varied and exact information,—had read so much, or remembered what he had read so accurately and well. He had infinite quickness of apprehension, a prodigious memory, and a certain rectifying and methodizing power of understanding, which extracted something precious out of all that was presented to it. His stores of miscellaneous knowledge were immense,—and yet less astonishing than the command he had at all times over them. It seemed as if every subject that was casually started in conversation with him, had been that which he had been last occupied in studying and exhausting;—such was the copiousness, the precision, and the admirable clearness of the information which he poured out upon it without effort or hesitation. Nor was this promptitude and compass of knowledge confined in any degree to the studies connected with his ordinary pursuits. That he should have been minutely and extensively skilled in chemistry and the arts, and in most of the branches of physical science, might perhaps have been conjectured; but it could not have been inferred from his usual occupations, and probably is not generally known, that he was curiously learned in many branches of antiquity, metaphysics, medicine, and etymology, and perfectly at home in all the details of architecture, music, and law. He was well acquainted, too, with most of the modern languages,—and familiar with their most recent literature. Nor was it at all extraordinary to hear the great mechanician and engineer detailing and expounding, for hours together, the metaphysical theories of the German logicians, or criticising the measures or the matter of German poetry. . . . His talk, too, though overflowing with information, had no resemblance to lecturing or solemn discoursing, but, on the contrary, was full of colloquial spirit and pleasantry. He had a certain quiet and grave humour, which ran through most of his conversation, and a vein of temperate jocularity, which gave infinite zest and effect to the condensed and inexhaustible information which formed its main staple and characteristic. There was a little air of affected testiness, and a tone of pretended rebuke and contradiction, with which he used to address his younger friends, that was always felt by them as an endearing mark of his kindness and familiarity,—and prized accordingly, far beyond all the solemn compliments that ever proceeded from the lips of authority. His voice was deep and powerful—though he commonly spoke in a low and somewhat monotonous tone, which harmonized admirably with the weight and brevity of his observations, and set off to the greatest advantage the pleasant anecdotes, which he delivered with the same grave brow, and the same calm smile playing soberly on his lips.

In his temper and dispositions he was not only kind and affectionate, but generous, and considerate of the feelings of all around him; and gave the most liberal assistance and encouragement to all young persons who showed any indications of talent, or applied to him for patronage or advice. His health, which was delicate from his youth upwards, seemed to become firmer as he advanced in years; and he preserved, up almost to the last moment of his existence, not only the full command of his extraordinary intellect, but all the alacrity of spirit, and the social gaiety, which had illumined his happiest days. His friends in this part of the country never saw him more full of intellectual vigour and colloquial animation,—never more delightful or more instructive,—than in his last visit to Scotland in autumn 1817. Indeed, it was after that time that he applied himself, with all the ardour of early life, to the invention of a machine for mechanically copying all sorts of sculpture and statuary;—and distributed among his friends some of its earliest performances, as the productions of a young artist just entering on his eighty-third year.

Francis Jeffrey (1773–1830)
Edinburgh Review

Robert Burns As A Child

Robert Burns was born in the 'Auld Clay Biggin' at Alloway, near Ayr. He was the eldest of the seven children of William Burness (he spelled his name in the old form), a gardener and small-holder—described by Captain Charles Gray as 'a thin, sinewy figure, about five feet eight or nine inches in height, somewhat bent with toil, his haffet-locks bare, with a dark, swarthy complexion'—and Agnes Broun—'a well-made, sonsy figure, with a beautiful red and white complexion . . . red hair, dark eyes and eyebrows with a fine square forehead'. Early toil beyond the strength of his youthful frame brought on that heart disease which we now know to have been the cause of his premature death.

I was born a very poor man's son.—For the first six or seven years of my life, my father was gardiner to a worthy gentleman of small estate in the neighbourhood of Ayr.—Had my father continued in that situation, I must have marched off to be one of the little underlings about a farm-house; but it was his dearest wish and prayer to have it in his power to keep his children under his own eye till they could discern between good and evil; so with the assistance of his generous Master my father ventured on a small farm in his estate.—At these years I was by no means a favorite with any body.—I was a good deal noted for a retentive memory, a stubborn, sturdy something in my disposition, and an enthusiastic, idiot piety.—I say idiot piety, because I was then but a child.—Though I cost the schoolmaster some thrashings, I made an excellent English scholar; and against the years of ten or eleven, I was absolutely a Critic in substantives, verbs and particles.—In my infant and boyish days too, I owed much to an old Maid of my Mother's, remarkable for her ignorance, credulity and superstition.—She had, I suppose, the largest collection in the county of tales and songs concerning devils, ghosts, fairies, brownies, witches, warlocks, spunkies, kelpies, elf-candles, deadlights, wraiths, apparitions, cantraips, giants, inchanted towers, dragons and other trumpery.—This cultivated the latent seeds of Poesy; but had so strong an effect on my imagination, that to this hour, in my nocturnal rambles, I sometimes kept a sharp look-out in suspicious places; and though nobody can be more sceptical in these matters than I, yet it often takes an effort of Philosophy to shake off these idle terrors. . . . The two first books I ever read in private, and which gave me more pleasure than any two books I ever read again, were, the life of Hannibal and the history of Sir William Wallace. —Hannibal gave my young ideas such a turn that I used to strut in raptures up and down after the recruiting drum and bagpipe, and wish myself tall enough to be a soldier; while the story of Wallace poured a Scottish prejudice in my veins which will boil along there till the flood-gates of life shut in eternal rest.

Robert Burns (1759–96)
Letter to John Moore, dated 2nd August 1787

The Making of The Poet

But, first an' foremost I should tell,
Amaist as soon as I could spell,
I to the crambo-jingle fell:
　　Tho' rude an' rough—
Yet crooning to a body's sel'
　　Does well enough.

I am nae poet, in a sense,
But just a rhymer like by chance,
An' hae to learning nae pretence;
　　Yet, what the matter?
Whene'er my muse does on me glance,
　　I jingle at her.

Your critic-folk may cock their nose,
And say, 'How can you e'er propose,
you wha ken hardly verse frae prose
　　To make a sang?'
But, by your leaves, my learned foes,
　　Ye're maybe wrang.

What's a' your jargon o' your schools—
Your Latin names for horns an' stools?
If honest nature made you fools,
    What sairs your grammars?
Ye'd better taen up spades and shools,
    Or knappin-hammers.

A set o' dull, conceited hashes
Confuse their brains in college-classes!
They gang in stirks, and come out asses,
    Plain truth to speak;
And syne they think to climb Parnassus
    By dint o' Greek.

Gie me ae spark o' nature's fire,
That's a the learning I desire;
Then tho' I drudge thro' dub an' mire
    At plough or cart,
My muse, tho' hamely in attire,
    May touch the heart.

                                        Robert Burns
                                From Epistle to J. Lapraik

Burns as a Youth

In my seventeenth year, to give my manners a brush, I went to a country dancing school.—My father had an unaccountable antipathy against these meetings; and my going was, what to this hour I repent, in absolute defiance of his commands.—My father, as I said before, was the sport of strong passions: from that instance of rebellion he took a kind of dislike to me, which, I believe was one cause of that dissipation which marked my future years.—I only say Dissipation, comparative with the strictness and sobriety of Presbyterean country life; for though the will-o'-wisp meteors of thoughtless Whim were almost the sole lights of my path, yet early engrained Piety and Virtue never failed to point me out the line of Innocence.—The great misfortune of my life was, never to have AN AIM.—I had felt early some stirrings of Ambition, but they were the blind gropins of Homer's Cyclops round the walls of his cave: I saw my father's situation entailed on me perpetual labor.—The only two doors by which I could enter the fields of fortune were, the most niggardly economy, or the little chicaning art of bargainmaking: the first is so contracted an aperture, I never could squeeze myself into it, the last, I always hated the contamination of the threshold.—Thus, abandoned of aim or view in life; with a strong appetite for sociability, as well

from native hilarity as from a pride of observation and remark; a constitutional
hypochondriac taint which made me fly solitude; add to all these incentives
to social life, my reputation for bookish knowledge, a certain wild, logical
talent, and a strength of thought something like the rudiments of good sense,
made me generally a welcome guest; so 'tis no great wonder that always
'where two or three were met together, there was I in the midst of them.'—
But far beyond all the other impulses of my heart was, *un penchant à l'adorable
moitiée du genre humain.*—My heart was compleatly tinder, and was eternally
lighted up by some Goddess or other: and like every warfare in this world, I
was sometimes crowned with success, and sometimes mortified with defeat.
—At the plough, scythe or reap-hook I feared no competitor, and set
Want at defiance; and as I never cared farther for my labors than while I
was in actual exercise, I spent the evening in the way after my own heart.—A
country lad rarely carries on an amour without an assisting confident.—I
possessed a curiosity, zeal and intrepid dexterity in these matters which
recommended me a proper Second in duels of that kind; and I dare say, I
felt as much pleasure at being in the secret of half the amours in the parish, as
ever did Premier at knowing the intrigues of half the courts of Europe.—

The very goosefeather in my hand seems instinctively to know the well-
worn path or my imagination, the favorite theme of my song; and is with
difficulty restrained from giving you a couple of paragraphs on the amours
of my Compeers, the humble Inmates of the farm-house and cottage; but
the grave sons of Science, Ambition or Avarice baptize these things by the
name of Follies.—To the sons and daughters of labor and poverty they are
matters of the most serious nature: to them, the ardent hope, the stolen
interview, the tender farewell, are the greatest and most delicious part of their
enjoyments.—

Another circumstance in my life which made very considerable alterations
in my mind and manners was, I spent my seventeenth summer on a smuggling
(coast) a good distance from home at a noted school, to learn Mensuration,
Surveying, Dialling, &c. in which I made a pretty good progress.—But I
made greater progress in the knowledge of mankind.—The contraband
trade was at that time very successful; scenes of swaggering riot and roaring
dissipation were as yet new to me; and I was no enemy to social life.—Here,
though I learned to look unconcernedly on a large tavern-bill, and mix
without fear in a drunken squabble, yet I went on with a high hand in my
Geometry; till the sun entered Virgo, a month which is always a carnival in
my bosom, a charming Fillette who lived next door to the school overset my
Trigonometry, and set me off in a tangeant from the sphere of my studies.—
I struggled on with my Sines and Co-sines for a few days more; but stepping
out to the garden one charming noon, to take the sun's altitude, I met with
my Angel,

—'Like Proserpine gathering flowers,
Herself a fairer flower'—

It was vain to think of doing any more good at school.—The remaining
week I staid, I did nothing but craze the faculties of my soul about her, or

steal out to meet with her; and the two last nights of my stay in the country, had sleep been a mortal sin, I was innocent. . . .

Robert Burns
Letter to John Moore dated 2nd August 1787

The Rigs O' Barley

It was upon a Lammas night,
  When corn rigs are bonie,
Beneath the moon's unclouded light,
  I held awa' to Annie;
The time flew by, wi' tentless heed;
  Till, 'tween the late and early,
Wi' sma' persuasion she agreed
    To see me thro' the barley.
    Corn rigs, an' barley rigs,
      An' corn rigs are bonie:
    I'll ne'er forget that happy night,
      Amang the rigs wi' Annie.

The sky was blue, the wind was still,
  The moon was shining clearly;
I set her down, wi' right goodwill,
  Amang the rigs o' barley:
I ken't her heart was a' my ain;
  I lov'd her most sincerely;
I kiss'd her owre and owre again,
  Amang the rigs o' barley.
    Corn rigs, an' barley rigs, etc.

I lock'd her in my fond embrace;
  Her heart was beating rarely:
My blessings on that happy place,
  Amang the rigs o' barley.
But by the moon and stars so bright,
  That shone that hour so clearly!
She ay shall bless that happy night
  Amang the rigs o' barley.
    Corn rigs, an' barley rigs, etc.

I hae been blythe wi' comrades dear;
  I hae been merry drinking;
I hae been joyfu' gath'rin' gear;

I hae been happy thinking:
But a' the pleasures e'er I saw,
  Tho' three times doubl'd fairly—
That happy night was worth them a',
  Among the rigs o' barley.
    Corn rigs, an' barley rigs, etc.

Robert Burns

Burns and Jean Armour

Burns's relationship with women tended to be either intellectually flirtatious, as with Margaret Chalmers and Maria Riddell, or purely sensual, as with Elizabeth Paton, Jenny Clow and Anna Park, all of whom bore his illegitimate children.

After his elderly 'mother confessor', Mrs Dunlop, the two principal women in Burns's adult life were Mrs Agnes Maclehose ('Clarinda') and Jean Armour (1767–1834), whom he first met in 1784 and who twice became pregnant by him before he suddenly and secretly married her in 1787. Jean was banished by her father in disgrace to Paisley on account of her second 'misdemeanour'. Burns, already involved with Mary Campbell ('Highland Mary') who died mysteriously in 1786, possibly bearing the poet's child, worked himself into an emotional frenzy to his friend David Brice over her alleged 'desertion' of him; and announced that he was sending off the manuscript of the 'Kilmarnock' poems to the press.

Poor, ill-advised, ungrateful Armour came home on friday last.—You have heard all the particulars of that affair; and a black affair it is.—What she thinks of her conduct now, I don't know; one thing I know, she has made me compleatly miserable.—Never man lov'd, or rather ador'd, a woman more than I did her: and, to confess a truth between you, and me, I do still love her to distraction after all, tho' I won't tell her so, tho' I see her, which I don't want to do.—My poor, dear, unfortunate Jean! how happy have I been in her arms!—It is not the losing her that makes me so unhappy; but for her sake, I feel most severely.—I foresee she is in the road to, I am afraid, eternal ruin; and those who made so much noise, and showed so much grief, at the thought of her being my wife, may, some day, see her connected in such a manner as may give them more real cause of vexation.—I am sure I do not wish it: may Almighty God forgive her ingratitude and perjury to me, as I from my very soul forgive her! and may His grace be with her and bless her in all her future life!—I can have no nearer idea of the place of eternal punishment than what I have felt in my own breast on her account.—I have tryed often to forget her: I have run into all kinds of dissipation and riot, Mason-meetings, drinking matches, and other mischief, to drive her out of my head, but all in vain: and now for a grand cure: the Ship is on her

way home that is to take me out to Jamaica; and then, farewel dear old
Scotland, and farewel dear, ungrateful Jean, for never, never will I see you
more!

You will have heard that I am going to commence Poet in print; and
tomorrow, my works go to the press.—I expect it will be a Volume of about
two hundred pages.—It is just the last foolish action I intend to do; and then
turn a wise man as fast as possible.

Robert Burns
Letter to David Brice, dated 22nd June 1786

Of A' the Airts the Wind Can Blaw

Of a' the airts the wind can blaw,
   I dearly like the West,
For there the bonie lassie lives,
   The lassie I lo'e best:
There's wild-woods grow, and rivers row,
   And money a hill between:
But day and night my fancy's flight
   Is ever wi' my Jean.

I see her in the dewy flowers,
   I see her sweet and fair:
I hear her in the tunefu' birds,
   I hear her charm the air:
There's not a bonie flower that springs,
   By fountain, shaw, or green;
There's not a bonie bird that sings
   But minds me o' my Jean.

Robert Burns

Burns In Edinburgh

*Josiah Walker was a private tutor in Edinburgh when Burns was taken up by
the Edinburgh literati and the Capital's aristocracy, becoming the sensation of the
1786/7 season. Walker met Burns on several occasions, and wrote an interesting
account of the poet which was used as a prefix to an edition of Burns's poems
published in 1811.*

His person, though strong and well knit, and much superior to what might
be expected in a ploughman, was still rather coarse in its outline. His stature,
from want of setting up, appeared to be only of the middle size, but was rather

above it. His motions were firm and decided, and though without any pretensions to grace, were at the same time so free from clownish constraint, as to shew that he had not always been confined to the society of his profession. His countenance was not of that elegant cast which is most frequent among the upper ranks, but it was manly and intelligent, and marked by a thoughtful gravity which shaded at times into sternness. In his large dark eye the most striking index of his genius resided. It was full of mind, and would have been singularly expressive, under the management of one who could employ it with more art, for the purpose of expression.

He was plainly, but properly dressed, in a style midway between the holiday costume of a farmer and that of the company with which he now associated. His black hair, without powder, at a time when it was very generally worn, was tied behind, and spread upon his forehead. Upon the whole, from his person, physiognomy, and dress, had I met him near a seaport, and been required to guess his condition, I should have probably conjectured him to be the master of a merchant vessel of the most respectable class.

In no part of his manner was there the slightest degree of affectation; nor could a stranger have suspected, from anything in his behaviour or conversation, that he had been for some months the favourite of all the fashionable circles of a metropolis.

In conversation he was powerful. His conceptions and expression were of corresponding vigour, and on all subjects were as remote as possible from commonplaces. Though somewhat authoritative, it was in a way which gave little offence, and was readily imputed to his inexperience in those modes of smoothing dissent and softening assertion which are important characteristics of polished manners. After breakfast I requested him to communicate some of his unpublished pieces . . . I paid particular attention to his recitation, which was plain, slow, articulate, and forcible, but without any eloquence or art. He did not always lay the emphasis with propriety, nor did he humour the sentiment by the variations of his voice. He was standing, during the time, with his face towards the window, to which and not to his auditors, he directed his eye; thus depriving himself of any additional effect which the language of his composition might have borrowed from the language of his countenance. In this he resembled the generality of singers in ordinary company, who, to shun any charge of affectation, withdraw all meaning from their features, and lose the advantage by which vocal performers on the stage augment the impression and give energy to the sentiment of the song.

Josiah Walker (1761–1831)

Scott Meets Burns

As for Burns, I may truly say, *Virgilium vidi tantum*. I was a lad of fifteen in 1786–7, when he came first to Edinburgh, but had sense and feeling enough to be much interested in his poetry, and would have given the world to know him: but I had very little acquaintance with any literary people, and still less with the gentry of the west country, the two sets that he most frequented. Mr Thomas Grierson was at that time a clerk of my father's. He knew Burns, and promised to ask him to his lodgings to dinner; but had no opportunity to keep his word; otherwise I might have seen more of this distinguished man. As it was, I saw him one day at the late venerable Professor Ferguson's, where there were several gentlemen of literary reputation, among whom I remember the celebrated Mr Dugald Stewart. Of course, we youngsters sat silent, looked and listened. The only thing I remember which was remarkable in Burn's manner, was the effect produced upon him by a print of Bunbury's, representing a soldier lying dead on the snow, his dog sitting in misery on one side,—on the other, his widow, with a child in her arms. These lines were written beneath:

> Cold on Canadian hills, or Minden's plain;
> Perhaps that mother wept her soldier slain:
> Bent o'er her babe, her eye dissolved in dew,
> The big drops, mingling with the milk he drew,
> Gave the sad presage of his future years,
> The child of misery baptised in tears.

Burns seemed much affected by the print, or rather by the ideas which it suggested to his mind. He actually shed tears. He asked whose the lines were; and it chanced that nobody but myself remembered that they occur in a half-forgotten poem of Langhorne's, called by the unpromising title of 'The Justice of Peace'. I whispered my information to a friend present; he mentioned it to Burns, who rewarded me with a look and a word, which, though of mere civility, I then received and still recollect with very great pleasure.

His person was strong and robust; his manners rustic, not clownish; a sort of dignified plainness and simplicity, which received part of its effect perhaps from one's knowledge of his extraordinary talents. His features are represented in Mr Nasmyth's picture; but to me it conveys the idea that they are diminished, as if seen in perspective. I think his countenance was more massive than it looks in any of the portraits. I should have taken the poet, had I not known what he was, for a very sagacious country farmer of the old Scotch school, i.e. none of your modern agriculturists who keep labourers for their drudgery, but the douce gudeman who held his own plough. There was a strong expression of sense and shrewdness in all his lineaments; the eye alone, I think indicated the poetical character and temperament, It was large, and of a dark cast, which glowed (I say literally glowed) when he spoke with feeling or interest. I never saw such another eye in a human head, though I have seen the most distinguished men of my time. His conversation expressed perfect self-confidence, without the slightest presumption. Among the men who were the most learned of their time and country, he expressed himself with perfect firmness, but without the least intrusive forwardness; and when he differed in opinion, he did not hesitate to express it firmly, yet at the same time with modesty. I do not remember any part of his conversation distinctly enough to be quoted; nor did I ever see him again, except in the street, where he did not recognize me, as I could not expect he should. He was much caressed in Edinburgh; but (considering what literary emoluments have been since his day) the efforts made for his relief were extremely trifling.

I remember, on this occasion I mention, I thought Burns's acquaintance with English poetry was rather limited: and also that, having twenty times the abilities of Allan Ransay and of Fergusson he talked of them with too much humility as his models; there was doubtless national predilection in his estimate.

This is all I can tell you about Burns. I have only to add, that his dress corresponded with his manner. He was like a farmer dressed in his best to dine with the laird. I do not speak *in malam partem*, when I say, I never saw a man in company with his superiors in station or information more perfectly free from either the reality or the affectation of embarrassment. I was told, but did not observe it, that his address to females was extremely deferential, and always with a turn either to the pathetic or humorous, which engaged their attention particularly.

J. G.Lockhart (1794–1854)
Life of Robert Burns

Sylvander to Clarinda

Between December 1787 and March 1788, Burns exchanged letters with a deserted Edinburgh 'grass-widow', Agnes Maclehose, of very modest means and a family of two young boys.

During the winter of 1787/8 the second of Burns's two Edinburgh 'seasons', when the poet was rather less 'the wonder of all the gay world' than he had been the previous winter, Burns carried on a passionate 'courtship' with her, calling himself Sylvander, she using the name Clarinda. The friendship had to be built up by correspondence because Burns was laid up with a damaged knee as the result of a fall from a coach.

But by 14th January 1788, he was declaiming:

Why have I not heard from you, Clarinda? To-day I expected it; and, before supper, when a letter to me was announced, my heart danced with rapture; but behold, 'twas some fool who had taken it into his head to turn poet,

and made me an offering of the first fruits of his nonsense . . . I am determined to see you, if at all possible, on Saturday evening. Next week I must
sing—

The night is my departing night,
   The morn's the day I maun awa':
There's neither friend nor foe of mine,
   But wishes that I were awa'!

What I hae done for lack o' wit,
   I never, never can reca';
I hope ye're a' my friends as yet,
   Gude night, and joy be wi' you a'.

If I could see you sooner, I would be so much the happier; but I would not
purchase the dearest gratification on earth, if it must be at your expense in
worldly censure, far less inward peace.

                              Robert Burns
                              Letter to Agnes Maclehose dated 14th January 1788

Clarinda to Sylvander

*The affair reached a climax on 26th January. Clarinda, who depended upon
financial help from her uncle, the judge Lord Craig, and was much under the
spiritual dominance of the Reverend James Kemp (1744–1808)—himself saved
only by his death from a scandal involving Lady Colquhoun of Luss—wrote
twice to Sylvander on the morning after.*

I am neither well nor happy to-day: my heart reproaches me for last night.
If you wish Clarinda to regain her peace, determine against everything but
what the strictest delicacy warrants.
   I do not blame you, but myself. I must not see you on Saturday, unless
I find I can depend on myself acting otherwise. Delicacy, you know, it was
which won me to you at once; take care you do not loosen the dearest, most
sacred tie that unites us! Remember Clarinda's present and eternal happiness
depends upon her adherence to Virtue. Happy Sylvander! that can be attached to Heaven and Clarinda together. Alas! I feel I cannot serve two
masters. God pity me!

                              Agnes Maclehose (1759–1841)
                              Letter to Burns dated 27th January 1788

The End of the Affair

When it was almost all over, Burns wrote a revealing letter to Clarinda dated 4th February. He commemorated their brief passion thereafter in one of his finest lyrics.

Oh, what a fool I am in love! what an extravagant prodigal of affection! Why are your sex called the tender sex, when I never have met with one who can repay me in passion! They are either not so rich in love as I am, or they are niggards where I am lavish.

O Thou, whose I am, and whose are all my ways! Thou see'st me here, the hapless wreck of tides and tempests in my own bosom: do Thou direct to thyself that ardent love, for which I have so often sought a return, in vain, from my fellow-creatures! If Thy goodness has yet such a gift in store for me, as an equal return of affection from her who, Thou knowest, is dearer to me than life, do Thou bless and hallow our band of love and friendship; watch over us, in all our outgoings and incomings, for good; and may the tie that unites our hearts be strong and indissoluble as the thread of man's immortal life!

Robert Burns
Letter to Agnes Maclehose dated 21st January 1788

Ae Fond Kiss

Ae fond kiss, and then we sever;
Ae fareweel, and then for ever!
Deep in heart-wrung tears I'll pledge thee,
Warring sighs and groans I'll wage thee,
Who shall say that Fortune grieves him,
While the star of hope she leaves him?
Me, nae cheerfu twinkle lights me;
Dark despair around benights me.

I'll ne'er blame my partial fancy,
Naething could resist my Nancy:
But to see her was to love her;
Love but her, and love forever.
Had we never lov'd sae kindly,
Had we never lov'd sae blindly,
Never met—or never parted,
We had ne'er been broken-hearted.

Fare-thee-weel, thou first and fairest!
Fare-thee-weel, thou best and dearest!
Thine be ilka joy and treasure,
Peace, Enjoyment, Love and Pleasure!
Ae fond kiss, and then we sever!
Ae fareweel, alas, for ever!
Deep in heart-wrung tears I'll pledge thee,
Warring sighs and groans I'll wage thee.

Robert Burns

Maria Riddell On Burns

Maria Riddell, wife of the brother of Burns's friend, Robert Riddell of Glenriddell, was the last of several intelligent women with whom the poet formed a deep friendship. It was an association temporarily broken by a quarrel with the Riddell family—probably with Robert Riddell's side of it—after which Burns wrote some insulting verses on Maria, who apparently had sided with her brother-in-law. But when Burns was taking a futile bathing cure at Brow Well, on the Solway Firth, Maria sent her coach for him. When he arrived, she recorded that the 'stamp of death was imprinted on his features.' His first salutation was: "Well, madam, have you any commands for the other world?". I replied, that it seemed a doubtful case which of us should be the soonest, and that I hoped he would yet live to write my epitaph.' A few weeks later Burns was dead, and Maria wrote a generous sketch of him.

If others have climbed more successfully the heights of Parnassus, none certainly ever outshone Burns in the charms—the sorcery I would almost call it—of fascinating conversation; the spontaneous eloquence of social argument, or the unstudied poignancy of brilliant repartee. His personal endowments were perfectly correspondent with the qualifications of his mind. His form was manly, his action energy itself, devoid in a great measure, however, of those graces, of that polish acquired only in the refinement of societies where in early life he had not the opportunity to mix; but where—such was the irresistible power of attraction that encircled him—though his appearance and manner were always peculiar, he never failed to delight and to excel. His figure certainly bore the authentic impress of his birth and original station in life; it seemed moulded by Nature for the rough exercises of agriculture rather than the gentler cultivation of *belles lettres*. His features were stamped with the hardy character of independence, and the firmness of conscious though not arrogant pre-eminence. I believe no man was ever gifted with a larger portion of the *vivida vis animi*: the animated expressions of his countenance were almost peculiar to himself. The rapid lightnings of his eye were always the harbingers of some flash of genius, whether they darted the fiery glances of insulted and indignant superiority, or beamed with the impassioned sentiment of fervent and impetuous affections. His voice alone could improve upon the magic of his eye; sonorous, replete with the finest modulations, it alternately captivated the ear with the melody of poetic numbers, the perspicuity of nervous reasoning, or the ardent sallies of enthusiastic patriotism.

Maria Riddell (1772–1808)
Memoir Concerning Burns

Mrs Alison Cockburn

Mrs Cockburn, one of the vigorous and talented ladies who adorned the eighteenth century scene, was born at Fairnilee, Selkirkshire, the daughter of Robert Rutherford, and was distantly related to Scott's mother. In 1731 she married Patrick Cockburn, and for sixty years was queen of Edinburgh society. She is remembered for her version of 'The Flowers of the Forest', said to be inspired not by Flodden, but by a wave of financial ruin which affected many families in the Ettrick Forest neighbourhood, and for her 'Letters', edited in 1900. She met Scott in his boyhood, and knew Burns during his Edinburgh stay. Scott said of her that she 'spoke both wittily and well', as her letters, mostly to the Reverend Dr Douglas, the parish minister at Galashiels, show.

I appointed this day, when free of interruption, to thank you for my birthday letter and to obey your pastoral instructions by looking back on a very long life. If I were to judge from the various scenes I have been placed in, my memory would make me believe that instead of 73, I have lived 300 years. I can this moment figure myself running as fast as a greyhound in a hot summer day to have the pleasure of plunging into Tweed to cool me. I see myself made up like a clew, with my feet wrapt in a peticoat, on the declivity of the hill at Fairnilee, letting myself roll down to the bottom with infinite delight. As for the chace of the silver spoon at the end of the rainbow, nothing could exceed my ardour except my faith, which excelled it. I can see myself the first favourite at Lamotte's dancing, and recollect turning pale and red with the ambition of applause. I advance to the age of admiration and assemblies. I was a prude when young; and remarkably grave. It was owing to a consciousness that I would not pass unobserved, and a fear of giving offence or incurring censure. I loved dancing exceedingly, because I danced well. At 17 my career was stopt. I was married, properly speaking, to a man of 75, my father-in-law. I lived with him 4 years, and as an ambition had seized me to make him fond of me, knowing also nothing could please his son so much, I bestowed all my time and study to gain his approbation. He disapproved of plays and assemblys: I never went to one. Soon the joys and cares of a mother fill'd my whole heart.

The various places of residence, the many uncommon joys and sorrows I have felt, the most acute sorrows with high strung passions makes it amazing how at so late a period I have strength to record it I was 22 years united to a lover and a friend; 50 years a happy tho' anxious mother, now 33 years a widow. See, then, if I have not lived 300 years. Now I feel all the blessings of old age, and thank my Creator and Preserver that he did not hear my prayers for death when my mind was in a tumult of passion and despair. I now seem to see myself seated on a height under a serene sky, looking back on the tempest I have escaped, and thankful to my Preserver for allowing me ease—tho' no strength—eyesight, and a capacity to be amused with it; kind friends and a heart grateful and cheered by their kindness; no anxious cares for futurity; no desires for what is out of my power; a wish to make everybody as happy as I am, or, at least less miserable: a violent desire to be more devout than I am. I pray to be so, for God himself only can infuse the love of himself into the human soul. And, waiting patiently, I answer myself, 'You are seeking pleasures here that belong to a future world.' Am I right? And now, for constitution of body, I think mine is what it ever was—never strong, but clean and free of gross humours. I never could eat as much as to feel repletion, nor drink as much as to feel any great degree of intoxication. Not but that I have often been enlivened with a glass of Fairnilee ale. You see, temperance is no virtue in me—merely constitutional. Now, my receit for health is also the same exactly—clean in my person, and, when needful, a dose of elixir. So endeth the chapter on egotism.

> Mrs Alison Cockburn (1713–94)
> *Letters*

Scotch Old Ladies

There was living at this time a singular race of excellent Scotch old ladies. They were a delightful set; strong headed, warm hearted, and high spirited; the fire of their tempers not always latent; merry even in solitude; very resolute; indifferent about the modes and habits of the modern world; and adhering to their own ways, so as to stand out, like primitive rocks above ordinary society. Their prominent qualities of sense, humour, affection, and spirit, were embodied in curious exteriors; for they all dressed, and spoke, and did, exactly as they chose; their language, like their habits, entirely Scotch, but without any other vulgarity than what perfect naturalness is sometimes mistaken for.

There sits a clergyman's widow, the mother of the first Sir David Dundas, the introducer of our German system of military manoeuvres, and at one time Commander-in-Chief of the British Army. We used to go to her house in Bunker's Hill, when boys, on Sundays between the morning and afternoon sermons, where we were cherished with Scotch broth and cakes, and many a joke. Age had made her incapable of walking even across the room; so, clad in a plain black silk gown, and a pure muslin cap, she sat half encircled by a high-backed black leather chair, reading; with silver spectacles stuck on her thin nose; and interspersing her studies with much laughter, and not a little sarcasm. What a spirit! There was more fun and sense around that chair than in the theatre or the church. I remember one of her grand-daughters stumbling, in the course of reading the newspapers to her, on a paragraph which stated that a lady's reputation had suffered from some indiscreet talk on the part of the Prince of Wales. Up she of four-score sat, and said with an indignant shake of her shrivelled fist and a keen voice— 'The dawmed villain! does he kiss and tell!'

And there is Lady Arniston, the mother of Henry Dundas, the first Lord Melville, so kind to us mischievous boys on the Saturdays. She was generally to be found in the same chair, on the same spot; her thick black hair combed all tightly up into a cone on the top of her head; the remains of considerable beauty in her countenance; great and just pride in her son; a good representative in her general air and bearing of what the noble English ladies must have been in their youth, who were queens in their family castles, and stood sieges in defence of them. Lady Arniston was in her son's house in George Square, when it was attacked by the mob in 1793 or 1794, and though no windows could be smashed at that time by the populace, without the inmates thinking of the bloody streets of Paris, she was perfectly firm, most contemptuous of the assailants, and with a heroic confidence in her son's doing his duty. She once wished us to go somewhere for her on an evening; and on one of us objecting that if we did, our lessons for next day could not be got ready—'Hoot man!' said she, 'what o' that? as they used to say in my day—it's only het hips and awa' again.' . . .

Lady Don (who lived in George Square) was still more highly bred, as was attested by her polite cheerfulness and easy elegance. The venerable faded beauty, the white well-coiled hair the soft hand sparkling with old brilliant rings, the kind heart, the affectionate manner, the honest gentle voice, and the mild eye, account for the love with which her old age was surrounded. She was about the last person (so far as I recollect) in Edinburgh who kept a private sedan chair. Hers stood in the loby, and was as handsome and comfortable as silk, velvet, and gilding could make it. And, when she wished to use it, two well-known respectable chairmen, enveloped in her livery cloaks, were the envy of her brethren. She and Mrs Rochead both sat in the Tron Church; and well I do remember how I used to form one of the group to see these beautiful relics emerge from the coach and the chair.

Lord Cockburn (1779–1874)
Memorials of His Time

Sir Henry Raeburn

Sir Henry Raeburn (1756–1823) was the greatest of a distinguished series of eighteenth and nineteenth century Scottish portrait painters, and the master of what we still recognize as a 'manly, dignified, and searching art' which gives him European significance.

Raeburn was a born painter of portraits. He looked people shrewdly between the eyes, surprised their manners in their face, and had possessed himself of what was essential in their character before they had been many minutes in his studio. What he was so swift to perceive, he conveyed to the canvas almost in the moment of conception . . . And so each of his portraits is not only (in Doctor Johnson's phrase) 'a piece of history', but a piece of biography into the bargain. It is devoutly to be wished that all biography were equally amusing, and carried its own credentials equally upon its face. These portraits are racier than many anecdotes, and more complete than many a volume of sententious memoirs.

Robert Louis Stevenson (1850–94)
Virginibus Puerisque

The Boy Scott at Smailholm Tower

Thus while I ape the measure wild
Of tales that charm'd me yet a child,
Rude though they be, still with the chime
Return the thoughts of early time;
And feelings, roused in life's first day,
Glow in the line, and prompt the lay.
Then rise those crags, that mountain tower,
Which charm'd my fancy's wakening hour.
Though no broad river swept along,
To claim, perchance, heroic song;
Though sigh'd no groves in summer gale,
To prompt of love a softer tale;
Though scarce a puny streamlet's speed
Claim'd homage from a shepherd's reed;
Yet was poetic impulse given,
By the green hill and clear blue heaven.
It was a barren scene, and wild,
Where naked cliffs were rudely piled;
But ever and anon between
Lay velvet tufts of loveliest green;
And well the lonely infant knew
Recesses where the wall-flower grew,

And honey-suckle loved to crawl
Up the low crag ruin'd wall.
I deem'd such nooks the sweetest shade
The sun in all its round survey'd;
And still I thought that shatter'd tower
The mightiest work of human power;
And marvell'd as the aged hind
With some strange tale bewitch'd my mind,
Of forayers, who, with headlong force,
Down from that strength had spurr'd their horse,
Their southern rapine to renew,
Far in the distant Cheviots blue,
And, home returning, fill'd the hall
With revel, wassel-rout, and brawl.
Methought that still with trump and clang,
The gateway's broken arches rang;
Methought grim features, seam'd with scars,
Glared though the window's rusty bars,
And ever, by the winter hearth,
Old tales I heard of woe or mirth,
Of lovers' slights, of ladies' charms,
Of witches' spells, of warriors' arms;
Of patriot battles, won of old
By Wallace wight and Bruce the bold;
Of later fields of feud and fight,
When, pouring from their Highland height,
The Scottish clans, in headlong sway,
Had swept the scarlet ranks away.
While stretch'd at length upon the floor,
Again I fought each combat o'er,
Pebbles and shells, in order laid,
The mimic ranks of war display'd;
And onward still the Scottish Lion bore,
And still the scatter'd Southron fled before.

Sir Walter Scott (1771–1832)
Thr Lady of the Lake

Scott Advertises the Trossachs

Robert Pearse Gillies, the son of an Arbroath bonnet-laird, was called to the Bar; but lost his fortune and, though befriended by Scott, led a more or less unsuccessful literary life, dying in London soon after spending two years in a debtor's prison. The Lady of the Lake was published in 1810.

The copyright of this poem was estimated at 4,000£., and in truth its success was unprecedented. The necessity of having it to read for fashion's sake precluded borrowing in many instances. It was a kind of disgrace, a losing of *caste*, not to possess it. But it found numberless intelligent, as well as fashionable readers. More especially were young hearts gained by this metrical story, for in it there was nothing which they could not understand. On the contrary, there was much which they had themselves perceived and felt, yet were not able to express, nor had heard expressed before ... In the autumn of that year a degree of homage was paid to the poet, such as has never been manifested before nor since. All the world, rich and poor, including crown-princes and *noblesse*, crowded to visit the scenery which he had depicted. Instead, of being, as usual, a dull, stupid village, whose inhabitants were all in a state of *cabbageism*, Callander of Menteith became a rallying point for all classes, a place wherein to study varieties of character. Truly *that* study was not very consolatory or edifying.

Robert Pearse Gillies (1788–1858)
Memoirs of a Literary Veteran

The Mystery of 'Waverley'

In 1814 Scott published *Waverley*—the first of those admirable and original prose compositions which have nearly obliterated the recollection of his poetry. Except the first opening of the Edinburgh Review, no work that has appeared in my time made such an instant and universal impression. It is curious to remember it. The unexpected newness of the thing, the profusion of original characters, the Scotch language, Scotch scenery, Scotch men and women, the simplicity of the writing, and the graphic force of the descriptions, all struck us with an electric shock of delight. I wish I could again feel the sensations produced by the first year of these two Edinburgh works. If the concealment of the authorship of the novels was intended to make mystery heighten their effect, it completely succeeded. The speculations and conjectures, and nods and winks, and predictions and assertions were endless, and occupied every company, and almost every two men who met and spoke in the street.

Lord Cockburn (1779–1854)
Memorials of his Time

An Abbotsford Day

It was a clear, bright September morning, with a sharpness in the air that

doubled the animating influence of the sunshine, and all was in readiness for
a grand coursing match on Newark Hill. The only guest who had chalked
out other sport for himself was that staunchest of anglers, Mr Rose; but he,
too, was there on his shelty, armed with his salmon-rod and landing-net,
and attended by his humorous squire Hinves, and Charlie Purdie, a brother
of Tom, in those days the most celebrated fisherman of the district. This little
group of Waltonians, bound for Lord Somerville s preserve, remained
lounging about to witness the start of the main cavalcade. Sir Walter,
mounted on Sybil, was marshalling the order of procession with a huge
hunting-whip; and, among a dozen frolicsome youths and maidens, who
seemed disposed to laugh at all discipline, appeared, each on horseback,
each as eager as the youngest sportsman in the troop, Sir Humphry Davy,
Dr Wollaston, and the patriarch of Scottish belles-lettres, Henry Mackenzie.
The Man of Feeling, however, was persuaded with some difficulty to resign
his steed for the present to his faithful negro follower, and to join Lady
Scott in the sociable until we should reach the ground of our battue. Laidlaw,
on a long-tailed wiry Highlander, yclept Hoddin Grey, which carried him
nimbly and stoutly, although his feet almost touched the ground as he sat,
was the adjutant. But the most picturesque figure was the illustrious inventor of the safety-lamp. He had come for his favourite sport of angling, and
had been practising it successfully with Rose, his travelling companion, for
two or three days preceding this, but he had not prepared for coursing
fields, or had left Charlie Purdie's troop for Sir Walter's on a sudden thought;
and his fisherman costume—a brown hat with flexible brims, surrounded
with line upon line, and innumerable fly-hooks—jack boots worthy of a
Dutch smuggler, and a fustian surtout dabbled with the blood of salmon,
made a fine contrast with the smart jackets white-cord breeches, and well-
polished jockey-boots of the less distinguished cavaliers about him. Dr
Wollaston was in black, and with his noble serene dignity of countenance
might have passed for a sporting archbishop. Mr Mackenzie, at this time
in the 76th year of his age, with a white hat turned up with green, green
spectacles, green jacket, and long brown leathern gaiters buttoned upon his
nether anatomy, wore a dog-whistle round his neck, and had all over the
air of as resolute a devotee as the gay captain of Huntly Burn. Tom Purdie
and his subalterns had preceded us by a few hours with all the greyhounds
that could be collected at Abbotsford, Darnick, and Melrose; but the giant
Maida had remained as his master's orderly, and now gambolled about Sybil
Grey, barking for mere joy like a spaniel puppy.

The order of march had been all settled and the sociable was just getting
under way, when the Lady Anne broke from the line, screaming with
laughter, and exclaimed—'Papa, papa, I knew you could never think of
going without your pet. —Scott looked round, and I rather think there was
a blush as well as a smile upon his face, when he perceived a little black pig
frisking about his pony, and evidently a self-elected addition to the party of
the day. He tried to look stern, and cracked his whip at the creature, but was
in a moment obliged to join in the general cheers. Poor piggy soon found a

strap round his neck, and was dragged into the background:—Scott, watching the retreat, repeated with mock pathos the first verse of an old song—

What will I do gin my hoggie die?
My joy, my pride, my hoggie!
My only beast, I had nae mae,
And wow! but I was vogie!

—the cheers were redoubled—and the squadron moved on.

J. G. Lockhart (1794–1857)
Life of Scott

Scott's Novels

Elizabeth Grant was the daughter of Sir John Grant, seventh Laird of Rothie-murchus. Although in 1829 she married Colonel Henry Smith, she used her maiden name when writing her memoirs, which appeared in 1897 edited by her niece, Lady Strachey.

Waverley came out, I think it must have been in the autumn of 1814, just before we went first to Edinburgh. It was brought to us at Doune, I know, by 'little Jemmy Simpson', as that good man, since so famous, was then most irreverently called. Some liked the book, he said; he thought himself it was in parts quite beyond the common run, and the determined mystery as to the author added much to its vogue. I did not like it. The opening English scenes were to me intolerably dull and lengthy, and so prosy, and the persons introduced so uninteresting, the hero contemptible, the two heroines unnatural and disagreeable, and the whole idea given of the Highlands so utterly at variance with truth. I read it again long afterwards, and remained of the same mind. Then burst out *Guy Mannering*, carrying all the world before it, in spite of the very pitiful setting the gipsies, the smugglers, and Dandie Dinmont are surrounded by. Here again is the copyist, the scenery Dumfries and Galloway, the dialect Forfar. People now began to feel these works could come but from one author, particularly as a few acres began to be added to the recent purchase of the old tower of Abbotsford, and Mrs Scott set up a carriage, a barouche landau built in London, which from the time she got it she was seldom out of.

I was never in company with Walter Scott; he went out very little, and when he did go he was not agreeable, generally sitting very silent, looking dull and listless, unless an occasional flash lighted up his countenance. In his own house, he was another character, especially if he liked his guests.

It was odd, but Sir Walter never had the reputation in Edinburgh he had elsewhere—was not the *lion*, I mean. His wonderful works were looked for, read with avidity, praised on all hands, yet the author made far less noise at home than he did abroad. The fat, vulgar Mrs Jobson, whose low husband had made his large fortune at Dundee by pickling herrings, on being congratulated at the approaching marriage of her daughter to Sir Walter Scott's son, said the young people were attached, otherwise her Jane might have looked higher; 'it was only a baronetcy, and quite a late creation.'

Elizabeth Grant (1797–1885)
Memoirs of a Highland Lady

The Financial Crash

In January 1826, the publishing house of Ballantyne, with which Scott had imprudently allowed himself to become involved without exercising financial supervision, failed on account of mismanagement. Its liabilities amounted to over a million pounds. Scott felt under a moral obligation to satisfy the firm's creditors, and although then fifty-five, he set himself the heroic task of paying off the firm's debts, an exertion which probably hastened his death.

I feel neither dishonoured nor broken down by the bad—now really bad news I have received. I have walked my last on the domains I have planted—sate the last time in the halls I have built. But death would have taken them from me if misfortune had spared them. My poor people whom I loved so well! There is just another die to turn up against me in this run of ill-luck; i.e. if I should break my magic wand in the fall from this elephant, and lose my popularity with my fortune. Then Woodstock and Bony may both go to the paper-maker, and I may take to smoking cigars and drinking grog, or turn devotee, and intoxicate the brain another way. In prospect of absolute ruin, I wonder if they would let me leave the Court of Session. I would like, methinks, to go abroad:

And lay my bones far from the Tweed.

But I find my eyes moistening, and that will not do. I will not yield without a fight for it. It is odd, when I set myself to work doggedly, as Dr Johnson would say, I am exactly the same that I ever was, neither low spirited nor distrait. In prosperous times I have sometimes felt my fancy and powers of language flag, but adversity is to me at least a tonic and bracer; the fountain is awakened from its inmost recesses, as if the spirit of affliction had troubled it in his passage.

Poor Mr Pole the harper sent to offer me £500 or £600, probably his all.

'There is much good in the world, after all. But I will involve no friend, either rich or poor. My own right hand shall do it—else will I be done in the slang language, and undone in common parlance.

Sir Walter Scott (1770-1832)
Journal. Entry for 22nd January 1826

Scott's Bankruptcy

The opening of the year 1826 will ever be sad to those who remember the thunderbolt which then fell on Edinburgh in the utterly unexpected bankruptcy of Scott, implying the ruin of Constable the bookseller, and of Ballantyne the printer. If an earthquake had swallowed half the town, it would not have produced greater astonishment, sorrow, and dismay. Ballantyne and Constable were merchants, and their fall, had it reached no further, might have been lamented merely as the casualty of commerce. But Sir Walter! The idea that his practical sense had so far left him as to have permitted him to dabble in trade, had never crossed our imagination. How humbled we felt when we saw him—the pride of us all, dashed from his lofty and honourable station, and all the fruits of his well-worked talents gone. He had not then even a political enemy. There was not one of those whom his thoughtlessness had so sorely provoked, who would not have given every spare farthing he possessed to retrieve Sir Walter.

Well do I remember Scott's first appearance after this calamity was divulged, when he walked into Court one day in January 1826. There was no affectation, and no reality, of facing it; no look of indifference or defiance; but the manly and modest air of a gentleman conscious of some folly, but of perfect rectitude, and of most heroic and honourable resolutions. It was on that very day, I believe, that he said a very fine thing. Some of his friends offered him, or rather proposed to offer him, enough money, as was supposed, to enable him to arrange with his creditors. He paused for a moment; and then, recollecting his powers, said proudly—'No! this right hand shall work it off!' His friend William Clerk supped with him one night after his ruin was declared. They discussed the whole affair, its causes and probable consequences, openly, and playfully; till at last they laughed over their noggins at the change, and Sir Walter observed that he felt 'something like Lambert and the other regicides, who, Pepys says when he saw them going to be hanged and quartered, were as cheerful and comfortable as any gentlemen could be in that situation.

Lord Cockburn (1779-1853)
Memorials of His Time

The Great Unknown Unmasked

It was during one of these small evening parties, when I remember Sydney Smith happened to be in Edinburgh, and spent that evening at our house, that my son Miles, returning from the Theatrical Fund dinner joined our party and announced that 'The Great Unknown' had, on Sir Walter Scott's health being drunk, risen and acknowledged himself to be the author of *Waverley*, *Guy Mannering*, etc. Though the fact was as well known, as if he had proclaimed it at the market cross, ten years before, this public and unexpected acknowledgment produced a great sensation not only on the people present, but throughout every circle in Edinburgh. The secret had been extracted from him by the unfortunate state of his affairs, involved as he was in Constable's bankruptcy.

Mrs Eliza Fletcher (1770–1858)
Autobiography

A Farewell Visit

On 18th July 1831, Sir Walter, accompanied by his son-in-law and future biographer Lockhart, set out for Douglasdale, so that Scott could gather material for his novel 'Castle Dangerous'. By then Scott himself had realized that his days were numbered, and that his powers were failing.

It was again a darkish cloudy day, with some occasional mutterings of distant thunder, and perhaps the state of the atmosphere told upon Sir Walter's nerves; but I had never before seem him so sensitive as he was all the morning after this inspection of Douglas. As we drove over the high tableland of Lesmahago, he repeated I know not how many verses from Winton, Barbour, and Blind Harry, with, I believe, almost every stanza of Dunbar's elegy on the deaths of the Makers [poets]. It was not that I saw him, such as he paints himself in one or two passages of his Diary but such as his companions in the meridian vigour of his life never saw him—'the rushing of a brook, or the sighing of the summer breeze, bringing the tears into his eyes not unpleasantly.' Bodily weakness laid the delicacy of the organisation bare, over which he had prided himself in wearing a sort of half-stoical mask. High and exalted feelings, indeed, he had never been able to keep concealed, but he had shrunk from exhibiting to human eye the softer and gentler emotions which now trembled to the surface. He strove against it even now, and presently came back from the Lament of the Makers to his Douglases, and chanted, rather than repeated, in a sort of deep and flowing, though not distinct recitative, his first favourite among all the ballads:

It was about the Lammas tide,
When husbandmen do win their hay,
That the Doughty Douglas bowne him to ride
To England to drive a prey,—

down to the closing stanzas, which again left him in tears:

My wound is deep—I fain would sleep—
Take thou the vanguard of the three,
And hide me beneath the bracken-bush,
That grows on yonder lily lea.

J. G. Lockhart (1794–1854)
Life of Scott

The Sun Upon the Weirdlaw Hill

The sun upon the Weirdlaw Hill,
  In Ettrick's vale, is sinking sweet;
The westland wind is hush and still,
  The lake lies sleeping at my feet.
Yet not the landscape to mine eye
  Bears those bright hues that once it bore;
Though evening, with her richest dye,
  Flames o'er the hills of Ettrick's shore.

With listless look along the plain,
  I see Tweed's silver current glide,
And coldly mark the holy fane
  Of Melrose rise in ruin'd pride.
The quiet lake, the balmy air,
  The hill, the stream, the tower, the tree,—
Are they still such as once they were,
  Or is the dreary change in me?

Alas, the warp'd and broken board,
  How can it bear the painter's dye!
The harp of strain'd and tuneless chord,
  How to the minstrel's skill reply!
To aching eyes each landscape lowers,
  To feverish pulse each gale blows chill;
And Araby's or Eden's bowers
  Were barren as this moorland hill.

Sir Walter Scott

The Death of Sir Walter Scott

While on an excursion to Naples and Rome during the Spring of 1832 in a vain search for health, Scott sank into a state of lethargy, suffering his fourth stroke followed by paralytic seizure on 9th June. He arrived home at Abbotsford on 11th July, and thereafter slowly declined. There is some reason to believe that Lockhart's account of the scene by the death-bed was romanticized in order to give a religious end to his father-in-law's life. It is deeply affecting, nonetheless.

At a very early hour on the morning of Wednesday the 11th, we again placed him in his carriage, and he lay in the same torpid state during the first two stages on the road to Tweedside. But as we descended the vale of the Gala he began to gaze about him, and by degrees it was obvious that he was recognizing the features of that familiar landscape. Presently he murmured a name or two—'Gala Water surely—Buckholm—Torwoodlee!' As we rounded the hill at Ladhope, and the outline of the Eildons burst on him, he became greatly excited, and when turning himself on the couch his eye caught at length his own towers, at the distance of a mile, he sprang up with a cry of delight. The river being in flood, we had to go round a few miles by Melrose bridge; and during the time this occupied, his woods and house being within prospect, it required occasionally both Dr Watson's strength and mine, in addition to Nicolson's, to keep him in the carriage. After passing the bridge, the road for a couple of miles loses sight of Abbotsford, and he relapsed into his stupor; but on gaining the bank immediately above it, his excitement became again ungovernable.

Mr Laidlaw was waiting at the porch, and assisted us in lifting him into the dining-room, where his bed had been prepared. He sat bewildered for a few moments, and then resting his eye on Laidlaw, said—'Ha! Willie Laidlaw! O man, how often have I thought of you!' By this time his dogs had assembled about his chair—they began to fawn upon him and lick his hands, and he alternately sobbed and smiled over them, until sleep oppressed him.

On Monday he remained in bed, and seemed extremely feeble; but after breakfast on Tuesday the 17th he appeared revived somewhat, and was again wheeled about on the turf. Presently he fell asleep in his chair, and after dozing for perhaps half an hour, started awake, and shaking the plaids we had put about him from off his shoulders, said—'This is sad idleness. I shall forget what I have been thinking of, if I don't set it down now. Take me into my own room, and fetch the keys of my desk.' He repeated this so earnestly, that we could not refuse; his daughters went into his study, opened his writing-desk, and laid paper and pens in the usual order, and I then moved him through the hall and into the spot where he had always been accustomed to work. When the chair was placed at the desk, and he found himself in the old position, he smiled and thanked us, and said—'Now give me my pen, and leave me for a little to myself.' Sophia put the pen into his hand, and he endeavoured to close his fingers upon it, but they refused their office—it dropped on the paper. He sank back among his pillows, silent tears rolling down his cheeks; but composing himself by and by, motioned to me to wheel him out of doors again. Laidlaw met us at the porch, and took his turn of the chair. Sir Walter, after a little while, again dropt into slumber. When he was awaking, Laidlaw said to me—'Sir Walter has had a little repose.'—'No, Willie,' said he, 'no repose for Sir Walter but in the grave.' The tears again rushed from his eyes. 'Friends,' said he, 'don't let me expose myself—get me to bed—that's the only place.'

As I was dressing on the morning of Monday, the 17th of September, Nicolson came into my room, and told me that his master had awoke in a state of composure and consciousness, and wished to see me immediately. I found him entirely himself, though in the last extreme of feebleness. His eye was clear and calm—every trace of the wild fire of delirium extinguished. 'Lockhart,' he said 'I may have but a minute to speak to you. My dear, be a good man—be virtuous—be religious—be a good man. Nothing else will give you any comfort when you come to lie here.'—He paused, and I said— 'Shall I send for Sophia and Anne?'—'No,' said he, don't disturb them. Poor souls! I know they were up all night—God bless you all!'—With this he sunk into a very tranquil sleep and indeed, he scarcely afterwards gave any sign of consciousness, except for an instant on the arrival of his sons. They, on learning that the scene was about to close, obtained a new leave of absence from their posts, and both reached Abbotsford on the 19th. About half-past one p.m. on the 21st of September, Sir Walter breathed his last, in the presence of all his children. It was a beautiful day—so warm, that every window was wide open—and so perfectly still, that the sound of all others most delicious to his ear, the gentle ripple of the Tweed over its pebbles, was distinctly audible as we knelt around the bed, and his eldest son kissed and closed his eyes.

J. G. Lockhart
Life of Scott

Scott's Nature

Mrs Fletcher, born Eliza Dawson at Oxton in 1770, married Andrew Fletcher, an Edinburgh advocate, in 1791. He was 45, she 21. Most of her life thereafter was spent in the Scottish Capital, where she died in 1858. Lord Brougham called her 'one of the most accomplished of her sex . . . with the utmost purity of life that can dignify female charms.'

Sir Walter was one of those great men who had an undue estimate of 'the pride of life'. He did not care for money, but he cared much for baronial towers and aristocratical distinction; and yet his taste was unaccompanied with haughtiness of disposition or manners. It was rather the romance of his character that led him to add acre to acre, and to found the family of Scott of Abbotsford; for there was nothing sordid in his nature; he was frank and kind-hearted, as much beloved by his poor neighbours as he was admired and courted by the great. It must always be regretted that the labours of a busy life failed to secure him an honourable independence in his advanced years; and yet he was never more truly great than when he said, on declaring himself insolvent, 'But this hand shall work me out of my difficulties;' and so it would, had his life been prolonged. There can be little doubt, however, that the painful excitement of the difficulties, which he met so bravely, broke down his constitution and shortened his life.

Mrs Eliza Fletcher (1770–1858)
Autobiography

Scots Judges: George Fergusson, Lord Hermaud

Hermand's external appearance was as striking as everything else about him. Tall and thin, with grey lively eyes, and a long face, strongly expressive of whatever emotion he was under, his air and manner were distinctly those of a well-born and well-bred gentleman. His dress for society, the style of which he stuck to almost as firmly as he did to his principles, reminded us of the olden time, when trousers would have insulted any company, and braces were deemed an impeachment of nature. Neither the disclosure of the long neck by the narrow bit of muslin stock, nor the outbreak of the linen between the upper and nether garments, nor the short coat sleeves, with the consequent length of bare wrist, could hide his being one of the aristocracy. And if they had, the thin and powdered grey hair, flowing down into a long thin gentleman-like pig-tail, would have attested it. His morning raiment in the country was delightful. The articles, rough and strange, would of themselves have attracted notice in a museum. But set upon George Fergusson, at his paradise of Hermand, during vacation, on going forth for a long day's work—often manual—at his farm with his grey felt hat and tall weeding hoe—what could be more agrestic or picturesque?

What was it that made Hermand such an established wonder and delight? It seems to me to have been the supremacy in his composition of a single quality—intensity of temperament, which was so conspicuous that it prevented many people from perceiving anything else in him. He could not be indifferent. Repose, except in bed, where however he slept zealously, was unnatural and contemptible to him. His constitutional animation never failed to carry him a flight beyond ordinary mortals. Those who only saw the operation of this ardour in public conflict, were apt to set him down as a phrenzied man. But to those who knew Hermand personally, the lamb was the truer type. When removed from contests which provoke impatience, and placed in the private scene, where innocent excesses are only amusing, what a heart! what conversational wildness! There never was a more pleasing example of the superiority of right affections over intellectual endowments in the creation of happiness. Had he depended on his understanding alone, or chiefly, he would have been wrecked every week. But honesty, humanity, social habits, and diverting public explosions, always kept him popular.

With very simple tastes, and rather a contempt of epicurism, but very gregarious, he was fond of the pleasures of the table. He had acted in more of the severest scenes of old Scotch drinking than any man at last living. Commonplace topers think drinking a pleasure: but with Hermand it was a virtue. . . .

Two young gentleman, great friends, went together to the theatre in Glasgow, supped at the lodgings of one of them, and passed a whole summer night over their punch. In the morning a kindly wrangle broke out, one of them was stabbed and died on the spot. The survivor was tried at Edinburgh, and was convicted of culpable homicide. It was one of the sad cases where the legal guilt was greater than the moral; and, very properly, he was sentenced to only a short imprisonment. Hermand, who felt that discredit had been brought on the cause of drinking, had no sympathy with the tenderness of his temperate brethren, and was vehement for transportation. 'We are told that there was no malice, and that the prisoner must have been in liquor. In liquor! Why, he was drunk! And yet he murdered the very man who had been drinking with him! They had been carousing the whole night; and yet he stabbed him after drinking a whole bottle of rum with him. Good God, my Laards, if he will do this when he's drunk, what will he not do when he's sober?'

Lord Cockburn (1779–1854)
Memorials of His Time

Scots Judges: Robert McQueen, Lord Braxfield

This sketch of the original 'Weir of Hermiston' is said by William Roughead to have been 'painted by a partisan brush with other people's colours'. Yet without Cockburn's vivid, if exaggerated, portrait, we might never have had Stevenson's greatest novel.

But the giant of the Bench was Braxfield. His very name makes people start yet. Strong built and dark, with rough eyebrows, powerful eyes, threatening lips, and a low growling voice, he was like a formidable blacksmith. His accent and his dialect were exaggerated Scotch; his language, like his thoughts, short, stront, and conclusive.

Our commercial jurisprudence was only rising when Braxfield was sinking, and, being no reader, he was too old both in life and in habit to master it familiarly; though even here he was inferior to no Scotch lawyer of his time except Ilay Campbell, the Lord President. But within the range of the feudal and civil branches, and in every matter depending on natural ability and practical sense, he was very great. His power arose more from the force of his reasoning and his vigorous application of principle, than from either the extent or the accuracy of his learning.

With this intellectual force, as applied to law, Braxfield's merits, I fear, cease. Illiterate and without any taste for refined enjoyment, strength of understanding only encouraged him to a more contemptuous disdain of all natures less coarse than his own. Despising the growing improvement of manners, he shocked the feelings even of an age, which, with more of the formality, had far less of the substance of decorum than our own. Thousands of his sayings have been preserved, and the staple of them is indecency; which he succeeded in making many people enjoy, or at least endure, by hearty laughter, energy of manner, and rough humour. Almost the only story of him I ever heard that had some fun in it without immodesty, was when a butler gave up his place because his lordship's wife was always scolding him. 'Lord!' he exclaimed, 'ye've little to complain o': ye may be thankfu' ye're no married to her'.

It is impossible to condemn Braxfield's conduct as a criminal judge too gravely, or too severely. It was a disgrace to the age. A dexterous and practical trier of ordinary cases, he was harsh to prisoners even in his jocularity, and to every counsel whom he chose to dislike. It may be doubted if he was ever so much in his element as when tauntingly repelling the last despairing claim of a wretched culprit, and sending him to Botany Bay or the gallows with an insulting jest. This union of talent, with a passion for rude domination, exercised in a very discretionary court, tended to create a formidable and dangerous judicial character.

Lord Cockburn
Ibid

Weir of Hermiston Eulogises Capital Punishment

My lord, after hanging up his cloak and hat, turned round in the lighted entry, and made him an imperative and silent gesture with his thumb, and with the strange instinct of obedience, Archie followed him into the house. . . .

The lamp was shaded, the fire trimmed to a nicety, the table covered deep with orderly documents, the backs of law books made a frame upon all sides that was only broken by the window and the doors.

For a moment Hermiston warmed his hands at the fire, presenting his back to Archie; then suddenly disclosed on him the terrors of the Hanging Face.

'What's this I hear of ye?' he asked.

There was no answer possible to Archie.

'I'll have to tell ye, then.' pursued Hermiston. 'It seems ye've been skirling against the father that begot ye, and one of his Maijesty's Judges in this land; and that in the public street, and while an order of the Court was being executit. Forbye which, it would appear that ye've been airing your opeenions in a Coallege Debatin' Society'; he paused a moment: and then, with extraordinary bitterness, added: 'Ye damned eediot.'

'I had meant to tell you,' stammered Archie. 'I see you are well informed.'

'Muckle obleeged to ye,' said his lordship, and took his usual seat. 'And so you disapprove of Capital Punishment?' he added.

'I am sorry, sir, I do,' said Archie.

'I am sorry, too,' said his lordship. 'And now, if you please, we shall approach this business with a little more parteecularity. I hear that at the hanging of Duncan Jopp—and, man! ye had a fine client there—in the middle of all the riff-raff of the ceety, ye thought fit to cry out, "This is a damned murder, and my gorge rises at the man that haangit him".'

'"No, sir, these were not my words,' cried Archie.

'What were yer words, then?' asked the Judge.

'I believe I said, "I denounce it as a murder!"' said the son. 'I beg your pardon—a God-defying murder. I have no wish to conceal the truth,' he added, and looked his father for a moment in the face.

'God, it would only need that of it next!' cried Hermiston. 'There was nothing about your gorge rising, then?'

'That was afterwards, my lord, as I was leaving the Speculative. I said I had been to see the miserable creature hanged, and my gorge rose at it.'

'Did ye, though?' said Hermiston. 'And I suppose ye knew who haangit him?'

'I was present at the trial; I ought to tell you that, I ought to explain. I ask your pardon beforehand for any expression that may seem undutiful. The position in which I stand is wretched,' said the unhappy hero, now fairly face to face with the business he had chosen. 'I have been reading some of your cases. I was present while Jopp was tried. It was a hideous business. Father, it was a hideous thing! Grant he was vile, why should you hunt him with a vileness equal to his own? It was done with glee—that is the word— you did it with glee; and I looked on, God help me! with horror.'

'You're a young gentleman that doesna approve of Caapital Punishment,' said Hermiston. 'Weel, I'm an auld man that does. I was glad to get Jopp haangit, and what for would I pretend I wasna? You're all for honesty, it seems; you couldn't even steik your mouth on the public street. What for should I steik mines upon the bench, the King's officer, bearing the sword, a dreid to evil-doers, as I was from the beginning, and as I will be to the end! Mair than enough of it! Heedious! I never gave twa thoughts to heediousness, I have no call to be bonny. I'm a man that gets through with my day's business, and let that suffice.'

The ring of sarcasm had died out of his voice as he went on; the plain words became invested with some of the dignity of the Justice-seat.

'It would be telling you if you could say as much,' the speaker resumed. 'But ye cannot. Ye've been reading some of my cases, ye say. But it was not for the law in them, it was to spy out your faither's nakedness, a fine employment in a son. You're splairging; you're running at lairge in life like a wild nowt. It's impossible you should think any longer of coming to the Bar. You're not fit for it; no splairger is. And another thing: son of mines or no son of mines, you have flung fylement in public on one of the Senators of the Coallege of Justice, and I would make it my business to see that you were never admitted there yourself. There is a kind of a decency to be observit. Then comes the next of it—what am I to do with ye next? Ye'll have to find some kind of a trade, for I'll never support ye in idleset. What do ye fancy ye'll be fit for? The pulpit? Na, they could never get diveenity into that blockhead. Him that the law of man whammles is no likely to do mauckle better by the law of God. What would ye make of hell? Wouldna your gorge rise at that? Na, there's no room for splaigers under the fower quarters of John Calvin. What else is there? Speak up. Have ye got nothing of your own?'

'Father, let me go to the Peninsula,' said Archie. 'That's all I'm fit for—to fight.'

'All? quo' he!' returned the Judge. 'And it would be enough too, if I thought it. But I'll never trust ye so near the French, you that's so Frenchifeed.'

'You do me injustice there, sir,' said Archie. 'I am loyal; I will not boast; but any interest I may have ever felt in the French—'

'Have ye been so loyal to me?' interrupted his father.

There came no reply.

'I think not,' continued Hermiston. 'And I would send no man to be a servant to the King, God bless him! that has proved such a shauchling son to his own faither. You can splairge here on Edinburgh street, and where's the hairm? It doesna play buff on me! And if there were twenty thousand eediots like yourself, sorrow a Duncan Jopp would hang the fewer. But there's no splairging possible in a camp; and if you were to go to it, you would find out for yourself whether Lord Well'n'ton approves of caapital punishment or not. You a sodger!' he cried, with a sudden burst of scorn. 'Ye auld wife, the sodgers would bray at ye like cuddies!'

As at the drawing of a curtain, Archie was aware of some illogicality in his position, and stood abashed. He had a strong impression, besides, of the essential valour of the old gentleman before him, how conveyed it would be hard to say.

'Well, have ye no other proposeetion?' said my lord again.

'You have taken this so calmly, sir, that I cannot but stand ashamed,' began Archie.

'I'm nearer voamiting, though, than you would fancy,' said my lord.

The blood rose to Archie's brow.

'I beg your pardon, I should have said that you had accepted my affront . . .

I admit it was an affront; I did not think to apologise, but I do, I ask your pardon; it will not be so again, I pass you my word of honour. . . . I should have said that I admired your magnanimity with—this—offender,' Archie concluded with a gulp.

'I have no other son, ye see,' said Hermiston. 'A bonny one I have gotten! But I must just do the best I can wi' him, and what am I to do? If ye had been younger, I would have wheepit ye for this rideeculous exhibeetion. The way it is, I have just to grin and bear. But one thing is to be clearly understood. As a faither, I must grin and bear it; but if I had been the Lord Advocate instead of the Lord Justice-Clerk, son or no son, Mr Erchibald Weir would have been in a jyle the night.'

Archie was no dominated. Lord Hermiston was coarse and cruel; and yet the son was aware of a bloomless nobility, an ungracious abnegation of the man's self in the man's office. At every word, this sense of the greatness of Lord Hermiston's spirit struck more home; and along with it that of his own impotence, who had struck—and perhaps basely struck—at his own father, and not reached so far as to have even nettled him.

'I place myself in your hands without reserve,' he said.

'That's the first sensible word I've had of ye the night,' said Hermiston 'I can tell ye, that would have been the end of it, the one way or the other; but it's better ye should come there yourself, than what I would have had to hirstle ye. Weel, by my way of it—and my way is the best—there's just the one thing it's possible that ye might be with decency, and that's a laird Ye'll be out of hairm's way at the least of it. If ye have to rowt, ye can rowt amang the kye; and the maist feck of the caapital punishment ye'll like to come across'll be guddling trouts Now, I'm for no idle lairdies; every man has to work, if it's only at peddling ballants; to work, or to be wheeped, or to be haangit. If I set ye down at Hermiston, I'll have to see you work that place the way it has never been workit yet; ye must ken about the sheep like a herd; ye must be my grieve there, and I'll see that I gain by ye. Is that understood?'

'I will do my best.' said Archie.

'Well, then, I'll send Kirstie word the morn, and ye can go yourself the day after,' said Hermiston. 'And just try to be less of an eediot!' he concluded, with a freezing smile, and turned immediately to the papers on his desk.

Robert Louis Stevenson (1850–94)
Weir of Hermiston

A Critic is Baited

Francis Jeffrey had two careers. Born in Edinburgh, and educated for the law at Glasgow and Oxford, his Whigism at first hindered his advancement after he had been called to the Scottish Bar in 1794. But he became Dean of the

Faculty of Advocates in 1829, and as Lord Advocate from 1830 onwards had a share in passing the Reform Bill insofar as it affected Scotland. He became Member of Parliament for Edinburgh in 1832, and in 1834 was elected to the Bench as Lord Jeffrey.

His literary career was as a critic and as editor of the 'Edinburgh Review' from 1802 until 1829. His failure to appreciate the poetry of the Romantics, and in particular his hostile critique on the work of the dying Keats, indicate the limitations of his taste.

His fellow lawyer Lockhart was a leading contributor to 'Blackwood's Magazine'. The work from which this extract is taken is a series of imaginary letters by a Welsh traveller in Scotland.

On looking into the room which had just received Lord Buchan, I observed him take his place among a row of musical cognoscenti, male and female, who already occupied a set of chairs disposed formally all around the centre of enchantment. By and bye, a young lady began thumping on the pianoforte, and I guessed, from the exquisite accompaniment of Mr Yaniewicz, that it was her design to treat us with some of the beautiful airs in the *Don Giovanni* of Mozart. Nothing, however, could be more utterly distressing than the mode in which the whole of her performance murdered that divine masterpiece, unless, indeed, it might be the nauseous sing-song of compliments which the ignorance or the politeness of the audience thundered out upon its conclusion.

After this blessed consummation had restored to us the free use of our limbs and tongues (I say free—for in spite of nods and whispers of rebuke administered by some of the Dowagers, our silence had never been much more complete than the music merited), I joined a small party which had gradually clustered around Mr Jeffrey, and soon found that the redoubtable critic had been so unfortunate as to fall into an ambush laid to entrap him by a skilful party of blue-stocking tirailleures. There he was pinioned up against the wall and listening with a greater expression of misery than I should have supposed to be compatible with his Pococurante disposition to the hints of one, the remarks of another, the suggestion of a third, the rebuke of a fourth, the dissertation of a fifth, and last, not least, in this cruel catalogue of inflictions, to the question of a sixth. 'Well now, Mr Jeffrey, don't you agree with me in being decidedly of opinion that Mr Scott is the true author of the *Tales of my Landlord*? O Lord! they're so like Mr Scott, some of the stories— one could almost believe one heard him telling them. Could not you do the same, Mr Jeffrey?' The shrug of ineffable derision which Mr Jeffrey vainly endeavoured to keep down in making some inaudible reply of two syllables to this did not a whit dismay another who forthwith began to ply him with query about the conduct of Lord Byron in deserting his wife—and whether or not he (Mr Jeffrey) considered it likely that Lord Byron had had himself (Lord Byron) in his eye in drawing the character of the Corsair—'and oh, now Mr Jeffrey, don't you think Gulnare so romantic a name? I wish I had been christened Gulnare. Can people change their names, Mr Jeffrey, without an estate?' 'Why, yes, Ma'am,' replied the critic—after a most malicious pause, 'by being married'.

John Gibson Lockhart (1794–1854)
Peter's Letters to his Kinsfolk

Bridge Builder and Road Maker

Thomas Telford (1752–1834), the son of an Eskdale shepherd in the Border hills, became perhaps the greatest bridge-builder and road-maker the world has known. During his long life, Britain abandoned her agricultural way of life and turned to industry.

Telford's canals and roads were the arteries of the manufacturing towns. In Scotland he provided roads, bridges and harbours, especially in the North-East, and he built the Caledonian Canal. The poet Robert Southey came North with Telford on the annual tour of inspection of his works in progress in 1819. Southey's brief portraits come respectively from the beginning, the middle and the final stages of the tour, which lasted from 17th August to 1st October.

Mr Telford arrived in the afternoon from Glasgow, so the whole party were now collected. There is so much intelligence in his countenance, so much frankness, kindness and hilarity about him, flowing from the never-failing well-spring of a happy nature, that I was upon cordial terms with him in five minutes . . .

Telford's is a happy life: everywhere making roads, building bridges, forming canals, and creating harbours—works of sure, solid, permanent utility; everywhere employing a great number of persons, selecting the most meritorious, and putting them forward in the world, in his own way. The plan upon which he proceeds in road-making is this: first to level and drain; then, like the Romans, to lay a solid pavement of large stones, the round or broad end downwards, as close as they can be set; the points are then broken off, and a layer of stones broken to about the size of walnuts, laid over them, so that the whole are bound together; over all a little gravel if it be at hand, but this is not essential. . . .

On the road we learnt that this was the last day of the races at Carlisle, and consequently that if we proceeded thither we should find no room. Of necessity therefore we stopt at Longtown, the cleanliness of the Inn there appearing to great advantage after the inns in Scotland. . . . Here we left Mr Telford, who takes the mail for Edinburgh. This parting company, after the thorough intimacy which a long journey produces between fellow travellers who like each other, is a melancholy thing. A man more heartily to be liked, more worthy to be esteemed and admired, I have never fallen in with; and therefore it is painful to think how little it is likely that I shall ever see him again—how certain that I shall never see *so* much.

Robert Southey (1774–1843)
Journal of a Tour in Scotland in 1819

The Painter Portrayed: Lord Cockburn

Lord Cockburn who, in 'Memorials of His Time', was himself a painter of word-portraits, is here the subject of a sketch by Lockhart.

It is, I think, a thousand pities that this gentleman should wear a wig in pleading; for when he throws off that incumbrance and appears in his natural shape nothing can be finer than the form of his head. He is quite bald, and his is one of those foreheads which, in spite of antiquity, are the better for wanting hair. Full of the lines of discernment and acumen immediately above the eyebrows, and over these again of the marks of imagination and wit, his skull rises highest of all in the region of veneration; and this structure, I apprehend, coincides exactly as it should do with the peculiarities of his mind and temperament. His face also is one of a very striking kind—pale and oval in its outline, having the nose perfectly aquiline, although not very large—the mouth rather wide, but nevertheless firm and full of meaning—the eyes beautifully shaped, in colour of a rich clear brown, and capable of conveying a greater range of expression than almost any I have seen. At first one sees nothing (I mean when he wears his wig) but a countenance of great shrewdness, and a pair of eyes that seem to be as keen as those of a falcon; but it is delightful to observe, when he gets animated with the subject of his discourse, how this countenance vibrates into harmony with the feelings he would convey, and how these eyes, above all, lose every vestige of their sharpness of glance, and are made to soften into the broadest and sweetest smile of good humour, or kindle with bright beams eloquent to overflowing of deepest sympathy in all the nobler and more mysterious workings of the human heart. It is when these last kinds of expression reveal themselves that one feels wherein Mr Cockburn is superior to all his more celebrated rivals. Of all the great pleaders of the Scottish Bar he is the only one who is capable of touching, with a bold and assured hand, the chords of feeling; who can, by one plain word and one plain look, convey the whole soul of tenderness, or appeal, with the authority of the true prophet, to a yet higher class of feelings which slumber in many bosoms, but are dead, I think, in none.

As every truly pathetic speaker must be, Mr Cockburn is a homely speaker; but he carries his homeliness to a length which I do not remember ever to have heard any other truly great speaker venture upon. He uses the Scottish dialect—always its music, and not unfrequently its words—quite as broadly as Mr Clerk, and perhaps, at first hearing, with rather more vulgarity of effect—for he is a young man, and I have already hinted that no young man can speak Scotch with the same impunity as an old one. Nevertheless I am sure no man who has witnessed the effect which Mr Cockburn produces upon a Scottish Jury would wish to see him alter anything in his mode of addressing them. He is the best teller of a plain story I ever heard. He puts himself completely upon a level with those to whom he speaks; he enters into all the feelings with which ordinary persons are likely to listen to the first statement from a partial mouth, and endeavours with all his might to destroy the impression of distrustfulness which he well knows he has to encounter. He utters no word which he is not perfectly certain his hearers understand, and he points out no inference before he has prepared the way for it by making his hearers understand perfectly how he himself has been brought to adopt it. He puts himself in the place of his audience; an obvious rule, no doubt; but in practice, above all others, difficult, and which it requires the skill of a very master in the knowledge of human nature to follow with precision. Instead of labouring, as most orators do, to impress on the minds of his audience a high notion of his own powers and attainments—this man seems to be anxious about nothing except to make them forget that he wears a gown, and to be satisfied that they are listening to a person who thinks, feels and judges exactly like themselves.

John Gibson Lockhart
Peter's Letters to his Kinsfolk

Thomas Carlyle Proposes

O Jane, Jane! Your half-jesting enumeration of your wooers does anything but make me laugh. A thousand and a thousand times have I thought the same thing in deepest earnest. That you have the power of making many good matches is no secret to me; nay it would be a piece of news for me to learn that I am not the very *worst* you ever thought of. And you add with the same tearful smile: 'Alas! we are married already.' Let me now cut off the interjection, and say simply what is true that we are *not* married already; and do you hereby receive further my distinct and deliberate declaration that it depends on yourself, and shall always depend on yourself whether we ever be married or not. God knows I do not say this in a vulgar spirit of defiance; which in our present relation were coarse and cruel; but I say it in the spirit of disinterested affection for you, and of fear for the reproaches of my own conscience should your fair destiny be marred by me, and you wounded in the house of your friends. Can you believe it with the good nature which I declare it deserves? It would absolutely give me satisfaction to know that you thought yourself entirely free of all ties to me, but those, such as they might be, of your own still-renewed election. It is reasonable and right that you should be concerned for your future establishment: look round with calm eyes on the persons you mention or may hereafter so mention; and if there is any one among them those Wife you had rather be—I do not mean whom you love better than me—but whose Wife, *all* things considered, you had rather be than mine, then *I* call upon you, I your Brother and Husband and friend thro' every fortune, to accept that man and leave me to my destiny. But if, on the contrary, my heart and my hand with the barren and perplexed destiny which promises to attend them, shall after all appear the *best* that this poor world can offer you, then take me and be content with me, and do not vex yourself with struggling to alter what is unalterable; to make a man who is poor and sick suddenly become rich and healthy. You tell me that you often weep when you think what is to become of us. It is unwise in you to weep: if you are reconciled to be *my Wife* (not the Wife of an ideal *me*, but the simple actual prosaic *me*), there is nothing frightful in the future. I look into it with more and more confidence and composure. Alas! Jane, you do not know me: it is not the poor, unknown, rejected Thomas Carlyle that you know, but the prospective rich, known and admired. I am reconciled to my fate as it stands or promises to stand ere long; I have pronounced the word *unpraised* in all its cases and numbers; and find nothing terrific in it, even when it means *unmonied*, and by the mass of his Majesty's subjects *neglected* or even partially *contemned*. I thank Heaven I have other objects in my eye than either *their* pudding or their breath. This comes of the circumstance that my Apprenticeship is ending, and yours still going on. O Jane! Jane! I could weep too: for I love you in my deepest heart.

These are hard sayings, my beloved Child; but I cannot spare them; and I hope, tho' better at first, they may not remain without wholesome influence. Do not get angry with me! Do not! I swear I deserve it not! Consider this as a true glimpse into my heart, which it is good that you contemplate with the gentleness and tolerance you have often shown me. I do not love you? If you judge it fit, I will clasp you to my bosom and my heart, as my wedded Wife, this very week: if you judge it fit, I will this very week forswear you forever.

Thomas Carlyle (1795–1881)
Letter to Jane Welsh dated 26th February 1826

Carlyle's Epitaph on His Wife

In her bright existence she had more sorrows than are common: but also a soft invincibility, a clearness of discernment, and a noble loyalty of heart, which are rare. For forty years she was the true and ever-loving helpmate of her husband: and by act and word unweariedly forwarded him, as none else could, in all of worth that he did or attempted. She died at London, 21st

April, 1866, suddenly snatched away from him, and the light of his life as if gone out.

Thomas Carlyle

John Galt Upon Himself

John Galt, one of Scotland's greatest novelists, was born at Irvine, Ayrshire, although when he was ten the family moved to Greenock, where he became in due course a Customs House clerk, and where later he entered business. He studied law at Lincoln's Inn, and in 1811 in Greece met Byron, whose life he later wrote. 'The Ayrshire Legatees' was followed by his masterpiece, 'Annals of the Parish' in 1821, then by 'The Steamboat', 'The Provost', 'Sir Andrew Wylie' and 'The Entail', all within a productive decade. They excel in the depiction of small-town Scots characters, and in the masterly use of colloquial Scots.

In 1825 he went to Canada as secretary of a land company, and two years later founded the town of Guelph. The town of Galt is named after him. Under suspiciously unfair circumstances, he found himself forced to resign in 1828. Broken in health, he eventually returned to Greenock, where he died after suffering a series of strokes.

The love of fame was my ruling passion, nor do I ever recollect being vain of any praise that my own judgment did not in some degree ratify as deserved. The consciousness of this has made me often assert, and I believe conscientiously, that those who thought me capable of being ruled by vanity mistook my character. I was much too sensitive to approbation ever to think of myself meritorious, a feeling the reverse of vanity, which always imagines itself entitled to more honour than it receives. But no man could inhale praise with a keener relish, and few so enterprising have received less of it in a substantial form. . . .

I was never vindictive, though often resentful; nor, when the indignation of the moment cooled, did I feel the sentiment of revenge,—the desire to inflict a vengeance for wrong. From the day I went to London till I returned a hopeless invalid, exceeded thirty years, and no man could, in his heart, accuse me, in that period, of having done any evil. When I left Scotland, I had not, I believe, an enemy.

Of the quality of my little talent I am more diffident to say what I think, because I am conscious of a great short-coming in endeavours to hopes. But my publications, in little more than twenty years, with long intervals of toilsome activity and of indisposition, prove my sedentory industry. I have never seen the clerk or amanuensis who could exhaust my assiduity, I might say, perhaps, whom I could not tire.

In my works I have not attained excellence, but some of them are considered not without merit, and those have made their way to their little prominence, without the advocacy of any associate, or any effort on my own part, directly or indirectly, to make them known. . . . Enough, however, of literature is before the public, by which my station as an author may be determined. But I shall not be justly dealt with if I am considered merely as a literary man: All that I have done ought to be taken into the estimate, and against many faults and blemishes many cares should be placed, disappoints, ill-requited struggles, and misfortunes of no common kind, with the depressing feeling, in calamitous circumstances, of how much I stood in the need of heartening from a friend.

But when my numerous books are forgotten, I shall yet be remembered. At a period when all the assurance of a provision for my family was announced to be a fallacy, I contrived the Canada Company, which will hereafter be spoken of among the eras of a nation destined to greatness. That project, flourishingly carried into effect, I not only projected, but established myself; and lands, now more extensive than all the arable land in Scotland are in process of settlement, and attractive to the super abundant population of the United Kingdom.

When having accomplished the establishment of so great an undertaking, I would have been satisfied; but my recompense was a mystery. However, convinced of my own rectitude I set myself to the renewal of my colonial schemes, and the British American Land Company is the result. Subsequently, when a little recovered from malady and depressions which induced me to give up my connections with that second project, the Secretary of State for the Colonies gave me leave to attempt the formation of a third Land Company, but which an indiscreet grant of a former Government rendered unavailing.

These endeavours placed me, I think, somewhat extra to common men; few so alone in the world and so environed with perplexities, have originated such undertakings with higher or with purer aims. . . . It is my fate to be thankful for less than I might expect, but a resolution to depend only on myself has often stifled complaint when perhaps it might have been justified, and I feel still my nature so unsubdued, that but for total lameness, and ever varying depression and infirmity, I see nothing that should not make me as independent in my conduct as other men.

John Galt 1779–1839
The Literary Life & Miscellanies

Livingstone on His Youth

David Livingstone was born at the village of Blantyre Works, Lanarkshire. He qualified both as a doctor and as a missionary with the London Missionary Society, who sent him not to China, as he had hoped, but to Africa. There, in many journeys of exploration, he won the admiration of the native tribes, and even of the Arab slavers, whom he opposed. Some of the discoveries of his later years were of considerable importance in the development of African hydrography. He whom Stanley called 'the strong and perseverant Scotch man', and whose own motto was: 'Fear God, and work hard', was by his inspiration a prime mover in raising European feeling against the slave trade to a pitch which dealt that evil practice its death blow.

The earliest recollection of my mother recalls a picture so often seen among the Scottish poor—that of the anxious housewife striving to make both ends meet. At the age of ten I was put into the factory as a 'piecer', to aid by my earnings in lessening her anxiety. With a part of my first week's wages I purchased Ruddiman's *Rudiments of Latin*, and pursued the study of that language for many years afterwards, with unabated ardour, at an evening school, which met between the hours of eight and ten. The dictionary part of my labours was followed up till twelve o'clock, or later, if my mother did not interfere by jumping up and snatching the books out of my hands. I had to be back in the factory by six in the morning, and continue my work, with intervals for breakfast and dinner, till eight o'clock at night. I read in this way many of the classical authors, and knew Virgil and Horace better at sixteen than I do now.

In reading, everything, that I could lay my hands on was devoured, except novels. Scientific works and books of travels were my especial delight; though my father, believing, with many of his time who ought to have known better, that the former were inimical to religion, would have preferred to have seen me poring over the *Cloud of Witnesses*, or Boston's *Fourfold State*. Our difference of opinion reached the point of open rebellion on my part, and his last application of the rod was on my refusal to peruse Wilberforce's *Practical Christianity*.

My reading while at work was carried on by placing the book on a portion of the spinning jenny, so that I could catch sentence after sentence as I passed at my work; I thus kept up a pretty constant study undisturbed by the roar of the machinery. To this part of my education I owe my present power of completely abstracting the mind from surrounding noises, so as to read and write with perfect comfort amidst the play of children or near the dancing and songs of savages. The toil of cotton-spinning, to which I was promoted in my nineteenth year, was excessively severe on a slim loose-jointed lad, but it was well paid for; and it enabled me to support myself while attending medical and Greek classes in Glasgow in winter, as also the divinity lectures of Dr Wardlaw, by working with my hands in summer. I never received a farthing of aid from any one, and should have accomplished my project of going to China as a medical missionary in the course of time by my own efforts, had not some friends advised me joining the London Missionary Society on account of its prefectly unsectarian character. It 'sends neither episcopacy, nor presbyterianism, nor independency, but the gospel of Christ to the heathen.' This exactly agreed with my ideas of what a Missionary Society ought to do; but it was not without a pang that I offered myself, for it was not quite agreeable to one accustomed to work his own way to become in a measure dependent on others. And I would not have been much put about, though my offer had been rejected.

Looking back now on that life of toil, I cannot but feel thankful that it formed such a material part of my early education; and, were it possible, I should like to begin life over again in the same lowly style, and to pass through the same hardy training.

David Livingstone (1813–73)

A Highland Nobleman: The Duke of Athole

When the 6th Duke of Athole died in 1864, his obituary was written for 'The Scotsman' by Dr John Brown, and later included in his 'Horae Subsecivae'.

He was a living, a strenuous protest, in perpetual kilt, against the civilization, the taming, the softening of mankind. He was essentially wild. His virtues were these of human nature in the rough and unreclaimed, open and insubdued as the Moor of Rannoch. He was a true autochthon, terrigena,—a son of the soil,—as rich in local colour, as rough in the legs, and as hot at the heart, as prompt and hardy, as heathery as a gorcock. Courage, endurance, staunchness, fidelity and warmth of heart, simplicity, and downrightness were his staples; and with them he attained to a power in his own region and among his own people quite singular. The secret of this was his truth and his pluck, his kindliness and his constancy. Other noblemen put on the kilt at the season, and do their best to embrown their smooth knees for six weeks, returning them to trousers and to town; he lived in his kilt all the year long, and often slept soundly in it and his plaid among the brackens; and not sparing himself, he spared none of his men or friends,—it was the rigour of the game,—it was Devil take the hindmost. Up at all hours, out all day and all night, often without food,—with nothing but the unfailing pipe,—there he was, stalking the deer in Glen Tilt or across the Gaick moors, or rousing before daybreak the undaunted otter among the alders of the Earn, the Isla, or the Almond; and if in his pursuit, which was fell as any hound's, he got his hand into the otter's grip, and had its keen teeth meeting in his palm, he let it have its will till the pack came up,—no flinching, almost as if without the sense of pain. It was this gameness and thoroughness in whatever he was about that charmed his people,—charmed his very dogs; and so it should.

There may be better pursuits for a man and a duke than otter-hunting, and crawling like a huge caterpillar for hours across bogs and rocks after a royal stag; but there may be worse; and it is no small public good to keep up the relish for and the exercise of courage, perseverance, readiness of mind and resource, hardihood,—it is an antidote against the softness and the luxury of a dainty world.

But he was not only a great hunter, and an organiser and vitaliser of hunting, he was a great breeder. He lived at home, was himself a farmer, and knew all his farmers and all their men; had lain out at night on the Badenoch heights with them, and sat in their bothies and smoked with them the familiar pipe. But he also was, as we have said, a thorough breeder, especially of Ayrshire cattle. It was quite touching to see this fierce, restless, intense man—*impiger, acer, iracundus*—at the great Battersea show doating upon and doing everything for his meek-eyed, fine-limbed, sweet-breathed kine. It was the same with other stock, though the Ayrshires were his pets to the end.

Then he revived and kept up the games of the country,—the throwing the hammer, and casting the mighty caber; the wild, almost naked, hillrace; the Ghillie-Callum [sword dance] and the study of the eldritch, melancholy pipes, to which, we think, distance adds not a little enchantment; all the natural fruits of human industry—the dyes, the webs, the hose—of the district. There might be much for Adam Smith and the Times to laugh at in all this, but it had and did its own good; and it made him a living centre,—a king. And who that ever was there does not remember the wonderful ball that closed the Athole Gathering, when delicate London girls were endued with miraculous spunk, when reel succeeded reel like the waves of the sea,—all innocent, and all happy, and all light of heel,—and when the jocund morn, far up in heaven, saw them 'doun by the Tummel and banks o' the Garry', or across into Lochaber by the grim Ben Aulder and utmost Dalnaspidal.

Let no man speak evil of those cordial and once-a-year jovialities. They did no harm to those who brought no harm with them, and they left the memory of honest mirth—of health and youth—rejoicing after its last Reel of Tulloch or Houlachan, to immerse itself in the loveliness of that nature which is the art of God, and go home to its bath, its breakfast, and its bed.

Dr John Brown (1810–82)
Horae Subsecivae

Robert Louis Stevenson In Youth

He was a fragile-looking youth of about eighteen, with a very noticeable stoop of the shoulders, and a poorly-developed chest, which suggested constitutional delicacy: and this impression was confirmed by his long hair, which made his face look emaciated. But as a set-off to these signs of physical weakness he had eyes that were quick-glancing and observant and brimful of humour, or, I should rather say, of banter. He had a large but expressive mouth, which led one to anticipate incisive speech: though in saying this

I am very likely reading into this first interview impressions derived from future intercourse . . .

At the University he enrolled as a student in the Greek class (Professor Blackie's), and then attended as seldom as possible. In the mathematical class, absenteeism could not be so easily practised, for here the discipline was strict. It began to be whispered that he would have himself to blame if his name did not appear on the Honours list: and this, he said, led to his conversion for the remainder of the session. His friends twitted him on his sudden devotion to triangles and trigonometry, and he said: 'I know how it would delight my father if even the shadow of the Mathematical Honours list fell on me, and I want to please him' . . .

The truth is that Stevenson never was a University student in the usual sense of the word. Not only was his attendance at classes intermittent, but he followed no regular curriculum. Then he took very little part in the work of the classes which he did attend. He used to sit on a far-back bench, pencil in hand and with a note-book before him, and looking as if he were taking notes of the lectures. But in reality he took no notes, and seldom listened to the lectures. 'I prefer,' he used to say, 'to spend the time in writing original nonsense of my own.' He always carried in his pocket a note-book, which he sometimes called his 'Book of Original Nonsense'; and not only during the class-hour, but at all odd times, he jotted down thoughts and fancies in prose and verse. Of course he generally gave class exams the go-by. And thus it came to pass that, except among his intimates, he was regarded as an idler. An idler, however, he never was. His time and energy, his heart and soul, were devoted to literature; and while he seemed to outsiders an idler, he was reading French and English classics, and filling note-books with attempts to imitate them. He was once spoken to seriously about taking a University degree. 'If literature,' said the friend, 'is to be your pursuit, a degree will be all but indispensable.' But he would not be persuaded. 'I would sooner commit to memory,' he said, 'the long bead-roll of names in the early chapters of the Book of Chronicles than cram for a degree-exam.' And so the matter ended.

Archibald Bisset
in Masson's *I Can Remember Robert Louis Stevenson*

Stevenson and Music

There is an unconscious pathos in Stevenson's fondness for his flageolet. He played it so badly, so haltingly, and as his letters show, he was always poking fun at himself in regard to it. Certainly, no one would get the impression that he was possessed of a very real love for music or that its deprivation left unanswered one of the most insistent appeals of his nature Yet

I believe that in a certain sense his whole life was starved in one of its essentials.

Looking back, I can recall how constantly he spoke of music. He would recur again and again to the dozen or so operas he had heard in his youth, repeating the names of the singers—all of them German mediocrities—in a zest of recollection; and he would talk with the same warmth and eagerness of the few great instrumentalists he had heard in London concerts. And it was always, of course, with an air of finality, as of a man speaking of past and gone experiences that could never be repeated. He bought an extraordinary amount of printed music—Chopin, Grieg, Bach, Beethoven, Mozart,—and would pore over it for hours at a time, trying here and there, and with endless repetitions, to elucidate it with his flageolet.

It was amazing the amount of pleasure he got out of the effort. The doleful, whining little instrument was one of his most precious relaxations. He played it persistently, and even attempted to write compositions of his own for it. He studied counterpoint; he was constantly transposing, simplifying, and rearranging music to bring it within the scope of his trumpery 'pipe'; the most familiar sound in Vailima was that strange wailing and squeaking that floated down from his study. To us at the time it all seemed very amusing, and Stevenson laughed as heartily as any one at our raillery But to me now it takes on a different aspect and my eyes are misty at the recollection.

At no time in his life had he ever musical friends. All of them except Henley were positively indifferent to music. Yet some humble little professional pianist, violinist, or singer, had Stevenson been fortunate enough to have had such an acquaintance, would have gladdened and enriched his life beyond measure. If only, indeed, he might have known intimately some of his own great musical contemporaries—Jean or Edouard de Reszke, for instance—Sarasate or Paderewski! Instead, he had nothing but his pitiful flageolet and those great stocks of music with no key to unlock them. The longing was there, the hunger, but how poor was the satisfaction!

To-day, when I see on every side those wonderful mechanical devices for the reproductions of vocal and instrumental music, I feel an almost unbearable regret that they have come too late for Stevenson . . . What a difference, for instance, they would have made to Stevenson, and what a surpassing joy and solace they would have been to him.

But all he had was his little flageolet and the far-away memories of his youth.

Lloyd Osbourne (1868–1947)
Introduction to the Vailima Edition of Stevenson

Stevenson in Samoa

I have seen him in all moods. I have seen him sitting on my table, dangling his long legs in the air, chatting away in the calmest manner possible; and I have seen him, becoming suddenly agitated, jump from that table and stalk to and fro across the floor like some wild forest animal, to which he has, indeed, already been compared. His face would glow and his eyes would flash, darkening, lighting, scintillating, hypnotizing you with their brilliance and the burning fires within. In calm they were eyes of strange beauty, with an expression that is almost beyond the power of pen to describe. 'Eyes half alert, half sorrowful,' said our common friend, Mr Carruthers, once; and I have neither read nor heard anything which seems to approach so near the mark. They carried in them a strange mixture of what seemed to be at once the sorrow and joy of life, and there appeared to be a haunting sadness in their very brightness . . .

Stevenson rose, as a rule, at six o'clock, though he was up, often enough, as early as four, writing by lamp-light. He wrote at all hours and at all times. Oftentimes he would come down town on 'Jack' and tell me he had got 'stuck' in some passage of a story and was out in search of an inspiration. 'The orange is squeezed out', he would say. He used generally to wear a little white yachting cap worth about twenty-five cents. As he was very thin and boyish in appearance, the cap suited him. I never saw him in a stiff shirt nor a stand-up collar in my life. Up at Vailima they all went about in their bare feet, except when expecting guests, and generally looked about half-dressed. When Stevenson came into Apia, he still looked only half-dressed. He always came down with a soft shirt on and generally white flannel trousers, sometimes with a red sash tied about the waist. He was very careless about his personal adornment, just 'a man of shirt-sleeves'; and his clothes invariably had the appearance of being a misfit, because of his extremely slight frame . . .

Stevenson was a charming host, and it mattered not whether he was receiving Europeans or natives. Everybody felt thoroughly at home at Vailima. There were invariably several dinner-parties there when a British or American warship put into port. In him the navy had a great champion, and he used to have a printed list of the warships that had been to Apia fixed up in front of his house, and every succeeding ship that arrived duly had its name printed there. To meet the officers from these ships a number of friends would be invited to Vailima, for the afternoon and evening. While dinner was being prepared the guests would sit on the wide veranda, smoking and talking, and an 'appetizer' would be handed round. Those were happy times. Stevenson the writer, the talker, the charmer, was in his element. He loved to have friends around him. Over the dinner plates he entertained the company with his anecdotes. But he never monopolized the conversation; he was as ready a listener as he was a ready talker. After dinner, music, or more smoking and more talking on the veranda—and coffee par excellence— coffee the sugar in which had first of all been soaked in burnt brandy!

H. J. Moor (b. 1854)
With Stevenson in Samoa

Stevenson's 'Supressio Veri'

I used to criticize the resolute, aggressive optimism of his philosophy, and accuse him of a certain deliberate *suppressio veri*—a tendency to cook his accounts with Destiny. One evening I had been talking in this strain, and saying, I suppose, that he did not make enough allowance for the amount of sheer boredom involved in existence. He was pacing up and down the drawing-room at Skerryvore, with his swift, somewhat feline tread, his arm in a sling, and a ragged cigarette in his fingers. As soon as he heard the word 'boredom', he turned sharply round upon me, and said with slow, impressive emphasis: 'I never was bored in my life!' I might have retorted, but probably didn't, that this was a fine example of the *suppressio veri* wherewith I reproached him.

William Archer (1865–1924)
in Masson's *I Can Remember Robert Louis Stevenson*

Keir Hardie

I first met Keir Hardie about the year 1887 or 1888. ... . I first saw him at his home in Cumnock ...

He was then about thirty years of age, I should judge, but old for his age. His hair was already becoming thin at the top of his head, and receding from the temples. His eyes were not very strong. At first sight he struck you as a remarkable man. There was an air of great benevolence about him, but his face showed the kind of appearance of one who has worked hard and suffered, possibly from inadequate nourishment in his youth. He was active and alert, though not athletic. Still, he appeared to be full of energy, and as subsequent events proved, he had an enormous power of resistance against long, hard and continued work. I should judge him to have been of a very nervous and high strung temperament. All that time, and I believe up to the end of his life, he was an almost ceaseless smoker, what is called in the United States 'a chain smoker'. He was a very strict teetotaller and remained so to the end, but he was no bigot on the subject and was tolerant of faults in the weaker brethren.

Nothing in his address or speech showed his want of education in his youth. His accent was of Ayrshire. I think he took a pride in it in his ordinary conversation. He could, however, to a great extent throw this accent aside, but not entirely. When roused and excited in public or private speech it was always perceptible. His voice was high-pitched but sonorous and very far carrying ... He never used notes, and I think never prepared a speech, leaving all to the inspiration of the moment. This suited his natural, unforced methods of speaking admirably. He had all the charm and some of the defects of this system. Thus, though he rose higher than I think it is possible to rise when a speech is prepared and committed to memory, he was also subject to very flat passages when he was not, so to speak, inspired. His chief merits as a speaker were, in my opinion, his homeliness, directness and sincerity; and his demerits were a tendency to redundancy and length, and a total lack of humour very rare in an Ayrshire Scot.

This was to me curious, as he had a considerable vein of pathos. He always opened his speeches in these days with 'Men', and finished with 'Now, men!'. This habit, which he also followed in his private speech—when two or three were gathered together—used to give great offence to numbers of paternal Baillies, councillors and other worthy men who had not much mental culture and failed to detect Hardie's sincerity, and took the familiar 'men' as something too familiar for their conversing.

Hardie's dress at this time was almost always a navy blue serge suit with a bowler hat. His hair was never worn long and his beard was well-trimmed and curly. Later on, to the regret of the 'judicious' he affected a different style of dressing entirely foreign to his custom when a little known man.

R. B. Cunninghame-Graham (1852–1936)
from *A Biography of J. Keir Hardie* by William Stewart

The Great McGonagall

William McGonagall (1830–1902?), born in Edinburgh, the son of an Irish weaver, spent most of his life in Dundee. He has been described as 'the only truly memorable bad poet'. In Scotland, his works sell in quantity second only to those of Burns, and not all readers appear to be aware of any marked qualitative difference. Neil Munro, the novelist born in Inveraray, Argyll, is remembered not only for such romantic tales as 'John Splendid' and 'Doom Castle', but as the creator of Para Handy, the skipper of 'The Vital Spark' Clyde puffer. His description of the sad baiting of McGonagall comes from a volume of autobiographical reminiscences originally published in the Glasgow 'Evening News', of which he was for a time editor.

Before 'the poet McGonagall' becomes wholly a creature of myth, his lineaments forgotten, his birthplace as much a subject of controversy as that of Homer; his authentic works confused with those of a score of contemporary imitators, and his character the subject of debate in suburban Literary Societies, I feel constrained to describe his first—and probably his last—public appearance in Glasgow.

The historian of the future will look in vain through newspaper files for any mention of this event. It was strictly incognito the poet came to Glasgow, to which he was not entirely a stranger, as may be gathered from his collected works.

On the occasion, I refer to, however, he came by special request, and for a specific purpose—to give a lecture on 'The Parlous State of Scottish Poetry,' with illustrations from his own poems and songs. It was in the year of the Diamond Jubilee—1897. What was called a Jubilee Ode of his had been widely quoted in the Press. One stanza, in particular, seemed to concentrate in itself not only the history of a great epoch, but most of the peculiar qualities of the McGonagallian muse.

For sixty glorious, magnificent years has reigned our noble Queen.
And her reign it has been the most beautiful that ever has been seen;
Since she went upon the Throne the world has grown.
For instance, we've seen the rise and progress of the bicycle, the telegraph,
    and the telephone.
Oh, Britons, upon this day of Jubilee let your voices rise in praise.
Sing 'God Save the Queen,' and all manner of lays.
Let the poets be not backward, too, in singing with great glee
In the year 1897 from Land's End to Dundee.

Such were the lines which induced a pseudo-Literary Society in Dennistoun, mainly composed of Forfarshire and Perthshire natives, to invite the poet of Dundee to a symposium in a licensed restaurant.

As a matter of fact, McGonagall never wrote the Jubilee Ode. It was composed in a Glasgow newspaper office by a townsman of his whose occasional recreation it was to parody the bard and gleefully watch with what rapidity a 'spoof' McGonagall lyric would go round the semi-comic Press of Great Britain.

The Jubilee Ode had been exceptionally popular with English newspapers; it even passed muster with Dr William Robertson Nicoll, who quoted it in the *British Weekly*. McGonagall himself was quite in ignorance whence such fictitious poems came, but never made any fuss about their being accredited to him; indeed, I suspect not a few of them of being reprinted afterwards by himself.

I went to the Dennistoun entertainment as a guest of Robert Ford, the editor of *Vagabond Songs and Ballads of Scotland*, and author, himself, of many poems and readings. He was chairman. McGonagall, who had been paid a fee for his attendance and his expenses, turned up in the most fantastic Highland costume, with a long feather in his bonnet, and with an old Volunteer officer's sword in lieu of a claymore.

Of middle height, shaven and puckered visage, long lyart locks, and a general aspect of being kippered like an East Coast herring, he looked as if deliberately made up for a part in *opera bouffe*. On his entry there was vociferous cheering, which he gravely acknowledged by repeated bowing. There was not the slightest evidence that he suspected any irony in the ovation. I already felt a little sorry for the poor old man, and wished I hadn't come. It was not a harmless, innocent 'character' I had been expecting, but rather a crafty merry-andrew deliberately playing up to the conception his employers for the time being had formed of him.

There was, I think, a supper of sorts to begin with; certainly there were toasts, all of a loyal or literary hue. At the start of the proceedings the Secretary read a series of telegrams and letters of apology for absence, ostensibly from some of the most distinguished literary men in England—such as the poet laureate and Rudyard Kipling. All of them expressed the loftiest admiration for the guest of the evening, who murmured his appreciation of these compliments.

Every speech of the evening was on the same note of fulsome adulation of McGonagall; the Chairman's was a masterpiece of sly mockery which would have been unbearably cruel were it not evident that its victim was hypnotized by the unaccustomed glory of these proceedings and incapable of realizing that his leg was being pulled.

The genius of Robert Burns was admitted, but only as secondary to that of 'the Bard of the Tay.' Shakespeare himself, it was agreed, had done nothing finer than the 'Jubilee Ode' and many other odes and lyrics which assured the guest of the evening of immortal fame.

In his reply to all this nonsense McGonagall forgot all about his lecture on 'The Parlous State of Scottish Poetry.' The speeches had evidently shown him that it was not so parlous as he had thought. While not disputing the verdict of the company that his own works were all that had been said of them, he must also plead that Shakespeare undoubtedly 'wrote a quite good poem.' So did Burns. What distinguished his (McGonagall's) poems from all others was that they were read and approved of by the highest in the land.

Thereupon, the guest of the evening, by request, proceeded to narrate how he had on one occasion made his way to London to pay his homage to Queen Victoria, from whom he had had a communication expressing her gratitude for a few examples of his verse which he had sent to her. Only the stupidity of a lackey at Her Majesty's front door had prevented him from seeing her in person.

The rest of the programme was made up of recitations by the bard of his own most notable poems. For this purpose the tables had to be removed, and an open space left in the middle of the hall. There was a perfect fury in his declamation; when it came to patriotic sentiment, the sword was drawn; the poet plunged up and down the room, and chased visionary Englishmen into the corners with thrusts from his trusty blade. Elocution was not his strong point, but he certainly knew all about broadsword play as it used to be practised in penny geggies.

Alas! the end of the evening was an anti-climax. Of all the company, probably McGonagall was the only total abstainer. To that extent he had the advantage of his gibers. There came a moment when this derisive joke was carried too far, and suspicions were roused in the poor old man that he was the butt of the company.

In a final speech he was made aware that before he left he was to get a presentation. With agreeable expectancy, he stood up to receive it at the chairman's hands, and there was suddenly produced for him on a salver, an enormous sausage of many pounds weight, all decorated with ribbons! . . . I felt painfully ashamed of myself.

It was pathetic to see the instant disillusionment of one, who a moment before was unsuspicious, at the fact that he was merely a laughing-stock for a convivial company of dubious taste. There was a tremor in his voice when he protested that he felt hurt and insulted by such a presentation as certainly no other poet in history had been offered. It took a little while and much diplomacy to soothe him down; convince him that the Brobdingnagian sausage was not stuffed with sawdust, and was as sensible an offering to a poet as the laureate's cask of Canary wine.

A few days later McGonagall wrote back from Dundee expressing his contrition for his touchiness about the sausage, which he now handsomely declared was the best he had ever tasted.

Neil Munro (1864–1930)

Scots Comic: Tommy Lorne

The funniest Scotsman who has appeared on the stage in my time was undoubtedly the late, great Tommy Lorne. Words cannot express the effect that this tall, gaunt figure with the craggy features and the big hands had on his audiences. Unlike most comedians, he was funny even off stage. I once saw him walk across Renfield Street from the Pavilion Theatre to Green's Playhouse. He was well dressed in a coat and a lounge suit. But, as he walked these few yards, everybody in his vicinity started smiling.

Tommy Lorne's real name was Hugh Corcoran, and early in his life he worked in Blochairn Steelworks in the drawing-office. He was a gangling, pleasant boy, but not overly interested in the work that was given him. On one occasion when the whole staff were working late, my father heard odd sounds coming from the drawing-office. He went along to investigate and found that Hugh Corcoran and another boy were practising tap dancing . . .

The change of name came about this way. Corcoran started his stage career with various partners under various names, but the time came when he got the chance to go on as a comic in his own right . . . At this time he greatly admired an English comic called Tom E. Hughes, so he decided he should be called Tom E. Lorne.

This name was 'phoned over to the bill-printer who interpreted it as Tommy Lorne and, after he'd seen it on the posters, Hugh Corcoran decided to leave it at that . . .

Tommy Lorne was an enormous success at the Princess's. It got so that he just had to walk on the stage and look at a bit of scenery and he had the audience in convulsions. He worked hard at the job of being a comic, and he was always going to odd places in Glasgow to get ideas for scenes and sketches. He took up popular Glasgow phrases at the time. When he cried in his creeking voice, 'In the name of the wee man!' or 'Ah'll get ye!', foreigners in the audience were amazed at the Glasgow reaction. Latterly he had only to say 'In the name!' and Glaswegians were prostrate.

Jack House (b. 1906)
Pavement in the Sun

A Writer at Work: Sir Compton Mackenzie

One of the most colourful figures on the Scottish scene through much of the twentieth century was Sir Compton Mackenzie (1883-1972) whose achievement takes in novels which are already classics, like 'Carnival' (1912) and 'Guy and Pauline' (1914) at one end of the literary spectrum; a range of popular comic novels on Scottish themes, of which 'Whisky Galore' (1947) is the best known since it was made into a film; and a remarkable autobiography in ten volumes, 'Octave'. The following word-picture of Mackenzie is by his fellow-novelist Eric Linklater, whose own picaresque novels like 'Juan in America' (1931) and 'Ripeness is All' (1935) themselves reflect a peculiarly Scottish variety of imaginative energy.

The toil of making books is so heavy—a persistent autogamy, the imagery of the male meeting twice-nightly female organization in the one system; the begetting, the load of pregnancy, the father's anxious fear, and parturition all burdened on a brain conceiving while still in labour—the toil is heavy, and few authors can spare for their own lives much of the colour, the adventuring, and vivacity of their work. There are exceptions, however: Byron the most redoubtable, Blunt in his Arab saddle, d'Annunzio well known, Graham the hidalgo, and like a plume on Scotland's dusky bonnet, Compton Mackenzie. As Byron fetched from the wild blood of the Gordons his excess of spirit, so I think could Mackenzie claim from the Seaforths a nimiety of Highland fervour. I have seen portraits of their chiefs that reproduce the dark and birdlike quality of his countenance. The broad but eager brow, the jutting nose, the blackness, and the lean asperity of the jaw were there. But in Mackenzie—what the Seaforth portraits lack—is the actor's gay but enervating mobility. To see him weary is to see a lean and anguished priest; to see him well and in unfriendly company is to see him harsh and arrogant; and to see him as a host, when entertainment is his aim, is to see a varying mask of all the emotions he may elect to show, the many characters he may choose to mime. To all who admit his virtue and his charm, he is the very top and flourish of good company.

His habit, however, is disconcertingly nocturnal. He sleeps by day because to be awake in sunlight would be, for him, an irresistible temptation to botanize, zoologize, nephelologize, and do no work. When I arrived in Barra he woke before his usual time—indeed quite early in the afternoon—and I saw him first in a lounging-suit, old rose in colour with lapels of a darker hue, of a thickened silk material. But this was not dandyism, for beneath it were pyjamas and a Fair Isle tunic most violently moresque: he was two days unshaven, and his hair hung like a mother raven shot upon the nest. His clothes resemble the adjectives in a poem by Gerard Manley Hopkins: chosen for their texture and colour, and often most arbitrarily joined.

He works with the persistence of a fanatic in circumstances of considerable luxury. In a high-backed padded chair in the corner of the room, a mere closet of a room but papered with gold, he will sit through the night under a funnelled lamp, the rest of the closet an aureate dusk, a hundred or so books of reference within easy reach; while in the adjacent room, the connecting door wide open, one of his secretaries . . . will feed a pair of enormous gramophones with continuous records, progressing in a single night, as may happen, from a symphony by Brahms, through a little César Franck and a few Beethoven quartets, to a Mozart concerto, and before the dawn an hour or so of Sibelius.

This arduous but mollified routine he will maintain, if he is alone, for weeks on end; but company is a temptation to which he yields. His conversation, like the delta of the Brahmaputra, flows from enormous reservoirs and will cover unpredictably far tracts of country.

Eric Linklater (b. 1899)
The Man on my Back

Mentor and Tormentor: C. M. Grieve

C. M. Grieve, alias Hugh MacDiarmid, was born at Langholm, Dumfries-shire, in 1892, where his English master was the composer Francis George Scott. After spending years in journalism in Montrose and London, his first volumes of poetry employing the Lowland Scots tongue, braced in vocabulary with words from Middle Scots and other sources (Lallans), were published; 'Sangschaw' (1925), 'Pennywheep' (1926) and 'A Drunk Man Looks at the Thistle' (1926): volumes which, a quarter of a century or so later, were to establish his reputation not only as one of Scotland's three greatest poets along with Dunbar and Burns, but a poet fully able to stand comparison with Yeats and Eliot. Though he spent the Second World War years working in and around Glasgow and his later years near Biggar, in Lanarkshire, during the 'thirties he settled in Shetland. William Power, a genial essayist and journalist of the between-the-war years, pictured MacDiarmid during this Shetland period.

And now we fare north to *Ultima Thule*, which has not even a telephone line to the mainland. There, on the island of Whalsay, surveying from the top of the map the Scotland of which he has for years been the mentor and tormentor, dwells Christopher Murray Grieve, better known as Hugh MacDiarmid . . .

Grieve came on the scene at a time when it was plain that Scotland would have to choose between national extinction and an enlargement of national consciousness. It is all very well to say that in identifying himself with this issue Grieve was departing from his proper business of lyrical self-expression; the issue was part of his inspiration, and Grieve could not, any more than Burns, dissociate himself from Scotland. His impulse was to express that which was high, profound, searching, bold and subtle; he could not do this except as a poet and a Scot . . .

Grieve has been a wild hitter at times . . . From some of his writings one might picture him as a truculently arrogant person. He is the very reverse. Unmistakably the genius, with tensely thoughtful features and smouldering, deep-set eyes . . . he is simple, modest, and friendly, and almost rustically Scots. His one piece of *panache* is the admirable habit of wearing a kilt and a plaid, both of bright tartan.

William Power (1873–1951)
Should Auld Acquaintance . . .

Hugh MacDiarmid

Physically he is a magnificent mouse of a man. I remember him best as he used to sit, sagged back in front of his fireplace, his legs plaited together and curled beneath his armchair, one hand, the left, lying indolently beside him while the right one gripped his black pipe. Then he would bend down forwards to tap out ash on the hearth and, as he did so, his head would turn sideways towards where I sat. That head looked huge. The hair curled up from it like the grey-brown smoke of a volcano and, though his expression betrayed no more than a quick slant of curiosity, the force of the man became apparent. The features were small and squeezed into the lower half of the face, the brow high and myriad wrinkled, the nose a sharp jut forwards, the eyes sunk in deep sockets as though eroded by a surfeit of sight; the whole composition denied his posture of repose. Then, at last, when he rose and walked across the room with that swift jerky gait of his, talking all the while, as though keeping time to his footsteps, in a learned staccato, one would glimpse the vigour that had written his twenty-odd books and his millions of words of invective.

By the time I met Hugh MacDiarmid he was over fifty but his physical appearance had probably changed very little since those days some twenty years before when he had published his first book of Scots lyrics, *Sangschaw*. At that time, he was already employed in the exercise of his vituperative genius. It was directed against such minor and local figures as, among others, Sir Hugh Roberton, the conductor of the Orpheus Choir. Since then he had enlarged the scope of his attacks, but they were still bitter and violent. The poems of those years possessed, however, an unusual delicacy and established him as the greatest lyric poet in Lowland Scots since at least the time of Burns.

Burns Singer (1928–64)
Scarlet Eminence

For Hugh MacDiarmid

You've walked on the waters quieter than God,
just listening
for Leviathan whudding his tail,
or the infinitesmal sound
of plancton,
like midges hung in still air.

When I put my ear to the great conch of your words
they bawl and hiss
of a universe in labour;
and hush to a woman's sigh
and quiet
when her waters break for a birth.

Light glowers off the darkness of your sea,
breaks up in
a lowe o' fun, and gathers
again, endlessly reforming
over amoebic depths
where life's too wee for hearing—

over slums where your moving surface refracts a heaven
of stony stars,
or admits a glimmer
of sun; in its swell
draws up a million
delicate lives and deaths.

You never whored the moon, naming her seas
Tranquillity—
but in the neep of our times gave
bloodstream, clenched brain,
your own miraculous tide
to her reflective light.

Morven Cameron (b. 1930)

A SHEAF OF BALLANTS

Edward, Edward

'Why does your brand sae drap wi' bluid,
             Edward, Edward,
Why does your brand sae drap wi' bluid,
    And why sae sad gang yee O?'
'O I hae killed my hawk sae guid,
             Mither, mither,
O I hae killed my hawk sae guid,
    And I had nae mair bot he O.'

'Your hawk's bluid was never sae reid,
             Edward, Edward,
Your hawk's bluid was never sae reid,
    My deir son, I tell thee O.'
'O I hae killed my reid-roan steid,
             Mither, mither,
O I hae killed my reid-roan steid,
    That erst was sae fair and free O.'

'Your steid was auld, and ye hae gat mair,
             Edward, Edward,
Your steid was auld, and ye hae gat mair,
    Some other dule ye dree O.'
'O I hae killed my fathir deir,
             Mither, mither,
O I hae killed my fathir deir,
    Alas, and wae is me O!'

'And whatten penance wul ye dree for that,
             Edward, Edward?
And whatten penance wul ye dree for that?
    My deir son, now tell me O.'
'I'll set my feet in yonder boat,
             Mither, mither,
I'll set my feet in yonder boat,
    And I'll fare over the sea O.'

16   241

'And what wul ye do wi' your towers and your ha',
  Edward, Edward.
And what wul ye do wi' your towers and your ha',
  That were sae fair to see O?'
'I'll let thame stand till they doun fa',
  Mither, mither,
I'll let thame stand till they doun fa',
  For here never mair maun I be O.'

'And what wul ye leave to your bairns and your wife,
  Edward, Edward?
And what wul ye leave to your bairns and your wife,
  When ye gang over the sea O?'
'The warld's room, let them beg through life,
  Mither, mither,
The warld's room, let them beg through life,
  For hame never mair wul I see O.'

'And what wul ye leave to your ain mither deir,
  Edward, Edward?
And what wul ye leave to your ain mither deir?
  My deir son, now tell me O.'
'The curse of hell frae me sall ye beir,
  Mither, mither,
The curse of hell frae me sall ye beir,
  Sic counseils ye gave to me O.'

Anonymous

Kinmont Willie

O have ye na heard o' the fause Sakelde?
  O have ye na heard o' the keen Lord Scroope?
How they hae ta'en bauld Kinmont Willie,
  On Haribee to hang him up?

Had Willie had but twenty men,
  But twenty men as stout as he,
Fause Sakelde had never the Kinmont ta'en,
  Wi' eight score in his companie.

They band his legs beneath the steed,
  They tied his hands behind his back;
They guarded him, fivesome on each side,
  And they brought him ower the Liddel-rack.

They led him thro' the Liddel-rack,
  And also thro' the Carlisle sands;
They brought him to Carlisle castell,
  To be at my Lord Scroope's commands.

'My hands are tied, but my tongue is free,
  And whae will dare this deed avow?
Or answer by the Border law?
  Or answer to the bauld Buccleuch?'

'Now haud thy tongue, thou rank reiver!
  There's never a Scot will set thee free:
Before ye cross my castle yate,   [gate
  I trow ye shall take farewell o' me.'

'Fear na ye that, my lord,' quo' Willie:
  'By the faith o' my body, Lord Scroope,' he said,
'I never yet lodged in a hostelrie
  But I paid my lawing before I gaed.'

Now word is gane to the bauld Keeper,
  In Branksome Ha', where that he lay,
That Lord Scroope has ta'en the Kinmont Willie,
  Between the hours of night and day.

He has ta'en the table wi' his hand,
  He garr'd the red wine spring on hie—
'Now Christ's curse on my head,' he said,
  'But avenged of Lord Scroope I'll be!

'O is my basnet a widow's curch?
  Or my lance a wand of the willow-tree?
Or my arm a ladye's lilye hand,
  That an English lord should lightly me!

'And have they ta'en him, Kinmont Willie,
  Against the truce of Border tide?
And forgotten that the bauld Buccleuch
  Is Keeper here on the Scottish side?

'And have they ta'en him, Kinmont Willie,
  Withouten either dread or fear?
And forgotten that the bauld Buccleuch
  Can back a steed, or shake a spear?

'O were there war between the lands,
  As well I wot that there is none,
I would slight Carlisle castell high,
  Though it were builded of marble stone.

'I would set that castell in a lowe,
  And sloken it with English blood!
There's never a man in Cumberland
  Should ken where Carlisle castell stood.

'But since nae war's between the lands,
  And there is peace, and peace should be;
I'll neither harm English lad or lass,
  And yet the Kinmont freed shall be!'

He has call'd him forty Marchmen bauld,
  I trow they were of his ain name,
Except Sir Gilbert Elliot, call'd
  The Laird of Stobs, I mean the same.

He has call'd him forty Marchmen bauld,
  Were kinsmen to the bauld Buccleuch;
With spur on heel, and splent on spauld,
  And gloves of green, and feathers blue.

There were five and five before them a',
  Wi' hunting-horns and bugles bright:
And five and five came wi' Buccleuch,
  Like Warden's men, array'd for fight.

And five and five, like a mason gang,
  That carried the ladders lang and hie;
And five and five, like broken men;
  And so they reach'd the Woodhouselee.

And as we cross'd the Bateable Land,
  When to the English side we held,
The first o' men that we met wi',
  Wha should it be but fause Sakelde?

'Where be ye gaun, ye hunters keen?'
  Quo' fause Sakelde; 'come tell to me!'
'We go to hunt an English stag,
  Has trespass'd on the Scots countrie.'

'Where be ye gaun, ye marshal men?'
   Quo' fause Sakelde; 'come tell me true!'
'We go to catch a rank reiver,
   Has broken faith wi' the bauld Buccleuch.'

'Where be ye gaun, ye mason lads,
   Wi' a' your ladders, lang and hie?'
'We gang to herry a corbie's nest,
   That wons not far fra Woodhouselee.'

'Where be ye gaun, ye broken men?'
   Quo' fause Sakelde; 'come tell to me!'
Now Dickie of Dryhope led that band,
   And the never a word of lear had he.

'Why trespass ye on the English side?
   Row-footed outlaws, stand!' quo' he;
The never a word had Dickie to say,
   Sae he thrust the lance through his fause bodie.

Then on we held for Carlisle toun,
   And at Staneshaw-bank the Eden we cross'd;
The water was great and meikle of spait,
   But the never a horse nor man we lost.

And when we reach'd the Staneshaw-bank,
   The wind was rising loud and hie;
And there the laird gar'd leave our steeds,
   For fear that they should stamp and nie.

And when we left the Staneshaw-bank,
   The wind began full loud to blaw;
But 'twas wind and weet, and fire and sleet,
   When we came beneath the castle wa'.

We crept on knees, and held our breath,
   Till we placed the ladders against the wa';
And sae ready was Buccleuch himsell
   To mount the first before us a'.

He has ta'en the watchman by the throat,
   He flung him down upon the lead-
'Had there not been peace between our lands,
   Upon the other side thou hadst gaed!

'Now sound out, trumpets!' quo' Buccleuch;
  'Let's waken Lord Scroope right merrilie!'
Then loud the Warden's trumpet blew—
  O wha daur meddle wi' me?

Then speedilie to wark we gaed,
  And raised the slogan ane and a',
And cut a hole through a sheet of lead,
  And so we wan to the castle ha'.

They thought King James and a' his men
  Had won the house wi' bow and spear;
It was but twenty Scots and ten,
  That put a thousand in sic a steir!

Wi' coulters, and wi' forehammers,
  We garr'd the bars bang merrilie,
Until we came to the inner prison,
  Where Willie o' Kinmont he did lie.

And when we came to the lower prison,
  Where Willie o' Kinmont he did lie—
'O sleep ye, wake ye, Kinmont Willie,
  Upon the morn that thou's to die?'

'O I sleep saft, and I wake aft;
  It's lang since sleeping was fley'd frae me,
Gie my service back to my wife and bairns,
  And a' gude fellows that spier for me."

The Red Rowan has hente him up,
  The starkest man in Teviotdale—
'Abide, abide now, Red Rowan,
  Till of my Lord Scroope I take farewell.

'Farewell, farewell, my gude Lord Scroope!
  My gude Lord Scroope, farewell!' he cried;
'I'll pay you for my lodging maill,
  When first we meet on the Border side.'

Then shoulder high, with shout and cry,
  We bore him down the ladder lang;
At every stride Red Rowan made,
  I wot the Kinmont's airns play'd clang!

'O mony a time,' quo' Kinmont Willie,
  'I have ridden horse baith wild and wud;
But a rougher beast than Red Rowan
  I ween my legs have ne'er bestrode.

'And mony a time,' quo' Kinmont Willie,
  'I've prick'd a horse out oure the furs;
But since the day I back'd a steed,
  I never wore sic cumbrous spurs!'

We scarce had won the Staneshaw-bank
  When a' the Carlisle bells were rung,
And a thousand men on horse and foot
  Cam wi' the keen Lord Scroope along.

Buccleuch has turned to Eden Water,
  Even where it flow'd frae bank to brim,
And he has plunged in wi' a' his band,
  And safely swam them through the stream.

He turn'd him on the other side,
  And at Lord Scroope his glove flung he;
'If ye like na my visit in merry England,
  In fair Scotland come visit me!'

All sore astonish'd stood Lord Scroope,
  He stood as still as rock of stane;
He scarcely dared to trow his eyes,
  When through the water they had gane.

'He is either himsell a devil frae hell,
  Or else his mother a witch maun be;
I wadna have ridden that wan water
  For a' the gowd in Christentie.

Anonymous

The Two Corbies

As I was walking all alane,
I heard twa corbies making a mane:
The tane unto the tither did say,
'Whar sall we gang and dine the day?'

'In behint yon auld fail dyke
I wot there lies a new slain knight;
And naebody kens that he lies there
But his hawk, his hound, and his lady fair.

'His hound is to the hunting gane,
His hawk to fetch the wild-fowl hame,
His lady's ta'en anither mate,
So we may mak our dinner sweet.

'Ye'll sit on his white hause-bane,   [neck-bone
And I'll pike out his bonny blue e'en:
Wi' ae lock o' his gowden hair
We'll theek our nest when it grows bare.   [thatch

'Mony a one for him maks mane,
But nane sall ken whar he is gane:
O'er his white banes, when they are bare,
The wind sall blaw for evermair.'

Anonymous

The Dowie Houms O' Yarrow

Late at e'en, drinkin' the wine,
  And ere they paid the lawin',
They set a combat them between,
  To fight it in the dawnin'.

'O stay at hame, my noble lord!
  O stay at hame, my marrow!
My cruel brother will you betray,
  On the dowie houms o' Yarrow.'

'O fare ye weel, my ladye gaye!
  O fare ye weel, my Sarah!
For I maun gae, tho' I ne'er return
  Frae the dowie banks o' Yarrow.'

She kiss'd his cheek, she kamed his hair,
  As oft she had done before, O;
She belted on his noble brand,
  An' he's awa to Yarrow.

O he's gane up yon high, high hill—
  I wat he ga'ed wi' sorrow—
And in a den spied nine arm'd men,
  I' the dowie houms o' Yarrow.

'O are ye come to drink the wine,
  As ye hae doon before, O?
Or are ye come to wield the brand,
  On the bonnie banks o' Yarrow?'

'I am no come to drink the wine,
  As I hae done before, O,
But I am come to wield the brand,
  On the dowie houms o' Yarrow.'

Four he hurt, and five he slew,
  On the dowie houms o' Yarrow,
Till that stubborn knight came him behind,
  An' ran his body thorrow.

'Gae hame, gae hame, good-brother John,
  An' tell your sister Sarah
To come an' lift her noble lord,
  Who's sleepin' sound on Yarrow.'

'Yestreen I dream'd a dolefu' dream;
  I ken'd there wad be sorrow;
I dream'd I pu'd the heather green,
  On the dowie banks o' Yarrow.'

She gaed up yon high, high hill—
  I wat she gaed wi' sorrow—
An' in a den spy'd nine dead men,
  On the dowie houms o' Yarrow.

She kiss'd his cheek, she kaim'd his hair,
  As aft she did before, O;
She drank the red blood frae him ran,
  On the dowie houms o' Yarrow.

'O haud your tongue, my dochter dear,
  For what needs a' this sorrow?
I'll wed you on a better lord
  Than him you lost on Yarrow.'

'O haud your tongue, my father dear,
   An' dinna grieve your Sarah;
A better lord was never born
   Than him I lost on Yarrow.

'Tak hame your ousen, tak hame your kye,
   For they hae bred our sorrow;
I wiss that they had a' gane mad
   When they cam first to Yarrow.'

Anonymous

The Wife of Usher's Well

There lived a wife at Usher's well,
   And a wealthy wife was she;
She had three stout and stalwart sons,
   And sent them o'er the sea.

They hadna been a week from her,
   A week but barely ane,
When word came to the carline wife
   That her three sons were gane.

They hadna been a week from her,
   A week but barely three,
When word came to the carline wife
   That her sons she'd never see.

'I wish the wind may never cease,
   Nor fishes in the flood,
Till my three sons come hame to me
   In earthly flesh and blood!'

It fell about the Martinmas,
   When nights are lang and mirk,
The carline wife's three sons came hame,
   And their hats were o' the birk.

It neither grew in skye nor ditch,
   Nor yet in ony sheugh;
But at the gates o' Paradise
   That birk grew fair eneugh.

'Blow up the fire, my maidens!
 Bring water from the well!
For a' my house shall feast this night,
 Since my three sons are well.'

And she has made to them a bed,
 She's made it large and wide;
And she's ta'en her mantle her about,
 Sat down at the bedside.

Up then crew the red, red cock,
 And up then crew the gray;
The eldest to the youngest said,
 ' 'Tis time we were away.'

The cock he hadna craw'd but once,
 And clapp'd his wings at a',
When the youngest to the eldest said,
 'Brother we must awa.'

'The cock doth craw, the day doth daw,
 The channerin' worm doth chide;
Gin we be miss'd out o' our place,
 A sair pain we maun bide.

'Fare ye weel, my mother dear!
 Fareweel to barn and byre!
And fare ye weel, the bonny lass
 That kindles my mother's fire!'

Anonymous

Waly, Waly

O waly, waly, up the bank,
 And waly, waly, doun the brae,
And waly, waly, yon burn-side,
 Where I and my Love wont to gae!
I lean'd my back unto an aik,
 I thocht it was a trustie tree;
But first it bow'd and syne it brak–
 Sae my true love did lichtlie me.

O waly, waly, gin love be bonnie
   A little time while it is new!
But when 'tis auld it waxeth cauld,
   And fades awa' like morning dew.
O wherefore should I busk my heid,
   Or wherefore should I kame my hair?
For my true Love has me forsook,
   And says he'll never lo'e me mair.

Now Arthur's Seat sall be my bed,
   The sheets sall ne'er be 'filed by me;
Saint Anton's well sall be my drink;
   Since my true Love has foresaken me.
Marti'mas wind, when wilt thou blaw,
   And shake the green leaves aff the tree?
O gentle Death, when wilt thou come?
   For of my life I am wearie.

'Tis not the frost, that freezes fell,
   Nor blawing snaw's inclemencie,
'Tis not sic cauld that makes me cry;
   But my Love's heart grown cauld to me.
When we cam in by Glasgow toun,
   We were a comely sicht to see;
My Love was clad in the black velvet,
   And I mysel in cramasie.

But had I wist, before I kist,
   That love had been sae ill to win,
I had lock'd my heart in a case o' gowd,
   And pinn'd it wi' a siller pin.
And O! if my young babe were born,
   And set upon the nurse's knee;
And I mysel were dead and gane,
   And the green grass growing over me!

Anonymous

The Bonny Earl O' Moray

Ye Highlands and ye Lawlands,
   O where hae ye been?
They hae slain the Earl o' Moray,
   And hae laid him on the green.

Now wae be to thee, Huntley!
  And whairfore did ye sae!
I bade you bring him wi' you
  But forbade you him to slay.

He was a braw gallant,
  And he rid at the ring;
And the bonny Earl o' Moray,
  O he might hae been a king!

He was a braw gallant,
  And he play'd at the ba';
And the bonny Earl o' Moray
  Was the flower amang them a'!

He was a braw gallant,
  And he play'd at the gluve;
And the bonny Earl o' Moray,
  O he was the Queen's luve!

O lang will his Lady
  Look owre the Castle Doune,
Ere she see the Earl o' Moray
  Come sounding through the toun!

Anonymous

Helen of Kirkconnell

I wish I were where Helen lies,
Night and day on me she cries;
O that I were where Helen lies,
  On fair Kirkconnell lea!

Curst be the heart that thought the thought,
And curst the hand that fired the shot,
When in my arms burd Helen dropt,
  And died to succour me!

O think na ye my heart was sair,
When my Love dropp'd and spak nae mair!
There did she swoon wi' meikle care,
  On fair Kirkconnell lea.

As I went down the water side,
None but my foe to be my guide,
None but my foe to be my guide,
   On fair Kirkconnell lea;

I lighted down my sword to draw,
I hackèd him in pieces sma',
I hackèd him in pieces sma',
   For her sake that died for me.

O Helen fair, beyond compare!
I'll mak a garland o' thy hair,
Shall bind my heart for evermair,
   Until the day I dee!

O that I were where Helen lies!
Night and day on me she cries;
Out of my bed she bids me rise,
   Says, 'Haste, and come to me!'

O Helen fair! O Helen chaste!
If I were with thee, I'd be blest,
Where thou lies low an' taks thy rest,
   On fair Kirkconnell lea.

I wish my grave were growing green,
A winding-sheet drawn owre my een,
And I in Helen's arms lying,
   On fair Kirkconnell lea.

I wish I were where Helen lies!
Night and day on me she cries;
And I am weary of the skies,
   For her sake that died for me.

Anonymous

Sir Patrick Spens

The King sits in Dunfermline town,
   Drinking the blude-red wine;
'O whare will I get a skeely skipper,
   To sail this new ship of mine?'—

O up and spake an eldern knight,
　　Sat at the King's right knee,—
'Sir Patrick Spens is the best sailor,
　　That ever sailed the sea.'—

Our King has written a braid letter,
　　And seal'd it with his hand,
And sent it to Sir Patrick Spens,
　　Was walking on the strand.

'To Noroway, to Noroway,
　　To Noroway o'er the faem;
The King's daughter of Noroway,
　　'Tis thou maun bring her hame.'

The first word that Sir Patrick read,
　　Sae loud loud laughed he;
The neist word that Sir Patrick read,
　　The tear blinded his ee.

'O wha is this has done this deed,
　　And tauld the King o' me,
To send us out, at this time of the year,
　　To sail upon the sea?

'Be it wind, be it weet, be it hail, be it sleet,
　　Our ship must sail the faem;
The King's daughter of Noroway,
　　'Tis we must fetch her hame.'—

They hoysed their sails on Monenday morn,
　　Wi' a' the speed they may;
They hae landed in Noroway,
　　Upon a Wodensday.

They hadna been a week, a week,
　　In Noroway, but twae,
When that the lords o' Noroway
　　Began aloud to say,—

'Ye Scottishmen spend a' our King's gowd,
　　And a' our Queenis fee.'—
'Ye lie, ye lie, ye liars loud!
　　Fu' loud I hear ye lie;

'For I brought as much white monie,
    As gane my men and me,
And I brought a half-fou of gude red gowd,   [eighth of a peck
    Out o'er the sea wi' me.

'Make ready, make ready, my merrymen a'!
    Our gude ship sails the morn.'—
'Now, ever alake, my master dear,
    I fear a deadly storm!

'I saw the new moon, late yestreen,
    Wi' the auld moon in her arm;
And, if we gang to sea, master,
    I fear we'll come to harm.'

They hadna sail'd a league, a league,
    A league but barely three,
When the lift grew dark, and the wind blew loud,
    And gurly grew the sea.   [boisterous

The ankers brak, and the topmasts lap,
    It was sic a deadly storm;
And the waves cam o'er the broken ship,
    Till a' her sides were torn.

'O where will I get a gude sailor,
    To take my helm in hand,
Till I get up to the tall top-mast,
    To see if I can spy land?'—

'O here am I, a sailor gude,
    To take the helm in hand,
Till you go up to the tall top-mast;
    But I fear you'll ne'er spy land.'—

He hadna gane a step, a step,
    A step but barely ane,
When a bout flew out of our goodly ship,   [bolt
    And the salt sea it came in.

'Gae, fetch a web o' the silken claith,
    Another o' the twine,
And wap them into our ship's side,   [wrap
    And let nae the sea come in.'—

They fetch'd a web o' the silken claith,
    Another o' the twine,
And they wapp'd them round that gude ship's side,
    But still the sea cam in.

O laith, laith, were our gude Scots lords
    To weet their cork-heel'd shoon!
But lang or a' the play was play'd,
    They wat their hats aboon.

And mony was the feather bed,
    That flotter'd on the faem;
And mony was the gude lord's son,
    That never mair cam hame.

The ladyes wrang their fingers white,
    The maidens tore their hair,
A' for the sake of their true loves;
    For them they'll see nae mair.

O lang, lang, may the ladyes sit,
    Wi' their fans into their hand,
Before they see Sir Patrick Spens
    Come sailing to the strand!

And lang, lang, may the maidens sit,
    With their gowd kaims in their hair,
A' waiting for their ain dear loves!
    For them they'll see nae mair.

Half-owre, half-owre to Aberdour,
    'Tis fifty fathoms deep,
And there lies gude Sir Patrick Spens,
    Wi' the Scots lords at his feet.

Anonymous

Proud Maisie

Proud Maisie is in the wood,
    Walking so early;
Sweet Robin sits on the bush,
    Singing so rarely.
17

'Tell me, thou bonny bird,
    When shall I marry me?'
'When six braw gentlemen
    Kirkward shall carry ye.'

'Who makes the bridal bed,
    Birdie, say truly?'
'The grey-headed sexton
    That delves the grave duly.

'The glow-worm o'er grave and stone
    Shall light thee steady.
The owl from the steeple sing,
    "Welcome, proud lady."'

Sir Walter Scott (1771–1832)
The Heart of Midlothian

Ravelston's Mourning Ghost

The murmur of the mourning ghost
    That keeps the shadowy kine.
O Keith of Ravelston,
    The sorrows of thy line!

Ravelston, Ravelston,
    The merry path that leads
Down the golden morning hill,
    And through the silver meads.

Ravelston, Ravelston,
    The stile beneath the tree,
The maid that kept her mother's kine
    The song that sang she!

She sang her song, she kept her kine,
    She sat beneath the thorn,
When Andrew Keith of Ravelston,
    Rode through, the Monday morn.

His henchmen sing, his hawk-bells ring,
    His belted jewels shine,
O Keith of Ravelston,
    The sorrows of thy line!

I lay my hand upon the stile,
    The stile is lone and cold,
The burnie that goes babbling by
    Says nought than can be told.

Yet, stranger, here from year to year,
    She keeps her shadowy kine.
O Keith of Ravelston,
    The sorrows of thy line!

Step our three steps where Andrew stood;
    Why blanch thy cheeks for fear?
The ancient stile is not alone,
    'Tis not the burn I hear!

She makes her immemorial moan,
    She keeps her shadowy kine.
O Keith of Ravelston,
    The sorrows of thy line!

Sydney Dobell (1824–74)

CREATURES

Robin at My Window

The air was cleart with white and sable clouds,
Hard frost, with frequent schours of hail and snaw;
Into the nicht the stormy wind with thouds
And baleful billows on the sea did blaw;
Men, beasts and fowls unto their beilds did draw,   [homes
Fain then to find the fruct of summer thrift,
When clad with snaw was sand, wood, crag and clift.

I sat at fire weil girdit in my gown;
The starving sparrows at my window cheeped;
To read ane while I to my book was bown,
In at ane pane the pretty progne peeped   [robin, but properly
And moved me for fear I should have sleeped,   swallow
To rise and set ane casement open wide
To see gif Robin would come in and bide.

Puir progne, sweetly I have heard ye sing
There at my window on the simmer day;
And now sen winter hither does ye bring
I pray ye enter in my hous and stay
Till it be fair, and then thous go thy way,
For trowlie thous be treated courteouslie
And nothing thralled in thy libertie.

Come in, sweet Robin, welcome verilie,
Said I, and down I sat me by the fire:
Then in comes robin reidbreist mirrilie,
And sups and lodges at my heart's desire:
But on ye morn, I him perceived to tire,
For Phoebus shining sweetly him allured,
I gave him leif, and furth guid robin furd.

James Melville (1556–1614)

A Wolf Hunt

The son of a baronet, Sir Thomas Dick Lauder was born at Haddington. He is remembered for his 'Account of the Great Floods in Morayshire in 1829' and his novel, 'The Wolf of Badenoch'.

'Hark,' said Hepborne, suddenly interrupting the enthusiastic greeting his friend was wafting towards his distant home—'hark! methinks I hear the sound of bugles echoing faintly through the woods below; dost thou not hear?'

'I do,' said Assueton, 'and methinks I also hear the yelling note of the sleuth-hounds.'

'That bugle note was my father's,' said Hepborne; 'I know it full well; I could swear to it anywhere. Nay, yonder they ride. Dost not see them afar off yonder, sweeping across the green alures and avenues, where the wood-shaws are thinnest? Now they cross the wide lawn yonder—and now they are lost amid the shade of these oakshaws. They come this way; let us hasten downward; we shall have ill luck an we meet them not at the bottom of the hill.'

Hepborne was so eager to embrace his father, that, forgetting his friend was a stranger to the perplexities of the way, he darted off, and descended through the brush-wood, leaving Assueton, in his turn, eager to overtake Hepborne, put down the point of his hunting-spear to aid him in vaulting over an opposing bush. There was a knot in the ashen shaft, and it snapt assunder with his weight. He threw it away, and, guided by the distant sounds of the bugle-blasts and the yells of the hounds, he pressed precipitately down the steep, but, in his ignorance, he took a direction different from that pursued by Hepborne.

As he was within a few yards of the bottom of the hill, he saw an enormous wolf making towards him, the oblique and sinister eyes of the animal flashing fire, his jaws extended, and tongue lolling out. Assueton regretted the loss of his hunting spear, but, judging him to be much spent, he resolved to attack him. He squatted behind a bush directly in the animal's path, and, springing at him as he passed, he grappled him by the throat with both hands, and held him with the grasp of fate. The furious wolf struggled with all his tremendous strength, and, before Assueton could venture to let go one hand to draw out his anelace, he was overbalanced by the weight of the creature, and they rolled over and over each other down the remainder of the grassy declivity, the knight still keeping his hold, conscious that the moment he should lose it he must inevitably be torn in pieces. There they lay tumbling and writhing on the ground, the exertions of the wolf being so violent as frequently to lift Assueton and drag him on his back along the green sward. Now he gained his knees, and, pressing down his savage foe, he at last ventured to loose his right hand to grope for his anelace, but it was gone—it had dropped from the sheath; and, casting a glance around him, he saw it glittering on the grass at some yards' distance. There was no other mode of recovering it, but by dragging the furious beast towards it, and this he now put forth all his strength to endeavour to effect. He tugged and toiled, and even succeeded so far as to gain a yard or two; but his grim foe was only rendered more ferocious by his resistance, by the additional force he employed. The wolf made repeated efforts to twist his neck round to bite, and more than once succeeded in wounding Assueton severely in the left arm, the sleeve of which was entirely torn off. As the beast lay on his back, too, pinned firmly down towards his head, he threw up his body, and thrust his feet against Assueton's face, so as completely to blind his eyes, and by a struggle more violent than any he had made before threw him down backwards.

The situation of the bold and hardy knight was now most perilous, for, though he still kept his grasp, he lay stretched on the ground; and whilst the wolf, standing over him, was now able to bring all his sinews to bear against him, from having his feet planted firmly on the ground, Assueton, was unable to use his muscles with much effect. The panting and frothy jaws, and the long sharp tusks of the infuriated beast, were almost at his throat, and the only salvation that remained for him was to prevent his fastening on it, by keeping the head of the brute at a distance by the strength of his arms. The muscles of the neck of a wolf are well known to be so powerful, that they enable the animal to carry off a sheep with ease; so that, with all his vigour of nerve, Assueton had but a hopeless chance for it. Still he held, and still they struggled, when the tramp of a horse was heard, and a lady came galloping by under the trees. She no sooner observed the dreadful strife between the savage wolf and the knight, than, alighting nimbly from her palfrey, she couched the light hunting-spear she carried and ran it through the heart of the half-choked animal. The blood spurted over the prostrate cavalier, and the huge carcass fell on him, with the eyes glaring in the head, and the teeth grinding together in the agony of death.

Sir Thomas Dick Lauder (1774–1848)
The Wolf of Badenach

To a Mouse

On Turning Her up in Her Nest with the Plough, November, 1785

Wee sleeket, cowrin' tim'rous beastie,
O, what a panic's in thy breastie!
Thou need na start awa' sae hasty,
   Wi' bickerin' brattle!
I wad be laith to rin an' chase thee,
   Wi' murderin' pattle!

I'm truly sorry man's dominion,
Has broken nature's social union,
An' justifies that ill opinion,
              Which makes thee startle
At me, thy poor, earth-born companion,
              An' fellow-mortal!

I doubt na, whyles, but thou may thieve;
What then? poor beastie, thou maun live!
A daimen icker in a thrave
              'S a sma' request;
I'll get a blessin' wi' the lave,
              An' never miss't!

Thy wee bit housie, too, in ruin!
Its silly wa's the win's are strewin'!
An' naething, now, to big a new ane,
              O' foggage green!
An' bleak December's winds ensuin',
              Baith snell an' keen!

Thou saw the fields laid bare an' waste,
An' weary winter comin' fast,
An' cozie here, beneath the blast,
              Thou thought to dwell—
Till crash! the cruel coulter past
              Out thro' thy cell.

That we bit heap o' leaves an' stibble,
Has cost thee mony a weary nibble!
Now thou's turn'd out, for a' thy trouble,
              But house or hald,
To thole the winter's sleety dribble,
              An' cranreuch cauld!

But Mousie, thou art no thy lane,
In proving foresight may be vain;
The best-laid schemes o' mice an' men
              Gang aft agley,
An' lea'e us nought but grief an' pain,
              For promis'd joy!

Still thou art blest, compar'd wi' me!
The present only toucheth thee:

But och! I backward cast my e'e,
>   On prospects drear!
An' forward, tho' I canna see,
>   I guess an' fear!

Robert Burns (1759–1796)

A Tyke

Toby was the most utterly shabby, vulgar, mean-looking cur I ever beheld: in one word, a tyke. He had not one good feature except his teeth and eyes, and his bark, if that can be called a feature. He was not ugly enough to be interesting; his colour black and white, his shape leggy and clumsy; altogether what Sydney Smith would have called an extraordinarily ordinary dog: and, as I have said, not even greatly ugly, or, as the Aberdonians have it, bonnie wi' ill-fauredness. My brother William found him the centre of attraction to a multitude of small blackguards who were drowning him slowly in Lochend Loch, doing their best to lengthen out the process, and secure the greatest amount of fun with the nearest approach to death. Even then Toby showed his great intellect by pretending to be dead, and thus gaining time and an inspiration. William bought him for twopence, and as he had it not, the boys accompanied him to Pilrig Street, when I happened to meet him, and giving the twopence to the biggest boy, had the satisfaction of seeing a general engagement of much severity, during which the two pence disappeared; one penny going off with a very small and swift boy, and the other vanishing hopelessly into the grating of a drain.

Toby was for weeks in the house unbeknown to any one but ourselves two and the cook, and from my grandmother's love of tidiness and hatred of dogs and of dirt, I believe she would have expelled 'him whom we saved from drowning', had not he, in his straightforward way, walked into my father's bedroom one night when he was bathing his feet, and introduced himself with a wag of his tail, intimating a general willingness to be happy. My father laughed most heartily, and at last Toby, having got his way to his bare feet, and having begun to lick his soles and between his toes with his small rough tongue, my father gave such an unwonted shout of laughter, that we—grandmother, sisters, and all of us—went in. Grandmother might argue with all her energy and skill, but as surely as the pressure of Tom Jones' infantile fist upon Mr Allworthy's forefinger undid all the arguments of his sister, so did Toby's tongue and fun prove too many for grandmother's eloquence. I somehow think Toby must have been up to all this, for I think he had a peculiar love for my father ever after, and regarded grandmother from that hour with a careful and cool eye.

Toby, when full grown, was a strong coarse dog; coarse in shape, in countenance, in hair, and in manner. I used to think that, according to the Pythagorean doctrine, he must have been, or been going to be, a Gilmerton carter. He was of the bull terrier variety, coarsened through much mongrelism and a dubious and varied ancestry. His teeth were good, and he had a large skull, and a rich bark as of a dog three times his size, and a tail which I never saw equalled—indeed it was a tail *per se*; it was of immense girth and not short, equal throughout like a policeman's baton; the machinery for working it was of great power, and acted in a way, as far as I have been able to discover, quite original. We called it his ruler.

When he wished to get into the house, he first whined gently, then growled, then gave a sharp bark, and then came a resounding, mighty stroke which shook the house; this, after much study and watching, we found was done by his bringing the entire length of his solid tail flat upon the door, with a sudden and vigorous stroke; it was quite a *tour de force* or a *coup de queue*, and he was perfect in it at once, his first bang authoritative, having been as masterly and telling as his last.

With all this inbred vulgar air, he was a dog of great moral excellence—affectionate, faithful, honest up to his light, with an odd humour as peculiar and as strong as his tail.

Dr John Brown (1810–82)
Horae Subecivae

The Dead Crab

A rosy shield upon its back,
That not the hardest storm could crack,
From whose sharp edge projected out
Black pin-point eyes staring about;
Beneath, the well-knit cote-armure
That gave to its weak belly power;
The clustered legs with plated joints
That ended in stiletto points;
The claws like mouths it held outside:—
I cannot think this creature died
By storm or fish or sea-fowl harmed
Walking the sea so heavily armed;
Or does it make for death to be
Oneself a living armoury?

Andrew Young (1885–1971)

On a Cat, Ageing

He blinks upon the hearth-rug,
   And yawns in deep content,

Accepting all the comforts
   That Providence has sent.

Louder he purrs and louder,
   In one glad hymn of praise
For all the night's adventures,
   For quiet restful days.

Life will go on for ever,
   With all that cat can wish;
Warmth and the glad procession
   Of fish and milk and fish.

Only—the thought disturbs him—
   He's noticed once or twice,
The times are somehow breeding
   A nimbler race of mice.

Sir Alexander Gray (1882–1968)

The Bubblyjock

It's hauf like a bird and hauf like a bogle   [ghost
And juist stands in the sun there and bouks.
It's a wunder its heid disna burst
The way it's aye raxin' its chouks.

Syne it twists its neck like a serpent
But canna get oot a richt note
For the bubblyjock swallowed the bagpipes   [turkey
And the blether stuck in its throat.

Hugh MacDiarmid (1892–1978)

The Proud Puddock

A puddock diddlin be a dub
Peer'd in to see himsel';
And, smirkin up his muckle gub,
Thocht: 'Man! I'm lookin weel'

He turn'd; and spied a corbie-craw
Upon a scroggie tree:
'Hullo! auld clouts, juist come awa
And tak a gowk at me.'

He puffl'd oot his puddy-breist:
He goggl'd in his pride:
He lowpit east, he lowpit west,
He lowpit heels-owre-head.

The corbie sherpen'd up his snoot;
And lauch't, and look't asclent:
'Ye little ken, my ginkie smout,
Hoo sune we'll be acquaint.'

William Soutar (1898–1943)

An Addition to the Family

A musical poet, collector of basset-horns,
was buttering his toast down in Dunbartonshire
when suddenly from behind the breakfast newspaper
the shining blade stopped scraping
and he cried to his wife, 'Joyce, listen to this!—
"Two basset-hounds for sale, house-trained, keen hunters"—
Oh we must have them! What d'you think?..' 'But dear,
did you say *hounds*?' 'Yes, yes, hounds, hounds—'
'But Maurice, it's *horns* we want, you must be over
in the livestock column, what would we do
with a basset-hound, you can't play a hound!'
'It's Beverley it says, the kennels are at Beverley—'
'But Maurice—' '—I'll get some petrol, we'll be there by
    lunchtime—'
'But a dog, two dogs, where'll we put them?'
'I've often wondered what these dogs are like—'
'You mean you don't even—' 'Is there no more marmalade?'
'—don't know what they look like? And how are we to feed
    them?
Yes, there's the pot dear.' 'This stuff's all peel, isn't it?'
'Well, we're at the end of it. But look, these two great—'
'You used to make marmalade once upon a time.'
'They've got ears down to here, and they're far too—'
'Is that half past eight? I'll get the car out.
See if I left my cheque-book on the—' 'Maurice,

are you mad? What about your horns?' 'What horns,
what are you talking about? Look Joyce dear,
if it's not on the dresser it's in my other jacket.
I believe they're wonderful for rabbits—' . . .

So the musical poet took his car to Beverley
with his wife and his cheque-book, and came back home
with his wife and his cheque-book and two new hostages
to the unexpectedness of fortune.
The creatures scampered through the grass, the children
came out with cries of joy, there seemed to be nothing
dead or dying in all that landscape.
Fortune bless the unexpected cries!
Life gathers to the point of wishing it,
a mocking pearl of many ventures. The house
rolled on its back and kicked its legs in the air.
And later, wondering farmers as they passed would hear
beyond the lighted window in the autumn evening
two handsome yellow-bosomed basset-hounds
howling to a melodious basset-horn.

Edwin Morgan (b. 1920)

PURSUITS AND PASTIMES

The Bewteis of the Fute-Ball

Brissit brawnis and broken banes,	[crushed muscles
Strife, discord, and wastit wanes,	
Crookit in cild, syne halt withal—	[age, lame
Thir are the bewteis of the fute-ball.	[these

Anonymous
The Maitland Manuscript (1570–85)

Dancing Before the Reformation

Thir shepherds and their wives sang many other melodies songs, the whilk
I have nocht in memory. Then after this sweet celestial harmony, they began
to dance in ane ring. Every auld shepherd led his wife be the hand, and
every young shepherd led her whom he lovit best. There were eight shepherds, and ilk ane of them had ane sundry instrument to play to the lave
[others]. The first had ane drone bagpipe, the next had ane pipe made of
ane bledder and of ane reed, the third playit on ane trump, the feyrd on ane
corn pipe, the fyft playit on ane pipe made of ane gait horn, the sext playit
on ane recorder, the sevent playit on ane fiddle, and the last playit on ane
whistle. King Amphion that playit so sweet on his harp when he keepit
his sheep, nor yet Appollo the God of Sapiens, that keepit King Admetus'
sheep, with his sweet minstrelsy, none of thir twa playit mair curiously nor
did thir eight shepherds; nor yet all the shepherds that Virgil maks mention
. . . nor Orpheus . . . nor Pan . . . nor Mercurius . . . I beheld nevir ane mair
delectable recreatioun. For first they began with twa beks and with a kiss.
Euripedes, Juvenal, Perseus, Horace, nor nane of the satiric poets, whilk
movit their bodies as they had been dansand when they pronoucit their
tragedies, none of them keepit more geometrical measure nor thir shepherds
did in their dancing . . . It was ane celestial recreation to behold their licht
lopene [leaping], gambolding [gamboling], stendling [striding], backward
and forward, dancing Basse Dances, Pavans, Gallierds, Turdions, Braulis
and Branles, Buffons, with many other licht dances, the whilk are ower
prolix to be rehearsit.

Anonymous
The Complaynt of Scotland, 1548

275

Hunting in the Highlands

In 1618, Ben Jonson, to the considerable amusement of his friends at the Mermaid Tavern, announced that he intended to walk to Scotland, one of his purposes being to converse with the Scottish poet William Drummond of Hawthornden. A few weeks later, a gusty Thames waterman, John Taylor, announced that he intended to follow the famous dramatist's example, 'not carrying any money to or fro, neither Begging, Borrowing, or asking Meate, Drinke or Lodging.' Taylor published a vigorous if eccentric account of his trip, 'The Pennylesse Pilgrimage', of which he sold 4,500 copies.

He penetrated the Highlands, his ready tongue apparently making him acceptable to the aristocracy; for on the Braes of Mar, where he felt so cold that his teeth began to chatter in his head 'like virginal's jacks', he found the Earl of Mar, the Earl of Enzie (a then recently acquired second title of the Marquis of Huntley) and the Earl of Buchan, who welcomed him to their sport.

Once in the yeere, which is the whole month of August and sometimes part of September, many of the nobility of the kingdom (for their pleasure) doe come into these highland countries to hunt, where they doe conform themselves to the habit of the Highlandmen, who for the most part speak nothing but Irish . . . Their habit is shoes with but one sole apiece; stockings (which they call short hose) made of a warm stuff of divers colours, which they call Tartan: as for breeches, many of them, nor their forefathers, never wore any, but a jerkin of the same stuff that their hose is of, their garters being bands or wreathes of hay or straw, with a plaid about their shoulders which is a mantle of divers colours, much finer and lighter stuff than their hose, with blue flat caps on their head, a handkerchief knit with two knots about their neck; and thus are they attired . . .

Their weapons are long bows and forked arrows, swords and targes, arquebusses, muskets, dirks and Lochaber axes . . . As for their attire, any man of what degree soever that comes amongst them must not disdain to wear it: for if they doe, then they will disdain to hunt, or willingly to bring in their dogs: but if men be kind unto them, and be in their habit, then they are conquered with kindness, and the sport will be plentiful . . .

Five or six hundred men doe rise early in the morning, and they doe dispose themselves divers ways, and seven, eight or ten miles compass. They doe bring or chase in the deer in many herds (two, three of four hundred in a herd) to such a place as the noblemen shall appoint them; then when day is come, the Lords and gentlemen of their companies doe ride or goe to the said place, sometimes wading up the middles through burns and rivers, and . . . doe lie on the ground till those foresaid scouts, who are called the Tinchel, doe bring down the deer . . .

After we had stayed there three hours or thereabouts, we might perceive the deer appear on the hills round about us (their heads making a show like a wood), which, being followed by the Tinchel, are chased down into the valley, on each side being way-laid with a hundred couple of strong Irish grey-hounds. They are let loose as occasion serves upon the herd of deer . . . With dogs, guns, arrows dirks and daggers, in the space of two hours four-score, fat deer were slain, which after are disposed of some one way, and some another, twenty and thirty miles, and more than enough left for us to make merry withall at our rendezvous.

John Taylor (1580–1653)
The Penniless Pilgrim

No Smoking, Please

Is it not the greatest sin of all, that you, the people of all sorts of this king-dom, who are created and ordained by God, to bestow both your persons and and goods, for the maintenance both of the honour and safety of your King and Commonwealth, should disable yourselves in both? In your persons having by this continual vile custom brought yourselves to this shameful imbecility, that you are not able to ride or walk the journey of a Jew's sab-bath, but you must have a reekie coal brought you from the next poor house to kindle your tobacco with? Whereas he cannot be thought able for any service in the wars, that cannot endure oftentimes the want of meat, drink and sleep, much more then must he endure the want of tobacco. In the times of the many glorious and victorious battles fought by this nation, there was no word of tobacco. But now if it were time of wars, and that you were to make some sudden cavalcade upon your enemies, if any of you should seek leisure to stay behind his fellow for taking of tobacco, for my part I should never be sorry for any evil chance that might befall him. To take a custom in any thing that cannot be left again, is most harmful to the people of any land . . .

Now how you are by this custom disabled in your goods, let the gentry of this land bear witness, some of them bestowing three, some four hundred pounds a year upon this precious stink, which I am sure might be bestowed upon many far better uses . . .

And for the vanities committed in this filthy custom, is it not both great vanity and uncleanness, that at the table, a place of respect, of cleanness, of modesty, men should not be ashamed to sit tossing of tobacco pipes and puffing of the smoke of tobacco one to another, making the filthy smoke and stink thereof, to exhale athwart the dishes and infect the air, when very often men that abhor it are at their repast? . . .

The public use whereof, at all times, and in all places, hath now so far prevailed, as divers men very sound both in judgment and complexion, have been at last forced to take it also without desire, partly because they were ashamed to seem singular . . . and partly, to be as one that was content to eat garlic (which he did not love) that he might not be troubled with the smell of it in the breath of his fellows. And is it not a great vanity, that a man cannot heartily welcome his friend now, but straight they must be in hand with tobacco. No, it is become in place of a cure, a point of good fellowship, and he that will refuse to take a pipe of tobacco among his fellows (though by his own election he would rather feel the favour of a sink) is accounted peevish and no good company, even as they do with tippling in the cold eastern countries. . . .

Moreover, which is a great iniquity, and against all humanity, the husband shall not be ashamed to reduce thereby his delicate, wholesome and clean-complexioned wife, to that extremity, that either she must also corrupt her sweet breath therewith, or else resolve to live in a perpetual stinking torment.

Have you not reason, then, to be ashamed, and to forbear this filthy novelty, so basely grounded, so foolishly received, and so grossly mistaken in the right use thereof; in your abuse thereof sinning against God, harming your selves both in persons and goods, and raking also thereby the marks and notes of vanity upon you; by the custom thereof making yourselves to be wondered at by all foreign civil nations, and by all strangers that come among you, to be scorned and contemned? A custom loathsome to the eye, hateful to the nose, harmful to the brain, dangerous to the lungs, and in the black stinking fume thereof, nearest resembling the horrible Stygian smoke of the pit that is bottomless.

James I and VI (1567–1625)
A Counterblaste to Tobacco

Golf

It seems probable that the game of golf was imported into Scotland from Holland. The earliest Scottish reference to golf is to be found in a parliamentary decree dated March 1457, when, it seems, so great was popular interest in the game that the more important pursuit of archery was being neglected.

We know nothing about James Arbuckle, except that he was a student at the University of Glasgow in 1721, and that he played his golf on Glasgow Green.

In Winter, too, when hoary frosts o'er spread
The verdant turf, and naked lay the mead,
The vig'rous youth commence the sportive war,
And, arm'd with lead, their jointed clubs prepare;
The timber curve to leathern orbs apply,
Compact, elastic, to pervade the sky:
These to the distant hole direct they drive;
They claim the stakes who hither first arrive.

Intent his ball the eager gamester eyes,
His muscles strains, and various postures tries
Th' impelling blow to strike with greater force,
And shape the motive orb's projective course.
If with due strength the weighty engine fall,
Discharged obliquely, and impinge the ball,
It winding mounts aloft, and sings in air;
And wondering crowds the gamester's skill declare.
But when some luckless wayward stroke descends,
Whose force the ball in running quickly spends,
The foes triumph, the club is cursed in vain;
Spectators scoff, and e'en allies complain.

Thus still success is followed with applause;
But ah! how few espouse a vanquished cause.

James Arbuckle

Scots Drink

When the Lowlanders want to drink a cheer-upping cup, they go to the public-house, called the Change House, and call for a chopin of pippany, which is a thin yeasty beverage, made of malt, not quite so strong as the table-beer of England. This is brought in a pewter stoup, shaped like a skittle; from whence it is emptied into a quaff, that is a curious cup made of different pieces of wood, such as box and ebany, cut into little staves, joined alternately, and secured with delicate hoops, having two ears or handles. It holds about a gill, is sometimes tipt round the mouth of a silver, and has a plate of the same metal at the bottom, with the landlord's cipher engraved.

The Highlanders, on the contrary, despise this liquor, and regale themselves with whisky, a malt spirit, as strong as geneva, which they swallow in great quantities, without any signs of inebriation: They are used to it from the cradle, and find it an excellent preservative against the winter cold, which must be extreme on these mountains—I am told that it is given with great success to infants, as a cordial, in the confluent smallpox, when the eruption seems to flag, and the symptoms grow unfavourable.

Tobias Smollett (1721-71)
Humphry Clinker

Highland Dress and Hospitality

Thomas Pennant, the descendant of a distinguished family which included on the paternal side several clerics including an Abbot and a poet who collected ancient Welsh manuscripts, was a scientist recognized alike in Sweden, where he was elected a Fellow of the Royal Society of Uppsala, and in his native England, where he was a Fellow of the Royal Society of London. He set out on the first of his Scottish tours in 1769, and made several extensive journeys throughout Scotland, his accounts of these journeys being widely read for many years after his death. At Inverness, he attended a Highland Fair.

The commodities were skins, various necessaries brought in by the Pedlars, coarse country cloths, cheese, butter and meal; the last in goat-skin bags; the butter lapped in cawls, or leaves of the broad *alga* or tang; and great quantities of birch wood and hazel cut into lengths for carts, etc., which had been floated down the river from Loch Ness.

The Fair was a very agreeable circumstance, and afforded a most singular group of Highlanders in all their motley dresses. Their *brechen* or plaid, consists of twelve or thirteen yards of a narrow stuff, wrapped round the middle with a belt . . . But in cold weather, it is large enough to wrap round the whole body from head to feet . . . It is frequently fastened at the shoulders with a pin, often of silver, and before with a brotche (like the *fibula* of the Romans) which is sometimes of silver . . . The stockings are short, and are tied below the knee. The *curan* is a sort of laced shoe made of a skin with the hairy side out, but now seldom worn . . . The *truis* were worn by the gentry, and were breeches and stockings made of one piece....

The *feil beg*, i.e. little plaid, also called *kelt* [kilt], is a sort of short petticoat reaching only to the knees, and is a modern substitute for the lower part of the plaid, being found to be less cumbersome, especially in time of action . .. The *dirk* was a sort of dagger stuck in the belt. I frequently saw this weapon in the shambles of Inverness, converted into a butcher's knife . . . The woman's dress is the *kirch*, or a white piece of linen, pinned over the foreheads of those that are married, and round the hind part of the head, falling behind over their necks. The single women wear only a ribband round their head, which they call a snood. The *tonnag* or plaid, hangs over their shoulders and is fastened before with a brotche; but in bad weather is drawn over their heads . . .

The manners of the native Highlanders may justly be expressed in these words: indolent to a high degree, unless roused to war, or to any animating amusement; or I may say, from experience, to lend any disinterested assistance to the distressed traveller, either in directing him on his way, or affording their aid in passing the dangerous torrents of the Highlands: hospitable to the highest degree, and full of generosity: are much affected with the civility of strangers, and have in themselves a natural politeness and address, which often flows from the meanest when least expected.

Thro' my whole tour I never met with a single instance of national reflection! Their forbearance proves them to be superior to the meanness of retaliation; I fear they pity us; but I hope not indiscriminately. Are excessively inquisitive after your business, your name, and other particulars of little consequence to them. ... Have much pride, and consequently are impatient of affronts, and revengeful of industries. Are decent in their general behaviour; inclined to superstition, yet attentive to the duties of religion, and are capable of giving a most distinct account of the principals of their faith. But in many parts of the Highlands, their character begins to be more faintly marked; they mix more with the world, and become daily less attached to their chiefs: the clans begin to disperse themselves through different parts of the country, finding that their industry and good conduct afford them better protection (since the due execution of the laws) than any of their chieftain can afford; and the chieftain, tasting the sweets of advanced rents the benefits of industry, dismisses from his table the crowds of retainers, the former instruments of his oppression and freakish tyrant.

Thomas Pennant (1726–98)
Tour of Scotland

A Justification of Travelling

Burns's 'honest Master Heron' was a native of Creehead, New Galloway. With his 'Memoir of the Life of Robert Burns—1797', Heron became the poet's first biographer. Although Heron studied at Edinburgh University, and was licensed to preach in the Church of Scotland, he was really a professional man of letters whose last days were spent in Newgate Debtors Prison, from whence he was removed to the Fever Hospital of St Pancras to die.

It is difficult to reconcile the habits of studious conduct with those of active life. The advantages naturally attached to one of these modes of employment are not easily communicated to the other. He who retires to cultivate his understanding in his closet, is liable to lose that dexterity of hand, and that quick perspicacity of eye, which are acquired on him through active external employments and amusements. The bustle of active life, again, is commonly unfavourable to our powers of recollection, of reasoning, and of abstraction. Books return us to theoretic speculation: and the business of the world has some tendency to unfit the imagination, and the reasoning faculty for that exercise. Men of study often have their minds filled with general notions, without a due proportion of particular facts; men of business are sometimes capable of little else than minute details.

Having been, for a series of years, subjected to many of the inconveniences, although perhaps, without reaping many of the advantages of a life of study and retirement, I lately resolved to try the benefits of a short excursion through some parts of my native country. I pleased myself with the hope that I might, in this way, quicken my powers of observation, by the view of those number-less, unconnected particulars, which in every country, meets the traveller's eye. Amongst such a diversity of objects comes some unavoidably interesting. And whenever the mind is interested, its attention is engaged. It is thus roused from that languor into which, in long confinement within a narrow sphere, it is apt to sink. Its faculties gain a new elasticity and energy, and become capable of nobler exertions.

A sedentary life, especially when one moves not in a very extensive, social circle, has a tendency to deaden and relax all the firmer nerves in the soul. These, diversity of social converse, and varied aspects of nature and of life will best restore to their proper tone.

Travelling, too, to anyone in any degree, more capable of observation than a post horse, must prove a distinct and highly beneficial line of study. There are certain classes of the arts, and of the objects of taste, with which an acquaintance cannot be obtained otherwise than by travelling, to examine them in their natural situations. Of the operations of agriculture, for instance, little knowledge can be gained from books alone: though not easily conceived in what manner nature and human industry conspired to make the earth yield her vegetables stores in richest abundance; unless we see the growing crops in the various stages of its progress, and observe the series of the husband-man's labours the minuter arts of life, too, which are not practised by distinct classes of artizans but by every individual, or every family, for themselves, can become known to us only by the same actual observation. Nor can books ever form taste or judge the beauties of natural or ornamentive scenery. The naturalist, in like manner, finds his most interesting cabinet in the wide range in which nature has originally disposed all the subjects of this science . . .

The feelings of the heart, too, may be bettered by a survey of the varied scenery of one's native country; by remarking the character and condition of its various inhabitants, and beholding how greatly the ingenious industry has improved the conveniences of nature. The attachments of patriotism are thus cherished in the breast. A generous desire that one may also contribute a mite however small, to the service of one's country, is awaked in the soul. And the relation of work and dignity of character is excited; the mean manners, and vicious conduct are regarded with increasing abhorence.

> Robert Heron (1764–1807)
> *Observations made on a Journey
> Through the Western Counties of
> Scotland*

Commerce and Vice Come to Gatehouse-of-Fleet

The increase of opulence, the growth of population and the rising activity of industry have . . . been astonishingly rapid and powerful. A second large edifice for a cotton work, has been directed by Messrs Birtwhistle. Another likewise, is being built by a Mr M'William. All intended as houses only for the spinning of cotton-yarn. By that machine, named the mule, between forty and fifty pounds of cotton-wool are made into yarn in a week. For, many have been induced to try this manufacture, who could not erect cotton-mills, and were therefore obliged to content themselves with spinning mules and Ginnees. A maker of these machines has settled here. A brass-foundry has also been established here, to supply those articles of wrought brass which are necessary to the construction of the spinning and weaving apparatus. Three hundred pounds of cotton-wool are spun into yarn in the week in the large cotton-work of Messrs Birtwhistle. Three hundred persons are employed in the labour; of them two hundred are children; and £50 of weekly wages are paid. On the Ginnees, a hundred pounds of cotton-wool are spun in the week. This yarn is all sold in Glasgow —and in the neighbourhood:—For the weaving of cotton-cloth begins to be carried on here with little less earnestness and success than the spinning of cotton-yarn. Nor is the spirit of the cotton-manufacture now confined exclusively to Gatehouse. It spreads fast through the whole country. Every person who can spare money enough to purchase a mule or a Ginnee, and a little raw cotton to begin with, eagerly turns Cotton-Spinner. The country weavers too either purchase yarn and make cotton-cloth for themselves —for which they find their ready sale,—or are employed by the manufacturers of Glasgow or of Gatehouse, to weave cotton-cloth for them. The ploughman forsakes his plough, the schoolmaster lays down his birch, the tanner deserts his tan-pits, the apothecary turns from the composition of pills, and the mixing of unguents; and all earnestly commence spinners of cotton-yarn or weavers of cotton-cloth . . . .

I wish I could honestly add, that the morals of these good people have been improved with their circumstances. But prostitution and breaches of chastity have lately become frequent here. Tippling houses are wonderfully numerous. I was informed by the excellent Excise man of the place, that not fewer than 150 gallons—of whisky alone—had been consumed here for every week of the last six months. The licentiousness of Gatehouse affords frequent business for the neighbouring Justices. The Clergyman of the Parish has found it necessary to act both as a Justice of the Peace and as a Clergyman; and although exceedingly active in the former of these capacities, has yet found it too hard for him to restrain the irregularities of these villagers. An assistant has been employed to aid him in the discharge of his clerical functions. Yet, both the pious assiduities of his assistant, and his own neighbours, clerical and juridical, have proved insufficient to maintain among the manufacturers of Gatehouse, all that purity of morals and decorum of manners which might be wished . . . As a moralist, I cannot but regret that crowded population, and the prosperity of manufacture should be so invariably attended with the extreme corruption of the lower orders. In this mind I should not wish to see Gatehouse increase greatly above its present population: and I would gladly see some expedience used to restrain the growth of vice, in a village where, but for vice, wanton idleness might be unknown. It has been the great error of the politicians and philosophers of the present age, that, in their care to multiply the numbers, to stimulate industry, and to increase the opulence of mankind, they have overlooked the important concern of checking their vices, and of encouraging their declining virtues.

Robert Heron
Ibid

Edinburgh Society, 1774/5

Twenty-four-year-old Edward Topham, son of Dr Topham of York, finished his Grand Tour by enduring the rigours of an Edinburgh winter. Not much escaped his enthusiastic scrutiny.

The married ladies of this City seldom entertain large sets of company, or have routs, as in London. They give the preference to private parties, and *conversatziones*, where they play at cards for small sums, and never run the risk of being obliged to discharge a debt of honour at the expence of their virtue and innocence. They often frequent the theatre, and show great taste and judgment in the choice of plays where Mr Digges performs a principal character.

As to exercise, they seldom ride on horseback; but find much pleasure in walking, to which the soil and country is peculiarly adapted, being dry, pleasant, and abounding in prospects, and romantic scenes. It is likewise customary for them to drive in their carriages to the sands at Leith and Musselburgh, and parade backwards and forwards, after the manner of Scarborough, and other public places of sea-bathing resort. For vivacity and agility in dancing, none excel the Scotch ladies; their execution in reels and country-dances is amazing; and the variety of steps which they introduce, and the justness of their ear is beyond description. They are very fond also of minuets, but fall greatly short in the performance of them, as they are deficient in grace and elegance in their motions. Many of them play on the harpsichord and guitar, and some have music in their voices: though they rather love to hear others perform than play themselves.

I do not think the Scotch ladies are great proficients in the languages. They rarely attempt any thing further than the French; which, indeed, they speak with great propriety, fluency, and good accent; but they make up for it by their accurate and just knowledge of their own. They talk very grammatically; and are peculiarly attentive to the conformity of their words to their ideas, and are great critics in the English tongue. They chiefly read history, and plaintive poetry: but elegies and pastorals are their favourites. Novels and romances they feel, and admire; and those chiefly which are tender, sympathetic, soothing or melancholy. Their hearts are soft and full of passion, and a well-told story makes a deep impression on them. Like virgin wax, a gentle heat mollifies their minds, which reflects the finest touches of art and sentiment —

Nor are the gentlemen in Edinburgh less rational in their diversions than the ladies. There is only one, in which I can censure their conduct: they rather pay too much respect to the divinity of Bacchus, and offer too copious libations at the shrine of that jovial deity . . .

The youths in this country are very manly in their exercises and amusements. Strength and agility seems to be most their attention. The insignicant pastimes of marbles, tops etc., they are totally unacquainted with. The diversion which is peculiar to Scotland, and in which all ages find great pleasure, is golf. They play at it with a small leathern ball, like a fives ball, and a piece of wood, flat on one side, in the shape of a small bat, which is fastened at the end of a stick, of three or four feet long, at right angles to it. The art consists of striking the ball with this instrument, into a hole in the ground, in a smaller number of strokes than your adversary. This game has the superiority of cricket and tennis, in being less violent and dangerous; but in point of dexterity and amusement, by no means to be compared with them. However, I am informed that some skill and nicety are necessary to strike the ball to the proposed distance and no further, and that in this there is a considerable difference in players. It requires no great exertion and strength, and all ranks and ages play at it. They instruct their children in it, as soon as they can run alone, and grey hairs boast their execution.

As to their other diversions, they dance, play at cards, love shooting, hunting, and the pleasures of the field; but they are proficient in none of them. When they are young, indeed, they dance, in the manner of their country, extremely well; but afterwards (to speak in the language of the turf) they train off, and are too robust and muscular to possess either grace or agility.

Edward Topham (1751–1819)
Letters from Edinburgh

An Edinburgh Ball

On Wednesday I gave a ball. How do ye think I contrived to stretch out this house to hold twenty-two people, and had nine couples always dancing? Yet this is true: It is also true that we had a table covered with divers eatables all the time, and that everybody eat when they were hungry and drank when were dry, but nobody ever sat down. I think my house, like my purse, is just the widow's cruse.

I must tell you of my party of dancers. Captain Bob Dalrymple was King of the Ball, as it was his bespeaking. Tell Lady Balcarres that, as a nephew she will delight in him: he is my first favourite. Well, for men, there was Bob and Hew, young men both; Peter Inglis, a Mr Bruce, a lawyer; then Jock Swinton and Jock Turnbull. Then, for women, there were Tibbie Hall, my two nieces, Agnes Keith, Christy Pringle, Babie Carnegie, Christy

Anderson, Jeanie Rutherford. Mrs Mure and Violy Pringle came and danced a reel, and went off. Now for our dance. Our fiddler sat where the cupboard is and they danced in both rooms; the table was stuffed into the window, and we had plenty of room. It made the bairns all vastly happy. Next day I went to the Assembly with all these misses.

Mrs Alison Cockburn (1713–94)
Letters

Music In Edinburgh

The building which Hugo Arnot, the historian of Edinburgh whose book was published in 1779, describes, is St Cecilia's Hall. When the New Town finally drew away the audiences, this beautiful hall became a sectarian chapel. Its final use during a long deterioration was as a dance hall. Restored again by Edinburgh University, it now houses the Russell Collection of keyboard instruments, and is once again a venue for chamber concerts.

The musical society of Edinburgh, whose weekly concerts form one of the most elegant entertainments of that metropolis, was first instituted in the year 1728.

Before that time, several gentlemen, performers on the harpsichord and violin, had formed a weekly club at the Cross-keys tavern, where the common entertainment consisted in playing the concertos and sonatas of Corelli, then just published; and the Overtures of Handel. That meeting becoming numerous, they instituted, in March 1728, a society of seventy members, for the purpose of holding a weekly concert. A governour, deputy-governour, treasurer and five directors, are annually chosen by the members, for regulating the affairs of this society. Its meetings have been continued since that period much on the same plan, only the place where they are held has been changed from St Mary's Chapel to their own hall. These meetings are only interrupted during three or four weeks of the vacation, in the months of September and October.

The present Concert hall, which is situated in a centrical part of the town, was built in A.D. 1762. The plan was drawn by Sir Robert Mylne, architect, of Blackfriars-bridge, after the model of the great opera-theatre at Parma but on a smaller scale; and the expence was defrayed by voluntary subscription among the members. The musical room is reckoned uncommonly elegant. It is of an oval form; the ceiling, a concave eliptical dome, lighted solely from the top by a lanthorn. Its construction is excellently adapted for musick; and the seats ranged in the room in the form of an amphitheatre, besides leaving a large area in the middle of the room, are capable of containing a company of about five hundred persons. The orchestra is at the upper end, which is handsomely terminated by an elegant organ.

The band consists of a *Maestro di capella*, an organist, two violins, two tenors, six or eight *ripienos*, a double or *contra*-bass, and harpsichord; and occasionally two French horns, besides kettle-drums, flutes, and clarinets. There is always one good singer, and there are sometimes two, upon the establishment. A few years ago, the celebrated Tenducci was at the head of this company . . .

Besides an extraordinary concert, in honour of St Cecilia, the patroness of music, there are usually performed, in the course of the year, two or three of Handel's oratorios. That great master gave this society the privilege of having full copies made for them, of all his manuscript oratorios. An occasional concert is sometimes given upon the death of a governour or director. This is conducted in the manner of a *concerto spirituale*. The pieces are of sacred music; the symphonies accompanied with the full organ, French-horns, clarinets and kettle-drums. Upon these occasions, the audience is in deep mourning, which, added to the pathetic solemnity of the musick, has a noble and striking effect upon the mind.

The musick generally performed, is a proper mixture of the modern and ancient stile. The former, although agreeable to the prevailing taste, is not allowed to debar the amusement of those, who find more pleasure in the old compositions. In every plan there are one or two pieces of Corelli, Handel, or Geminiani.

Among the number of members, which is now increased to 200, there are many excellent performers, who take their parts in the orchestra, especially in extraordinary concerts, where sometimes a whole act is performed solely by the gentlemen-members.

Formerly some of the members of this society instituted a catch-club, which met after the concert. On the great concert, in honour of St Cecilia, the governour and directors were in use to invite a few of their friends, and strangers of fashion, to an entertainment of this kind, after the concert, where select pieces of vocal musick were performed, intermingled with Scots songs, duets, catches, and glees. There were many excellent voices in the catch-club, who sung each their part at sight. . . .

By an uniform adherence to the spirit and rules of the society, and a strict economy in the management of their funds, the musical society has subsisted these fifty years, with great honour and reputation; and, at present, it is esteemed one of the most elegant and genteel entertainments, conducted upon the most moderate expence, of any in Britain.

Hugo Arnot (1749–86)
The History of Edinburgh

A Director of the Musical Society

The concert was, from its early hour (beginning at six, afterwards at half past six, and latterly at seven, and ending at nine or half past nine) and the unceremoniousness of only a common dinner dress being required, an entertainment excellently well adapted to men of business, of whom most of the resident members consisted. Lord Kames was a constant attendant, relaxing at the concert from his labours both judicial and literary, and indulging in that playful homage to the ladies which he was proud to indulge in and to exhibit. His great favourites, the daughters of Chief Baron Ord, were very seldom absent, and being all extremely musical, and speaking Italian, then no common accomplishment in Edinburgh, they sat in a particular seat near the orchestra, and had much communication with the principal performers.

I was admitted a member about the year 1778, and a director ten or twelve years after. I had the honour of being a director for a good many years, in conjunction with Lord Haddington, governor of the institution; Sir W. Forbes; Mr Mitchelson and Mr Tytler, both uncommonly good performers on the German Flute; and we used to meet occasionally at very pleasant suppers, on the business of the Society.

When the New Town attracted the people of fashion, when Stabilini ceased to be a novelty and grew very careless about the Concert, the place of their hall was felt as extremely inconvenient, and the concerts began to be neglected, tho' the directors did all they could to bolster them up, by giving tea between the acts, and appointing some musical lady of rank and fashion to be a sort of patroness for the night; but all their exertions were fruitless. I was very desirous, on account of my old friend Mr Tytler, whose favourite object the Concert had been for more than half a century, that it should survive *him*. This object I attained; one of the last concerts was a funeral one to his memory, and after languishing a short time, it expired; the property was sold, and the subscribers lost nothing by the adventure.

Henry Mackenzie (1745–1831)
Anecdotes and Egotisms

Music and Dancing in Glasgow

Robert Reid, who contributed many articles to 'The Glasgow Herald' around the middle years of the nineteenth century, wrote under the pen-name 'Senex'. His recollections of music and dancing about the year 1800 were set down in 1849. The Assembly Rooms to which he refers were built in 1796 by Robert Adam. They stood in Ingram Street, on the site of what is now the site of the Post Office. Demolished in 1893, the central arch was rebuilt on Glasgow Green the following year, and again in 1922, where it now forms one of the entrances to the Green. Adam's Trades Hall we still have.

Music, both vocal and instrumental, and also dancing, were then taught in

Glasgow with fewer flourishes than now; the former was professed and taught to classes of both sexes by various individuals; and among them was Mr Rivin, as he was usually called (Ruthvin was the name), who was precentor in the Ram's-horn Kirk, and who taught numerous parties of young people to sing; he often led them in such a manner that their sweet voices had small chance against his pipe.

In that, he was not unlike some of the more modern precentors now in churches, who, instead of merely raising and conducting tunes to congregations while engaged in the soul-stirring exercise of psalmody, seem to think it their duty to sing with such exertion of lungs and larynx that ordinary mortals are held at bay.

Pianofortes ... were then much rarer instruments in houses in this city than they are now, even in proportion to its wealth and population ...

Dancing was then confined almost to the walking of the minuet and *contredanse*, with Roger de Coverley, or bab-at-the-bolster and Highland fling. Waltzes, quadrilles, gallopades, and polkas were at that period either unknown here, or not in fashion.

On the evening of the King's birthday there was always a grand ball in the Assembly Rooms, where the scions of the Glasgow aristocracy figured on 'the light fantastic toe;' but the balls, concerts, and practisings of schools were mostly in the Trades' Hall. In those days ladies going to parties in the evening were usually carried in sedan chairs, of which there was a great number in town, carried mostly by Highlanders; and on any grand occasion, especially without moonlight, it was a sight worth seeing, that of these chairs being hobbled along, each of them with a lantern dangling from its pole, and making darkness visible even when the street lamps were burning; but before the introduction of gas the oil lamps with which the streets were supplied were often on a windy evening nearly all extinguished, leaving the thoroughfares of the city after business hours in almost total darkness.

Robert Reid-'Senex' (1773–1865)
Glasgow Past and Present

The Highland Family Piper

Our landlord is a man of consequence in this part of the country; a cadet from the family of Argyle, and hereditary captain of one of his castles—his name, in plain English, is Dougal Campbell; but as there are a great number of the same appellation, they are distinguished (like the Welsh) by patronymics; and as I have known an ancient Briton called Madoc ap-Morgan, ap-Jenkin, ap-Jones, our Highland chief designs himself Dou'l Mac-amish, mac-'oul ich-Ian, signifiying in the course of his education, and is disposed to make certain alterations in his domestic economy: but he finds it impossible

19

to abolish the ancient customs of the family: some of which are ludicrous enough. His piper, for example, who is an hereditary officer of the household, will not part with the least particle of his privileges. He has a right to wear the kilt, or ancient Highland dress, with the purse, pistol, and dirk- a broad yellow ribbon, fixed to the chanter-pipe, is thrown over his shoulder, and trails along the ground, while he performs the functions of his minstrelsy; and this, I suppose, is analogous to the pennon or flag, which was formerly carried before every knight in battle. He plays before the laird every Sunday in this way to the kirk, which he circles three times, performing the family march, which implies defiance to all the enemies of the clan; and every morning he plays a full hour by the clock, in the great hall, marching backwards and forwards all the time, with a solemn pace, attended by the laird's kinsmen, who seem much delighted with the music. In this exercise he indulges them with a number of pibrochs or airs, suited to the different passions which he would either excite or assuage.

Mr Campbell himself, who performs very well on the violin, has an invincible antipathy to the sound of the Highland bagpipe, which sings in the nose with a most alarming twang, and, indeed, is quite intolerable to ears of common sensibility, when aggravated by the echo of a vaulted hall. He, therefore, begged the piper would have some mercy upon him, and dispense with this part of the morning service. A consultation of the clan being held on this occasion, it was unanimously agreed, that the laird's request could not be granted, without a dangerous encroachment upon the customs of the family. The piper declared he could not give up for a moment the privileges he derived from his ancestors; nor would the laird's relations forego an entertainment which they valued above all others. There was no remedy; Mr Campbell being obliged to acquiesce, is fain to stop his ears with cotton, to fortify his head with three or four nightcaps, and every morning retire into the penetralia of his habitation, in order to avoid this diurnal annoyance.

Tobias Smollett (1721–71)
Humphry Clinker

A Bagpipe Competition

In the Autumn of 1784, the French geologist Faujas St Fond visited Edinburgh while on his Scottish tour. The man he met most often seems to have been 'that venerable philospher, Adam Smith', author of 'The Wealth of Nations'. They talked of Voltaire and of Rousseau, whom Smith had met when he lived in Paris. They also talked about music. One day, at nine o'clock in the morning, Smith came to St Fond's lodgings and took him off to 'a spacious concert-room' full of people; landlords from the Highlands and Islands, Smith explained, come to

judge a piping competition. To Scots who enjoy the music of the pipes, St Fond's
description will seem unsympathetic. It is nevertheless an amusingly-written
and wholly understandable reaction from someone possessed of non-Scottish
ears.

A few moments later, a folding door opened at the bottom of the room, and
to my great surprise, I saw a Scottish Highlander enter . . . playing upon the
bagpipe, and walking up and down an empty space with rapid steps and a
military air, blowing the noisiest and most discordant sounds from an
instrument which lacerates the ear. The air he played was a kind of sonata,
divided into three parts. Smith begged me to give it my whole attention,
and to tell him afterwards the impression it made on me.

But I confess that at first I could distinguish neither air nor design. I
only saw the piper marching always with rapidity, and with the same warlike
countenance. He made incredible efforts both with his body and his fingers
to bring into play at once the different pipes of his instrument, which made
an insupportable uproar.

He received nevertheless great applause from all sides. A second musician
followed into the arena, wearing the same martial look and walking to and
fro with the same martial air . . .

After having listened to eight pipers in succession, I began to suspect that
the first part was connected with a warlike march and military evolutions:
the second with a sanguinary battle, which the musician sought to depict by
the noise and rapidity of his playing and by his loud cries. He seemed then
to be convulsed; his pantomimical gestures resembled those of a man engaged
in combat; his arms, his hands, his head, his legs, were all in motion; the
sounds of his instrument were all called forth and confounded together at
the same moment. This fine disorder seemed keenly to interest every one.
The piper then passed, without transition, to a kind of andante; his convulsions suddenly ceased; the sounds of his instrument were plaintive, languishing, as if lamenting the slain who were being carried off from the field of
battle. This was the part which drew tears from the eyes of the beautiful
Scottish ladies. But the whole was so uncouth and extraordinary; the impression which this wild music made upon me contrasted so strongly with
that which it made upon the inhabitants of the country, that I am convinced
we should look upon this strange composition not as essentially belonging to
music, but to history . . .

The same air was played by each competitor, of whom there was a considerable number. The most perfect equality was maintained among them;
the son of the laird stood on the same footing with the simple shepherd,
often belonging to the same clan, bearing the same name, and having the
same garb. No preference was shown here save to talent, as I could judge
from the hearty plaudits given to some who seemed to excel in that art. I
confess it was impossible for me to admire any of them. I thought them all of
equal proficiency: that is to say, the one was as bad as the other; and the

air that was played as well as the instrument itself, involuntarily put me in
mind of a bear's dance.

B. Faujas St Fond (1741–1819)
Travels in England and Scotland

Burns's 'Poor Namesake'

*Margaret Burns (or Matthews, as was probably her real name), was young,
beautiful and lived in Rose Street, Edinburgh, where, in 1789 with one Sally
Sanderson, she set up a brothel immediately opposite the back of Lord Swinton's
house. The neighbours complained and Miss Burns was ordered to leave the
City by the magistrate, bookseller William Creech—Burns's 'little, upright,
pert, tart tripping wight'. Miss Burns appealed against her sentence, first un-
successfully before Lord Dreghorn at the Court of Session, and then successfully,
when she reclaimed to the Inner House in December 1789. Soon after her
health failed, and she died at Rosslyn in 1792.*

*Burns got to hear of her plight before the success of her appeal was known,
and on 2nd February, 1790 wrote in compassionate but amusing terms to his
friend the Edinburgh bookseller, Peter Hill.*

How is the fate of my poor Namesake Mademoiselle Burns, decided? Which
of their grave *Lordships* can lay his hand on his heart and say that he has not
taken advantage of such frailty; nay, if we may judge by near six thousand
years experience, can the World do without such frailty; O Man! but for
thee, and they selfish appetites and dishonest artifices, that beauteous form,
and that once innocent and still ingenious mind, might have shone conspicuous and lovely in the faithful wife and the affectionate mother; and shall
the unfortunate sacrifice to thy pleasures have no claim on thy humanity?
As for those flinty-bosomed, puritanic Prosecutors of Female Frailty, and
Prosecutors of Female Charms—I am quite sober—I am dispassionate—to
shew you that I am so I shall mend my pen ere I proceed—It is written, 'Thou
shalt not take the name of the Lord thy God in vain,' so I shall neither say,
G— curse them! nor G— blast them! nor G— damn them! But may Woman
curse them! May Woman blast them! May Woman damn them! May her
lovely hand inexorably shut the Portal of Rapture to their most earnest
Prayers and fondest essays for entrance! And when many years and much
port and great business have delivered them over to Vulture Gouts and
Aspen Palsies, *then* may the dear bewitching Charmer in derision throw
open the blissful Gate to tantalise their impotent desires when all their
powers to give or receive enjoyment, are for ever asleep in the sepulchre of
their fathers! ! !

Robert Burns (1759–96)
Letters

New Social Customs

Before this year, the drinking of tea was little known in the parish, saving among a few of the heritors' houses on a Sabbath evening; but now it became very rife: yet the commoner sort did not like to let it be known that they were taking to the new luxury, especially the elderly women, who, for that reason, had their ploys in out-houses and by-places, just as the witches lang syne had their sinful possets and galravitchings; and they made their tea for common in the pint-stoup, and drank it out of caps and luggies, for there were but few among them that had cups and saucers. Well do I remember one night in harvest, in this very year, as I was taking my twilight dauner aneath the hedge along the back side of Thomas Thorl's yard, meditating on the goodness of Providence, and looking at the sheaves of victual on the field, that I heard his wife, and two three other carlins, with their Bohea in the inside of the hedge, and no doubt but it had a lacing of the conek, for they were all cracking like pen-guns. But I gave them a sign, by a loud host, that Providence sees all, and it skailed the bike; for I heard them, like guilty creatures, whispering and gathering up their truck-pots and trenchers, and cowering away home. . . .

I should not, in my notations, forget to mark a new luxury that got in among the commonality at this time. By the opening of new roads, and the traffic thereon with carts and carriers, and by our young men that were sailors going to the Clyde, and sailing to Jamaica and the West Indies, heaps of sugar and coffee-beans were brought home, while many, among the kail-stocks and cabbages in their yards, had planted groset and berry bushes; which two things happening together, the fashion to make jam and jelly, which hitherto had only been known in the kitchens and confectionaries of the gentry, came to be introduced into the clachan. All this, however, was not without a plausible pretext; for it was found that jelly was an excellent medicine for a sore throat, and jam a remedy as good as London candy for a cough, or a cold, or a shortness of breath. I could not, however, say that this gave me so much concern as the smuggling trade, only it occasioned a great fasherie to Mrs Balwhidder; for, in the berry time, there was no end to the borrowing of her brass-pan to make jelly and jam, till Mrs Toddy of the Cross-Keys bought one, which, in its turn, came into request, and saved ours.

John Galt (1779–1839)
Annals of the Parish

Tea-Smuggling

Shortly after the revival of the smuggling, an exciseman was put among us. The first was Robin Bicker, a very civil lad that had been a flunkey with Sir Hugh Montgomerie, when he was a residenter in Edinburgh, before the old

Sir Hugh's death. He was a queer fellow, and had a coothy way of getting in about folk, the which was very serviceable to him in his vocation. Nor was he overly gleg: but when a job was ill done, and he was obliged to notice it, he would often break out on the smugglers for being so stupid; so that for an exciseman he was wonderful well liked, and did not object to a waught of brandy at a time, when the auld wives ca'd it well-water. It happened, however, that some unneighbourly person sent him notice of a clecking of tea-chests, or brandy kegs, at which both Jenny and Betty Pawkie were the howdies; and Robin could not but enter their house. However, before going in, he just cried at the door to somebody on the road, so as to let the twa industrious lasses hear he was at hand. They were not slack in closing the trance-door, and putting stoups and stools behind it, so as to cause trouble, and give time before anybody could get in. They then emptied their chaff-bed, and filled the tikeing with tea, and Betty went in on the top, covering herself with the blanket, and graining like a woman in labour. It was thought that Robin Bicker himself would not have been overly particular in searching the house, considering there was a woman seemingly in the dead-thraws; but a sorner, an incomer from the east country, that hung about the change-house as a divor hostler, and would rather gang a day's journey in the dark, than turn a spade in daylight, came to him as he stood at the door, and went in with him to see the sport. Robin, for some reason, could not bid him go away, and both Betty and Janet were sure he was in the plot against them. Indeed, it was always thought that he was an informer; and no doubt he was something not canny, for he had a down look.

It was sometime before the doorway was cleared of the stoups and stools: and Jenny was in great concern, and flustered, as she said, for her poor sister, who was taken with a heart-colic. 'I'm sorry for her,' said Robin: 'but I'll be as quiet as possible'. And so he searched all the house, but found nothing; at the which his companion, the divor hostler, swore an oath that could not be misunderstood. Without more ado, but, as all thought, against the grain, Robin went up to sympathise with Betty in the bed, whose groans were loud and vehement. 'Let me feel your pulse,' said Robin; and he looted down as she put forth her arm from aneath the clothes, and, laying his hand on the bed, cried, 'Hey! what's this? This is a costly filling.' Upon which Betty jumpet up quite recovered, and Jenny fell to the wailing and railing; while the hostler from the east country took the bed of tea on his back, to carry it to the change-house, till a cart was gotten to take it to the custom house at Irville.

Betty Pawkie, being thus suddenly cured, and grudging the loss of property, took a knife in her hand, and, as the divor was crossing the burn at the stepping-stones that lead to the back of the change-house, she ran after him and ripped up the tikeing, and sent all the tea floating away on the burn.

John Galt
Ibid

The Taking of the Salmon

A birr! a whirr! a salmon's on,
  A goodly fish! a thumper!
Bring up, bring up the ready gaff,
And if we land him we shall quaff
    Another glorious bumper!
      Hark 'tis the music of the reel,
        The strong, the quick, the steady;
      The line darts from the active wheel,
        Have all things right and ready.

A birr! a whirr! the salmon's out,
  Far on the rushing river;
Onward he holds with sudden leap,
Or plunges through the whirlpool deep,
    A desperate endeavour!
      Hark to the music of the reel!
        The fitful and the grating;
      It pants along the breathless wheel,
        Now hurried, now abating.

A birr! a whirr! the salmon's off!—
  No, no, we still have got him;
The wily fish is sullen grown,
And, like a bright imbedded stone,
    Lies gleaming at the bottom.
      Hark to the music of the reel!
        'Tis hush'd, it hath forsaken;
      With care we'll guard the magic wheel,
        Until its notes rewaken.

A birr! a whirr! the salmon's up,
  Give line, give line and measure;
But now he turns! keep down ahead,
And lead him as a child is lead,
    And land him at your leisure.
      Hark to the music of the reel!
        'Tis welcome, it is glorious;
      It wanders thro' the winding wheel,
        Returning and victorious.

A birr! a whirr! the salmon's in,
  Upon the bank extended;

The princely fish is gasping slow,
His brilliant colours come and go,
   All beautifully blended.
     Hark to the music of the reel!
      It murmurs and it closes;
     Silence is on the conquering wheel,
      It's wearied line reposes.

No birr! no whirr! the salmon's ours,
   The noble fish—the thumper:
Strike through his gill the ready gaff,
And bending homewards, we shall quaff
   Another glorious bumper!
     Hark to the music of the reel!
      We listen with devotion;
     There's something in that circling wheel
      That wakes the heart's emotion!

Thomas Tod Stoddart (1810–80)

The Garden at Dungair

In spite of the usual disappointments, wounded vanity and mornings after, I have always regarded this world as a rather pleasant place. I think the reason is that I spent so much of my little years in the garden at Dungair. It was a wide and sheltered close, with the house against the north, seven tall ash trees and a wall against the east and the cart shed against the west. It lay open to the south and gathered all the warmth of the sun into its arms. Fruit bushes filled the east border, strawberries the middle and vegetables the west, while the big flower border swept round in front of the house. An old apple tree grew in the middle of the strawberry bed. Sometimes it bore a harvest of sour unsociable little apples, but more often it was only a choir for the multitudinous sparrows that swung there gently in the breeze, like little pirate boats on a quiet tide, waiting a chance to raid the strawberry beds below. There was an arbour between the east wall and the house where a small thatched bower nestled under the golden laburnums. The bower contained a spacious seat made out of a mahogany bed and a number a mattresses, where old lady visitors like Miss Betsy, the sewing woman, used to take their rest on summer afternoons and add a somnulent burden to the sweeter humming of the bees.

The garden was my grandmother's own particular world where she spent every hour she could spare from her duties in the house. It is thus I remember her best, a little old woman in a soiled gown and sacking apron, her nails cracked, her hands torn and a smudge of earth on her face, moving slowly among the bushes with a pruning knife, going stiffly down on her knees to weed the seedlings, or gathering fruit so gently that her touch seemed a caress. She was not a beautiful woman poised against an exquisite garden. She herself was the gardener; she was part of the garden. It was her greatest joy to care for it, and it repaid her most bountifully. She had had a hard life. She had built castles in the quicksands of human nature and had seen them fall in ruins. She had tried to pattern life after her own ideas but it had defied her and delivered her unto sorrow. Now in her old age she had learned wisdom to let human kind gang its ain gait. She was content to cultivate her garden.

John R. Allan (1847–1907)
The Farmer's Boy

Doon the Watter

Since that August day of 1812 when the first practical steam ship—Henry Bell's 'Comet'—made its unsteady way down the Clyde from Glasgow to Greenock the pleasures of sailing on the Clyde—or 'Doon the Watter', as the pastime became popularly known—increased steadily throughout Victorian times, and survived until the 1960s. Of the several hundred steamers that plied on the Clyde over the century and a half during which pleasure-sailing was a popular pastime, none was more famous than Macbrayne's paddle-steamer the R.M.S. 'Columba'. Built in 1878, she survived until 1936—long enough to enable the present writer to savour the delights of sailing on her in the annual ritual of moving from Glasgow to the family summer-house at Innellan.

We were to set out, I think, on the first day of July—mother and father, nurse, four children, dog, cat and goldfish—the packing was done systematically during the last days of June. I do not think I slept much on the night before the day of our departure. It began early. We got up at five in the morning, and had breakfast half an hour later. For some reason, that breakfast had a special quality of its own. Its ingredients were those of many another breakfast eaten since—porridge, bread and butter and a boiled egg— but I can still remember the extra flavour those comestibles seemed to acquire that morning. . . .

After breakfast, we children were expected to keep out of the way of our elders, for a horse-drawn lorry arrived outside the house at 6 o'clock to cart the luggage down to the quay. I was given the job of guarding the cat while the luggage was being grunted and manoeuvred round the bends of the staircase. The cat, a venerable beast who lived to be eighteen and would then be about twelve, had the idea that if he managed to escape while the front door stood open to let the carters move freely in and out, he would not have to undergo his annual holiday ordeal of transportation by basket; hence the need for one of the family to stand guard.

At last the luggage had rumbled away, the cat had been safely basketed, and it was time to prepare ourselves for the arrival of the taxi. That taxi-drive itself was something of a novelty. Usually I went to children's parties in a cab, a musty affair upholstered in faded green and driven by a red-nosed, mufflered coachman, whose characteristic smell was almost as strong as that of the horse that pulled the contraption.

Ordinary mortals who go about their affairs during the hours of daylight would do well to take an occasional ride through an industrial city at half past six in the morning, if only to remind themselves how large a section of the community has to do 'day labour, light denied' in order to keep essential public services running. The new sun shone out from a clean sky this July morning, glistening the roof-tops of the tenements, and lighting up even the drabbest side-streets with the promise of a fair day.

The *Columba* lay on the south side of the river, her two red-and-black funnels setting off nobly her huge, gilded paddle boxes. The moment you climbed up her gangway, your nostrils were assailed by a peculiar aroma that was all her own. After some years I discovered that it was a mixture of heated engine oil, good galley cooking and well-scrubbed cleanliness, to which, down the river, the scudding tang of salt spray was added. But at that time, analysis did not matter. The smell was wholly entrancing. We were to establish ourselves in the cabin, or 'saloon' as it was more grandly called. The saloon consisted of a number of seated bays lined with dark red-velvet plush, and richly draped with similar hangings.

It gave an impression of well-established opulence and time-saturated sea-going. All went well at first. I carried the cat's basket down the com-panionway, and the cat remained obligingly silent. But at the entrance to the saloon, a liveried steward looked at me and my burden with an unmistakable air of hostility.

'What's in that basket?' he demanded.

'Provisions', I answered, with a happier promptitude than I have dis-played on many a more important occasion since. He grunted and let us past. We chose an empty bay, and comfortably dispersed our bits and pieces.

Those final moments of waiting seemed the most interminable of all. Above our heads, busy feet tapped out their walking patterns on the deck. In the orange glow of the engine-room, the great gleaming monsters hissed and sizzled quietly to themselves, as if anticipating the moment when the flicker of a dial and the loosening of a lever would send them plunging backward and forward in all their pride of power.

Seven o'clock! Five minutes past! and then the mishanter occurred. A long, thin stream of clear liquid suddenly raced down the floor. Its place of origin was unmistakably the basket at my feet. In a moment the steward was at my side.

'Your provisions seem to be leaking, sir,' he observed acidly. (That 'sir', to one of my tender years, seemed an additional humiliation.) 'You'd better take them on deck.'

I was delighted. I certainly had no desire to spend my first voyage in the feminine confines of the cabin. Now, someone would *have* to stay on deck to see that the cat was not shipped prematurely ashore.

Up there, things were happening. The captain, an impressive and recognizably Highland figure even beneath the disguising weight of his gold braid, was pacing his bridge, which straddled the ship from one paddle-box to the other between the two funnels. (It has always seemed strange to me that until about 1920, it apparently never occurred to the designers of paddle-steamers that the funnel was a fairly major obstacle in the way of the helmsman's vision.) The captain took one final look at his watch—then he pulled the clanging brass levers at his side. The paddles began to thresh the water, nosing the ship's bow out towards the centre of the river—with a couple of dirty splashes, the ropes were tossed into the water, to be retrieved fussily by puffing steam capstans at bow and stern—and then the long, lean hull, shuddering a little at first, began to slide slowly forward.

Past close miles of shipyard, resounding with the racket of the riveters putting together the rusty hulks of the ships that would sail tomorrow's seas; past docks full of towering ocean-going liners, and queer-looking tramp ships with foreign characters scrawled across their stern; past grumphed-up dirty old dredgers, squatting in the middle of the river, digging away the mud that forever strives to slip back into its ancient bed; past low-built hoppers carrying the City's sewage far down the Firth to be dumped in the deeps around Ailsa Craig; past the chain-drawn car ferries of Renfrew and Earskine; past Bowling, with its stone pencil monument to Henry Bell, and its huge oil port and depot cut back into the hills; past Greenock and Gourock, and over the broadening Firth to Dunoon and Innellan, names which sounded music to my senses.

Maurice Lindsay (*b.* 1918)
Portrait of Glasgow

MYSTICISM

Thomas the Rhymer

True Thomas lay on Huntlie bank;
   A ferlie he spied wi' his e'e;   [marvel
And there he saw a ladye bright
   Come riding down by the Eildon Tree.

Her skirt was o' the grass-green silk,
   Her mantle o' the velvet fyne;
At ilka tett o' horses mane   [tuft
   Hung fifty siller bells and nine.

True Thomas he pu'd aff his cap,
   And louted low down on his knee:
'Hail to thee, Mary, Queen of Heaven!
   For thy peer on earth could never be.'

'O no, O no, Thomas,' she said,
   'That name does not belang to me;
I'm but the Queen o' fair Elfland.
   That am hither come to visit thee.

'Harp and carp, Thomas,' she said;   [play and recite
   'Harp and carp along wi' me;
And if ye dare to kiss my lips,
   Sure of your bodie I will be.'

'Betide me weal, betide me woe,
   That weird shall never daunten me.'   [doom
Syne he has kiss'd her rosy lips,
   All underneath the Eildon Tree.

'Now ye maun go wi' me,' she said,
   'True Thomas, ye maun go wi' me;
And ye maun serve me seven years,
   Thro' weal or woe as may chance to be.'

303

She's mounted on her milk-white steed,
  She's ta'en true Thomas up behind;
And aye, whene'er her bridle rang,
  The steed gaed swifter than the wind.

O they rade on, and farther on,
  The steed gaed swifter than the wind;
Until they reach'd a desert wide,
  And living land was left behind.

'Light down, light down now, true Thomas,
  And lean your head upon my knee;
Abide ye there a little space,
  And I will show you ferlies three.

'O see ye not yon narrow road,
  So thick beset wi' thorns and briers?
That is the Path of Righteousness,
  Though after it but few inquires.

'And see ye not yon braid, braid road,
  That lies across the lily leven?   [lawn
That is the Path of Wickedness,
  Though some call it the Road to Heaven.

'And see ye not yon bonny road
  That winds about the fernie brae?
That is the Road to fair Elfland,
  Where thou and I this night maun gae.

'But, Thomas, ye sall haud your tongue,
  Whatever ye may hear or see;
For speak ye word in Elfyn-land,
  Ye'll ne'er win back to your ain countrie.'

O they rade on, and farther on,
  And they waded rivers abune the knee;
And they saw neither sun nor moon,
  But they heard the roaring of the sea.

It was mirk, mirk night, there was nae starlight,
  They waded thro' red blude to the knee;
For a' the blude that's shed on the earth
  Rins through the springs o' that countrie.

Syne they came to a garden green,
  And she pu'd an apple frae a tree:
'Take this for thy wages, True Thomas;
  It will give thee the tongue that can never lee.'

'My tongue is my ain,' true Thomas said;
  'A gudely gift ye wad gie to me!
I neither dought to buy or sell
  At fair or tryst where I might be.

'I dought neither speak to prince or peer,
  Nor ask of grace from fair ladye!'—
'Now haud thy peace, Thomas,' she said,
  'For as I say, so must it be.'

He has gotten a coat of the even cloth,   [smooth
  And a pair o' shoon of the velvet green;
And till seven years were gane and past,
  True Thomas on earth was never seen.

Anonymous

A Definition of Fairies

Perhaps it is not without significance that the seventeenth century, which con-
tained the religious upheavals associated with the two Covenants, also encom-
passed an attempt to systematize the occult; by applying so-called standards of
proof in the trial of witches at one end of the period, and by attempting to lay
down the nature of creatures of occult fancy at the other. First in distinction
among those who undertook to map out the fairy world was the Reverend
Robert Kirk, a seventh son whose numerical position in his family led him to
believe that he had special insight regarding such matters. Minister first at
Balquidder, Perthshire, and later at Aberfoyle, he was twice married and made a
Gaelic translation of the Bible. He completed 'The Secret Commonwealth' in
1691, and a year later was seized by fairies on a dun-shi or fairy hill, and
spirited off to Fairyland, where presumably he is still held. The fairies managed
to prevent publication of his work until 1815.

The Siths, or Fairies, they call Sleagh Maith (or the Goodpeople, it would
seem, to prevent the dint of their ill attempts), are said to be of a middle
nature betwixt man and angel, as were demons thought to be of old, of
intelligent studious spirits, and light changeable bodies (like those called
astral), somewhat of the nature of a condensed cloud, and best seen in
twilight. These bodies be so pliable through the subtlety of the spirits that
agitate them, that they can make them appear or disappear at pleasure. Some

20

have bodies or vehicles so spongeous, thin, and defecate that they are fed by only sucking into some fine spirituous liquors, that pierce like pure air and oil; others feed more gross on the abundance or substance of corn and liquors, or corn itself that grows on the surface of the earth, which these fairies steal away, partly invisible, partly preying on the grain, as do crows and mice; wherefore in this same age they are sometimes heard to break bread, strike hammers, and to do such like services within the little hillocks they most do haunt; some whereof of old, before the Gospel dispelled Paganism, and in some barbarous places yet, enter houses after all are at rest, and set the kitchens in order, cleansing all the vessels. Such drudgs go'under the name of Brownies. When we have plenty, they have scarcity at their hames; and, on the contrary (for they are not empowered to catch as much prey everywhere as they please), their robberies, notwithstanding, oft-time occasion great ricks of corn not to bleed so well (as they call it), or prove so copious by very far as was expected by the owner.

Their bodies of congealed air are sometimes carried aloft, other whiles grovel in different shapes, and enter into any cranny or cleft of the earth where air enters, to their ordinary dwellings; the earth being full of cavities and cells, and their being no place, no creature, but is supposed to have other animals (greater or lesser) living in or upon it as inhabitants; and no such thing as a pure wilderness in the whole universe. . . .

They are distributed in tribes and orders, and have children, nurses, marriages, deaths , and burials in appearance, even as we (unless they so do for a mock-show, or to prognosticate some such things among us).

They are clearly seen by these men of the second sight to eat at funerals and banquets. Hence many of the Scottish–Irish will not taste meat at these meetings, lest they have communion with, or be poisoned by, them. So are they seen to carry the bier or coffin with the corpse among the middle-earth men to the grave. Some men of that exalted sight (whether by art or nature) have told me they have seen at these meetings a double man, or the shape of some man in two places; that is a super-terranean and a sub-terranean inhabitant, perfectly resembling one another in all points, whom he, notwithstanding, could easily distinguish one from another by some secret tokens and operations, and so go and speak to the man, his neighbour and familiar, passing by the apparition or resemblance of him. They avouch that every element and different state of being has animals resembling those of another element; as there be fishes sometimes at sea resembling monks of late order in all their hoods and dresses; so as the Roman invention of good and bad demons, and guardian angels particularly assigned, is called by them an ignorant mistake, sprung only from this original. They call this reflex man a co-walker, every way like the man, as a twin brother and companion, haunting him as his shadow, as is oft seen and known among men (resembling the original), both before and after the original is dead; and was often seen of old to enter a house, by which the people knew that the person of that likeness was to visit them within a few days. This copy, echo, or living picture, goes at last to his own herd. It accompanied that person so long and frequently for ends best known to itself, whether to guard him from the secret assaults of some of its own folk, or only as a sportful ape to counterfeit all his actions. However, the stories of old witches prove beyond contradiction that all sorts of people, spirits which assume light airy bodies, or crazed bodies coacted by foreign spirits, seem to have some pleasure (at least to assuage some pain or melancholy) by frisking and capering like satyrs, or whistling and screeching (like unlucky birds) in their unhallowed synagogues and Sabbaths. If invited and earnestly required, these companions make themselves known and familiar to men; otherwise, being in a different state and element, they neither can nor will easily converse with them. They avouch that a heluo or great eater has a voracious elve to be his attender, called a joint-eater or just-halver, feeding on the pith and quintessence of what the man eats; and that, therefore, he continues lean like hawk or heron, notwithstanding his devouring appetite; yet it would seem they convey that substance elsewhere, for these subterraneans eat but little in their dwellings, their food being exactly clean, and served up by pleasant children, like enchanted puppets....

Their houses are called large and fair, and (unless at some odd occasions) unperceivable by vulgar eyes, like Rachland and other enchanted islands, having fir lights, continual lamps, and fires, often seen without fuel to sustain them. Women are yet alive who tell they were taken away when in child-bed to nurse fairy children, a lingering voracious image of them being left in their place (like their reflection in a mirror), which (as if it were some insatiable spirit in an assumed body) made first semblance to devour the meats that it cunningly carried by, and then left the carcass as if it expired and departed thence by a natural and common death. The child and fire, with food and all other necessaries, are set before the nurse how soon she enters, but she neither perceives any passage out, nor sees what those people do in other rooms of the lodging. When the child is weaned, the nurse dies, or is conveyed back, or gets it to her choice to stay there.

Robert Kirk (1630–92)
The Secret Commonwealth

King Duff Bewitched

Though this be well known to all who read our Scots Histories, yet it will not be amiss to insert it here, as in its own place, for their sake especially who have not heard of it. While the King was about the setling of the Countrey, and punishing the Troublers of the Peace, he began to be sore afflicted in his Body with a new and unheard of Disease, no Causes of his Sickness appearing in the least. At length, after that several Remedies and Cures were made use of to no purpose, a Report is spread, the Authors thereof being uncertain, that the King was brought to that sickness and Trouble by Witches.

This suspicion arose, from an unusual Sweating he was under, his Body pining and withering away by little and little and his strength failing day by day. And since all his Physicians had done their utmost, and yet no appearance of recovery, it was supposed his case was extraordinary, therefore all men being vehemently intent upon the Event, news came to Court that Night-meetings were kept at Forres, a town in Murray, for taking away the life of the King. This was presently received and believed for truth, because no other thing did occur for the present more probable.

Whereupon Trusty and Faithful men are presently sent away to one Donald, Governour of the Castle there, in whom the King had the greatest Trust and Confidence. This man having gotten some knowledge of the business from a certain young Wench, whose Mother was under a bad report of being skilful in this Black-Art, found out and discovered the whole matter. The young Harlot is taken, because she had spoken some words rashly anent the King's sickness, and that within a few days his life would be at an end. Some of the Guard being sent, found the Lass's Mother, with some Haggs, such as her self, roasting before a small moderate fire, the King's Picture made of Wax. The design of this horrid Act, was that as the Wax by little and little did melt away, so the King's Body, by a continual sweating, might at last totally decay. The Waxen-Image being found and broken, and those old Haggs being punished by death, the King did in that same moment recover. Compare this with the first Relation, and you will find them jump and agree exactly.

George Sinclair (c. 1624–96)
Satan's Invisible World Discovered

The Pawky Auld Kimmer

There's a pawky auld Kimmer wons low i' the glen;
Nane kens how auld Kimmer maun fecht and maun fen;
Kimmer gets maut, and Kimmer gets meal,
And cantie lives Kimmer, right couthie an' hale;
Kimmer gets bread, an' Kimmer gets cheese,
An' Kimmer's uncannie een keep her at ease.
'I rede ye speak lowne, lest Kimmer should hear ye;   [reckon . . . speak soft
Come sain ye, come across ye, an' Gude be near ye!'

Kimmer can milk a hale loan of kye,
Yet sit at the ingle fu' snug an' fu' dry;
Kimmer a brown cowte o' poor Laurie made,
Whan she posted to Locherbrigg last Hallowmass rade.
Kimmer can sit i' the coat tails o' the moon,
And tipple gude wine at Brabant brewin'.

'I rede ye speak lowne, lest Kimmer should hear ye,
Come sain ye, come cross ye, an' Gude be near ye!'

Kimmer can sit an' say—'E'en be't sae!'
An' red jowes the Nith atween banking an' brae;
Kimmer can cast owre it her cantraips an' spells,
An' feerie can cross it in twa braid cockle shells.
The Laird spake to Kimmer for his barren ladie,
An' soon gaed my ladie coats kilted fu' hie.
'I rede ye speak lowne, lest Kimmer should hear ye;
Come sain ye, come cross ye, an' Gude be near ye!'

Kimmer was nae bidden whan the cannie wives gade,
But for Kimmer they ran, an' for Kimmer they rade:
Kimmer an' I are right couthie an' kin
Or the Laird's ae daughter wad ne'er hae been mine:
I creshed weel Kimmer's loof wi' howdying fee,
Or a cradle had ne'er a been totched for me!
'I rede ye speak lowne, lest Kimmer should hear ye;
Come sain ye, come cross ye, an' Gude be near ye!'

Anonymous

The Deil of Ardrossan

Ae day a merchant of Dumbarton sailed in his ship from that town. After
they had sailed several days, they got a great storm and were shipwrecked
on the coast of a desert island. All the crew were drowned except himself.
He, wandering about, found a cave on the shore, and he took his abode in it.
A mermaid found him there. She had a fondness towards the stranger. And
they afterwards lived together in that cave. The mermaid every day went to
her own element, or the sea, and brought provisions. And after a whole
year's residence, and his mermaid spouse being from home, he saw a ship,
and he hailed her. The ship's crew sent a boat ashore, and they entered into
conversation with this forlorn merchant, who related the take of his captivity,
and his living in a cave with a mermaid; and how that she brocht rowth of
food, and gowd, and sillar, and gows [jewels] and wine to him, so much as he
kenna what to do wi' them. They, being outward bound, requested him to
gar the beloved mermaid gather all the stores she possibly could, and they
hecht to cum again after a year and a day, and tak' him wi' the valuable
spuilyie, or boothie. They cam at the time appointed, and the mermaid
being out, they made quick dispatch to get all the stores on board before she
cam, which done, they sailed away, and she cam home she found the cave
desolated and herrid. She pursued and over-took the ship. She demanded

her husband and stores. The Skipper cast off a bundle [to the mermaid] of books, and hecht her to get her husband after she counted them. Which she did and requested her love, and the skipper gave her another bundle, again and again, till they reached Gourock and Lawrence Bay.

The Dumbarton trafficker being on dry land refused to go with the mermaid again. But this mermaid told him that he must meet her at the cave where they spent sae monie happie days, a year and a day hence, and she committed her bairn (or mongrel half fish and man) which she bore to the merchant, to its father, telling him to nurse it and give it much lair, as he had plenty of sillar, belangan to her: and she gave him a book whilk he wisna to let the miraculous bairn see, till it was able to read it perquier and squarolie; and the bairn after the directions he sall find in that buke, after he soud be able to read it, could do what he liked, such as to order the foul Thief do onie thing when he pleased. The mermaid's bairn took up his abode in the auld castle of Ardrossan. He went under the name of Michael Scott.

J. Mitchell and J. Dickie
The Philosophy of Witchcraft (1839)

Tam O' Shanter

A Tale

Of Brownyis and of Bogillis full is this Buke.

Gawin Douglas

When chapman billies leave the street,
And drouthy neibors, neibors meet;
As market days are wearing late,
An' folk begin to tak the gate;
While we sit bowsing at the nappy,
An' getting fou and unco happy,
We think na on the lang Scots miles,
The mosses, waters, slaps, and styles,
That lie between us and our hame,
Where sits our sulky, sullen dame,
Gathering her brows like gathering storm,
Nursing her wrath to keep it warm.

    This truth fand honest TAM O' SHANTER,
As he frae Ayr ae night did canter:
(Auld Ayr, whom ne'er a town surpasses,
For honest men and bonie lasses).

O Tam! hadst thou but been sae wise,
As taen thy ain wife Kate's advice!
She tauld thee weel thou was a skellum,
A bletherin', blusterin', drunken blellum;
That frae November till October,
Ae market-day thou was na sober;
That ilka melder wi' the miller,
Thou sat as lang as thou had siller;
That ev'ry naig was ca'd a shoe on
The smith and thee gat roarin' fou on;
That at the L—d's house, ev'n on Sunday,
Thou drank wi' Kirkton Jean till Monday.
She prophesied that, late or soon,
Thou wad be found, deep drown'd in Doon,
Or catch'd wi' warlocks in the mirk,
By Alloway's auld haunted kirk.

Ah, gentle dames! it gars me greet,
To think how mony counsels sweet,
How mony lengthen'd sage advices,
The husband frae the wife despises!

But to our tale:—Ae market night,
Tam had got planted unco right,
Fast by an ingle, bleezing finely,
Wi' reaming swats, that drank divinely;
And at his elbow, Souter Johnie,
His ancient, trusty, drouthy cronie:
Tam lo'ed him like a very brither;
They had been fou for weeks thegither.
The night drave on wi' sangs an' clatter;
And ay the ale was growing better:
The Landlady and Tam grew gracious,
Wi' secret favours, sweet and precious:
The Souter tauld his queerest stories;
The Landlord's laugh was ready chorus:
The storm without might rair and rustle,
Tam did na mind the storm a whistle.

Care, mad to see a man sae happy,
E'en drown'd himsel amang the nappy.
As bees flee hame wi' lades o' treasure,
The minutes wing'd their way wi' pleasure:
Kings may be blest, but Tam was glorious,
O'er a' the ills o' life victorious!

But pleasures are like poppies spread,
You seize the flow'r, its bloom is shed;
Or like the snowfall in the river,
A moment white—then melts for ever;
Or like the borealis race,
That flit ere you can point their place;
Or like the rainbow's lovely form
Evanishing amid the storm.
Nae man can tether Time nor Tide,
The hour approaches Tam maun ride—
That hour, o' night's black arch the key-stane,
That dreary hour Tam mounts his beast in;
And sic a night he taks the road in,
As ne'er poor sinner was abroad in.

The wind blew as 'twad blawn its last;
The rattling showers rose on the blast;
The speedy gleams the darkness swallow'd;
Loud, deep, and lang the thunder bellow'd;
That night, a child might understand,
The deil had business on his hand.

Weel mounted on his grey mare, Meg,
A better never lifted leg,
Tam skelpit on thro' dub and mire,
Despising wind, and rain, and fire;
Whiles holding fast his gude blue bonnet,
Whiles crooning o'er an auld Scots sonnet,
Whiles glow'ring round wi' prudent cares,
Lest bogles catch him unawares;
Kirk-Alloway was drawing nigh,
Where ghaists and houlets nightly cry.

By this time he was 'cross the ford,
Where in the snaw the chapman smoor'd;
And past the birks and meikle stane,
Where drunken Charlie brak's neck-bane;
And thro' the whins, and by the cairn,
Where hunters fand the murder'd bairn;
And near the thorn, aboon the well,
Where Mungo's mither hang'd hersel.
Before him Doon pours all his floods,
The doubling storm roars thro' the woods,
The lightnings flash frae pole to pole,
Near and more near the thunders roll,
When, glimmering thro' the groaning trees,

Kirk-Alloway seem'd in a bleeze,
Thro' ilka bore the beams were glancing,
And loud resounded mirth and dancing.

Inspiring, bold John Barleycorn!
What dangers thou canst make us scorn!
Wi' tippenny, we fear nae evil;
Wi' usquabae, we'll face the devil!
The swats sae ream'd in Tammie's noddle,
Fair play, he car'd na deils a boddle,
But Maggie stood, right sair astonish'd,
Till, by the heel and hand admonish'd,
She ventur'd forward on the light;
And, wow! Tam saw an unco sight!

Warlocks and witches in a dance:
Nae cotillion, brent new frae France,
But hornpipes, jigs, strathspeys, and reels,
Put life and mettle in their heels.
A winnock-bunker in the east,
There sat auld Nick, in shape o' beast;
A towzie tyke, black, grim, and large,
To gie them music was his charge:
He screw'd the pipes, and gart them skirl,
Till roof and rafters a' did dirl.—
Coffins stood round, like open presses,
That shaw'd the dead in their last dresses;
And (by some devilish cantraip sleight)
Each in its cauld hand held a light,
By which heroic Tam was able
To note upon the haly table,
A murderer's banes, in gibbet-airns;
Twa span-lang, wee unchristen'd bairns;
A thief, new-cutted frae a rape,
Wi' his last gasp his gab did gape;
Five tomahawks, wi' blude red-rusted;
Five scymitars, wi' murder crusted;
A garter, which a babe had strangled;
A knife, a father's throat had mangled,
Whom his ain son of life bereft,
The grey hairs yet stack to the heft;
Wi' mair of horrible and awfu',
Which even to name wad be unlawfu.

As Tammie glowr'd, amaz'd, and curious,
The mirth and fun grew fast and furious;

The piper loud and louder blew,
The dancers quick and quicker flew,
They reel'd, they set, they cross'd, they cleekit,
Till ilka carlin swat and reekit,
And coost her duddies on the wark,
And linket at it in her sark!

    Now Tam, O Tam! had they been queans,
A' plump and strapping in their teens!
Their sarks, instead o' creeshie flannen,
Been snaw-white seventeen hunder linen!—
Thir breeks o' mine, my only pair,
That ance were plush, o' guid blue hair,
I wad hae gien them off my hurdies,
For ae blink o' the bonie burdies!
But wither'd beldams, auld and droll,
Rigwoodie hags wad spean a foal,
Louping an' flinging on a crummock,
I wonder did na turn thy stomach.

    But Tam kent what was what fu' brawlie:
There was ae winsome wench and waulie.
That night enlisted in the core,
Lang after kenn'd on Carrick shore
(For mony a beast to dead she shot,
And perish'd mony a bonie boat,
And shook baith meikle corn and bear,
And held the country-side in fear);
Her cutty sark', o' Paisley harn,
That while a lassie she had worn,
In longitude tho' sorely scanty,
It was her best, and she was vauntie.
Ah! little kent thy reverend grannie,
That sark she coft for her wee Nannie,
Wi' two pund Scots ('twas a' her riches),
Wad ever grace'd a dance o' witches!

    But here my Muse her wing maun cour,
Sic flights are far beyond her power;
To sing how Nannie lap and flang
(A souple jade she was and strang),
And how Tam stood, like ane bewitch'd,
And thought his very een enrich'd;
Even Satan glowr'd, and fidg'd fu' fain,

And hotch'd and blew wi' might and main:
Till first ae caper, syne anither,
Tam tint his reason a' thegither,
And roars out, 'Weel done, Cutty-sark!'
And in an instant all was dark:
And scarcely had he Maggie rallied,
When out the hellish legion sallied.

As bees bizz out wi' angry fyke,
When plundering herds assail their byke;
As open pussie's mortal foes,
When, pop! she starts before their nose;
As eager runs the market-crowd,
When 'Catch the thief!' resounds aloud;
So Maggie runs, the witches follow,
Wi' mony an eldritch skriech and hollow.

Ah, Tam! ah, Tam! thou'll get thy fairin'!
In hell they'll roast thee like a herrin'!
In vain thy Kate awaits thy comin'!
Kate soon will be a woefu' woman!
Now, do thy speedy utmost, Meg,
And win the key-stane o' the brig;
There, at them thou thy tail may toss,
A running stream they dare na cross.
But ere the key-stane she could make,
The fient a tail she had to shake!
For Nannie, far before the rest,
Hard upon noble Maggie prest,
And flew at Tam wi' furious ettle;
But little wist she Maggie's mettle!
Ae spring brought off her master hale,
But left behind her ain grey tail:
The carlin caught her by the rump,
And left poor Maggie scarce a stump.

Now, wha this tale o' truth shall read,
Each man, and mother's son, take heed:
Whene'er to drink you are inclin'd,
Or Cutty-sarks rin in your mind,
Think! ye may buy the joys o'er dear,
Remember Tam o' Shanter's mare.

Robert Burns (1759–96)

Bonny Kilmeny

Bonny Kilmeny gaed up the glen,
But it wasna to meet Duneira's men,
Nor the rosy monk of the isle to see,
For Kilmeny was pure as pure could be.
It was only to hear the yorlin sing,   [yellow-hammer
And pu' the cress-flower round the spring;
The scarlet hypp and the hindberrye,   [raspberry
And the nut that hung frae the hazel tree;
For Kilmeny was pure as pure could be.
But lang may her minny look o'er the wa',
And lang may she seek i' the green-wood shaw;
Lang the laird of Duneira blame,
And lang, lang greet or Kilmeny come hame! ...

    When many a day had come and fled,
When grief grew calm, and hope was dead,
When mass for Kilmeny's soul had been sung,
When the bedes-man had prayed, and the dead bell rung,
Late, late in a gloamin' when all was still,
When the fringe was red on the westlin hill,
The wood was sere, the moon i' the wane,
The reek o' the cot hung over the plain,
Like a little wee cloud in the world its lane;
When the ingle lowed with an eiry leme,   [uncanny fiery glow
Late, late in the gloamin' Kilmeny came hame!
'Kilmeny, Kilmeny, where have you been?
Lang hae we sought baith holt and dean;
By linn, by ford, and green-wood tree,
Yet you are halesome and fair to see.
Where gat you that joup o' the lily schene?   [bodice
That bonny snood of the birk sae green?   [ribbon
And these roses, the fairest that ever were seen?
Kilmeny, Kilmeny, where have you been?'

    Kilmeny looked up with a lovely grace,
But nae smile was seen on Kilmeny's face;
As still was her look, and as still was her ee,
As the stillness that lay on the emerant lea,
Or the mist that sleeps on a waveless sea.
For Kilmeny had been she knew not where,
And Kilmeny had seen what she could not declare;
Kilmeny had been where the cock never crew,
Where the rain never fell, and the wind never blew;
But it seemed as the harp of the sky had rung,

And the airs of heaven played round her tongue,
When she spake of the lovely forms she had seen,
And a land where sin had never been;
A land of love, and a land of light,
Withouten sun, or moon, or night;
Where the river swa'd a living stream,
And the light a pure celestial beam:
The land of vision it would seem,
A still, an everlasting dream. . . .

When seven lang years had come and fled;
When grief was calm, and hope was dead;
When scarce was remembered Kilmeny's name,
Late, late in a gloamin' Kilmeny came hame!

James Hogg (1770–1835)
from *Kilmeny*

By Moonlight

It was upon Rathan Head that I first heard their bridle-reins jingling
clear . . .

I shall never forget that night. I rowed over towards the land in our little
boat, which was commonly drawn up in the cove of Rathan Isle, and lay a
great time out on the clear still flow of a silver tide that ran inwards, drifting
slowly up with it . . . My skiff lay just outside the loom of the land, the black
shadow of the Orraland shore on my left hand; but both boat and I as clear
in the moonlight as a fly on a sheet of white paper.

There was a brig at anchor in the bay, and it was along the cliffs towards
her that I saw the horsemen ride. They were, I knew, going to run the
cargo into shelter. I was thinking of how fine they looked, and wondering
how long it would be till my father let me have a horse from the stable and a
rope over my shoulder to go out to the Free Trade among the Manx-men
like a lad of spirit, when all at once I got a sudden, horrid surprise.

I could hear the riders laughing and wagering among themselves, but
I was too far away to hear what the game might be. Suddenly one of the
foremost whipped a musket to his shoulder. I was so near the shore that I
saw the flash of moonlight run along the barrel as he brought it to his eye.
I wondered what he could be aiming at—a sea bird belike.

'Clip! Splash!' went something past my head and through the bow of the
boat. Then on the back of the crack of the gun came a great towrow of
laughter from the cliff edge.

'A miss! a palpable miss!' cried someone behind. 'Haud her nose doon,
ye gowk!'

'Noo, Gil, ye are next. See you an' mak' a better o't.'

I was somewhat dazed with the suddenness of the cowardly assault, but I seized my oars of instinct and rowed shorewards. I was in the black of the shadows in three strokes, and not a moment oversoon, for another ball came singing after me. It knocked the blade of my left oar into flinders, just as the water dripped silver off it in the moonlight for the last time before I was submerged in the shadow. Again the laughter rang loud and clear, but heartless and hard.

'Guid e'en to ye, gowk fisherman,' cried the man who had first spoken. 'The luck's wi' ye the nicht; it's a fine nicht for flounders.'

I could have broken his head, for I was black angry at the senseless and causeless cruelty of the shooting. My first thought was to make for home: my second to draw to shore, and find out who they might be that could speed the deadly bullet with so little provocation at a harmless lad in his boat in the bay. So without pausing to consider of wisdom and folly (which indeed I have but seldom done in this life with profit), I sculled softly to the mainland with the unbroken oar.

Barefoot and bareleg I got into the shallow water, taking the little cleek anchor ashore and pushing the boat out that she might ride freely, for as I said, the tide was running upwards like a mill-race.

Then I struck through the underbush till I came to the wall of the deserted and overgrown kirkyard of Kirk Oswald. There stands a great old tomb in the corner from which, it ran in my mind, I might observe the shore and the whole route of the riders, if they were on their way to unload the brig in the offing.

There was a broad splash of moonlight on the rough grass between me and the tomb of the MacLurgs. The old tombstones reeled across it drunkenly, yet all was still and pale. I had almost set my foot on the edge of this white patch of moonshine to strike across it, when, with a rustle like a brown owl alighting swiftly and softly, someone took me by the hand, wheeled me about, and ere I had time to consider, carried me back again into the thickest of the wood.

Yet I looked at my companion as I ran, you may be sure. I saw a girl in a light dress, high-kilted—May Mischief of Craigdarroch, what other? But she pointed to her lip to show that there was to be no speech; and so we ran together even as she willed it to an angle of the old wall, where, standing close in the shade, we could see without being seen.

Now this I could not understand at all, for May Mischief never had a civil word for me as far back as I remember, but so many jibes and jeers that I never could endure the girl. Yet here we were, jinking hand in hand under the trees in the moonlight, for all the world like lad and lass playing at hide-and-seek. Soon we heard voices, and again the bits and chains rattling as the horses, suddenly checked, tossed their heads. Then the spurs jingled as the riders dismounted, stamping their feet as they came to the ground.

Twenty yards below us a man set his head over the wall. He whistled low and shrill.

'All clear, Malcolm?' he cried. I remember to this day the odd lilt of his voice. He was a Campbell, and gave the word Malcolm a strange twist, as if he had turned it over with his tongue in his mouth—to this day the mark of a Cantyre man.

A man stepped out of the doorway of the MacLurg tomb with a gun in his hand. May Maxwell looked up at me with something triumphant in her eyes, which I took to mean, 'Where had you been now, if it had not been for me?' And indeed the two shots at the boat in the moonlight told me where I would have been, and that was on the sward with a gunshot through me.

A dozen or more men came swarming over the broken wall. They carried a long black coffin among them—the coffin, as it seemed, of an extraordinarily large man. Straight across the moon-whitened grass they strode, stumbling on the flat tombs and cursing one another as they went. There was no solemnity as at a funeral, for the jest and laughter ran light and free.

'We are the lads,' cried one. 'We can lay the spirits and we can raise the dead!'

They went into the great tomb of the MacLurgs with the long, black coffin, and in a trice came out jovially, abusing one another still more loudly for useless dogs of peculiar pedigrees, and dealing great claps on each other's backs. It was a wonder to me to see these outlaws at once so cruel and so merry.

Some of them went down by the corner of the kirkyard opposite to us. May Maxwell, who had kept my hand, fearing, I think, that we might have to run for it again round the circle of shade, plucked me sharply over to see what they were doing.

They were opening a grave, singing catches as their picks grated on the stones. I shivered a little, and a great fear of what we were about to see came over me. I think if May Maxwell had not gripped me by the hand I had fairly run for it.

The man we had first seen came out of the tomb and took a look at the sky. Another stretched himself till I heard his joints crack, and said, 'Hech, How!' as though he were sleepy. Whereat the others railed on him, calling him, 'Lazy vagabond.'

Then all of them turned their ears towards the moors as though they listened for something of importance.

'Do the Maxwells ride tonight?' asked one.

'Wheesh,' said another. 'Listen!'

This he said in so awe-stricken a tone that I also was struck with fear, and listened till my flesh crept.

From the waste came the baying of a hound—long, fitful, and very eerie. There was a visible, uneasy stir among the men.

'Let us be gone,' said another, making for the wall; ' 'tis the Loathly Dogs. The Black Deil hunts himsel' the nicht. I'm gaun hame.'

'Stop!' cried one with authority (I think the man that was called Gil). 'I'll put an ounce of lead through your vitals gin ye dinna stand in your tracks.'

But the others stayed neither for threat nor lead.

'It'll be waur for ye gin the Ghaistly Hounds get a grip o' your shins, Gil, my man. They draw men quick to hell!'

So, at the word, there seized the company a great fear, and they took to their heels, every man hastening to the wall. Then, from the other side, there was a noise of mounting steeds, and a great clattering of stirrup-irons.

May Mischief came nearer to me, and I heard her breath come in little broken gasps, like a rabbit that is taken in a net and lies beating its life out in your hands. At which I felt a man for the sole time that night.

But not for long, for I declare that what we saw in the next moment brought us both to our knees, praying silently for mercy. Over the wall at the corner farthest from us there came a fearsome pair. First a great grey dog, that hunted with its head down and bayed as it went. Behind it lumbered a still more horrible beast, big as an ox, grim and shaggy also, but withal clearly monstrous, and not of the earth, with broad, flat feet that made no noise, and a demon mark in scarlet on its side, which told that the foul fiend himself that night followed the chase. May Mischief clung to my arm, and I thought she had swooned away. But the beasts passed some way beneath us, like spirits that flit by without noise, save for the ghostly baying which made one sweat with fear.

As the sounds broke farther from us that were in the graveyard, the horsemen dispersed in a wild access of terror. We could hear them belabouring their horses and riding broadcast over the fields, crying tempestuously to each other as they went. And down the wind the bay of the ghostly hunters died away.

S. R. Crockett (1860–1914)
The Raiders

Fairy Chorus

How beautiful they are,
The lordly ones
Who dwell in the hills,
In the hollow hills.

They have faces like flowers,
And their breath is a wind
That blows over summer meadows,
Filled with dewy clover.

Their limbs are more white
Than shafts of moonshine:
They are more fleet
Than the March wind.

They laugh and are glad
And are terrible:
When their lances shake and glitter,
Every green reed quivers.

How beautiful they are,
How beautiful
The lordly ones
In the hollow hills.

'Fiona Macleod', William Sharp (1855–1905)
The Immortal Hour

Unlucky Boat

That boat has killed three people. Building her
Sib drove a nail through his thumb, and died in his croft
Bunged to the eyes with rust and penicillin.
One evening when the Flow was a bar of silver
Under the moon, and Mansie and Tom with wands
Were putting a spell on cuithes, she dipped a bow
And ushered Mansie, his pipe still in his teeth,
To meet the cold green angels. They hauled her up
Among the rocks, right in the path of Angus,
Whose neck, rigid with pints from the Dounbymarket,
Snapped like a barley stalk . . . There she lies,
A leprous unlucky bitch, in the quarry of Moan.

Tinkers, going past, make the sign of the cross.

George Mackay Brown (*b.* 1921)

RELIGION

The Legend of Holyrood Abbey

At this time wes with the king ane man of singulare and devout life, namit Alkwine, cannon eftir the ordour of Sanct Augustine, whilk wes lang time confessoure, afore, to King David in Ingland, the time that he wes Erle of Huntingtoun and Northumberland. This religious man dissuadit the king, by mony reasons, to pass to this huntis; and allegit the day wes so solempne, by reverence of the holy croce, that he suld gif him over, for that day, to contemplation than ony othir exersition. Noctheles, his dissuasions litill availit; for the king wes finalie so provokit, by inoportune solicitatioun of his baronis that he passed, noctwithstanding the solempnite of this day, to his hounts. At last, when he wes cumin throw the vail that lyis to the gret east fra the said castell, whare now lyis the Cannongait, the staik past throw the wood with sic noyis and din of rachis and bugillis, that all the bestis were rasit fra thair dennis.

Now wes the king cumin to the fute of the crag, and all his nobles severit, here and thair, fra him at thair game and solace; when suddenlie apperit to his sicht the farist hart that evir wes sene afore with levand creatour. The noise and din of this hart rinnand, as apperit, with auful and braid tindis [points], maid the kingis hors so effrayit, that na reins micht hald him; bot ran, perforce, owre mirc and mosses, away with the king and his hors to the ground. Than the king cast abak his handis betuix the tindis of this hart, to haif savit him fra the strak thairof; and the haly croce slaid, [slid], incontinent, in [to] his handis.

The hart fled away with great violence, and evanist in the same place whare now springs the Rude Well. The pepil, richt affrayitly, returnit to him out of all parts of the wood, to comfort him efter his trubill, and fell on kneis, devoutly adoring the haly croce; for it was not cumin but some hevinly providence, as weill appears, for thair is na man can schaw of what mater it is of, metal or tree. Soon eftir, the king returnit to his castel; and in the nicht following he was admonist, by ane vision in his sleip, to bigg [build] ane abbay of cannons regular in the same place whare he got the croce. Als soon as he was awalkinnit, he schew his vision to Alkwine, his confessour; and he na thing suspendit his gude mind, bot ever inflammit him with maist fervent devotion thairto.

The king, incontinent, send his traist servandis in France and Flanders, and brocht richt crafty masonis to bigg this abbay; syne dedicat it in the honour of this haly croce. The croce remanit continewally in the said abbay, to the time of King David Bruce; whilk was unhappily tane with it at Durame, whare it is holden yit in gret veneration.

Hector Boece (1465?–1536)
History of Scotland, translated from the Latin by John Bellenden in 1533

Of the Nativity of Christ

Rorate celi desuper!
Heavens distill your balmy schours,
For now is risen the bricht day ster,   [star
Fro the rose Mary, flour of flours:
The clear sun, whom no clud devours,
Surmounting Phoebus in the east,
Is cumin of his heavenly tours;   [towers
Et nobis Puer natus est.   ['Unto us a child is born' (Isaiah)

Archangels, angels and dompnations,   [dominions
Thrones, potestats and martyrs seir,   [various
And all ye heavenly operations,
Ster, planet, firmament and sphere,
Fire, erd, air and watter clear,
To him gife loving, most and lest,
That come in to so meek mannere;
Et nobis Puer natus est.

Sinners be glad, and pennance do,
And thank your Makar hairtfully;
For he that ye micht nocht come to,
To yow is cumin full humbly,
Your saulis with his blud to buy,
And lous yow of the feind's arrest,
And only of his awin mercy;
Pro nobis Puer natus est.

All clergy do to him incline,
And bow unto that barne benyng,   [bairn
And do your observance divine
To him that is of kingis King;
Insence his altar, read and sing   [incense
In haly kirk, with mind digest,

Him honouring atour all thing,   [above
Qui nobis Puer natus est.

Celestial fowlis in the air
Sing with your nottis upon hicht;   [notes
In firthis and in forrests fair
Be mirthful now, at all your micht,
For passit is your dully nicht,
Aurora has the cluddis perst,   [pierced
The sun is risen with glaidsum licht,
Et nobis Puer natus est.

Now spring up flours fra the root,
Revert yow upwart naturally,
In honour of the blissit frute
That rais up fro the rose Mary;
Lay out your leavis lustily,
Fro deid tak life now at the lest
In worschip of that Prince worthy,
Qui nobis Puer natus est.

Sing heaven imperial, most of hicht,
Regions of air mak harmony;
All fish in flud and foul of flicht,
Be mirthful and mak melody:
All *Gloria in excelsis* cry,
Heaven, erd, sea, man, bird and best,   [beast
He that is crowned abone the sky
Pro nobis Puer natus est.

William Dunbar (*c.* 1460–1520)

Cradle Song for the New Year

O my dear Heart, young Jesus sweet,
Prepare Thy cradle in my spreit,
And I sall rock Thee in my heart
And nevermare fra Thee depart.

Bot I sall praise Thee evermore
With sangis sweet unto Thy gloir,
The knees of my heart sall I bow,
And sing that richt Balulalow.

Gloir be to God eternally
Whilk gave His only Son for me;
The angellis joyis for to hear
The gracious gift of this New Year.

The Wedderburn Brothers
from 'Ane Sang of the Birth of Christ'
Gude and Godly Ballatis (1567)

O Jesu Parvule

'Followis ane sang of the birth of Christ, with the tune of Baw lu la law'—
'Godly Ballatis'

His mither sings to the bairnie Christ
Wi' the tune o' *Ba lu la law*.
The bonnie wee craturie lauchs in His crib
An' a' the starnies an' he are sib.   [blood related
        Baw, baw, my loonikie, baw, balloo.

'Fa' owre, ma hinny, fa' owre, fa' owre,
A'body's sleepin' binna oorsels.'
She's drawn Him in tae the bool o' her breist
But the byspale's nae thocht o' sleep i' the least.
        Balloo, wee mannie, balloo, balloo.

Hugh MacDiarmid (1892–1978)

Flemish Primitive

Soft petals fell out of a brooding air
Like blossoms of the apple or the pear,

Soft magic, like the feathers of a dove,
Fell on this lady and her little love.

Up in the inn, the travellers sat to dine,
Pouring hot spices in their steaming wine.

Out on the street, the sentry stamped and swore,
Knowing his guard must last for one hour more.

The Three Wise Kings were on their homeward road,
Their hearts unburdened of the ruler's load,

While Herod slept; but, dreaming of disaster,
He felt his heart, that nightmare, beat the faster.

Back on the hill, a Shepherd scratched his head
To find the sense of what the Angels said.

But in her dark Byzantine green and gold,
This sleeping miracle repelled the cold.

The green was fodder, and the gold was straw;
And Mary sang a lullaby and saw

Azure and gilt around her; the intense
And choking fragrance of the frankincense

Swirled in her dream. A thought of stillness was
Sick longing in her soul. She wished to pause

From thought, from movement, and from grief; to rest
For ever with the baby at her breast.

G. S. Fraser (1915–1980)

All My Luve, Leave Me Not

All my luve, leave me not,
Leave me not, leave me not,
All my luve leave me not
        Thus mine alone.
With ane burden on my back
I may not bear it I am sa waik,
Luve, this burden fra me tak
        Or else I am gone.

With sins I am laden sore,
Leave me not, leave me not,
With sins I am laden sore
        Leave me not alone.
I pray Thee, Lord, therefore,

Keep not my sins in store,
Loose me or I be forlore,
   And hear my moan.

With Thy hands Thou has me wrocht,
Leave me not, leave me not,
With Thy hands Thou has me wrocht
   Leave me not alone.
I was sold and Thou me bocht,
With thy blude Thou has me coft   [purchased
Now am I hither socht
   To Thee, Lord, alone.

I cry and I call to Thee.
To leave me not, to leave me not,
I cry and I call to Thee
   To leave me not alone.
All they that laden be
Thou biddis come to Thee
Then sall they savit be
   Through Thy mercy alone.

The Wedderburn Brothers
Gude and Godly Ballatis (1567)

Of the Resurrection of Christ

Done is a battle on the dragon black,
Our campioun Christ confoundit has his force;   [champion
The yetts of hell are broken with a crack,   [gates
The sign triumphal rasit is of the croce,
The devil trimmillis with hideous voce,
The sauls are borrowit and to the bliss can go,
Surrexit Dominus de sepulchro.

Dungin is the deidly dragon Lucifer,
The cruel serpent with the mortal stang;
The auld keen tiger with his teeth on char,   [ajar
Whilk in a wait has lyen for us so lang,
Thinkand to grip us in his clawis strang;
The merciful Lord wald nocht that it were so,
He made him for to felye of that fang: [fail ... prize
Surrexit Dominus de sepulchro.

He for our sake that sufferit to be slain,
And like a lamb in sacrifice wes dicht,   [made ready
Is like a lion risen up again,
And as gyane raxit him on hicht;   [giant
Sprungin is Aurora radious and bricht,
On loft is gone the glorious Appollo,
The blissful day depairtit fro the nicht:
Surrexit Dominus de sepulchro.

The grit victour again is risen on hicht
That for our quarrel to the death was woudit;
The sun that wox all pale now shinis bricht,
And, derkness clearit, our faith is now refoundit;
The knell of mercy fra the heaven is soundit,
The Christian are deliverit of their woe,
The Jewis and their error are confoundit:
Surrexit Dominus de sepulchro.

The foe is chassit, the battle is done cease,
The prison broken, the jevellours fleit and flemit;   [jailors fled and banished
The fetters lowsit and dungeon temit,   [released . . . emptied
The ransom made, the prisoners redeemit;
The field is won, owrecomin is the foe,
Dispulit of the treasure that he yemit: [kept
Surrexit Dominus de sepulchro.

                                        William Dunbar (*c.* 1460–1520)

Lament for The Makars

I that in heill was and gladness,   [health
Am trublit now with great seikness,
And feeblit with infirmity;
    Timor mortis conturbat me.

Our pleasance here is all vainglory,
This fals world is but transitory,
The flesh is bruckle, the Feind is slee;   [brittle . . . cunning
    Timor mortis conturbat me.

The state of man does change and vary,
Now sound, now seik, now blythe, now sary,   [sorry
Now dansand merry, now like to dee;   [dancing
    Timor mortis conturbat me.

No state in Erd here standis sicker;   [Earth . . . sure
As with the wind wavis the wicker,   [willow
So wavis this warld's vanitie;
   Timor mortis conturbat me.

Unto the deid goes all Estatis,
Princes, Prelates and Potestatis,   [potentates
Baith rich and puir of all degree;
   Timor mortis conturbat me.

He taks the knichtis in to field
Enarmit under helm and schield;
Victor he is at all mêlée;
   Timor mortis conturbat me.

That strang unmerciful tyrand
Taks, on the mother's breist sowkand,   [sucking
The babe full of benignitie;
   Timor mortis conturbat me.

He taks the campioun in the stour,   [champion . . . fight
The captain closit in the touer,
The lady in bour full of beautie;
   Timor mortis conturbat me.

He spares no lord for his piscence,   [puissance
Na clerk for his intelligence;
His awful strak may no man flee;   [stroke
   Timor mortis conturbat me.

Art-magicians and astorloggis,
Rethors, logicians and theologgis,   [rhetoreticians
Them helpis no conclusions slee;
   Timor mortis conturbat me.

In medecine the most practicians,
Leeches, surgeons and physicians,
Themselves fra Death may not supplee;   [save
   Timor mortis conturbat me.

I see that makars amang the lave   [poets . . . others
Plays here their pageant syne goes to grave;   [then
Sparit is nocht their facultie;
   Timor mortis conturbat me.

He has done piteouslie devour
The noble Chaucer, of makars flour,
The Monk of Bury, and Gower, all three;
Timor mortis conturbat me.

The guid Sir Hew of Eglintoun,
And eik Heriot and Wyntoun,   [also
He has tane out of this countrie;
Timor mortis conturbat me.

That scorpion has done infeck
Maister John Clerk, and James Afflek,
Fra ballat-making and tragedie;
Timor mortis conturbat me.

Holland and Barbour he has berevit,
Alas! that he nocht with us levit
Sir Mungo Lockhart of the Lee;
Timor mortis conturbat me.

Clerk of Tranent eik he has tane
That made the Anters of Gawaine;   [adventures
Sir Gilbert Hay endit has he;
Timor mortis conturbat me.

He has Blind Harry and Sandy Traill
Slain with his schour of mortal hail,
Whilk Patrick Jonstoun micht nocht flee;
Timor mortis conturbat me.

He has reft Merseir his endite   [inditing
That did in luve so lively write,
So short, so quick, of sentence hie;
Timor mortis conturbat me.

He has tane Roull of Aberdeen,
And gentle Roull of Corstorphine;
Two better fellows did no man see;
Timor mortis conturbat me.

In Dunfermline he has done roune   [whispered
With Maister Robert Henrysoun;
Sir John the Ross enbrast has he;   [embraced
Timor mortis conturbat me.

And he has now tane, last of aa,
Guid gentle Stobo and Quintin Shaw,
Of whom all wichtis has pitie;   [people
   Timor mortis conturbat me.

Guid Maister Walter Kennedy
In point of deid lies verily;
Great ruth it were that so suld be;
   Timor mortis conturbat me.

Sen he has all my brither tane
He will nocht let me live alane;
On force I maun his next prey be;
   Timor mortis conturbat me.

Sen for the deid remeid is none,
Best is that we for deid dispone,   [make disposition
Eftir our deid that live may we;
   Timor mortis conturbat me.

William Dunbar

A Covenanter's Sermon

*While Charles II was nominally a Covenanted King, there was a feeling of
revulsion against Presbyterianism after the Restoration. English politicians
would have none of it. By its Acts Recissory of 1661, the Scots Parliament
swept away all legislation passed since 1633. The two Covenants were annulled,
and James Sharp, minister of Crail, became Archbishop of St Andrews, proceeding to appoint bishops for the rest of the Scottish sees. Presbyterians were
left to worship as they pleased. The restoration of Episcopacy might have been
regarded as merely a formal framework, but for a decree by the Scottish Privy
Council on 1st October 1622, whereby all ministers had to have the backing of a
patron and a bishop, or vacate their charges. The ensuing upheaval only ended
with the settlement of 1688, and drove the Stuarts from their throne.*

   *This account of Alexander 'Hoodiecraw' Peden's last sermon, and related
happenings, is by John Mackay Wilson, a native of Tweedsmouth, who
began his career as a printer's apprentice in Berwick and finished it as Professor
of Humanity at the University of St Andrews.*

On the 4th day of October 1662, a council, under the commission of the
infatuated and ill-advised Middleton, was held at Glasgow; and, in an hour
of brutal intoxication, it was resolved and decreed that all those ministers of

the Church of Scotland who had, by a popular election, entered upon their cures since the year 1649, should, in the first instance, be arrested, nor permitted to resume their pulpits, or draw their stipends, till they had received a presentation at the hands of the lay patrons, and submitted to induction from the diocesan bishop. In other words, Presbytery, which had been so dearly purchased, and was so acceptable to the people of Scotland, was to be superseded by Prelacy; and the mandate of the Prince, or of his privy council, was to be considered in future as law, in all matters, whether civil or ecclesiastical. It was not to be supposed that the descendants and admirers of Knox, and Hamilton, and Welsh, and Melville could calmly and passively submit to this; and accordingly the 20th day of October—the last Sabbath which, without conformity to the orders in council, the proscribed ministers were permitted to preach—was a day anticipated with anxious feelings, and afterwards remembered to their dying day, by all who witnessed it. It was our fortune, in early life, to be acquainted with an old man, upwards of ninety, an inhabitant of the village of Glenluce, whose grandfather was actually present at the farewell sermon which Mr Peden, the author of the famous prophecies which bear his name, delivered on this occasion to his parishioners. We have conversed with this aged chronicler so frequently and so fully upon the subject, that we believe we can give a pretty faithful report of what was then delivered by Peden.

'I remember well (continued, according to my authority, the old chronicler) —I mind it well, it seems but as yesterday—the morning of this truly awful and not-to-be-forgotten day. It had been rain in the night-time, and the morning was dark and cloudy—the mist trailed like the smoke o' a furnace, white and ragged, alang the hill-taps. The heavens above seemed, as it were, to scowl upon the earth beneath. I rose early, as was my wont on the Sabbath morning, and hitched away towards the tap o' the Briok. I had only continued, it micht be, an hour in private meditation and prayer, when I heard the eight o'clock bells beginning to toll. Indeed, I could hear, from the place where I was, I may say, every bell in the presbytery. The sound o' these bells is still in my ears—it was unusually sweet and melodious; and yet there was something very melancholy in the sound, and I thought on the sad alteration which a few hours would produce, when the pulpits would be deserted by the worthy Presbyterian ministers who filled them, and be filled, it micht be, by Prelatical curates—wolves in sheep's clothing, and fushionless preachers at the best.

'The doors o' the kirk o' New Luce had been thrown open early in the morning; but, owing to an immense concourse of people, a tent had been latterly erected on the brow face, immediately opposite to the kirk-stile, and when we arrived the multitude were settling down on all sides of it. A portion of the Thirty-second Psalm had been selected by the precentor, when Peden made his appearance above the brow of the adjoining linn. He advanced with the pulpit Bible under his arm, and with a rapid, though occasionally a hesitating, step. His figure was diminutive, but his frame athelic and his step elastic. He wore a blue bonnet, from beneath which his dark hair flowed

out over his shoulders, long, lank and dishevelled. His complexion was sallow
but his eyes dark, keen and penetrating. He had neither gown nor band, but
had his shirt-neck tied up with a narrow stock of uncommon whiteness.
Thus habited, he approached the congregation, who rose up to make way
for him, ascended the ladder attached to the back door of the tent, and forthwith proceeded to the duties of the day.

"Therefore watch and remember; for the space of three years I ceased
not to warn everyone, night and day, with tears."

'These words of the text were read out in a firm though somewhat shrill
and squeaking tone of voice; and as he lifted up his eyes from the sacred
page, and looked east and west around him, there was a general preparatory
cough, and adjustment of position and dress, which clearly bespoke the
protracted attention which was about to be given. And, truly, although he
continued to discourse from twelve o'clock till dusk, I cannot say that I felt
tired or hungry. Nor did it appear that the speaker's strength or matter
failed him—nay, he even rose into a degree of fervid and impressive eloquence towards the close which none who were present ever heard equalled.

"And now, my friends," continued he, in a concluding appeal to their
consciences—"and now I am gaun to warn ye anent the future, as weel as
to admonish you o' the past. Ye'll see and hear nae mair o' puir Sandy
Peden after this day's wark is owre. See ye that puir bird" (at this moment a
hawk had darted down, in view of the whole congregation, in pursuit of its
prey)—"see ye that puir panting laverock, which has now crossed into that
dark and deep lin, for safety and for refuge, from the claws and the beak of
its pursuer? I'll tell ye what, my freends—the twasome didna drift down this
way for naething. They were sent, they were commissioned; and if ye had
risen to your feet, ere they passed, and cried, 'Shue!' ye couldna hae frichtened
them oot o' their mission. They cam to testify o' a persecuted remnant and
o' a cruel pursuing foe—o' a Kirk which will soon hae to betak hersel like a
bird to the mountains, and o' an enemy which will not allow her to rest, by
night nor by day, even in the dark recesses o' the rocks, or amidst the damp
and cauld mosses o' the hills. They cam, and they war welcome, to gie auld
Sandy a warning, too, and to bid him tak the bent as fast as possible; to
flee, even this very nicht, for the pursuer is even nigh at hand. But, hooly,
sirs, we mauna part till our wark is finished; as an auld writer has it—till
our work is finished, we are immortal. I hae e'en dune my best, as saith an
apostle, amang ye; and I hae this day the consolation, and that's no sma', to
think that my puir exertions hae been rewarded wi' some sma' success. And
had it been His plan, of His pleasure, to have permitted me to lay down my
auld banes, when I had nae mair use for them, beneath ane o' the through-
stanes there, I canna say but I wad hae been content. But, since it's no His
guid and sovereign pleasure, I hae ae request to mak before we separate this
nicht, never in this place to meet again." (Hereupon the sobbing and the
bursting forth of hitherto suppressed sorrow was almost universal.) "Ye
maun a' stand upon your feet, and lift up your hands, and swear, before the
great Head and Master o' the Presbyterian Kirk o' Scotland" (there was a

general rising and show of hands, whilst the speaker continued), "that, till an independent Presbyterian minister ascend the pulpit, you will never enter the door o' that kirk mair; and let this be the solemn league and covenant betwixt you and me, and betwixt my God and your God, in all time coming! Amen!—so let it be!"

'In this standing position, which we had thus almost insensibly assumed, the last prayer or benediction was heard, and the concluding psalm was sung:

> For He in His pavilion shall
> Me hide in evil days,
> In secret of His tent me hide,
> And on a rock me raise.

'I never listened to a sound or beheld a spectacle more overpowering. The night-cloud had come down the hill above us—the sun had set. It was twilight; and the united and full swing of the voice of praise ascended through the veil of evening, from the thousands of lips, even to the gate of heaven. Whilst we continued singing, our venerable pastor descended from the tent—the Word of God in his hand, and the accents of praise on his lips; and at the concluding line he stood fairly and visibly out by himself, upon the entry to the seat door of the kirk. Having shut the door and locked it, in the view and in the hearing of the people, he knocked upon it thrice with the back of the pulpit Bible, accompanying this action with these words, audibly and distinctly pronounced:

"I arrest thee in my Master's name, that none ever enter by thee, save those who enter by the door of Presbytery." So saying, he ascended the wall at the kirk-stile, spread his arms abroad to their utmost stretch, and in the most solemn and impressive manner dismissed the multitude.'

J. M. Wilson (1804-44)
Tales of the Borders

Tolerant Religion

Sir George Mackenzie, son of the 2nd Earl of Seaforth, was educated at the Universities of St Andrews and Aberdeen, and at Bourges. Admitted to the Scots Bar in 1659, he achieved distinction by his unsuccessful defence of the Marquis of Argyll, accused of supporting Cromwell. In 1677 he became Lord Advocate. His persecution of Covenanters and his acceptance of torture as a legitimate means of obtaining information (still in many countries the usual method) earned him the nickname of 'Bluidy Mackenzie'. As such he was celebrated by Scott in 'The Heart of Midlothian' and 'Wandering Willie's Tale.'

22

Although he refused to support James VII's Catholicism, he also refused to vote for that sovereign's deposition in favour of William of Orange, so retired to Oxford and London. He founded the Advocates Library in Edinburgh, and is buried in Greyfriar's Churchyard. His two finest prose-works are 'Aretino' (1660) and 'Religio Stoici.'

It pleases my humour to contemplat, how that albeit all religions war against one another, yet are all of them governed by the same principles, and even by these principles, in effect, which they seem to abominat. . . . It is remarkable, that albeit infallibility be not by all conceded to any militant church, yet it is assumed by all. Neither is there any church under the sun, which would not fix the name of heretick, and account him (almost) reprobat, who would refuse to acknowledge the least rational of their principles; and thus these church-men pull up the ladders from the reach of others, after they have by them scal'd the walls of preferment themselves. That church-men should immerse themselves in things civil, is thought excentrick to their sphere, even *in ordine ad spiritualia*: and yet, even the Capuchins, who are the greatest pretenders to abstract Christianity and mortification, do, of all others, dipth most in things civil. The Phanaticks enveigh against presbyterian gowns. The Presbyterian tears the episcopal lawn sleeves, and thinks them the whore of Babel's shirt. The Episcopist flouts at the parish robes, as the livery of the beast. The Antinomian emancipats his disciples from all obedience to the law. The Protestant enjoyns good works, and such are commanded, but place no merit in them. The Roman-Catholick thinks he merits in his obedience. The Phanatick believs the Lords Supper but a ceremony, though taken with very little outward respect. The Presbyterian allowes it, but will not kneel. The Episcopist kneels, but will not adore it. The Catholick mixeth adoration with his kneeling. And thus, most of all religions are made up of the same elements, albeit their asymbolick qualities predomine in some more then in others. And if that maxime hold, that *majus et minus non variant speciem*, we may pronounce all of them to be one religion.

The church, like the River Nilus, can hardly condescend where it's head lyes; and as all condescend that the church is a multitude of Christians, so joyn all their opinions, and you shall find that they will have it to have, like the multitude, many heads. But in this (as in all articles, not absolutely necessar for being saved) I make the laws of my countrey to be my creed. And that a clear decision herein is not absolutely necessar for salvation, is clear from this, that many poor clowns shall be saved, whose conscience is not able to teach their judgements how to decide this controversie, wherein so many heads have been confounded, so many have been lost, and so many have been shrewdly knockt against one another; from which flinty collisions much fire, but little light, hath ever burst forth.

Sir George Mackenzie (1636–97)
Religio Stoici

The Sad Estranger

William Drummond, son of the 1st Laird of Hawthornden, Midlothian, trained in law at Edinburgh, Paris and Bourges. At twenty-four, he succeeded to the beautiful castle perched above the Esk, where he spent his time reading widely in foreign authors, and producing some of the finest and best-chiselled poems to be written in English by a Scot, as well as a magnificent prose meditation upon death, 'A Cypresse Grove'. He was buried in Lasswade Cemetery.

Death is the sad estranger of acquaintance, the eternall divorcer of marriage, the ravisher of the children from their parents, the stealer of parents from the children, the interrer of fame, the sole cause of forgetfulnesse, by which the living talke of those gone away as of so manie shadowes, or fabulous paladincs. All strength by it is enfeebled, beautie turned in deformite and rottonnesse, honour in contempt, glorie into basenesse. It is the un-reasonable breaker off of all the actions of vertue, by which wee enjoye no more the sweete pleasures on earth, neither contemplate the statelie revolutions of the heavens; the sunne perpetuallie setteth, starres never rise unto us; it in one moment depriveth us of what with so great toyle and care in manie yeeres wee have heaped together. By this are successions of lineages cut short, kingdomes left heireless, and greatest states orphaned. It is not overcome by pride, smoothed by gaudie flatterie, tamed by intreaties, bribed by benefites, softened by lamentations, diverted by time. Wisedome, save this, can alter and helpe anie thing. By death wee are exiled from this faire citie of the world. It is no more a world unto us, nor wee anie more people into it. The ruines of phanes, palaces, and other magnificent frames, yeeld a sad prospect to the soule; and how should it consider the wracke of such a wonderful maisterpiece as is the bodie without horrour?...

If thou doest complaine, that there shall bee a time in the which thou shalt not bee, why doest thou not too grieve, that there was a time in the which thou wast not, and so that thou art not as olde, as that enlifening planet of time? For, not to have beene a thousand yeeres before this moment, is as much to bee deplored, as not to bee a thousand after it, the effect of them both beeing one. That will bee after us which long, long ere wee were was. Our children's children have that same reason to murmure that they were not young men in our dayes, which wee now, to complaine that wee shall not be old in theirs. The violets have their time, though they empurple not the winter, and the roses keepe their season, though they disclose not their beautie in the spring.

Empires, states, kingdomes, have by the doome of the supreame pro-vidence their fatall periods; great cities lye sadlie buried in their dust; artes and sciences have not onelie their eclipses, but their wainings and deathes; the gastlie wonders of the world, raised by the ambition of ages, are overthrowne and trampled; some lights above (deserving to bee intitled starres) are loosed and never more seene of us; the excellent fabrike of this universe it selfe shall one day suffer ruine, or a change like a ruine, and poore earthlings thus to bee handled complaine!

William Drummond (1585–1649)
A Cypresse Grove

To Heaven On Clatty Feet

The muddled imagery and inflated rhetoric which did service for substance in many a Scottish sermon from the seventeenth century onwards, derives in no small degree from the effusions of Rutherford, a native of Nisbet, Roxburghshire, whose pamphlet 'Lex Rex' was burned by the common hangman in 1661. He spent his ministry in the Parish of Anwoth in Galloway, but ended his days as Principal of the New (St. Mary's) College, St Andrews.

In the words and sacraments, Christ now takes you into the chariot with himself, and draws your hearts after him. Be Satan's nor the world's footmen no longer; for it is a wearysome life; but ride with Christ in his chariot, for it is all paved with love; the bottom of it is the love of slain Christ, ye must sit there upon love. Love is a soft cushion, but the devil and the world make you sweat at the sore work of sin, and run upon your own foot too; but it is better to be Christ's horsemen to ride, than to be Satan's trogged footmen, and to travel upon clay. Christ says He has washen you today; sin no more; keep yourselves clean; go not to Satan's sooty houses, but take you to your husband the fairest among ten thousand, that your lovely husband may make your robes clean in the blood of the Lamb. Ye are going into a clean Heaven and an undefiled city: Take not filthy clatty hands and clatty feet with you. What say ye of your new husband? Please ye your new husband well, may not his servants say in his name, that he is heartily welcome to you? A plain answer; Ye cannot well want an half-marrow, no soul ever dwell a single life. Now, seeing you must marry, marry Christ; Ye will never get a better husband; Take Him and his father's blessing; Fall too and woo him; Be holy and get a good name, and Christ will not want you.

It is many a day since ye were invited to his banquet; Why should ye bide from it? Ye are not uncalled; And Christ both sitteth and eateth with you; And standeth and serve with you; Christ both said the Grace to-day and praised my Father's blessing at the banquet. Your father cries, Divorce, Divorce all other lovers, go and agree with Christ your cautioner, and purchase a discharge if you can. It is better holding than drawing; better to say, Hear He is, than, hear He was, and slippery-fingered I held him, and would not let him go. Rive all his cloaths, and he will not be angry at you: In death he held a strait grip of you: Hell, devils, and wrath of God, the curse of the law could not all loose his grips of you. Christ got a claught of you in the water, and he brought you all with him. Look up by faith to him. You could never have been set up by angels.

May not Christ say, The law soon took a cleik off me, and threw me among thieves for your cause; and was not that strong love, that humble Christ cared not what they did to him, so being he might get you? In that night our Lord was betrayed, he ordained the supper for you upon his death-bed, he made his testament, and left it in legacy to you; In death he had more mind of you, his wife, than he had of himself; In the garden, on the cross, in the grave, his silly lost sheep was aye in his mind. Love has a bra' memory and cannot forget; He has graven you on the palms of his hands, and, when he looks upon his hands he says, My sheep I cannot forget; Yea, in my death, my sister, my spouse, was aye in my mind; She took my night's sleep from me, that night I was sweating in the garden for her.

> Samuel Rutherford (1600–61)
> *An exaltation at Communion to a*
> *Scots Congregation in London*

O God of Bethel!

In 1781 the General Assembly of the Church of Scotland adopted a collection of sixty-seven hymns for use in Church services. Hitherto only the psalms had been officially used. Those which were versified accounts of scriptural texts were known as paraphrases.

Three or four of the best and most frequently sung were in their present form the work of Michael Bruce, who came from Kinnesswood, a small village above Loch Leven. The son of a weaver, Bruce studied for the Secession Church, but like so many undernourished divinity students from country places in the eighteenth century, died of consumption before he qualified. A fellow-student to whom the young poet's manuscripts had been entrusted by Alexander Bruce, the father, appropriated a number of them, including the paraphrases, or 'Gospel Sonnets' as Bruce's friends who had heard him recite them, called them. In due course the Reverend John Logan put them out in his own 'Poems', also published in 1781, and in many quarters has been wrongly allowed to take the credit for them ever since.

O God of Bethel! by whose hand
  thy people still are fed;
Who through this weary pilgrimage
  hast all our fathers led:

Our vows, our pray'rs we now present
  before thy throne of grace;

God of our fathers! be the God
  of their succeeding race.

Through each perplexing path of life
  our wand'ring footsteps guide;
Give us each day our daily bread
  and raiment fit provide.

O spread thy cov'ring wings around
  till all our wand'ring cease,
And at our Father's loved abode
  our souls arrive in peace.

Such blessings from thy gracious hand
  our humble prayers implore;
And Thou shalt be our chosen God,
  and portion evermore.

> Michael Bruce (1746–67)
> Based on a hymn, 'Jacob's Vow', written by Dr Philip
> Dodderidge in 1736, and on Genesis xxvii, 20–22.

Behold! The Mountain of the Lord

Behold! the mountain of the Lord
  in latter days shall rise
On mountain tops above the hills,
  and draw the wond'ring eyes.

To this the joyful nations round,
  all tribes and tongues shall flow;
Up to the hill of God, they'll say,
  and to his house we'll go.

The beam that shines from Sion hill
  shall lighten ev'ry land;
The king who reigns in Salem's tow'rs
  shall all the world command.

Among the nations he shall judge;
  his judgments truth shall guide;
His sceptre shall protect the just,
  and quell the sinner's pride.

No strife shall rage, nor hostile feuds
  disturb those peaceful years;
To ploughshares men shall beat their swords,
  to pruning-hooks their spears.

No longer hosts encount'ring hosts
  shall crowds of slain deplore;
They hang the trumpet in the hall,
  and study war no more.

Come then, O house of Jacob! come
  to worship at his shrine;
And, walking in the light of God,
  with holy beauties shine.

> Michael Bruce
> After the version in Ralph Erskine's *Scripture Songs* (1752),
> *Translations and Paraphrases* (1745), and Isaiah ii, 2–6.

Equally in the Dark

The close of life indeed, to a reasoning eye is

> ... dark as was chaos, ere the infant sun
> Was roll'd together, or had try'd his beams
> Athwart the gloom profound ...

But the honest man has nothing to fear. If we lie down in the grave, the whole man a piece of broke machinery, to moulder with the clods of the valley—so be it; at least there is an end of pain, care, woes and wants: if that part of us called Mind, does survive the apparent destruction of the man—away with old-wife prejudices and tales! Every age and every nation has had a different set of stories: and as the many are always weak, of consequence they have often, perhaps always been deceived: a man, conscious of having acted an honest part among his fellow-creatures; even granting that he may have been the sport, at times, of passions and instincts; he goes to a great unknown Being who could have no other end in giving him existence but to make him happy; who gave him those passions and instincts, and well knows their force.

    These, my worthy friend, are my ideas. . . . It becomes a man of sense to think for himself; particularly in a case where all are equally interested, and where, indeed, all men are equally in the dark.

> Robert Burns (1759–96)
> *Letter to Robert Muir, 7th March 1788*

Holy Willie's Prayer

And send the godly in a pet to pray.=Pope

O Thou, who in the heavens does dwell,
Who, as it pleases best Thysel,
Sends ane to heaven, an' ten to hell,
   A' for thy glory,
And no for ony gude or ill
   They've done afore Thee!

I bless and praise Thy matchless might,
When thousands Thou hast left in night,
That I am here afore Thy sight,
   For gifts an' grace
A burning and a shining light
   To a' this place.

What was I, or my generation,
That I should get sic exaltation,
I wha deserve most just damnation
   For broken laws,
Five thousand years ere my creation,
   Thro' Adam's cause.

When frae my mither's womb I fell,
Thou might hae plungèd me in hell,
To gnash my gums, to weep and wail,
   In burnin' lakes,
Where damned devils roar and yell,
   Chain'd to their stakes.

Yet I am here a chosen sample,
To show Thy grace is great and ample;
I'm here a pillar o' Thy temple,
   Strong as a rock,
A guide, a buckler, and example,
   To a' Thy flock.

O L—d, Thou kens what zeal I bear,
When drinkers drink, an' swearers swear,
An' singin' there, an' dancin' here,
   Wi' great and sma';
For I am keepit by Thy fear
   Free frae them a'.

But yet, O L—d! confess I must,
At times I'm fashed wi' fleshly lust:
An' sometimes, too, in warldly trust,
   Vile self get in;
But Thou remembers we are dust,
   Defil'd wi' sin.

O L—d! yestreen Thou kens, wi' Meg—
Thy pardon I sincerely beg,
O! may't ne'er be a livin' plague
   To my dishonour,
An' I'll ne'er lift a lawless leg
   Again upon her.

Besides, I farther maun allow,
Wi' Leezie's lass three times I trow—
But L—d, that Friday I was fou,
   When I cam near her;
Or else, Thou kens, Thy servant true
   Wad never steer her.

Maybe Thou lets this fleshly thorn
Buffet Thy servant e'en and morn,
Lest he owre proud and high shou'd turn,
   That he's sae gifted:
If sae, Thy han' maun e'en be borne,
   Until Thou lift it.

L—d, bless Thy chosen in this place,
For here Thou hast a chosen race:
But G—d confound their stubborn face,
   An' blast their name,
Wha bring Thy elders to disgrace
   An' public shame.

L—d, mind Gaw'n Hamilton's deserts;
He drinks, an' swears, an' plays at cartes,
Yet has sae mony takin' arts,
   Wi' great and sma',
Frae G—d's ain priest the people's hearts
   He steals awa'.

An' when we chasten'd him therefor,
Thou kens how he bred sic a splore,
An' set the warld in a roar
   O' laughing at us;—

Curse Thou his basket and his store,
      Kail an' potatoes.

L—d, hear my earnest cry and pray'r,
Against that Presbyt'ry o' Ayr;
Thy strong right hand, L—d, make it bear
      Upo' their heads;
L—d, visit them, an' dinna spare,
      For their misdeeds.

O L—d, my G—d! that glib-tongu'd Aiken,
My vera heart and flesh are quakin'
To think how we stood sweatin', shakin',
      An' p—d wi' dread,
While Auld, wi' hingin' lip, gaed sneakin',
      And hid his head.

L—d, in Thy day o' vengeance try him,
L—d, visit them wha did employ him,
And pass not in Thy mercy by them,
      Nor hear their pray'r,
But for Thy people's sake destroy them,
      An' dinna spare.

But, L—d, remember me an' mine
Wi' mercies temporal an' divine,
That I for grace an' gear may shine,
      Excell'd by nane,
And a' the glory shall be Thine,
      Amen, Amen!

Robert Burns

The Disruption

The law-courts of Scotland having invaded the spiritual independence of the Church of Scotland, the Evangelical party of the Church seceded, and formed the Free Church of Scotland.

8th June, 1843. The crash is over!
   Dr Welsh, Professor of Church History in the University of Edinburgh, having been Moderator last year, began the proceedings by preaching a

sermon before his Grace the Commissioner in the High Church, in which what was going to happen was announced and defended. The Commissioner then proceeded to St Andrew's Church, where the Assembly was to be held. The streets, especially those near the place of meeting, were filled, not so much with the boys who usually gaze at the annual show, as by grave and well-dressed grown people of the middle rank. According to custom, Welsh took the chair of the Assembly. Their very first act ought to have been to constitute the Assembly of this year by electing a new Moderator. But before this was done, Welsh rose and announced that he and others who had been returned as members held this not to be a free Assembly—that, therefore, they declined to acknowledge it as a Court of the Church—that they meant to leave the very place, and, as a consequence of this, to abandon the Establishment. In explanation of the grounds of this step he then read a full and clear protest. It was read as impressively as a weak voice would allow, and was listened to in silence by as large an audience as the church could contain.

As soon as it was read, Dr Welsh handed the paper to the clerk, quitted the chair, and walked away. Instantly, what appeared to be the whole left side of the house rose to follow. Some applause broke from the spectators, but it checked itself in a moment. 193 members moved off, of whom about 123 were ministers, and about 70 elders. Among these were many upon whose figures the public eye had been long accustomed to rest in reverence. They all withdrew slowly and regularly amidst perfect silence, till that side of the house was left nearly empty. They were joined outside by a large body of adherents, among whom were about 300 clergymen. As soon as Welsh, who wore his Moderator's dress, appeared on the street, and people saw that principle had really triumphed over interest, he and his followers were received with the loudest acclamations. They walked in procession down Hanover Street to Canonmills, where they had secured an excellent hall, through an unbroken mass of cheering people, and beneath innumerable handkerchiefs waving from the windows. But amidst this exultation there was much sadness and many a tear, many a grave face and fearful thought; for no one could doubt that it was with sore hearts that these ministers left the Church, and no thinking man could look on the unexampled scene and behold that the temple was rent, without pain and sad forebodings. No spectacle since the Revolution reminded one so forcibly of the Covenanters.

Henry, Lord Cockburn (1779–1854)
Journal

Dr Chalmers Preaches

His gestures are neither easy nor graceful; but, on the contrary, **extremely** rude and awkward—his pronunciation is not only broadly national, but broadly provincial—distorting almost every word he utters into some barbarous novelty which, had his hearer leisure to think of such things, might be productive of an effect at once ludicrous and offensive in a singular degree.

But of a truth these are things which no listener *can* attend to while this great preacher stands before him, armed with all the weapons of the most commanding eloquence and swaying all around him with its imperial rule. At first, indeed, there is nothing to make one suspect what riches are in store. He commences in a low drawling key which has not even the merit of being solemn—and advances from sentence to sentence, and from paragraph to paragraph, while you seek in vain to catch a single echo that gives promise of that which is to come. There is, on the contrary, an appearance of constraint about him that effects and distresses you—you are afraid that his breast is weak and that even the slight exertion he makes may be too much for it. But then with what tenfold richness does this dim preliminary curtain make the glories of his eloquence to shine forth when the heated spirit at length shakes from its chill, confining fetters and bursts out elate and rejoicing in the full splendour of its dis-imprisoned wings! . . .

I have heard many men deliver sermons far better arranged in regard to argument, and have heard very many deliver sermons far more uniform in elegance both of conception and of style. But most unquestionably I have never heard, either in England or Scotland or in any other country, any preacher whose eloquence is capable of producing an effect so strong and irresistible as this.

J. G. Lockhart (1794–1854)
Peter's Letters to His Kinsfolk

A Highland Church Service

Elizabeth Grant was the eldest son of Sir John Peter Grant, 7th Laird of Rothiemurchus and an advocate. Born in Edinburgh, she passed the vacations in the law terms at The Doune, the family house on the Rothiemurchus estate. Debt caused her father to move to the Continent at one point, but he was later appointed a judge in Bombay, and thereafter had a distinguished career. In India, Elizabeth met and married Colonel Henry Smith, who had succeeded to the family estate of Baltiboys, in Ireland, where Mrs Smith spent the rest of her life, restoring a ruined estate by thrift and good management. Her 'Memoirs of a Highland Lady' end with her return from India in 1830. The book was edited by her niece, Lady Strachey, and published in 1897, but the church service she describes took place in 1809.

The minister gave out the psalm; he put a very small dirty volume up to one eye, for he was near-sighted, and read as many lines of the old version of the rhythmical paraphrase (we may call it) of the Psalms of David as he thought fit, drawling them out in a sort of sing-song. He stooped over the pulpit to hand his little book to the precentor, who then rose and calling out aloud the tune—'St George's tune,' 'Auld Aberdeen,' 'Hondred an' fifteen,' etc.— began himself a recitative of the first line on the key-note, then taken up and repeated by the congregation; line by line, he continued in the same fashion, thus doubling the length of the *exercise*, for really to some it was no play— serious severe screaming quite beyond the natural pitch of the voice, a wandering search after the air by many who never caught it, a flourish of difficult execution and plenty of the *tremolo* lately come into fashion. The dogs seized this occasion to bark (for they always came to the kirk with the family), and the babies to cry. When the minister could bear the din no longer he popped up again, again leaned over, touched the precentor's head, and instantly all sound ceased. The long prayer began, everybody stood up while the minister asked for us such blessings as he thought best. . . . The prayer over, the sermon began; that was the time for making observations. 'Charity' and 'Solomon's Lillies,' soon required no further attention. Few save our own people sat around; old grey-headed rough-visaged men that had known my grandfather and great-grandfather, black, red, and fair hair, belonging to such as were in the prime of life, younger men, lads, boys—all in the tartan. The plaid as a wrap, the plaid as a drapery, with kilt to match on some, blue trews on others, blue jackets on all. The women were plaided too, an outside shawl was seen on none, though the wives wore a large handkerchief under the plaid, and looked picturesquely matronly in their very white high caps . . . The wives were all in homespun, home-dyed, linsey-woolscy gowns, covered to the chin by the modest kerchief worn outside the gown. The girls who could afford it had a Sabbath day's gown of like manufacture and very bright colour, but the throat was more exposed, and generally ornamented with a string of beads, often amber; some had to be content with the best blue flannel petticoat and a clean white jacket, their ordinary and most becoming dress, and few of these had either shoes or stockings; but they all wore the plaid, and they folded it round them very gracefully.

They had a custom in the Spring of washing their beautiful hair with a decoction of the young buds of the birch trees. I do not know it if improved or hurt the hair, but it agreeably scented the kirk, which at other times was wont to be overpowered by the combined odours of snuff and peat reek, for the men snuffed immensely during the delivery of the English sermon; they fed their noses with quills fastened by strings to the lids of their mulls, spooning up the snuff in quantities and without waste. The old women snuffed too, and groaned a great deal, to express their mental sufferings, their grief for all the backslidings supposed to be thundered at from the pulpit; lapses from faith was their grand self-accusation, lapses from virtue were alas! little commented on; temperance and chastity were not in the Highland code of morality . . .

There was no very deep religious feeling in the Highlands up to this time. The clergy were reverenced in their capacity of pastors without this respect extending to their persons unless fully merited by propriety of conduct. The established form of faith was determinately adhered to, but the *kittle questions*, which had so vexed the Puritanic south, had not yet troubled the minds of their northern neighbours. Our mountains were full of fairy legends, old clan tales, forebodings, prophecies, and other superstitions, quite as much believed in as the Bible. The Shorter Catechism and the fairy stories were mixed up together to form the innermost faith of the Highlander, a much gayer and less metaphysical character than his Saxon-tainted countryman.

Elizabeth Grant (1797–1885)
Memoirs of a Highland Lady

A Scottish Sunday

A Sunday in Scotland is for the traveller like a thunderstorm at a picnic. You get wet, you can't go on and all your good humour vanishes. We had seen all the sights of Stirling and were horrified at the thought that for the next twenty-four hours we should have nothing to entertain us but an old copy of *The Times* and a silent table d'hôte. Fortunately an early train had mercy on us which, despite the fact that there are no Sunday trains in Scotland, took us at about ten or eleven in the morning to the ancient city of Perth so often famed in song.

This business of an early train which thus desecrates the Sunday is very like that of champagne on the table of a Turk—it passes under another name. This Sunday train is really a Saturday evening train. The thing works as follows. The Great Northern Railway, which traverses England and Scotland from head to foot, runs a daily express which leaves London in the evening; now if a traveller boards it in London on a Saturday evening with the intention of going to Perth and Aberdeen *via* Edinburgh, this is entirely in accordance with prevailing law and custom; even the church-mindedness of a Scot can hardly object to it. After all, it isn't the traveller's fault that the express doesn't go faster than it actually does, and consequently the Saturday has to borrow a bit of Sunday. It is only the act of making use of the train after it has actually touched Scottish soil that is frowned upon ... but there is no limit to the licence accorded to foreigners.

Theodor Fontane (1819–98)
Jenseit des Tweed, Bilder und Briefe aus Schottland

Christmas Thoughts

To be honest, to be kind—to earn a little and to spend a little less, to make upon the whole a family happier for his presence, to renounce when that shall be necessary and not be embittered, to keep a few friends but these without capitulation—above all, on the same grim condition, to keep friends with himself—here is a task for all that a man has of fortitude and delicacy, He has an ambitious soul who would ask more; he has a hopeful spirit who would look in such an enterprise to be successful. There is indeed one element in human destiny that not blindness itself can controvert: whatever else we are intended to do, we are not intended to succeed; failure is the fate allotted. It is so in every art and study; it is so above all in the continent art of living well. Here is a pleasant thought for the year's end or for the end of life: only self-deception will be satisfied, and there need be no despair for the despairer.

R. L. Stevenson (1850–94)
Later Essays

A Sermon

Two steadfast and intolerable eyes
  Burning beneath a broad and rugged brow;
The head behind it of enormous size,
  And as black fir-groves in a large wind bow,
Our rooted congregation, gloom-arrayed,
By that great sad voice deep and full were swayed:—

O melancholy Brothers, dark, dark, dark!
O battling in black floods without an ark!
  O spectral wanderers of unholy Night!
My soul hath bled for you these sunless years,
With bitter blood-drops running down like tears:
  Oh, dark, dark, dark, withdrawn from joy and light!

My heart is sick with anguish for your bale!
Your woe hath been my anguish; yea, I quail
  And perish in your perishing unblest.
And I have searched the heights and depths, the scope
Of all our universe, with desperate hope
  To find some solace for your wild unrest.

And now at last authentic word I bring,
Witnessed by every dead and living thing;
   Good tidings of great joy for you for all:
There is no God; no friend with names divine
Made us and tortures us; if we must pine,
   It is to satiate no Being's gall.

It was the dark delusion of a dream,
That living Person conscious and supreme,
   Whom we must curse for cursing us with life;
Whom we must curse because the life He gave
Could not be buried in the quiet grave,
   Could not be killed by poison or by knife.

This little life is all we must endure,
The grave's most holy peace is ever sure,
   We fall asleep and never wake again;
Nothing is of us but the mouldering flesh,
Whose elements dissolve and merge afresh
   In earth, air, water, plants, and other men.

We finish thus; and all our wretched race
Shall finish with its cycle, and give place
   To other beings, with their own time-doom
Infinite aeons ere our kind began;
Infinite aeons after the last man
   Has joined the mammoth in earth's tomb and womb.

We bow down to the universal laws,
Which never had for man a special clause
   Of cruelty or kindness, love or hate:
If toads and vultures are obscene to sight,
If tigers burn with beauty and with might,
   Is it by favour or by wrath of fate?

All substance lives and struggles evermore
Through countless shapes continually at war,
   By countless interactions interknit:
If one is born a certain day on earth,
All times and forces tended to that birth,
   Not all the world could change or hinder it.

I find no hint throughout the Universe
Of good or ill, of blessing or of curse;
   I find alone Necessity Supreme;
With infinite Mystery, abysmal, dark,

Unlighted ever by the faintest spark
  For us the flitting shadows of a dream.

O Brothers of sad lives! they are so brief;
A few short years must bring us all relief:
  Can we not bear these years of labouring breath?
But if you would not this poor life fulfil,
Lo, you are free to end it when you will,
  Without the fear of waking after death.—

The organ-like vibrations of his voice
  Thrilled through the vaulted aisles and died away;
The yearning of the tones which bade rejoice
  Was sad and tender as a requiem lay:
Our shadowy congregation rested still
As brooding on that 'End it when you will.'

James Thomson (1834–82)
The City of Dreadful Night

Here and Now

For whether earth already to its doom
Reels orbit slipped, or whether decades hence,
Or next year, or to-morrow, or to-day
The weight of ice amassed at either pole
Shall change our axis till a deluge wipe
The citied world away, and glacial drift
Plough up the earth and harrow it again;
Or whether flame consume us comet-struck;
Or the earth's crust fall in; or to the sun
Returning whence it sprang, our orb effete,
Enwombed in pristine fire once more, become
The brilliant seed of stars to be, we know
That men shall cease: their speech, their deeds, their arts,
The wonder of their being, passion, love,
Ambition, charity, transcendent thought
Shall leave no memory, token, sign, or sigh
In any speck of dust, or nook of space;
We know that here and now is Heaven-and-Hell;
This is the Promised Land, the Golden Age,

This, the Millennium, and the Aftertime.
The fixed, eternal moment, sounding on.

John Davidson (1857–1909)
from *The Testament of a Prime Minister*

Approaches to God

There is still a Church of Scotland—ostensibly more powerful than ever, having recently amalgamated with its great rival, the United Free Church. There are still innumerable ministers of the Kirk to be met with in the leafy manse walks, the crowded Edinburgh streets, the gatherings of conferences and associations and the like. There is still the trickle of the kirkward folk on a Sabbath morning in summer, when the peewits hold their unending plaint over the greening fields and the young boys linger and kick at the thistles by the wayside, the young girls step daintily down whin-guarded paths and over the cow-dung pats by this and that gate. There is still the yearly Assembly of the Kirk in Edinburgh—the strangest of functions ... There are still old men and women who find sustenance and ease and comfort in the droned chantings of the risen God, in symbolic cannibal feastings upon the body of the dead God at time of Communion ... But it is little more now than a thin and tattered veil upon the face of the Scottish scene ...

Catholicism was more mellow and colourful and poetic: it was also darker and older and more oppressed by even more ancient shames. It produced an attitude of mind more soft than the Presbyterian: and also infinitely more servile. Sex has always been a tabu and shameful thing to the Catholic mind, a thing to be *transmuted*—in the fashion of gathering a lovely lily from its cheerful dung and transmuting it into a glassy ornament for a sterile altar.

Episcopalianism is in a different category. From the first it was more a matter of social status than of theological conviction; it was rather a grateful bourgeois acknowledgement of Anglicization than dissent with regard to the methods of worshipping a God ... The Episcopalian Church in Scotland gave to life and ritual mildly colourful trappings, a sober display; it avoided God with a shudder of genteel taste.

The modern Free Church member is the ancient Presbyterian who has learned nothing and forgotten nothing. As certain unfortunate children abandon mental development at the cretinaceous age of eight, Free Church doctrine, essentially un-Christian, abandoned development with the coming of the Kelts. It is a strange and disgusting cult of antique fear and antique spite. It looks upon all the gracious and fine things of the human body—particularly the body of woman—with sickened abhorrence, it detests music and light and life and mirth, the God of its passionate conviction is a kind of immortal Peeping Tom, an unsleeping celestial sneak-thief ... As fantastically irrelevant to contemporary Scottish affairs as the appendix is to the human body, its elimination may be brought about rather by advances in social hygiene than by surgical operation.

Lewis Grassic Gibbon (1901–35)
Scottish Scene

Sabbath

'*Come unto me, all ye that are heavy-laden*'.

The portly paunches trundled
the few short steps (O merciful religion!)
from the car to the door of the kirk,
the loaded furs lurching
from limousines to cushioned pews—

Pagan, I paused,
the Sunday papers under my infidel arm,
amazed at the joyful vision of
gentle Jesus
kicking camel-fat backsides
through a needle's eye.

Alexander Scott (*b.* 1920)

Mammon's Argument

John Davidson, a kind of inverted Calvinist, was brought up in Greenock, became a teacher in Perth and Glasgow, earned a difficult living as a writer in London, and walked into the sea in the erroneous belief that he was suffering from cancer.

(Mammon tries to convert the aged Papal Legate, Anselm, to renounce Christianity and to follow him. Florimond is Mammon's Chancellor.)

Mammon: This is the huge insanity of the world,
            The time-old morbid mind that fears itself,
            Unknowing and unknown. How great are men
            To fashion out of ignorance and dread
            Such greatness! For I know your spirit-world
            Better than any prophet, poet, priest,
            Philosopher, occultist, mystic, seer.
            Hear me expound your dual universe:—

Man is a spirit, and his various life,
A bodying forth of the invisible;
The Universe and forms of time and space—
The garment and the symbolism of God;
The elements, the stars, earth and its brood—
The self-analysis, precipitation,
Pomp and deployment of the absolute:
The visible's the immaterial;
And only spirit's matter and momentous.
A noble Universe whose furthest nook
Is still a suburb of the City of God;
Where every star and every blade of grass,
Where every pulse and every thought reveals
The hallowed presence of divinity!

Anselm: You sin against the light knowing so well
What apparition matter is, and all
The Universe a mere similitude
And mutable appurtenance of God.

Mammon: No God; no spirit; only matter. God?
The cowardice of men flung forth to fill
With welcome shadow an imagined void—
Which never was, which by no chance can be.
The unconscious ether fills the universe,
Omnipotent, omniscient, omnipresent:
No interstice in matter anywhere
Even for the daintiest elf of other world;
And in the infinite no interval
To harbour alien immaterial dreams.

Anselm: But spirit, God, may be material stuff,
Of the same substance as the stars and us.

Mammon: Not spirit, then; not God. You *know*!

Anselm: I do.
And may God pardon me my flash of sin!

Mammon: Afraid of mystery men explained the unknown
As something immaterial—spirit, God.
But there's no mystery hidden in the unknown;
There's nothing in the unknown; there's no
                                     unknown.

Anselm: O King, the darkness! There the unknown hides!

Mammon: Darkness?—negation; nil. Light?—wonder;
                                    woven
Magnificence of seven mysterious stains,
Ethereal substance of the Universe.

Anselm: Bethink you, King; the silence of the night—

Mammon: Silence that misanthropes have praised so, golden
Against the silver sound of speech, is dull

Inanity: the mystery of the whole resides
In music—substance of the ether tuned
To audible enchantment. Time's a lie,
And space a trick. Eternity's the truth:
Infinitude, the all-dynamic vast,
Mystery of mysteries, known to any one,
The everlasting durability
Of the immeasurable universe;
For all is matter, all is mystery, all
Is known: we are the universe become
Self-conscious; and nothing anywhere exists
Not us. All men are great, all men: unmade,
Incomparable, immeasurable, free—
The eternal Universe become self-conscious.
I'll have you understand this here and now,
Accept its truth and change the world with
                                                    me.
My patience ends: I bring the greatest news;
I'll have it welcomed. We ourselves are fate;
We are the universe; we are all that is:
Outside of us nothing that is not us
Can be at all. No room! The universe
Is full of us, the matter of the stars;
The all-pervading ether seen as light,
Elaborate purity of rainbows; heard
As music, woven of elemental sounds;
And smelt in perfume, the poetry of flowers
Exhaled from sex, which in all plants and
                                                    beasts
Secretes and sows the ethereal universe.
Seen in the light, in music heard, and smelt
In subtle odour of a thousand flowers,
In us the ether consciously becomes
Imagination, thought, religion, art.
We are the ether, we are the universe,
We are eternity; not sense, not spirit,
But matter; but the whole become self-conscious.
Whatever Heaven there is, whatever Hell,
Here now we have it; and I cannot wait
On God, the nothing, and his damned event
That mocked the world for sixty centuries;
Nor will I linger eating out my heart
While this new proxy of divinity
Your specious evolution, blunders on
From tedious age to age. I'll carve the world
In my own image, I, the first of men

To comprehend the greatness of mankind;
I'll melt the earth and cast it in my mould,
The form and beauty of the universe.
Say after me 'Get thee behind me, God;
I follow Mammon.' Say it, say it!

Anselm: God
Is God, eternal and unchangeable,
The God of my salvation.

Mammon: (*seizes Anselm by the throat*)
                                        Hideous liar,
Abominably old and impotent!
You know there is no God, no soul at all,
But only matter, ether polarised,
Condensed and shown and felt and understood,
Beholding, feeling, thinking, comprehending,
The subject-object of the Universe.
'Get thee behind me, God; I follow Mammon.'
Say it, before I fling you at my feet,
Abhorred senility, and stubborn past
Of the world! Say it, antiquity!

Anselm: Release
Me, King.

        (*Mammon flings Anselm from him violently.
        Anselm staggers and falls with a loud cry.*)

Mammon Old craven heart of man, from truth
Divorced, God's creature, famulus and fool,
Go back to Rome and tell the triple-crown—

Florimond: (*who has entered quickly and is kneeling beside
                                                Anselm*)
He'll ne'er see Rome again: the legate's dead.

Mammon: Dead! Anselm dead! How dead?
Dead in the spirit—
Like all the world to all material truth,
Senseless and dead.

Florimond: Dead as a carcase, King.
How quickly he grows cold!

Mammon: Why should he die?
A wine-glass falls and breaks. Is human stuff
As brittle? Come; help him to his feet.

Florimond: The man is dead. His heart: to-day the world
Trembles with broken hearts; the pace of life
Exceeds our staying power.

                                John Davidson (1857–1909)
                                from *Mammon and his Message*

Two Memories

Religion? Huh! Whenever I hear the word
It brings two memories back to my mind.
Choose between them and tell me which
You think the better model for mankind.

Fresh blood scares sleeping cows worse than anything else on earth.
An unseen rider leans far out from his horse with a freshly-skinned
Weaner's hide in his hands, turning and twisting the hairy slimy thing
And throwing the blood abroad on the wind.

A brilliant flash of lightning crashes into the heavens.
It reveals the earth in a strange yellow-green light,
Alluring yet repelling, that distorts the immediate foreground
And makes the grey and remote distance odious to the sight.

And a great mass of wraithlike objects on the bed ground
Seems to upheave, to move, to rise, to fold and undulate
In a wavelike mobility that extends to an alarming distance.
The cows have ceased to rest: they are getting to their feet.

Another flash of lightning shows a fantastic and fearsome vision.
Like the branches of some enormous grotesque sprawling plant
A forest of long horns waves, and countless faces
Turn into the air, unspeakably weird and gaunt.

The stroke of white fire is reflected back
To the heavens from thousands of bulging eyeballs,
And into the heart of any man who sees
This diabolical mirroring of the lightning numbing fear falls.

Is such a stampede your idea for the human race?
Haven't we milled in it long enough? My second memory
Is of a flight of wild swans. Glorious white birds in the blue October heights
Over the surly unrest of the ocean! Their passing is more than music to me
And from their wings descends, and in my heart triumphantly peels
The old loveliness of earth that both affirms and heals.

Hugh MacDiarmid (1892–1978)

The Heart of the Matter

Dogma founded on faith, and designed to manipulate human beings into moulds justifying pre-conceived ends, has probably produced more human misery than any other single cause. Edwin Muir once described theosophists as "people willing to believe anything about everything". The work of intellectual destruction carried out upon Marxism in the twentieth century by Popper no more deters Marxists from practising unspeakable cruelties than did Hume's similar treatment of Christianity in the eighteenth century.

Since Hume's observations on religion—as, indeed, his observations upon the impossibility of achieving any kind of certainty—have never been refuted, the following passage, tinged as it is with his gentle irony, makes a satisfactory pendant to this section, and follows naturally after MacDiarmid's poem.

Our most holy religion is founded on Faith, not on reason; and it is a sure method of exposing it to put it to such a trial as it is by no means fitted to endure. To make this more evident, let us examine those miracles related in Scripture; and not to lose ourselves in too wide a field, let us confine ourselves to such as we find in the Pentateuch, which we shall examine, according to the principles of those pretended Christians, not as the word or testimony of God Himself, but as the production of a mere human writer and historian. Here then we are first to consider a book, presented to us by a barbarous and ignorant people, written in an age when they were still more barbarous, and in all probability long after the facts which it relates, corroborated by no concurring testimony, and resembling those fabulous accounts which every nation gives of its origin. Upon reading this book, we find it full of prodigies and miracles. It gives an account of the state of the world and of human nature entirely different from the present; of our fall from that state: of the age of man extended to near a thousand years: of the destruction of the world by a deluge: of the arbitrary choice of one people as the favourites of heaven, and that people the countrymen of the author: of their deliverance from bondage by prodigies the most astonishing imaginable: I desire any one to lay his hand upon his heart, and after a serious consideration declare, whether he thinks that the falsehood of such a book, supported by such a testimony, would be more extraordinary and miraculous than all the miracles it relates; which is, however, necessary to make it be received, according to the measures of probability above established.

What we have said of miracles may be applied, without any variation, to prophecies; and indeed, all prophecies are real miracles, and as such only can be admitted as proofs of any revelation. If it did not exceed the capacity of human nature to foretell future events, it would be absurd to employ any prophecy as an argument for a divine mission or authority from heaven. So that, upon the whole, we may conclude that the Christian Religion not only was at first attended with miracles, but even at this day cannot be believed by any reasonable person without one. Mere reason is insufficient to convince us of its veracity; and whoever is moved by Faith to assent to it is conscious of a continued miracle in his own person, which subverts all the principles of his understanding, and gives him a determination to believe what is most contrary to custom and experience.

David Hume (1711–1776)
Of Miracles.

COUNTRYSIDE CONCERNS

A Countryman Observes the Seasons

Robert Henryson lived at Dunfermline, and probably taught in the Abbey School. He was a shrewd and kindly observer of the ways of beasts and men, as his thirteen verse Fables based on Aesop show. Unlike many courtly poets of his time, he was familiar with the day-to-day changes in the seasons, as this extract from one of his Fables makes plain.

Yet nevertheless we may have knawledging
Of God Almychty by his creatouris;
That He is gude, fair, wise and bening;
Example tak be thir jolie flouris,
Richt sweet of smell and plesand of colouris,
Some green, some blue, some purpour, white and reid
Thus distribute by gift of His Godheid.

The firmament paintit with starnis cleir
From east to west rolland in circle round,
And every planet in his proper spheir
In moving makand harmony and sound;
The fire, the air, the water and the ground—
Til understand it is aneuch, I wis,
That God in all His workis wittie is....

The summer with his jolie mantle green
With flouris fair furrit on everilk fent,
Whilk Flora goddess, of the flouris queen,
Has to that lord as for his seasoun lent,
And Phoebus, with his golden bemis gent,   [graceful
Has purfillit and payntit plesandly,
With heat and moisture stilland from the sky....

Syne winter wan, when austerne Eolus,
God of the wind, with blastis boreal
The green garment of summer glorious
Has al to-rent and riven in piecis small;
That flouris fair, fadit with frost mon fall,
And birdis blythe changit their notis sweet
In still murning, near slain with snow and sleet.

The dalis deep with dubbis drownit is,
Baith hill and holt heillit with frostis hair;
And boughis bene laifit bare of bliss,
By wicked windis of the winter wair,
All wild beastis then from the bentis bare
Drawis for dread unto their denis deep
Couchand for cauld in covis thame to keep.

Syne cumis ver, when winter is away,
The secretar of summer with his seal,
When columbine upkeikis through the clay,
Whilk fleit was before with frostis fell;
The mavis and the merle begynnis to mell;
The lark on loft, with other birdis small,
Then drawis forth fra derne owre down and dale.

The samyn season, into ane soft morning,
Richt blythe that bitter blastis were ago,
Unto the wood, to see the flouris spring,
And hear the mavis sing and birdis mo,
I passit forth, syne lookit to and fro,
To see the soil whilk was richt seasonable,
Sappie, and to receive all seedis able.

Moving thusgait, great mirth I took in mind,
Of labouraris to see the business,
Some makand dyke, and some the pleuch can wynd,
Some sowand seidis fast from place to place,
The harrowis hoppand in the sowers' trace:
It was great joy to him that luvit corn
To see them labour baith at even and morn.

Robert Henryson (?1430–?1500)
from *The Fable of the Swallow and the Other Birds*

The Comin' o' the Spring

There's no a muir in my ain land but's fu' o' sang the day,
Wi' the whaup, and the gowden plover, and the lintie upon the brae.
The birk in the glen is springin', the rowan-tree in the shaw,
And every burn is rinnin' wild wi' the meltin' o' the snaw.

The wee white clouds in the blue lift are hurryin' light and free,
Their shadows fleein' on the hills, where I, too, fain wad be;
The wind frae the west is blawin, and wi' it seems to bear
The scent o' the thyme and gowan thro' a' the caller air.

The herd doon the hillside's linkin'. O licht his heart may be
Whose step is on the heather, his glance ower muir and lea!
On the Moss are the wild ducks gatherin', whar the pules like diamonds lie,
And far up soar the wild geese, wi' weird unyirdly cry.

In mony a neuk the primrose lies hid frae stranger een,
An' the broom on the knowes is wavin' wi' its cludin' o' gowd and green;
Ower the first green springs o' heather the muir-fowl faulds his wing,
And there's nought but joy in my ain land at the comin' o' the Spring!

Lady John Scott (1810–1900)

Choosing a Site for Your Villa

*Friend of the poet Allan Ramsay, Sir John Clerk of Penicuik, landowner,
Member of Parliament, and composer—as a young man he was a pupil of
Corelli in Rome—wrote a still unpublished poem, 'The Country Seat', which
reposes in the archives of Register House, Edinburgh. It illustrates delightfully
the eighteenth-century attitude to Nature.*

Tho' every beauteous villa should be placed
In open view of Neptune's wise domain,
Yet shun his borders with your utmost care.
Here, noise and tumult reign, for winds and waves
Insult the shore, and with united force
Seem bent to ruin once again the world.
Here, liquid mountains, rising to the sky,
Disclose the gloomy caverns of the deep,
Unknown rocks with banks of sinking sands
And certain death in many dreadful shapes.
Here ships distress'd and many wrecks appear,
The shattered fortunes of the mariner;
Piratick ambuscades affright the shoar,
And piercing winds the tender plants devour.
Yet at some certain points the sea will yield
A noble prospect to the neighbouring fields,
The noise will cease and Neptune's awful form

Be hid in distance. All his kingdom seems
A peaceful lake, or beauteous azure plain.
So there are pictures done with utmost art,
Which must at proper distances be seen;
For when the bold rough strokes are brought too nigh,
They lose their beauty and offend the eye.

Still other harsh and frightful objects be
Which not a little grace a country seat;
If only brought within the bounds of sight;
Deep rapid rivers, wide extended lakes,
Hige tow'ring rocks and rising cataracts.
Such rivers from a thousand urns pour forth
A central deluge; all their flowr'y banks
Sapt and deformed appear; no animal
However urg'd by violent heat or thirst
Dares to attempt the raging turbid flood.
Thus with uncertain channel on they roll,
Unless where rugged rocks their force withstand.
Lakes from afar will charm the eye and seem
Huge silver mirrors set in verdant frames.
But come we nearer, feeble Nature shrinks
To find them hideous gulph with perilous banks,
Rocks whose tumultuous noise will echo back
Loud peel of thunder from the cataract.
But yet all these, tho' Nature's spots and stains,
Or of the delug'd world the dire remains,
With wondrous beauty variegate the plains.

Sir John Clerk (1676–1755)
The Country Seat

Border Rivers

Tweed said to Till,
'What gars ye rin sae still?'
Till said to Tweed,
'Though ye rin wi' speed,
And I rin slaw,
Whar ye droon ae man,
I droon twa.'

Anonymous

Spring

By lichened tree and mossy plinth
   Like living flame of purple fire,
Flooding the wood, the hyacinth
   Uprears its heavy-scented spire.

The redstart shakes its crimson plume,
   Singing alone till evening's fall
Beside the pied and homely bloom
   Of wallflower on the crumbling wall.

Now dandelions light the way,
   Expecting summer's near approach;
And, bearing lanterns night and day,
   The great marsh-marigolds keep watch.

John Davidson (1857–1909)

Spring

Come, gentle Spring, etheral mildness, come;
And from the bosom of yon dropping cloud,
While music wakes around, veiled in a shower
Of shadowing roses, on our plains descend . . .
   As yet the trembling year is unconfirmed,
And Winter oft at eve resumes the breeze,
Chills the pale morn, and bids his driving sleets
Deform the day delightless; so that scarce
The bittern knows his time, with bill engulfed
To shake the sounding marsh; or from the shore
The plovers when to scatter o'er the heath,
And sing their wild notes to the listening waste.
   At last from Aries rolls the bounteous sun,
And the bright Bull receives him. Then no more
The expansive atmosphere is cramped with cold;
But, full of life and vivifying soul,
Lifts the light clouds sublime, and spreads them thin,
Fleecy, and white o'er all surrounding heaven.
   Forth fly the tepid airs; and unconfined,
Unbinding earth, the moving softness strays.
Joyous, the impatient husbandman perceives

Relenting Nature, and, and his lusty steers
Drives from their stalls, to where the well-used plough
Lies in the furrow loosened from the frost.
There, unrefusing, to the harnessed yoke
They lend their shoulder, and begin their toil,
Cheered by the simple song and soaring lark.
Meanwhile incumbent o'er the shining share
The master leans, removes the obstructing clay,
Winds the whole work, and sideling lays the glebe.
    White through the neighbouring fields the sower stalks
With measured step, and liberal throws the grain
Into the faithful bosom of the ground:
The harrow follows harsh, and shuts the scene . . .
    Nor only through the lenient air this change
Delicious breathes: the penetrative sun,
His force deep-darting to the dark retreat
Of vegetation, sets the steaming power
At large, to wander o'er the vernant earth
In various hues; but chiefly thee, gay green!
Thou smiling Nature's universal robe!
United light and shade! where the sight dwells
With growing strength and ever new delight.

James Thomson (1700–48)
from *The Seasons*

High Noon

*Alexander Hume, son of the 5th Lord Polwarth, was a Presbyterian minister
who spent much of his life at Logie, Stirlingshire, and wrote one distinguished
poem (which must surely have been known to Coleridge), celebrating the rise and
fall of a summer day.*

The ample heaven of fabric sure
    In cleanness does surpass
The crystal and the silver pure,
    Or clearest poleist glass.

The time sa tranquil is and still,
    That na where sall ye find—
Saif on ane high and barren hill-
    Ane air of peeping wind.

All trees and simples great and small,
   That balmy leaf do bear,
Nor they were painted on a wall
   Na mair they move or steir.

Calm is the deep and purpour sea,
   Yea, smoother nor the sand;
The wawis that welt'ring wont to be,
   Are stable like the land.

Sa silent is the cessile air,
   That every cry and call,
The bills, and dales, and forest fair
   Again repeats them all.

The rivers fresh, the caller streams
   Owre rocks can softly rin,
The water clear like crystal seems,
   And makes a pleasant din.

The flourishes and fragrant flowers,
   Throw Phoebus' fost'ring heat,
Refresh'd with dew and silver showers,
   Casts up ane odour sweet.

The clogg'd, busy humming bees,
   That never thinks to drown,
On flowers and flourishes of trees,
   Collects their liquor brown....

The breathless flocks draws to the shade,
   The frechure of their fald,
The startling nolt as they were mad
   Runs to the river cald.

The herbs beneath some leafy tree,
   Amids' the flowers they lie;
The stable ships upon the sea
   Tends up their sails to dry.

Back from the blue paymented whun,
   And from ilk plaister wall,
The hot reflexing of the sun
   Inflames the air and all.

24

The labourers that timely raise,
  All weary, faint, and weak
For heat, down to their houses gais,
  Noon-meat and sleep to take.

The caller wine in cave is sought,
  Men's brothing breists to cool,
The water cauld and clear is brought,
  And sallets steep'd in oil.

Some plucks the honey plum and pear,
  The cherry and the peach;
Some like the remand London beer,
  The body to refresh.

Alexander Hume (?1560–1609)
from *Of The Day Estivall*

June Evening

*The first translation of Virgil's 'Aeneid' into any of the languages of this island
was the Scots translation into heroic couplets made by Bishop Gavin Douglas of
Dukeld. A son of the 5th Earl of Angus, known as 'Archibald Bell-the-Cat', the
poet belonged to the pro-English faction during the minority of James V, and the
triumph of the Regent Albany's pro-French 'nationalist' faction eventually
forced Douglas into English exile, where he died of the plague.*

*Each of the thirteen books of his version of the 'Aeneid' has an original
Prologue, from the thirteenth of which this evocative description of a long June
evening is taken.*

All birnand red gan wax the even sky:
The sun enfirit hail as to my sicht
Whirlit about his ball with bemis bricht,   [beams
Declinand fast toward the north in deed.
And fiery Phlegon his dim nichtis steed
Dowkit his head sa deep in fludis gray,   [dipped
That Phoebus rollis doun under hell away,
And Hesperus in the west with bemis bricht
Upspringis, as fore-rider of the nicht.
Amang the haughs and every lusty vale   [level land, near a river
The recent dew beginnis doun to scale,
To meys the birning whare the sun had shine,   [soothe
Whilk tho was to the nether world decline.
At every polis point and cornis crops   [grass-blade

The techrys stude, as lemand beryl drops,   [dewdrops
And on the halesome herbis, clene bot weeds,
Like crystal knoppis or small silver beads.   [knobs
The licht begouth to quinkle out and fail
The day to darken, decline and devaill;   [descend
The gummis rises, down falls the donk rime,   [vapours: dank
Baith here and there scuggis and shadows dim.   [shades
Up goes the bat, with her pelit leathern flicht,
The lark descendis from the skyis hicht
Singand her complin sang eftir her guise,
To tak her rest at matin hour to rise
Ont oure the swyre swimmis the sops of mist,   [shallow valley
The nicht furthsped her cloak with sable list
That all the beauty of the fructuous field
Was with the earthis umbrage clere ourheild.   [covered
Baith man and beast, firth, flood and woodis wild
Involvit in the shadowis weren sild.   [covered
Still were the fowlis fleeis in the air,
All stoc and cattle seysit in their lair,   [settled
And everything, whareso them likis best
Bownis to tak the halesome nichtis rest   [prepares
After the dayis labour and the heat.

                    Gavin Douglas (1475?–1522)
                    from Prologue XIII, *The Aeneid*

In the Highlands

In the highlands, in the country places,
Where the old plain men have rosy faces,
And the young fair maidens
Quiet eyes;
Where essential silence cheers and blesses,
And for ever in the hill-recesses
Her more lovely music
Broods and dies.

O to mount again where erst I haunted;
Where the old red hills are bird-enchanted,
And the low green meadows
Bright with sward;
And when even dies, the million-tinted,
And the night has come, and planets glinted,

Lo! the valley hollow
Lamp-bestarred.

O to dream, O to awake and wander
There, and with delight to take and render,
Through the trance of silence,
Quiet breath;
Lo! for there, among the flowers and grasses,
Only the mightier movement sounds and passes;
Only winds and rivers,
Life and death.

Robert Louis Stevenson (1850–94)

Byre

The thatched roof rings like heaven where mice
Squeak small hosannahs all night long,
Scratching its golden pavements, skirting
The gutter's crystal river-song.

Wild kittens in the world below
Glare with one flaming eye through cracks,
Spurt in the straw, are tawny brooches
Splayed on the chests of drunken sacks.

The dimness becomes darkness as
Vast presences come mincing in,
Swagbellied Aphrodites, swinging
A silver slaver from each chin.

And all is milky, secret, female.
Angels are hushed and plain straws shine.
And kittens miaow in circles, stalking
With tail and hindleg one straight line.

Norman MacCaig (b. 1910)

Collies

We quite well remember sitting on a dike by the roadside for nearly an
hour with a shepherd of those parts, whilst, at our request, he despatched

his dog over to the opposite hill, the face of which rose steeply backwards for nearly two miles, and stretched for double that space to right and left. The intelligence displayed by the creature was infinitely beyond anything we could have previously conceived. The moment he had compelled the brigade of bleaters to perform the evolution which his master's first signal had dictated, he sat down in his distant position with his eyes fixed on him; and, though certainly not nearer to us than half-a-mile to a mile, as the crow would fly, he at once caught up every successive signal, however slight, of his commanding officer, and put the troops into active motion, to carry the wished-for manoeuvre into effect. In this manner, they were made to visit every part of the hill-face in succession—at one time keeping in compact phalanx, as if prepared to receive cavalry, and at another scouring away and scattering themselves over the mountain, as if skirmishing, like *tirailleurs* against some unseen enemy advancing from over the hill-top beyond; and it appeared to us that, great as we had already considered the talents of Lieutenant Lightbody, the able adjutant of the distinguished corps we had then recently left, we must feel ouselves compelled to declare that he was a mere tyro compared to this wonderful canine tactician.

And then, as to council, as well as war, we have seen some half-dozen of these highly gifted animals meet together from different parts of the mountains and glens, as if by appointment, at a sunny nook of some *fauld dike*, and then, seated on their haunches, hold a conference in which we, who were watching them, could have no doubt matters of vital importance to the collie population of the parish were discussed. No body of Presbyterian elders of kirks could have behaved with greater decorum, or could have shaken their heads more wisely; and when the conference broke up, we had not a single lingering doubt in our mind that the important business which had been under discussion, had been temperately settled in the wisest and most satisfactory manner.

Sir Thomas Dick Lauder (1784–1848)
Scottish Rivers

Milk-wort and Bog-cotton

Cwa' een like milk-wort and bog-cotton hair!
I love you, earth, in this mood best o' a'
When the shy spirit like a laich wind moves
And frae the lift nae shadow can fa'
Since there's nocht left to throw a shadow there
Owre een like milk-wort and milk-white cotton hair.

Wad that nae leaf upon anither wheeled
A shadow either and nae root need dern

In sacrifice to let sic beauty be!
But deep surroondin' darkness I discern
Is aye the price o' licht. Wad licht revealed
Naething but you, and nicht nocht else concealed.

Hugh MacDiarmid (1892–1978)

The Gowk

Half doun the hill, whaur fa's the linn
Far frae the flaught o' fowk,
I saw upon a lanely whin
A lanely singin' gowk:
Cuckoo, cuckoo;
And at my back
The howie hill stude up and spak:
Cuckoo, cuckoo.

There was nae soun': the loupin' linn
Hung frostit in its fa':
Nae bird was on the lanely whin
Sae white wi' fleurs o' snaw:
Cuckoo, cuckoo;
I stude stane still;
And saftly spak the howie hill:
Cuckoo, cuckoo.

William Soutar (1898–1943)

Poaching

They set off for the river, going single file. A milky haze was over the sky,
and here and there a star shone faintly. Hamish set a smart pace, for it was
not very dark, as though a slim moon had risen somewhere, or an afterglow
from the summer's day still dwelt in the high air. A clean, fresh night, with
now and then a tang of scent that went straight into the blood.

A peewit swung up, crying. Hamish stopped and cursed it with a soft
intensity. As they stood, they heard the noises of living things, and the earth
itself was not asleep but lying quietly, with all her secret brood alive. Even
the bushes in their sleep seemed watchful and hid under their skirts sudden

scurryings and rustlings. A tiny stream sang, the song that haunts the mind and won't stop. Iain's eyes were moving about him, his hearing drawn fine as a bat's cry.

The river was near when Hamish stopped.

'You go straight on with the bag,' he said, 'and I'll go up and round by the bridge. You'll find the coil of string on top, tied to the net's back line. Wait till you hear me whistle. Fix a stone to the string and have it over. Right?'

'Right,' said Hughie, and Hamish disappeared.

Iain and Hughie came by the pool, and after much hearkening and careful scouting around they settled.

'Not a soul in the world!' said Hughie, feeling for the coil of string.

'Wait a bit,' said Iain. 'Plenty of time.'

Hughie laughed and forebore hauling the net out of the bag. Iain was trying to get his ears used to the sound of the water as it rumbled over boulders into the pool, so that they could pick up a new sound.

'Hearing things?' asked Hughie with sly but friendly humour.

'No,' answered Iain.

'Queer, all the same, the things you do hear when you listen.'

'On a stunt like this, you come alive.'

'I suppose that's it.'

'As if you didn't know!'

They smiled in friendship, in warm adventure.

'It's good, this,' said Iain, confidence coming round him as his senses tuned themselves to the moment and to the night.

'Nothing better,' agreed Hughie. 'I wouldn't swop a night like this for a king's ransom.'

'If we're caught—you'll have to swop it for much less!'

'I'd have to clear out. And my parents depending on me!'

'And if Finlay even whispered to Major Grant that I was suspected—oh lord!'

They laughed softly, but still hearkening, vividly aware of movement and sound and silence.

'And you can't even take a bit of salmon home with you,' said Hughie.

'I know. It's pure madness,' said Iain.

'Danger.'

'Yes—and more.' Iain peered around him, his eyes going from one shape to another, to the pool, lifting to the sky, while his fingers of their own accord felt round the ledge of rock like a blind man's feeling a face.

Hughie's fingers had found a stone under the water, in shape like a big matchbox, and were now tying an end of the stout string round it.

A whistle came across the pool and they went into action. Hughie got the coil of string ready, stood up, whistled, and heaved the stone so that it would pass over the dim figure on the opposite bank. Presently he felt a jerk on the line and said, 'He's got it.' Iain picked up the net and they started moving down the ledge of rock where the pool, broadening slightly, grew fairly still. On their knees, with great care, they paid out the net as Hamish hauled from the other side.

Like small dark otter heads, the corks went across the pool, like living things with their arrows of water. Sometimes Hughie stood upright, lifting the net against the sky to clear a ravelling, and ensure that the rounded lead sinkers would draw the net to its natural wall. At last a jerk came along the back line. The net had reached the other bank; the river was spanned.

The moment of all moments had come, and suspense squatted in its own hollow. Each of them had a hand on the back line, waiting for the swimming salmon to hit the net. The surge of the river came from the pool's throat, rose into the still night, and their listening pierced it, hearkening for other sounds in between it and beyond it, but hardly consciously, for the stream of their instincts ran into their hands, ran so finely, so expectantly, that breathing itself was all but suspended between their open lips.

This was the moment of ecstasy before the act. This is what they always remembered as the state of delight and of freedom, for at this point a million hunting years distilled their drop of pure being.

When expectancy could draw itself no finer, the signal came to their hands. Small tugs at the back line—tug-tug—tug-tug—and they felt the fish nosing into the net, knew the shape of the fish, saw it with an inner eye and eased the back line a little, and then the pool's face was riven as the silver body rose above the surface and thrashed within the loose light meshes of the net.

Carefully but firmly they drew in the net, for the salmon had meshed near the bank, and now the thrashing white body was on the pool's edge, was drawn clear, and they fell on it. A sharp rap on the dark nape, and Iain pulled away the fish, gleaming against the sky's light. They had their moment of adoration; then he went up over the bank with it.

Confidence now rose like laughter. They were freed—the deed done— and nothing had come at them out of the night.

'Fifteen pounds,' called Hughie across the pool in an almost open voice. 'Good lads!'

And the net was being drawn away again, drawn back by Hamish whose voice had echoed their gaiety.

Once more the net was set and they crouched on their heels by the water's edge, waiting. But expectancy had lost its first tension, and now, having sunk deep into the mood of the night, they chuckled at quick, small jokes, at words thrown like pebbles, at a picture of Finlay, the gamekeeper, leading his partner to the dance. Because they love the night so much, they feel friendly to Finlay, to those having authority, to everyone, for have they not stepped beyond that world into this?

So subtle with mystery and wonder is their mirth that presently it knows why the pool has gone dead. The wise fish have seen or felt, have become aware of dark danger, and are keeping their distance from its otter's teeth.

'I'll go and stone the top of the pool,' spoke Hughie. He had hardly finished when the voice from the other side called, 'Stone it.'

'Great minds think alike,' murmured Iain, squatting now squarely and taking the back line between both hands.

'I'll shift them!' declared Hughie.

Iain laughed softly.

Hughie stepped lightly on to the rock ledge which swept up towards the throat of the pool. It was a narrow ledge some two feet above water, with wide cracks and crannies in the rock wall that rose behind it, eight to ten feet.

He had taken three or four paces along this ledge when an extraordinary thing happened to him. His body side-stepped into a cavity in the rock wall and stood there keyed to a quivering pitch. It was not that he had consciously heard or seen anything. 'Suddenly I felt something coming,' was the only way he could explain his action afterwards. 'For,' as he added, 'if I had seen or heard anything, naturally I would have given the signal.'

A figure was suddenly there between him and the pool. The figure stooped. He could have touched it with his hand. Then he smelt it, smelt tobacco from its tweeds, and in an instant knew, from the smell and shape of the head, of the cap, that it was Major Grant.

Neil M. Gunn (1891–1973)
The Drinking Well

Picking Apples

Apple time, and the trees brittle with fruit.
My children climb the bent, half-sapping branches
to where the apples, cheeked with the hectic flush
of Autumn, hang. The children bark their haunches

and lean on the edge of their balance. The apples are out
of reach; so they shake the tree. Through a tussle of leaves
    and laughter
the apples thud down; thud on the orchard grasses
in rounded, grave finality, each one after

the other dropping; the muffled sound of them dropping
like suddenly hearing the beats of one's own heart
falling away, as if shaken by some storm
as localized as this. Loading them into the cart,

the sweet smell of their bruises moist in the sun,
their skins' bloom tacky against the touch,

I experience fulfilment, suddenly aware
of some ripe, wordless answer, knowing no such
answers exist; only questions, questions, the beating years,
the dropped apples . . . the kind of touch and go
that poetry makes satisfactions of;
reality, with nothing more to show
than a brush of branches, time and the apples falling,
and shrill among the leaves, children impatiently calling.

                                        Maurice Lindsay (b. 1918)

Winter Storm

Then issues forth the storm with sudden burst,
And hurls the whole precipitated air
Down in a torrent. On the passive main
Descends the ethereal force, and with strong gust
Turns from its bottom the discoloured deep.
Through the black night that sits immense around,
Lashed into foam, the fierce-conflicting brine
Seems o'er a thousand raging waves to burn.
Meantime the mountain-billows, to the clouds
In dreadful tumult swelled, surge above surge,
Burst into chaos with tremendous roar,
And anchored navies from their stations drive
Wild as the winds, across the howling waste
Of mighty waters; now the inflated wave
Straining they scale, and now impetuous shoot
Into the secret chambers of the deep,
The wintry Baltic thundering o'er their head.
Emerging thence again, before the breath
Of full-exerted heaven they wing their course,
And dart on distant coasts—if some sharp rock
Or shoal insidious break not their career,
And in loose fragments fling them floating round,
    Nor less at land the loosened tempest reigns.
The mountain thunders, and its sturdy sons
Stoop to the bottom of the rocks they shade.
Lone on the midnight steep, and all aghast,
The dark wayfaring stranger breathless toils,
And, often falling, climbs against the blast.
Low waves the rooted forest, vexed, and sheds
What of its tarnished honours yet remain—

Dashed down and scattered, by the tearing wind's
Assiduous fury, its gigantic limbs.
Thus struggling through the dissipated grove,
The whirling tempest raves along the plain;
And, on the cottage thatched or lordly roof
Keen-fastening, shakes them to the solid base.
Sleep frighted flies; and round the rocking dome,
For entrance eager, howls the savage blast.
Then too, they say, through all the burdened air
Long groans are heard, shrill sounds, and distant sighs,
That, uttered by the demon of the night,
Warn the devoted wretch of woe and death.
Huge uproar lords it wide. The clouds, commixed
With stars swift-gliding, sweep along the sky.
All Nature reels: till Nature's King, who oft
Amid tempestuous darkness dwells alone,
And on the wings of the careering wind
Walks dreadfully serene, commands a calm;
Then straight air, sea, and earth, are hushed at once.

James Thomson (1700–48)
from *The Seasons*

The Moray Floods

*In August 1829, as a result of torrential rain on the Cairngorms and the
Monadhliath, the rivers flowing to the Moray Firth came down in such heavy
spate that they rose as much as twenty feet above their usual level, flooding all
the surrounding country. Houses far above the usual high-water mark were
surrounded; many people were drowned; and terrible destruction was wrought.
The extracts that follow are by Sir Thomas Dick Lauder, one of the local lairds,
who recorded the experience of the people, as far as he could in their own words.*

Below Orton, the Duke of Gordon's small tenants of the Ellie were clustered
together in a little hamlet, or as a boy emphatically called it, 'a bourrach o'
hooses.' Some of these dwellings were not more than six feet above the level
of the Spey, and between these and the houses on the higher ground there
is an old river course. The flood made its way into this on the evening of the
3rd, and whilst some escaped at the risk of their lives, it unexpectedly cut
off all chance of retreat from others. About seven o'clock, the water began to
spread over the fields, and to approach the houses. That of a very poor and
industrious man, called John Geddes, built on a somewhat elevated spot,
had entirely escaped in the floods of 1768 and 1799, when the neighbouring
cottages were inundated to considerable depth. Alarmed by the rapid growth

of the river, the people of the other cottages crowded as night fell towards
that belonging to Geddes, firmly believing that they should be perfectly
safe in it. There nine men and women, and four children, sat shivering over
the fire in their wet garments. The faggots were heaped high, and as John
Geddes himself says, 'We soon begud to grow braw an' hearty, whan John
Forsyth an' me gaed oot to big up the stable-door, an' saw the water growin'
terrible! "Ye're a' very, merry, Sirs," said I, as I gaed in, "but ye'll no be
lang sae. Ye had better stir your stumps, an' put things oot o' the gate, an'
look till your ain safety." The words were hardly oot o' my mouth, whan in
cam' the river on us. We lifted the meal-kist, pat the wife and her bit weane
and the bairnies into the bed, an' the rest got up on kists an' tables. We pat
the fire on the girdle, hung the girdle on the crook in the lum, an stuck the
lamp up on the wa'. But the water soon drooned oot the fire, and rose into
the bed. I then pat twa chairs i' the bed, and the wife sat upon them wi' the
little anes in her lap; but the water soon got up to them there. Syne I cut the
ceilin' aboon the bed—pat a door atween the twa chair backs—laid a cauf-
bed on the door—set the wife an' little anes aboon that—and then gaed up
mysel' to the couplebaulk, an' held the door firm wi' my feet, an had an
axe ready to cut the hoose roof in case o' need. The rest o' the fouk stowed
themsels awa frae the water as weel as they could, on chairs on the tap o'
tables an' kists. We ware lang in this way, an' I cheered them the best I
could, an' telt them the hours every noo an' than by my watch, that I hung
up on the couple-leg i' my sight. But the water raise an' raise, till aboot twa
o'clock, whan it drooned oot the lamp, an' left us a' i' the dark thegither.
There was a groan, an' a cry that there was naething for us noo but death.
"Trust in Providence," says I till them; "trust in Providence, neebours.
But dinna think ye can be saved unless ye mak' use o' the raison an' the
faculties that God has bestowed on ye. I'll cut the roof the moment I see
that naething else will do." But in trouth, it was an' aw'some night, what wi'
the roar an' ragin' o' the water, the howlin' o' the wind, an' the blatterin' o'
the rain without, an' the cries an' prayers o' the terrified fouk, an' the
greetin' o' the bairns within; an' a' thing dark; an' we, as a body might say,
hingin' atween the twa warlds, ilka moment expectin' the hoose to gie way
bodily; an' the very tables an' chairs the fouk war standin' on shakin' an'
floatin' aneath them. Auld Jean Stronach, fourscore years o' age, sat the
hale night, amid a' the jost'ling, wi' a clocking hen and a wheen chuckens in
her apron. Some ane said till her, that she might hae ither things in her
mind than a hen 'an chuckens, when she was on the brink of eternity.
"Poor things," quo' Jean, "I couldna think o' lettin' them be drooned."
Aweel! when we war a' in the height o' despondency, Maggie Christie
heard tongues thereoot, an', wi' very joy, she jumpit doon frae the kist she
was stanin' on; but, I trow, she gat sic a gliff o' the water, that she gied a
roar, an' lap upon the hearth, gruppit at the cruik to save hersel', an' wi'
that she climbed up the lum, an' pat her head oot at the tap, wi' her face as
black as a suttyman's. "Oh! Jamie Mill, Jamie Mill," cried she, "ye're the
blythest sight that ever I saw!" "Keep us a!" is that you Maggie?" quo'

Jamie Mill; "weel, I've seen blyther sights than you are at this precious moment; but, black though ye be, I maun hae ye oot o' that." An' sae he crap up the roof an' pu'ed her oot o' the lum into the boat. Whan they cam' round to the door, the hoose was so deep wi' water, that there was barely space to thrust our heads atween the stream and the door lintel, so that I was forced to dip the bit bairnies i' the water afore I could get them oot. That did gang to my very heart! Poor Jean Stronach lost five o' her chuckens, as they were draggin' her oot through the water into the boat; an' we were a' sae benumbed wi' cauld an' weet, that, I'm sure she an' the bairnies wad hae died had we been muckle langer there.' The boat was so full that, to prevent its sinking, some of the men were compelled to creep on the house-top, and to wait there till it could return.

The Ellie presented a miserable scene after the waters had subsided; the houses, furniture, and crops being ruined, buried, or swept off. Among the cattle carried away and drowned, was poor John Geddes' cow: 'But the thrawsome brute,' as he said himself, 'was drooned by her ain obstinacy, for she wad gang nae gaet but what she likit.'

Sir Thomas Dick Lauder (1784–1848)
*An Account of the Great Floods in the Province
of Moray*

Winter in Town and Country

To town and country Winter comes alike, but to each he comes in different fashion. To the villager, he stretches a bold frosty hand; to the townsman, a clammy one. To the villager, he comes wrapt in cold clear air; to the towns-man, in yellow fogs, through which the gas-lamps blear at noon. To the villager, he brings snow on the bare trees, frosty spangles on the roadways, exquisite silver chasings and adornments to the ivies on the walls, tumults of voices and noises of skating-irons, smouldering orange sunsets that distain the snows, make brazen the window-panes, and fire even the icicles at the cottage eaves. To the townsman, he brings influenzas, secret slides on unlighted pavements, showers of snow-balls from irreverent urchins, damp feet, avalanches from the roofs of houses six stories high, cab fares woefully begrudged, universal slush. Winter is like a Red Indian, noble in his forests and solitudes, deteriorated by cities and civilization. The signs of his approach are different in the town and in the village. To a certain northern city, whose spires fret my sky-line of a morning, his proximity is made known by the departure of the last tourist and the arrival of the first student; by brown papers taken from windows in fashionable streets and squares; by the reassembling of schools and academies; and by advertisements in the newspapers relative to the opening of the University. By these signs, rather than by the cawing of uneasy rooks, or the whirling away of the last red leaf, the inhabitants know that the stern season is at hand; a salvo of inagural addresses announces that he is in their midst, and the reappearance of lawyers in the long-deserted halls of the Parliament House, is regarded as a prophecy of snow. In that famous northern city, winter is disagreeable, as in other cities. Lawyers, doctors, and professors tumble out of bed, and shave by gas-light. The entire population catches cold, and the clergymen are coughed down on Sundays. The falling snow covers the pavements— except the spaces in front of the bakers' shops, which are wet, and black, and steaming; in due time it makes dumb the streets, muffling every sound of wheel and hoof; it slips its moorings, and hangs in icicles and avalanches from the roofs of houses, but it does not appear in any perfection; it has lost all purity, and is dingy as a city sparrow. It is regarded as a nuisance; shop-keepers scrape it from their doors, deft scavengers built it in mounds along the streets; in a couple of days thaw sets in, and from roof, and eave, and cornice, from window-sill, gargoyle, and spout, there is a universal sound of weeping, like that which was heard in the old Norse world, when gods and men lamented the death of Balder, the Beautiful. On frosty mornings, cab-horses, whose shoes are never sharpened in preparation, although the previous night every star was sparkling like steel, are tumbling on the hilly streets, and the fare gesticulates from the window, and one man holds down the head of the terrified animal, whose breath is like a wreath of incense, and the driver, clothed in a drab great-coat, with a comforter up to his nose, is busy with the girths, and small boys gather round, and attempt to blow some warmth into their benumbed fingers. Up from the sea comes a wicked harr, shedding disastrous twilight; church spires are visible half way up and dis-appear; the lights in shops are yellow smears on the darkness; at crossings, vehicles burst on you in a moment, and in another moment are swallowed up; and on the obscure pavement all ties of relationship and acquaintanceship are dissolved.

Alexander Smith (1830–67)
Last Leaves

In December

I watch the dung-cart stumble by
  Leading the harvest to the fields,
That from cow-byre and stall and sty
  The farmstead in the winter yields.

Like shocks in a reaped field of rye
  The small black heaps of lively dung
Sprinkled in the grass-meadow lie
  Licking the air with smoky tongue.

This is Earth's food that man piles up
  And with his fork will thrust on her,
And Earth will lie and slowly sup
  With her moist mouth through half the year.

Andrew Young (1885–1971)

LOVERS

Blest, Blest and Happy He

Blest, blest and happy he
Whose eyes behold her face,
But blessed more whose ears hath heard
Thy speeches framed with grace

And he is half a god
That these thy lips may kiss,
Yet god all whole that may enjoy
    Thy body as it is.

Anonymous (c. 1610)

A Thanksgiving for Love

James I of Scotland was captured at sea on his way to France by an English pirate in 1406, and handed over to Henry IV. For eighteen years the young Scots king was held captive, although he accompanied Henry V to France, where that monarch died. Terms of release were then negotiated, the Scots being compelled to pay for the maintenance of their king.

During the close of his stay in England, James saw from a window the Lady Joan Beaufort, daughter of the Duke of Somerset, and fell in love, whereupon, he tells us, there ran

> *. . . sudden abate, anon asterte,*
> *The blude of all my body to my hert.*

He related his love in a long poem, 'The King's Quhair' (Book). Apparently finished after his marriage, when he was back in Scotland, the close of the poem contains one of the earliest celebrations of married love in Scots literature.

Blissit mot be the heyë goddis all
So fair that glitteren in the firmament!
And blissit be their might celestial
That have convoyit hale with one assent

387

My luve, and to so glad a consequent!
And thankit be Fortunis axletree
And wheel, that thus so well has whirlit me.

Thankit mot be and fair in luve befall
The nychtingale, that with so gude intent,
Sang there of luve the notis swete and small,
Where my fair hertis lady was present,
Her with to glad or that she forthir went.
And thou geraflour, mot y-thankit be   [gillyflower
All other flouris for the luve of thee.

And thankit be the fairë castle wall
Where as I whilom lookit furth and lent,
Thankit mot be the sanctis martial
That me first causit hath this accident,
Thankit mot be the grenë bewis bent
Through whom and under first fortunyt me
My hertis heal and my comfort to see.

For to the presence, swete and delitable,
Richt of this flour that full is of plesance,
By process and by meanis favourable,
First of the blisful goddis purveyance,
And syne through long and true continuance
Of veray faith in luve and true service
I comin am, and forthir in this wise.

Unworthy, lo, bot only of her grace
In luvis yoke that easy is and sure,
In guerdoun eke of all my luvis space
She hath me tak, her humble creature,
And thus befell my blisful aventure
In youth, of love, that now from day to day
Floureth aye new, and yit forthir, I say. . . .

And thus endeth the fatal influence
Causit from heaven, where power is commit
Of governance by the magnificence
Of Him that hiest in the heaven sit,
To Whom we thank that all our life hath writ,
Who couth it read, agone sen mony a year,
High in the heavenis figure circulere.

King James I of Scotland (1394–1437)
The King's Quhair

The Self-Righteous Lover

My heart is heich above,
  My body is full of bliss,
For I am set in luve,
  As weil as I wald wiss;
I luve my lady pure,
  And she luvs me again;
I am her serviture,
  She is my soverane.

Shc is my vcry heart,
  I am her hope and heal;
She is my joy inwart,
  I am her luvar leal;
I am her bound and thrall,
  She is at my command;
I am perpetual
  Her man, both fute and hand.

The thing that may hcr plcase
  My body sall fulfil;
Whatever her disease,
  It does my body ill.
My bird, my bonnie ane,
  My tender babe venust,   [beautiful
My luve, my life alane,
  My liking and my lust.

We interchange our hairts
  In others armis soft;
Spreitless we twa departs
  Usand our luvis oft;
We murne when licht day daws,
  We plain the nicht is short,   [complain
We curse the cock that craws.
  That hinders our disport.

I glowffin up agast,   [stare
  When I her miss on nicht,
And in my oxter fast
  I find the bowster ticht;   [bolster
Then langour on me lies,
  Like Morpheus the mair,
Whilk causis me uprise   [which
  And to my sweet repair:

And then is all the sorrow
  Furth of remembrance,
That ever I had aforrow
  In luvis observance.
Thus never do I rest,
  So lusty a life I lead,
When that I list to test   [choose
  The well of womanheid.

Luvars in pain, I pray
  God send you sic remead   [such remedy
As I have nicht and day,
  You to defend from deid;
Therefore be ever true
  Unto your ladies free,
And they will on you rue,
  As mine has done on me.

Anonymous
The Bannatyne Manuscript (completed 1568)

Lo' What It Is To Luve

Lo! what it is to luve,
  Learn ye, that list to pruve,
Be me, I say, that no ways may
  The grund of grief remuve,
Bot still decay, both nicht and day:
  Lo! what it is to luve.

Luve is ane fervent fire,
  Kendillit without desire:
Short plesour, lang displesour,
  Repentance is the hire;
Ane puir tressour without messour:
  Luve is ane fervent fire.

To luve and to be wise,
  To rege with gud advice,
Now thus, now than, so goes the game,
  Incertain is the dice:
There is no man, I say, that can
  Both luve and to be wise.

Flee always from the snare;
  Learn at me to be ware;
It is ane pain and double trane   [temptation
  Of endless woe and care;
For to refrain that danger plain,
  Flee always from the snare.

Alexander Scott (*c.* 5130–84?)

Robene and Makyne

Robene sat on gude green hill
Keepand a flock of fe: [sheep
Merry Makyne said him til,   [said to him
'Robene, thou rue on me;
I have thee luvit loud and still,
Thir yearis twa or three;
My dule in dern bot gif thou dill,   [if you don't soothe my secret sorrow
Doubtless bot dreid I die.   [without doubt

Robene answer it, 'Be the rude,
Naething of luve I know,
Bot keepis my sheep under yon wood,
Lo where they raik on raw: [range in order
What has marrit thee in thy mood,
Makyne, to me thou shaw;
Or what is luve, or to be lo'ed?
Fain wald I leir that law.'   [learn

'At luvis lair gif thou will leir,
Tak there an a b c:
Be heynd, courteous, and fair of feir,   [skilful: bearing
Wise, hardy, and free;
So that no danger do thee deir,   [injure
What dule in dern thou dree;   [secret grief you endure
Press thee with pain at all power,
Be patient and privie.'

Robene answerit her again,
'I wait nocht what is luve;
Bot I have marvel in certain
What makis thee thus wanrufe: [disturbed
The weddir is fair, and I am fain,

My sheep gois hale abufe;
An we suld play us in this plain,
They wald us baith reprufe.'

'Robene, tak tent unto my tale,
And work all as I rede,
And thou sall have my hairt all haill,
Eke and my maidenheid.
Sen God sendis bute for bale,   [remedy for sorrow
And for murning remeid,   [mourning, remedy
In dern with thee bot gif I deal,   [unless in secret
Doubtless I am bot deid.'

'Makyne, to-morne this ilka tide,
An ye will meet me here,
Peraventure my sheep may gang beside,
Whill we have liggit full near;   [lain
Bot maugre haif I, an I bide   [annoyance
Fra they begin to steir;   [stir
What lyis on hairt I will nocht hide;
Makyne, than mak gude cheer.'

'Robene, thou reivis my roif and rest;   [robs peace
I luve bot thee alane.'
'Makyne, adieu, the sun gois west,
The day is near hand gane.'
'Robene, in dule I am so drest,   [I am so sad
That luve will be my bane.'
'Ga luve, Makyne, wherever thou list,
Far leman I lo'e nane.'

'Robene, I stand in sic a styll;   [state
I sich, and that full sair.'   [sigh
'Makyne, I have been here this while;
At hame God gif I were.'
'My honey, Robene, talk ane while,
Gif thou wilt do na mair.'
'Makyne, some other man beguile,
For hameward I will fare.'

Robene on his wayis went,
As licht as leaf of tree;
Makyne murnit in her intent,
And trow'd him never to see.   [swore

Robene braid attour the bent;   [moved over the little
Then Makyne cryit on hie,   hillock
'Now may thou sing, for I am shent!   [disarmed
What ailis luve at me?'

Makyne went hame withouthin fail,
Full weary eftir couth weep.
Then Robene in a full fair dale
Assemblit all his sheep.
Be that, some pairt of Makyne's ail   [then
Outhrow his hairt coud creep;
He followit her fast there til assail,   [to accost
And til her tuke gude keep.

'Abide, abide, thou fair Makyne,
A word for ony thing;
For all my luve it sall be thine,
Withouthin depairting.
All haill thy heart for til have mine
Is all my coveting;
My sheep to-morne whill houris nine   [till
Will need of no keeping.'

'Robene, thou has heard sung and say,
In gestis and stories auld,   [tales
The man that will nocht when he may
Sall have nocht when he wald.   [shall
I pray to Jesus every day
Mot eke their carës cauld,
That first presses with thee to play,
Be firth, forest or fauld.'   [by

'Makyne, the nicht is soft and dry.
The weddir is warm and fair,
And the green wood richt near us by
To walk attour all where;
There may na janglour us espy,   [tale-carrier
That is to luve contrair:
Therein, Makyne, baith ye and I
Unseen we may repair'

'Robene, that warld is all away
And quite brocht til ane end,
And never again thereto, perfay,

Sall it be as thou wend;   [you think
For of my pain thou made it play,
And all in vain I spend:
As thou has done, sa sall I say,
Murne on, I think to mend.'

'Makyne, the hope of all my heal,   [health
My hairt on thee is set,
And evermair to thee be leal,   [true
While I may live but let;
Never to fail, as others feill,   [others do
What grace that ever I get.'
'Robene, with thee I will nocht deal;
Adieu, for thus we met.'

Makyne went hame blyth aneuch,   [enough
Attour the holtis hair;   [dusky wood
Robene murnit, and Makyne leuch;   [laughed
She sang, he sichit sair;
And so left him, baith wo and wreuch,   [wretched
In dolour and in care,
Keepand his herd under a heuch,   [cliff
Amangis the holtis hair.

                                        Robert Henryson

A Warning on Second Marriages

Amang follies, ane grit folly I find—
When that ane man past fifty years of age
That in his vain conceit growis sa blind
As for to join himself in mairriage
With ane young lass; whare blude is in ane rage
Thinkand that he may serve hir appetite—
Whilk, gif he fail, then scho will him despite.   [which, if

Aged men suld joice in moral tales,   [rejoice
And nocht in tails: for folly is to mairry   [having sex
Fra time that baith thair strength and nature fails
To tak ane wife, and bring themselves in tairy: [into difficulty
For fresch May and cauld January
Agreeis nocht upon ane sang in June—
The treble wants that suld be sung abune.

Men suld tak voyage at the larkis sang
And nocht at e'en, when passit is the day;
Efter mid-age, the luvar lies full lang;
When that his hair is turnit lyart gray,   [hoary
And auld gray beird on ane white mouth to lay
Into ane bed, it is ane piteous sicht—
The ane crys 'Help!', the other wantis micht.

Sir Richard Maitland of Lethington (1496–1586)
from *The Folly of Ane Auld Man*

Inconstancy Reproved

I do confess thou'rt smooth and fair,
    And I might have gone near to love thee,
Had I not found the slightest prayer
    That lips could speak, had power to move thee;
But I can let thee now alone
As worthy to be loved by none.

I do confess thou'rt sweet; yet find
    Thee such an unthrift of thy sweets,
Thy favours are but like the wind
    That kisseth everything it meets:
And since thou canst with more than one,
Thou'rt worthy to be kiss'd by none.

The morning rose that untouch'd stands
    Arm'd with her briers, how sweet she smells!
But pluck'd and strain'd through ruder hands,
    Her sweets no longer with her dwell:
But scent and beauty both are gone,
And leaves fall from her, one by one.

Such fate ere long will thee betide
    When thou hast handled been awhile,
Like fair flowers to be thrown aside;
    And thou shalt sigh, when I shall smile,
To see thy love to everyone
Hath brought thee to be loved by none.

Sir Robert Ayton (1570–1638)

O Werena My Heart Licht I wad Dee

*Grizell, daughter of Sir Patrick Hume, afterwards Earl of Marchmont.
married George Baillie of Jerviswood. As a child she aided her father and her
future husband's father during the years of Cromwellian prosecution, sharing
their exile in Utrecht.*

There ance was a may, and she loo'd na men;
She biggit her bonnie bower doun in yon glen;
But now she cries, dool! and well-a-day!
Come doun the green gait and come here away!

When bonnie young Johnnie cam' ower the sea,
He said he saw naething sae lovely as me;
He hecht me baith rings and mony braw things,—
And werena my heart licht I wad dee.

He had a wee titty that loo'd na me,   [sister
Because I was twice as bonnie as she;
She raised such a pother 'twixt him and his mother
That werena my heart licht I wad dee.

The day it was set, and the bridal to be:
The wife took a dwam, and lay doun to dee;
She maned and she graned out o' dolour and pain,
Till he vow'd he never wad see me again.

His kin was for ane of a higher degree,
Said, What had he to do wi' the like of me?
Albeit I was bonnie, I wasna for Johnnie,—
And werena my heart licht I wad dee.

They said I had neather cow nor calf,
Nor dribbles o' drink rins through the draff,
Nor pickles o' meal rins through the mill-e'e;
And werena my heart licht I wad dee.

His titty she was baith wylie and slee;
She spied me as I cam' ower the lea;
And then she ran in and made a loud din,—
Believe your ain een an' trow na me.

His bonnet stood aye fu' round on his brow,—
His auld ane look'd aye as weel as some's new;
But now he lets 't wear ony gait it will hing,
And casts himself dowie upon the corn-bing.

And now he gaes daund'ring about the dykes,
And a' he dow do is to hund the tykes:
The live-lang nicht he ne'er steeks his e'e;
And werena my heart licht I wad dee.

Were I but young for thee, as I hae been,
We should hae been gallopin' doun on yon green,
And linkin' it on the lily-white lea,—
And wow! gin I were but young for thee!

Lady Grizel Baillie (1665–1746)

A Cavalier Lyric

My dear and only love, I pray
   That little world of thee
Be governed by no other sway
   Than purest monarchy;
Or if confusion have a part,
   Which virtuous souls abhor,
And hold a synod in thine heart,
   I'll never love thee more.

As Alexander I will reign,
   And I will reign alone;
My thoughts did ever more disdain,
   A rival on my throne.
He either fears his fate too much,
   Or his deserts are small,
That dares not put it to the touch
   To gain or lose it all....

But if thou wilt prove faithful then,
   And constant of thy word,
I'll make thee glorious by my pen,
   And famous by my sword;
I'll serve thee in such noble ways
   Was never heard before;
I'll crown and deck thee all with bays,
   And love thee more and more.

Montrose (1612–50)

Glad Am I, Glad Am I

Glad am I, glad am I,
my mother is gone to Henislie;
steiche the door and catch me,   [shut
lay me doun and stretch me,
ding me, and dang me,
ye, gif I cry hang me—
ye, gif I die of the same,
bury me, bury in godis name.

Alexander Montgomerie (1556?–1610)

The Key o' Love

Kissin' is the key o' love,
An' clappin' is the lock,
An' makin' o's the best thing
That e'er a young thing got.

Sung to the boy Burns by his mother, Agnes Burns, nee Broun (1732–1820)

My Peggy

My Peggy is a young thing
    Just enter'd in her teens,
Fair as the day, and sweet as May,
Fair as the day, and always gay.
    My Peggy is a young thing.
    And I'm na very auld,
Yet weel I like to meet her at
    The wauking o' the fauld.

My Peggy speaks sae sweetly,
    Whene'er we meet alane,
I wish nae mair to lay my care,
I wish nae mair o' a' that's rare.
    My Peggy speaks sae sweetly,
    To a' the lave I'm cauld,
But she gars a' my spirits glow
    At wauking o' the fauld.

My Peggy smiles sae kindly
  Whene'er I whisper love,
That I look doun on a' the toun,
That I look doun upon a croun.
  My Peggy smiles sae kindly,
    It makes me blythe and bauld,
  An' naething gies me sic delight
    As wauking o' the fauld.

My Peggy sings sae saftly
  When on my pipe I play,
By a' the rest it is confest,
By a' the rest that she sings best.
  My Peggy sings sae saftly,
    And in her sangs are tauld
Wi' innocence, the wale o' sense,
    At wauking o' the fauld.

Allan Ramsay (1686–1758)

If Doughty Deeds

If doughty deeds my lady please,
  Right soon I'll mount my steed;
And strong his arm and fast his seat,
  That bears frae me the meed.
I'll wear thy colours in my cap,
  Thy picture in my heart,
And he that bends not to thine eye
  Shall rue it to his smart!
    Then tell me how to woo thee, Love;
      O tell me how to woo thee!
    For they dear sake nae care I'll take,
      Tho' ne'er another trow me.

If gay attire delight thine eye
  I'll dight me in array;
I'll tend thy chamber door all night,
  And squire thee all the day;
If sweetest sounds can win thine ear,
  These sounds I'll strive to catch;
Thy voice I'll steal to woo thysel',
  That voice that nane can match.

But if fond love they heart can gain,
   I never broke a vow;
Nae maiden lays her skaith to me,
   I never loved but you.
For you alone I ride the ring,
   For you I wear the blue;
For you alone I strive to sing,
   O tell me how to woo!
     Then tell me how to woo thee, Love;
      O tell me how to woo thee!
     For thy dear sake nae care I'll take,
      Tho' ne'er another trow me.

            Robert Cunninghame-Graham of Gartmore (1735–97)

False Luve

False luve! and hae ye played me this,
   In the simmer, 'mid the flowers?
I sall repay ye back again,
   In the winter 'mid the showers.

But again, dear luve, and again, dear luve,
   Will ye not turn again?
As ye look to ither women,
   Sall I to ither men.

            from David Herd's *Scottish Songs*, 1776

Auld Robin Gray

Daughter of James Lindsay, 5th Earl of Balcarres, Anne married Andrew Barnard, who later became Colonial Secretary of Cape Town. 'Auld Robin Gray' was written in 1771 and published anonymously, authorship still being thought unladylike in the eighteenth century. She confessed her authorship, however, to Scott in 1823. Her letters were published in 1901 inder the title 'South Africa a Century Ago.'

When the sheep are in the fauld, and the kye at hame,
And a' the warld to rest are gane,
The waes o' my heart fa' in showers frae my e'e,
While my gudeman lies sound by me.

Young Jamie lo'ed me weel, and sought me for his bride;
But saving a croun he had naething else beside:
To make the croun a pund, young Jamie gaed to sea;
And the croun and the pund were baith for me.

He hadna been awa' a week but only twa,
When my father brak his arm, and the cow was stown awa';
My mother she fell sick,—and my Jamie at the sea—
And auld Robin Gray came a-courtin' me.

My father couldna work, and my mother couldna spin;
I toil'd day and night, but their bread I couldna win;
Auld Rob maintain's them baith, and wi' tears in his e'e
Said, 'Jennie, for their sakes, O, marry me!'

My heart it said nay; I look'd for Jamie back;
But the wind it blew high, and the ship it was a wrack;
His ship it was a wrack—Why didna Jamie dee?
Or why do I live to cry, Wae's me!

My father urged me sair: my mother didna speak;
But she look'd in my face till my heart was like to break
They gi'ed him my hand, tho' my heart was in the sea;
Sae auld Robin Gray he was gudeman to me.

I hadna been a wife a week but only four,
When mournfu' as I sat on the stane at the door,
I saw my Jamie's wraith,—for I couldna think it he,
Till he said, 'I'm come hame to marry thee.'

O sair, sair did we greet, and muckle did we say;
We took but ae kiss, and we tore ourselves away;
I wish that I were dead, but I'm no like to dee;
And why was I born to say, Wae's me!

I gang like a ghaist, and I carena to spin;
I daurna think on Jamie, for that wad be a sin;
But I'll do my best a gude wife aye to be,
For auld Robin Gray he is kind unto me.

Lady Anne Barnard (1750–1825)

A Red, Red Rose

O, my luve's like a red, red rose,
    That's newly sprung in June:
O, my luve's like the melodie
    That's sweetly played in tune.

As fair art thou, my bonnie lass,
    So deep in luve am I;
And I will luve thee still, my dear,
    Till a' the seas gang dry.

Till a' the seas gang dry, my dear,
    And the rocks melt wi' the sun:
And I will luve thee still, my dear,
    While the sands o' life shall run.

And fare thee well, my only luve!
    And fare thee well a while!
And I will come again, my luve,
    Though it were ten thousand mile.

Robert Burns (1759–96)

John Anderson, My Jo

John Anderson, my jo, John,
    When we were first acquent;
Your locks were like the raven,
    Your bonie brow was brent;
But now your brow is beld, John,
    Your locks are like the snow;
But blessings on your frosty pow,
    John Anderson, my jo.

John Anderson, my jo, John,
    We clamb the hill thegither;
And mony a cantie day, John,
    We've had wi' ane anither:
Now we maun totter down, John,
    And hand in hand we'll go,
And sleep thegither at the foot,
    John Anderson, my jo.

Robert Burns

Florine

Could I bring back lost youth again
  And be what I have been,
I'd court you in a gallant strain,
  My young and fair Florine.

But mine's the chilling age that chides
  Devoted rapture's glow,
And Love—that conquers all besides—
  Finds Time a conquering foe.

Farewell! we're severed by our fate
  As far as night from noon;
You came into the world too late,
  And I depart so soon.

Thomas Campbell (1777–1844)

Mary's Song

I was ha'e gi'en him my lips tae kiss,
Had I been his, had I been his;
Barley breid and elder wine,
Had I been his as he is mine.

The wanderin' bee it seeks the rose;
Tae the lochan's bosom the burnie goes;
The grey bird cries at evenin's fa',
'My luve, my fair one, come awa'.'

My beloved sall ha'e this he'rt tae break,
Reid, reid wine and the barley cake,
A he'rt tae break, an' a mou' tae kiss,
Tho' he be nae mine, as I am his.

Marion Angus (1866–1946)

The Tryst

O luely, luely, cam she in
And luely she lay doun:

I kent her by her caller lips   [cold
And her breists sae sma' and roun'.

A' thru the nicht we spak nae word
Nor sinder'd bane frae bane:
A' thru the nicht I heard her hert
Gang soundin' wi' my ain.

It was about the waukrife hour
Whan cocks begin to craw
That she smool'd saftly thru the mirk
Afore the day wud daw.

Sae luely, luely, cam she in
Sae luely was she gaen;
And wi' her a' my simmer days
Like they had never been.

William Soutar (1898–1943)

O Wha's Been Here Afore Me, Lass

O wha's the bride that cairries the bunch
O' thistles blinterin white?
Her cuckold bridgegroom little dreids
What he sall ken this nicht.

For closer than gudeman can come
And closer to'r than hersel,'
Wha didna need her maidenheid
Has wrocht his purpose fell.

O wha's been here afore me, lass,
And hoo did he get in?
   —A man that deed or I was born
   This evil thing has din.

And left, as it were on a corpse,
Your maidenheid to me?
   —Nae lass, gudeman, sin time began
   'S hed ony mair to gie.

But I can gie ye kindness, lad,
And a pair o willin hands,
And ye sall hae my briests like stars,
My limbs like willow wands.

And on my lips ye'll heed nae mair,
And in my hair forget,
The seed o a' the men that in
My virgin womb hae met. . . .

from *A Drunk Man Looks At The Thistle*
Hugh MacDiarmid (1892–1978)

Under The Eildon Tree

*Sydney Goodsir Smith's poem, one of the masterpieces of twentieth-century
Scottish literature, consists of twenty-three Elegies, variating upon the theme
of love.*

Elegy XIII

i

I got her i the Black Bull
    (The Black Bull o Norroway),
Gin I mynd richt, in Leith Street,
Doun the stair at the corner forenent
The Fun Fair and Museum o Monstrosities,
    The Tyke-faced Loun, the Cunyiars Den
        And siclike.
I tine her name the nou, and cognomen for that—
Aiblins it was Deidre, Ariadne, Calliope,
Gaby, Jacquette, Katrina, Sandra,
    Or· sunkots; exotic, I expeck.
A wee bit piece
    O' what our faithers maist unaptlie
    But romanticallie designatit 'Fluff'.
My certie! Nae muckle o Fluff
    About the hures o Reekie!
Dour as stane, the like stane
As biggit the unconquerable citie
Whar they pullulate,
                        Infestan
The wynds and closes, squares

And public promenads
　　　—The bonnie craturies!
　　　　　—But til our winter's tale.

ii

Fou as a puggie, I, the bardic ee
In a fine frenzie rollan,
Drunk as a fish wi sevin tails,
Purpie as Tiberio wi bad rum and beerio,
　　　(Io! Io! Iacche! Iacche, Io!)
—Sevin nichts and sevin days
　　　(A modest bout whan aa's dune,
　　　Maist scriptural, in fack)
Was the Makar on his junketins
　　　(On this perticular occasioun
　　　O' the whilk we tell the nou
　　　Here i the records, for the benefit
　　　O' future putative historians)
Wi sindrie cronies throu the wastage-land
O' howffs and dancins, stews
And houses o assignatioun
I' the auntient capital.

—Ah, she was a bonnie cou!
Ilka a pennie I had she teuk,
Scoffed the halicarnassus lot,
As is the custom, due
And meet and mensefu,
Proper and proprietous,
　　Drinkan hersel to catch up wi me
　　That had a sevin-day stert on her
　　　—O' the whilk conditioun
Nae smaa braggandie was made at the time
Here' and yont about the metropolis—
　　And mysel drinkan me sober again
For reasouns ower obvious
Till needcessitate descriptioun,
　　　　　　　Explanatioun,
　　　　　　　　Or ither.

Nou, ye canna ging lang at yon game
And the hour cam on at length
That the Cup-bearer did refuse

The provision of further refreshment
—Rochlie, I mynd, and in a menner
Wi the whilk I amna uised,
  Uncomformable wi my lordie spreit,
  A menner unseemlie, unbefittan
  The speakin-til or interlocutioun
  O' a Bard and Shennachie,
      Far less a Maister o Arts,
      —The whilk rank and statioun I haud
      In consequence and by vertue
      O' unremittan and pertinacious
      Applicatioun til the bottle
      Ower a period no exceedan
      Fowr year and sax munce or moneths
(The latter bean a *hiatus* or *caesura*
For the purposes o rusticatioun
Or *villeggiatura* 'at my place in the country'):
  Aa the whilk was made sufficient plain
Til the Cup-bearer at the time—
  Losh me, what a collieshangie!
Ye'd hae thocht the man affrontit
  Deeplie, maist mortallie
      And til the hert.
Ay, and I cried him Ganymede,
  Wi the whilk address or pronomen
      He grew incensed.
'Run, Ganymede!" quo I,
  'Stay me wi flagons!'
                    (Or maybe tappit-hens)
      —But I digress.
It was rum, I mynd the nou, rum was the bree,
Rum and draucht Bass.
                —Sheer *hari-kiri!*

                        iii

—Ah, she was a bonnie cou!
Saxteen, maybe sevinteen, nae mair,
Her mither in attendance *comme il faut*
Pour les jeunes filles bien élevées,
  Drinkan like a bludie whaul tae!
Wee breists, round and ticht and fou
Like sweet Pomona i the oranger grove
Her shanks were lang, but no ower lang, and plump,
  A lassie's shanks,

Wi the meisurance o Venus—
   Achteen inch the hoch frae heuchle-bane til knap,
   Achteen inch the cauf frae knap til cuit
As is the true perfectioun calculate
By the Auntients efter due regaird
For this and that,
                   The true meisurance
   O' the Venus dei Medici,
   The Aphrodite Anadyomene
And aa the goddesses o hie antiquitie—
   Siclike were the shanks and hochs
O' Sandra the cou o the auld Black Bull.
   Her een were, naiturallie, expressionless,
Blank as chuckie-stanes, like the bits
O' blae-green gless ye find by the sea.
              —Nostalgia! Ah, sweet regrets!—
   Her blee was yon o sweet sexteen,
Her lyre as white as Dian's chastitie
   In yon fyle, fousome, clartie slum.
Sound the tocsin, sound the drum!
The Haas o Balclutha ring wi revelrie!
The Prince sall dine at Hailie Rude the nicht!

iv

The lums o the reikan toun
Spreid aa ablow, and round
As far as ye could leuk
The yalla squares o winnocks
Lit ilkane by a nakit yalla sterne
Blenkan, aff, syne on again,
Out and in and out again
As the thrang mercat throve,
   The haill toun at it
Aa the lichts pip-poppan
   In·and out and in again
     I' the buts and bens
      And single ends,
        The banks and braes
   O' the toueran cliffs o lands,
Haill tenements, wards and burghs, counties,
   Regalities and jurisdictiouns,
      Continents and empires
      Gien ower entire
Til the joukerie-poukerie!
Hech, sirs, whatna feck of fockerie!

Shades o Knox, the hochmagnadie!
  My bonie Edinburrie,
    Auld Skulduggerie!
Flat on her back sevin nichts o the week,
Earnan her breid wi her hurdies' sweit.

—And Dian's siller chastitie
Muved owre the reikan lums,
Biggan a ferlie toun o jet and ivorie
That was but blackened stane
Whar Bothwell rade and Huntly
And fair Montrose and aa the lave
Wi silken leddies doun till the grave.
    —The hoofs strak siller on the causie!
        And I mysel in cramasie!

v

There Sandra sleepan, like a doe shot
I' the midnicht wuid, wee paps
Like munes, munc-aipples gaithert
  I' the Isles o Youth,
Her flung straucht limbs
A paradisal archipelagie
Inhaudan divers bays, lagoons,
Great carses, strands and sounds,
Islands and straits, peninsulies,
  Whar traders, navigators,
  Odyssean gangrels, gubernators,
  Mutineers and maister-marineers,
And aa sic outland chiels micht utilise wi ease
Cheap flouered claiths and beads,
Gawds, wire and sheenan nails
  And siclike flichtmafletherie
In fair and just excambion
For aa the ferlies o the southren seas
That chirm in thy deep-dernit creeks,
  —My Helen douce as aipple-jack
    That cack't the bed in exstasie!
Ah, belle nostalgie de la boue!

—Sandra, princess-leman o a nicht o lust,
    That girdelt the fishie seas
    Frae Leith til Honolulu,
Maistress o the white mune Cytherean,
    Tak this bardic tribute nou!

Immortalitie sall croun thy heid wi bays,
    Laurel and rosemarie and rue!
You that spierit me nae questions,
    Spierit at me nocht,
        Acceptit me and teuk me in
        A guest o the house, nae less;
Teuk aa there was to gie
        (And yon was peerie worth),
Gied what ye didna loss—
        A bien and dernit fleeman's-firth
        And bodie's easement
        And saft encomfortin!
O Manon! Marguerite! Camille!
        And maybe tae the pox—
                            Ach, weill!

Sydney Goodsir Smith (b. 1914)
from *Under the Eildon Tree*

Continent o Venus

She lies ablow my body's lust and love,
A country dearly-kent, and yet sae fremd   [strange
That she's at aince thon Tir-nan-Og I've dreamed,   [land of youth
The airt I've lived in, whar I mean to live,   [place
And mair, much mair, a mixter-maxter warld
Whar fact and dream are taigled up and snorled.   [tangled
                                                           and knotted

I ken ilk bay o aa her body's strand,
Yet ken them new ilk time I come to shore,
For she's the uncharted sea whar I maun fare
To find anither undiscovered land,
To find it fremd, and yet to find it dear,
To seek it aye, and aye be bydan there.   [staying
                                Alexander Scott (b. 1920)

HUMOUR

The Ballad of Kind Kittok

My gudame was a gay wife, but she was richt gend,   [grandmother . . . simple
   She dwelt furth far into France, upon Falkland Fell;
They callit her Kind Kittok, whaso her weil kenned:
   She was like a cauldron cruke, clear under kell;   [hook . . . coif
They threepit that she dee'd of thirst, and made a guid end.
   Eftir her deid, she dreidit nocht in Heaven for to dwell,
And sa to Heaven the hieway dreidless she wend,
   Yet she wanderit and yeid by to ane elritch well.   [went . . . elfin
               She met there, as I wene,   [believe
               Ane ask ridand on a snail   [newt
               And cryit, 'Outrane fellow, hail!'
               And rade an inch behind the tail,
               Till it was near even.   [evening

Sa she had hap to be horsit to her hebry   [carried on horseback . . . lodging
   At ane alehous near Heaven, it nichtit them there;   [benighted
So deeit of thirst in this warld, that gart her be so dry,
   She never eat, but drank owre measure and mair.
She sleepit till the morn at noon, and rais airly;
   And to the yetts of Heaven fast can the wife fare,
And by Sanct Peter, in at the yett she stole privilie:
   God lukit and saw her latten in, and leuch his hert sair.
         And there yearis seven
            She levit a guid life,
            And was Our Lady's hen-wife:
            And held Sanct Peter at strife,
         Ay while she was in Heaven.

She lookit out on a day and thocht richt lang
   To see the alehous beside, intil an evil hour;
And out of Heaven the hie gait couth the wife gang   [did . . . go
   For to get her ane fresh drink, the ale of Heaven was sour.
She came again to Heaven's yett; when the bell rang,   [gate
   Sanct Peter hit her with a club, till a great clour   [bump
Rais in her heid, because the wife yeid wrang.   [went
   Then to the alehous again she ran the pitchers to pour,
         And for to brew and bake.
         Friends, I pray you hertfully,

Gif ye be thirsty or dry,   [if
   Drink with my gudame, as ye ga by,
Aince for my sake.

attributed to William Dunbar (c. 1460–1520)

How the First Highlandman Was Made

God and Saint Peter was gangand by the way   [going
Heich up in Argyll where their gait lay.   [way
Saint Peter said to God, in ane sport word—
'Can ye nocht mak a Hielandman of this horse turd?'
God turned owre the horse turd with his pykit staff,
And up start a Hielandman black as ony draff.
Quod God to the Hielandman, 'Where wilt thou now?'
'I will doun to the Lawland, Lord, and there steal a cow.'
'And thou steal a cow, carle, there they will hang thee.'   [fellow
'What reck, Lord, of that for aince mon I dee.'   [once
God then he leuch and owre the dyke lap,
And out of his sheath his gully outgat.   [fell ou
Saint Peter socht the gully fast up and doun,
Yet could not find it in all that braid roun.   [all round about
'Now,' quod God, 'here a marvell, how can this be,
That I suld want my gully, and we here bot three.'
'Humf,' quod the Hielandman, and turned him about,
And at his plaid neuk the gully fell out.   [from the fold of his plaid
'Fy,' quod Saint Peter, 'thou will never do weill;
And thou bot new made and sa soon gais to steal.'   [goes
'Humf,' quod the Hielandman, and sware by yon kirk,
'Sa lang as I may get gear to steal, I will never wirk.'

Anonymous
The Bannatyne Manuscript (completed 1568)

Get Up and Bar The Door

It fell about the Martinmas time,
   And a gay time it was then,
When our goodwife got puddings to make,
   And she's boil'd them in the pan.

The wind sae cauld blew south and north,
   And blew into the floor;
Quoth our goodman to our goodwife,
   'Gae out and bar the door.'—

'My hand is in my hussyfskap,
   Goodman, as ye may see;
An' it shou'dna be barr'd this hundred year,
   It's no be barr'd for me.'

They made a paction 'tween them twa,
   They made it firm and sure,
That the first word whae'er shou'd speak,
   Shou'd rise and bar the door.

Then by there came two gentlemen,
   At twelve o'clock at night,
And they could neither see house nor hall,
   Nor coal nor candle-light.

'Now whether is this a rich man's house,
   Or whether it is a poor?
But ne'er a word wad ane o' them speak,
   For barring of the door.

And first they ate the white puddings,
   And then they ate the black.
Tho' muckle thought the goodwife to hersel'
   Yet ne'er a word she spake.

Then said the one unto the other,
   'Here, man, tak ye my knife;
Do ye tak aff the auld man's beard,
   And I'll kiss the goodwife.'—

'But there's nae water in the house,
   and what shall we do than?'—
'What ails ye at the pudding-broo,
   That boils into the pan?'

O up then started our goodman,
   An angry man was he:
'Will ye kiss my wife before my een,
   And sca'd me wi' pudding-bree?'

Then up and started our goodwife,
   Gied three skips on the floor:
'Goodman, you've spoken the foremost word!
   Get up and bar the door.'

Anonymous

Codicil to a Will

*David Hume, the philosopher, enjoyed a strong friendship with John Home, the
author of 'Douglas: A Tragedy'. Home got into trouble with the Church of
Scotland for writing the play, but was never actually unfrocked. Indeed, the
defiance of Alexander 'Jupiter' Carlyle of a ban on clergymen attending the play
did much towards the eventual defeat of the Kirk's opposition to the
theatre. Home and Hume did not allow their differences of opinion on religious
matters to come between them, though apparently other differences, including the
spelling of their commonly pronounced name, gently rankled. Wrote Hume:*

I leave to my friend Mr John Home of Kilduff ten dozen of my old claret,
at his choice; and one single bottle of that other liquor called port. I also
leave him six dozen of port provided he attests under his hand signed John
Hume that he has himself alone finished that bottle at two sittings. By this
concession he will at once terminate the only two differences that ever arose
between us on temporal matters.

David Hume (1711–76)

Joking Judges

The gravest English judges sometimes indulge in a pun or joke. Lord
Ellenborough, not at all a man disposed to joke, asked a musician who was
offered as bail, 'Are you possessed of property to the *tune* of a thousand
pounds?'—And Lord Mansfield, on a Jew offered as bail who was covered
with gold lace appearing in Court, and objected to by the prosecutor's
counsel, said, 'Really, I think he must be accepted; he would *burn* for the
money.'

Our Scots judges (perhaps from the paucity of wit among us often
mentioned by our Southern neighbours) rarely indulge in jokes. Yet one of
the gravest, Lord Auchinleck, uttered a good enough pun on occasion of a
prosecution brought against the Italian musician Piscatori for firing a
pistol at a man who was attempting to get into his house to visit his daughter

with whom he was believed to have an intrigue; the justification pleaded for
the defendant was that a man was entitled to fire on a *fur nocturnus*.—'I
believe,' said Lord Auchinleck, 'he was not a *fur nocturnus*.—but I believe
he was a *furnicator*.'

Henry Mackenzie (1745–1831)
Anecdotes and Egotisms

The Cameronian Cat

*When church discipline was at its strictest, it was thought sinful to use the
actual words of the scripture for choir rehearsal purposes. Paraphrase-like sets
of doggerel verse, many of them revealing human qualities beneath the veneer
of hypocrisy, were invented to get over this difficulty. The following anonymous
verses (wittily set to music by the Scottish composer Francis George Scott) are
perhaps the most famous.*

There was a Cameronian cat
  A-seeking for its prey,
Went ben the hose and caught a moose
  Upon the Sabbath day.

The Elders they were horrified
  And they were véxed sair,
Sae straight they took that wicked cat
  Afore the meenistair.

The meenistair was sairly grieved
  And much displeased did say:
'Oh, bad perverted pussy-cat
  Tae break the Sabbath day!'

'The Sabbath's been, frae days o' yore,
  An Institution:
Sae straightway tak this wicked cat
  Tae Execution!'

Anonymous

A Border Incident

Last year, when the dalesmen were cried out in sic a hurry for the Durham
raide, there was ane o' Fairniehirst's troopers got strong breastplates o' steel
27

made to defend his heart. There was ane Brogg Paterson in Hawick, a wag that I kenned weel, was employed to fit the harnessing to the clothes; and learning that the raide was to be early in the morning, an' nae leisure for shifting, an' seeing the trooper so intent on protecting his heart, instead o' putting the steel plates in the inside o' his doublet, Paterson fastened them in the seat of his trews. After passing the Time, the Scots encamped within a half moon of an impervious brake, and sent out a party of foragers, among whom was this trooper Turnbull. The party was pursued by a body of English horse, and several of them slain; but Turnbull reaching the brake, plunged into it, horse and man. The horse stuck fast, and just as poor Turnbull was trying to extricate himself, by scrambling over the horse's head, an Englishman came riding fiercely up, and struck such a blow with his lance behind as would have spitted him on the neck,—but hitting right on the steel plate, he made him fly heels-o'er-head over the brake, and into a place of safety. A comrade perceiving, came to assist him, and found Turnbull lying on the ground, repeating to himself these words with the utmost devotion:—'God bless Brogg Paterson in Hawick! God bless Brogg Paterson in Hawick!' 'Wherefore that?' said the other. 'Because,' said Turnbull, 'he kend better where my heart lay than I did.'

James Hogg (1770–1835)
The Three Perils of Man

Presbyterian Eloquence

While it is unlikely that Presbyterian divines have talked more nonsense than those of any other persuasion, there was often a couthy homeliness about their less happy efforts at verbal illustration. In 1692, under the pseudonym 'Jacob Curate', some seventeenth-century gems of pulpit imagery were brought together in a tract title 'The Scotch Presbyterian Eloquence'.

Mr Robert Blair, that famous presbyterian preacher at St Andrews, was very much thought of for his familiar way of preaching. He preached often against the observation of Christmas, and once in this Scotch jingle, 'You will say, Sirs, "Good old Youle-day;" I'll tell you, "Good old Fool-day." You will say, "It is a brave Haly-day;" I tell you, "It is a brave Belly-day." You will say, "These are bonny formalities;" but I tell you, they are bonny fartalities. . . .'

Another, preaching against drunkenness, told the hearers . . . 'For all my preaching against drunkenness, they will go into a change-house after sermon, and the first thing they'll get, is a meikle cup full of hot ale, and they will say, "I wish we had the minister in the midst of it."'

After sermon, the Clerk gives him up the name of a fornicatrix, whose name was Ann Cantly. 'Here is,' saith he, 'one upon the stool of repentance. They call her Cantly. She saith herself she is an honest woman, but I trow scantly.'

Anonymous
The Scotch Presbyterian Eloquence

Cuddie Headrig About to Confront the Privy Council

At that moment his shoulder was seized by old Mause, who had contrived to thrust herself forward into the lobby of the apartment.

'O hinny, hinny!' said she to Cuddie, hanging upon his neck, 'glad and proud and sorry and humbled am I, a' in ane and the same instant, to see my bairn ganging to testify for the truth gloriously with his mouth in council, as he did with his weapon in the field.'

'Whisht, whisht, mither!' cried Cuddie impatiently. 'Odds, ye daft wife, is this a time to speak o' thae things? I tell ye I'll testify naething either ae gate or anither. I hae spoken to Mr Poundtext, and I'll tak the Declaration, of whate'er they ca' it, and we're a' to win free off if we do that—he's gotten life for himsell and a' his folk, and that's a minister for my siller; I like nane o' your sermons that end in a psalm at the Grassmarket.'

'O, Cuddie, man, laith wald I be they suld hurt ye,' said old Mause, divided grievously between the safety of her son's soul and that of his body, 'but mind, my bonny bairn, ye hae battled for the faith, and dinna let the dread o' losing creature comforts withdraw ye frae the gude fight.'

'Hout, tout, mither,' replied Cuddie, 'I hae fought e'en owre muckl already, and to speak plain, I'm wearied o' the trade. I hae swaggered wi' a' thae arms, and muskets and pistols, buff-coats and bandoliers lang eneugh, and I like the pleugh-paidle a hantle better. I ken naething suld gar a man fight (that's to say, when he's no angry) by and out-taken the dread o' being hanged or killed if he turns back.'

'But, my dear Cuddie,' continued the persevering Mause, 'your bridal garment! Oh, hinny, dinna sully the marriage garment.'

'Awa, awa, mither,' replied Cuddie, 'dinna ye see the folk waiting for me— Never fear me—I ken how to turn this far better than ye do—for ye're bleezing awa about marriage, and the job is how we are to win by hanging.'

Sir Walter Scott (1771–1832)
Old Mortality

The Village of Balmaquhapple

D'ye ken the big village of Balmaquhapple,
The great muckle village of Balmaquhapple?
'Tis steep'd in inquity up to the thrapple,
An' what's to become o' poor Balmaquhapple?
Fling a' aff your bannets, an' kneel for your life, fo'ks,
And pray to St Andrew, the god o' Fife fo'ks;
Gar a' the hills yout wi' sheer vociferation,
And thus you may cry on sic needfu' occasion:

'O, blessed St Andrew, if e'er ye could pity fo'k,
Men fo'k or women fo'k, country or city fo'k,
Come for this aince wi' the auld thief to grapple,
An' save the great village of Balmaquhapple
Frae drinking and leeing, an' flyting an' swearing,
An' sins that ye wad be affrontit at hearing,
An' cheating an' stealing; O, grant them redemption,
All save an' except that few after to mention:

'There's Johnny the elder, wha hopes ne'er to need ye,
Sae pawkie, sae holy, sae gruff, an' sae greedy;
Wha prays every hour as the wayfarer passes,
But aye at a hole where he watches the lasses;
He's cheated a thousand, an' e'en to this day yet,
Can cheat a young lass, or they're leears that say it
Then gie him his gate; he's sae slee an' sae civil,   [sly
Perhaps in the end he may wheedle the devil.   [persuade

'There's Cappie the cobbler, an' Tammie the tinman,
An' Dickie the brewer, an' Peter the skinman,
An' Geordie our deacon, for want of a better,
An' Bess, wha delights in the sins that beset her.
O, worthy St Andrew, we canna compel ye,
But ye ken as weel as a body can tell ye,
If these gang to heaven, we'll a' be sae shockit,
Your garret o' blue will but thunly be stockit.

'But for a' the rest, for the women's sake, save them,
Their bodies at least, an' their sauls, if they have them;
But it puzzles Jock Lesly, an' sma' it avails,
If they dwell in their stamocks, their heads, or their tails.   [stomachs
An' save, without word of confession auricular;
The clerk's bonny daughters, an' Bell in particular;

For ye ken that their beauty's the pride an' the staple
Of that great wicked village of Balmaquhapple!'

James Hogg (1770–1835)

Godly Girzie

For Burns, sex was an earlier leveller than death. He kept a collection of bawdy
verses, which he circulated among a few chosen friends. This disappeared from
his bedside a short time after his death. It may have fallen into the hands of the
poet's biographer, Dr John Currie, the reformed teetotaller who was to use
Burns most shamefully as an object-lesson upon the consequences of drunkenness.
In any case, around 1800, 'The Merry Muses of Caledonia' made its first
printed appearance, some of the pieces already clearly not the work of Burns.
Later, successive clandestine nineteenth-century editions tended to gather in
additional inferior Irish and English bawdy verse.

'Godly Girzie', however, does have the marks of authenticity. Its apt reflection
of the age-long connection between evangelical religious fervour and sexual
licence, touched upon also in 'Holy Willie's Prayer', is deftly satirized.

While Girzie herself would no doubt have preferred to see these verses in either
the Love or Religion sections of this anthology, at the risk of seeming ungallant to
her canting memory, I have allocated her a place among Scots humour.

The night it was a haly night,
   The day had been a haly day;
Kilmarnock gleamed wi' candlelight,
   As Girzie hameward took her way.
A man o' sin, ill may he thrive!
   And never haly-meeting see!
Wi' godly Girzie met belyve,
   Amang the Craigie hills sae hie.

The chiel' was wight, the chiel' was stark,
   He wad na wait to chap nor ca',
And she was faint wi' haly wark,
   She had na pith tae say him na.
But ay she glowr'd up to the moon,
   And ay she sigh'd most piouslie;
'I trust my heart's in heaven aboon,
   Whare'er your sinfu' p—e 'be'.

Robert Burns (1759–96)
The Merry Muses of Caledonia

Wet Feet

'Bless me, Major!' exclaimed the lady in a tone of alarm. 'Is it possible that you have been walking? And the roads are quite wet! Why did you not tell me you were going out, and I would have ordered the carriage for you, and have gone with you, although I believe it is the etiquette for a married lady to be at home for some time;' then observing a spot of mud on his boot, 'And you have got your feet quite wet; for Heaven's sake, Major, do go and change your boots directly! I see they are quite wet!'

The major looked delighted at this proof of conjugal tenderness, but protested that his feet were quite dry, holding up a foot in appeal to the company.

'Now, how can you say so, Major, when I see they are quite damp? Do, I entreat you, put them off; it makes me perfectly wretched to think of your sitting with wet feet; you know you have plenty of boots. I made him get a dozen pairs when we were at York, that I might be quite sure of his always having dry feet. Do, my love, let Caesar help you off with these for any sake!—for my sake, Major. I ask it as a personal favour.'

This was irresistible; the Major prepared to take the suspected feet out of company with a sort of vague, mixed feeling floating in his brain, which, if it had been put into words, would have been thus rendered—

'What a happy dog am I to be so tenderly beloved by such a charming girl; and yet what a confounded deal of trouble it is to be obliged to change one's boots every time my wife sees a spot of mud on them!' 'Now, you won't be long, Major?' cried the lady, as the Major went off, attended by Caesar. 'The Major is so imprudent, and takes so little care of himself, he really makes me quite wretched; but how do you think he looks?' . . .

At that moment the Major entered, with a very red face and a pair of new boots, evidently too tight.

'You see what it is to be under orders,' said he, pointing to his toes and trying to smile in the midst of his anguish.

'It's lucky for you, Major, I'm sure, that you are; for I don't believe there ever was anybody in earth so careless of themselves as you are. What do you think of his handing Lady Fairacre to her carriage yesterday in the midst of the rain, and without his hat, too? But I hope you'll change your stockings as well as your boots, Major?'

'I assure you, upon my honour, my dear, neither of them were the least wet.'

'Oh! now, Major, you know if you haven't changed your stockings I shall be completely wretched,' cried the lady, all panting with emotion. 'Good gracious! To think of your keeping on your wet stockings—I never knew anything like it!'

'I assure you, my dear Bell,'—began the Major. 'Oh!, now, my dearest Major, if you have the least regard for me, I beseech you put off your stockings this instance. Oh! I am certain you have got cold already—how hot you are', taking his hand; 'and don't you think his colour very high? Now I am quite wretched about you.'

In vain did the poor Major vow and protest as to the state of his stockings —it was all in vain; the lady's apprehensions were not to be allayed. And again he had to limp away to pull off boots which the united exertions of himself and Caesar had with difficulty got on.

'I really think my wife will be for keeping me in a band box,' said he, with a sort of sardonic smile, the offspring of flattered vanity and personal suffering ...

The poor Major once more made his appearance re-booted, and trying to look easy under the pressure of his *extreme* distress.

'Now, are you quite sure you changed your stockings, Major? Are you not teasing me? Caesar, did the Major change his stockings?'

Caesar, with a low bow, confirmed the important fact, and that interesting question was at length set at rest.

Susan Ferrier (1782–1854)
Inheritance

The Press Gang

On a Saturday night, as I was on the eve of stepping into my bed, (I shall never forget it—Mrs Pawkie was already in, and as sound as a door-nail—and I was just crooking my mouth to blow out the candle), I heard a rap. As our bedroom window was over the door, I looked out. It was a dark night; but I could see by a glaik of light from a neighbour's window, that there was a man with a cocked hat at the door. 'What's your will?' said I to him, as I looked out at him in my night-cap. He made no other answer, but that he was one of His Majesty's officers, and had business with the justice.

I did not like this Englification and voice of claim and authority; however, I drew on my stockings and breeks again, and taking my wife's flannel coaty about my shoulders—for I was then troubled with rheumatiz—I went down, and, opening the door, let in the Lieutenant.

'I come,' said he, 'to show you my warrant and commission, and to acquaint you that, having information of several able-bodied seamen being in the town, I mean to make a search for them.'

I really did not well know what to say at the moment. I begged him, for the love of peace and quietness, to defer his work till the next morning; but he said he must obey his orders, and he was sorry that it was his duty to be on so disagreeable a service,—with many other things that showed something like a sense of compassion that could not have been hoped for in the Captain of a pressgang.

When he had said this, he then went away, saying,—for he saw my tribulation,—that it would be as well for me to be prepared in case of any riot. This was the worst news of all; but what could I do? I thereupon went again to Mrs Pawkie, and shaking her awake, told her what was going on, and a terrified woman she was. I then dressed myself with all possible expedition, and went to the town-clerk's, and we sent for the town-officers, and then adjourned to the council-chamber to wait the issue of what might betide.

In my absence, Mrs Pawkie rose out of her bed, and by some wonderful instinct collecting all the bairns, went with them to the minister's house, as to a place of refuge and sanctuary.

Shortly after we had been in the council-room, I opened the window and looked out; but all was still: the town was lying in the defencelessness of sleep, and nothing was heard but the clicking of the town-clock in the steeple over our heads. By-and-by, however, a sough and pattering of feet was heard approaching; and shortly after, in looking out, we saw the press-gang, headed by their officers, with cutlasses by their side, and great club-sticks in their hands. They said nothing; but the sound of their feet and the silent stones of the causey was as the noise of a dreadful engine. They passed, and went on; and all that were with me in the council stood at the windows and listened. In the course of a minute or two after, two lasses, with a callan, that had been out, came flying and wailing, giving the alarm to the town. Then we heard the driving of the bludgeons on the doors, and the outcries of terrified women; and presently after we saw the poor chased sailors running in their shirts, with their clothes in their hands, as if they had been felons and blackguards caught in guilt, and flying from the hands of justice.

The town was awakened with the din as with the cry of fire; and lights came starting forward, as it were, to the windows. The women were out with lamentations and vows of vengeance. I was in a state of horror unspeakable. Then came some three or four of the pressgang with a struggling sailor in their clutches, with nothing but his trousers on—his shirt riven from his back in the fury. Syne came the rest of the gang and their officers, scattered as it were with a tempest of mud and stones, pursued and battered by a troop of desperate women and weans, whose fathers and brothers were in jeopardy. And these were followed by the wailing wife of the pressed man, with her five bairns, clammering in their agony to heaven against the King and Government for the outrage. I could not listen to the fearful justice of their outcry, but sat down in a corner of the council-chamber with my fingers in my ears.

In a little while a shout of triumph rose from the mob, and we heard them returning, and I felt, as it were, relieved; but the sound of their voices became hoarse and terrible as they drew near, and, in a moment, I heard the jingle of twenty broken windows rattle in the street. My heart misgave me; and, indeed, it was my own windows. They left not one pane unbroken; and nothing kept them from demolishing the house to the groundstone but the exaltations of Major Pipe, who, on hearing the uproar, was up and out, and did all in his power to arrest the fury of the tumult. It seems the mob had taken it into their heads that I had signed what they called the press-warrants; and on driving the gang out of the town, and rescuing the man, they came to revenge themselves on me and mine,—which is the cause that made me say it was a miraculous instinct that led Mrs Pawkie to take the family to Mr Pittle's; for, had they been in the house, it is not to be told what the consequences might have been.

Before morning the riot was ended, but the damage to my house was very great. I was intending, as the public had done the deed, that the town should have paid for it. 'But,' said Mr Keelivine, the town-clerk, 'I think you may do better; and this calamity, if properly handled to the Government, may make your fortune.' I reflected on the hint; and accordingly, the next day, I went over to the regulating captain of the pressgang, and represented to him the great damage and detriment which I had suffered, requesting him to represent to Government that it was all owing to the part I had taken in his behalf. To this, for a time, he made some scruple of objection; but at last he drew up, in my presence, a letter to the Lords of the admiralty, telling what he had done, and how he and his men had been ill-used, and that the house of the chief magistrate of the town had been in a manner destroyed by the rioters.

By the same post I wrote off myself to the Lord Advocate, and likewise to the Secretary of State, in London; commending, very properly, the prudent and circumspect manner in which the officer had come to apprise me of his duty, and giving as faithful an account as I well could of the riot, concluding with a simple notification of what had been done to my house, and the outcry that might be raised in the town were any part of the town's funds to be used in the repairs.

Both the Lord Advocate and Mr Secretary of State wrote me back by retour of post, thanking me for my zeal in the public service; and I was informed that, as it might not be expedient to agitate in the town the payment of the damage which my house had received, the Lords of the Treasury would indemnify me for the same; and this was done in a manner which showed the blessings we enjoy under our most venerable constitution, for I was not only thereby enabled, by what I got, to repair the windows, but to build up a vacant steading,—the same which I settled last year on my dochter, Marion, when she was married to Mr Geery, of the Gatherton Holme.

John Galt (1779–1839)
The Provost

Drink and Tobacco

At a prolonged drinking bout, one of the party remarked 'What gars the laird of Garskadden luk sae gash.' 'Ou', says his neighbour, the Laird of Kilmardinny, 'Garscadden's been wi' his Makar these twa hours; I saw him step awa, but I dinna like to disturb company!' . . .

Smoking does not appear to have been practised more in Scotland than in England, and if Scotchmen are sometimes intemperate in the use of snuff it is certainly a more innocent excess than intemperance in whisky. I recollect, amongst the common people in the north, a mode of taking snuff which showed a determination to make the most of it, and which indicated something of intemperance in the enjoyment; this was to receive it, not through a pinch between the fingers, but through a quill or little bone ladle, which forced it up the nose. . . .

The inveterate snuff-taker, like the dram drinker, felt severely the being deprived of his accustomed stimulant . . .

A severe snow-storm in the Highlands, which lasted for several weeks, having stopped all communication betwixt neighbouring hamlets, snuff-takers were reduced to their last pinch. Borrowing and begging from all the neighbours within reach was resorted to, but this soon failed, and all were alike reduced to the extremity which unwillingly-abstinent sufferers alone know. The minister of the parish was amongst the unhappy number; the craving was so intense, that study was out of the question. As a last resort, the beadle was despatched, through the snow, to a neighbouring glen in the hope of getting a supply; but he came back as unsuccessful as he went. 'What's to be dune, Jock?' was the minister's pathetic inquiry. John shook his head, as much as to say, that he could not tell; but immediately thereafter started up, as if a new idea had occurred to him. He came back in a few minutes, crying, 'Hae'. The minister, too eager to be scrutinizing, took a long, deep pinch, and then said, 'Whaur did ye get it?' 'I soupit the poupit' was John's expressive reply. The minister's superfluous Sabbath snuff now came into good use.

Dean Edward Bannerman Ramsay (1793–1872)
Reminiscences of Scottish Life and Character

The Pawky Duke

There aince was a very pawky duke,
  Far kent for his joukery-pawkery,
Wha. owned a hoose wi' a gran' outlook,
  A gairden an' a rockery.
Hech mon! The pawky duke!
  Hoot ay! An' a rockery!
For a bonnet laird wi' a sma' kailyaird
  Is naethin' but a mockery!

He dwalt far up a Heelant glen
  Where the foamin' flood an' the crag is,
He dined each day on the usquebae
  An' he washed it doon wi' haggis.

Hech mon! The pawky duke!
  Hoot ay! An' a haggis!
For that's the way that the Heelanters dae
  Whaur the foamin' flood an' the crag is!

He wore a sporran an' a dirk,
  An' a beard like besom bristles,
He was an elder o' the kirk
  And he hated kists o' whistles!   [church organ
Hech mon! The pawky duke!
  An' doon on kists o' whistles!
They're a' reid-heidit fowk up North
  Wi' beards like besom bristles!

His hair was reid as ony rose,
  His legs was lang an' bony,
He keepit a hoast an' a rubbin'-post
  An' a buskit cockernony!
Hech mon! The pawky duke!
  An' a buskit cockernony!
Ye ne'er will ken true Heelantmen
  Wha'll own they hadna ony!

An' if he met a Sassenach,
  Attour in Caledonia,
He gart him lilt in a cotton kilt
  Till he took an acute pneumonia!
Hech mon! The pawky duke!
  An' a Sassenach wi' pneumonia!
He lat him feel that the Land o' the Leal
  'S nae far frae Caledonia!

Then aye afore he socht his bed
  He danced the Gillie Callum,
An' wi's Kilmarnock owre his neb   [bonnet
  What evil could befall him!
Hech mon! The pawky duke!
  What evil could befall him?
When he cast his buits an' soopled his cuits   [ankles
  Wi' a gude-gaun Gillie Callum!

But they brocht a joke, they did indeed,
  Ae day for his eedification,
An' they needed to trephine his heid
  Sae he deed o' the operation!

Hech mon! The pawky duke!
 Wae's me for the operation!
For weel I wot this typical Scot
 Was a michty loss to the nation!

David Rorie (1867–1946)

The Deil O' Bogie

Sir Alexander Gray's renderings of poems from other tongues into Scots goes far beyond mere translation. The 'feel' of the new idiom amounts to little short of re-creation.

When I was young, and ower young,
I wad a deid-auld wife;
But ere three days had gane by,
 Gi-Ga-Gane-by,
I rued the sturt and strife.

Sae to the Kirk-yaird furth I fared,
And to the Deil I prayed:
'O, muckle Deil o' Bogie,
 Bi-Ba-Bogie,
Come, tak the runkled jade.'

When I got hame, the soor auld bitch
Was deid, ay, deid eneough.
I yokkit the mare to the dung-cairt,
 Ding-Dang-Dung-cairt,
And drove her furth—and leuch!

And when I cam to the place o' peace,
The grave was howked, and snod:
'Gae canny wi' the corp, lads,
 Ci-Ca-Corp, lads,
You'll wauk her up, by God!

Ram in, ram in the bonnie yird
Upon the ill-daein wife.
When she was hale and herty,
 Hi-Ha-Herty,
She plagued me o' my life.'

But when I gat me hame again,
The hoose seemed toom and wide.

For juist three days I waited,
  Wit-Wat-Waited,
Syne took a braw young bride.

In three short days my braw young wife
Had ta'en to lounderin me.
'Gie's back, dear Deil o' Bogie,
  Bi-Ba-Bogie,
My auld calamitie!'

Sir Alexander Gray (1882–1968)

Glasgow Singing

There is always a lot of singing in Glasgow, everybody does it. It was the thing that most struck two French girls from the melodious south who spent a holiday with my family some years ago. They had never heard anything like the incessant urge of Glaswegians to burst into song. Burns songs, pop songs, folk songs, operatic songs, patriotic songs, all kinds of songs. But mostly, in terms of sheer bulk, passionately sentimental songs.

Every wedding in Glasgow proves that every family in Glasgow has at least one singing uncle, usually called Uncle Willie, I have sometimes noticed. He either carries his well-worn music in his pocket on the chance that he may be persuaded to favour the company, or is prepared to go on unaccompanied. The Uncle Willies tend to choose songs with a bit of tone, like 'Red, Red Rose', or the 'Rowan Tree'. Both of these are certain death to amateur singers, but they die happy and proud. They take pride in a good-going tremolo, produce very rolling r's, very broad a's, and o's so narrow you could slice a cheese with them, and whatever the tempo, when they hit a good note fair and square, they hang on to it till they've milked it of every drop of passion.

All traditional Glasgow singers do this, drunk or sober—give their best notes all the time they need. It may express their rugged independence of restrictive practices like Time.

Singing is not permitted by law in Glasgow pubs, because Glasgow understands the dangerous power of music, which inflames as readily as it soothes; especially as pub singers would always be liable to come up with 'The Wild Colonial Boy', or 'Ra Sash my Farra Wore', either of them guaranteed to spark off a crusade. But buskers sing outside the pubs, and customers sing after they leave the pubs. They still cling to their ancient favourites, for instance:

Ra pale mune was raaaaaaaaaaaaaaaa-ising,
Above rgrnmounte-e-e-e-e-e-e-e-e-ens . . .

Or the song that is the Glasgow drunkard's national anthem, although Glasgow (and Will Fyfe) gave the rest of the world 'I Belong to Glasgow' for the world's drinking parties. Glasgow's own choice is 'The Bonnie Wells o' Wearie', pronounced 'Rab Onie Wells a Wee-a-rie'. Glaswegians never sing this song sober because it is believed to bring rain.

Cliff Hanley (b. 1922)
Dancing in the Streets

Scots Scarts

Scotch God
Kent His
Faither.

Scotch Religion
Damn
Aa.

Scotch Education
I tellt ye
I tellt ye.

Scotch Prostitution
Dear,
Dear.

Scotch Liberty
Agree
Wi me.

Scotch Equality
Caa the feet frae
Thon big bastard.

Scotch Passion
Forgot
Mysel.

Scotch Poets
Wha's
T'ither?

Alexander Scott (b. 1920)
A selection from *Scotched*

An Apprentice Angel

Try on your wings; I ken vera weel
It wadna look seemly if ony ane saw
A Glasgow Divine ga'en flutherin' aboot
In his study like a drunk craw.

But it 'ud look waur if you'd to bide
In an awkward squad for a month or mair
Learnin' to flee afore you could join
Heaven's air gymnkhana aince you get there.

Try on your wings, and gi'c a bit flap,
Pot belly and a', what does it maitter?
Seriously prepare for your future state
—Tho' that's never been in your natur'!

Hugh MacDiarmid (1892–1978)

Nemo Canem Impune Lacessit

I kicked an Edinbro dug-luver's dug,
leastways, I tried: my timing wes owre late,
It stopped whit it wcs dacin on my gate
and skelpit aff to find some ither mug.

Whit a sensation! If a clockwark thug
suid croun ye wi a brolly owre yir pate,
the Embro folk wad leave ye to yir fate;
it's you, maist like, wad get a flee in yir lug.

But kick the Friend of Man! Or hae a try!
The Friend of Wummin, even, that's far waur
a felony, mair dangerous, forby.

Meddle wi puir dumb craiturs gin ye daur.
That maks ye a richt cruel bruitt, my! my!
And whit d'ye think yir braw front gate is for?

Robert Garioch (1909–1981)

Last Lauch

The Minister said it wald dee,
   the cypress buss I plantit.   [bush
But the buss grew til a tree,
   naething dauntit.

It's growan, stark and heich,
   derk and straucht and sinister,
kirkyairdie-like and dreich.
   But whaur's the Minister?

Douglas Young (1913-1973)

THE SCOTS CHARACTER

Freedom

Ah! freedom is a noble thing!
Freedom mays man to haiff liking;   [makes
Freedom all solace to man gives:
He lives at ease that freely lives.
A noble hart may haiff nane ease
Na ellis nocht that him may please,   [nor anything else
Gif freedom fail: for free liking   [if
Is yarnit owre all other thing.   [above
Na he that ay has livit free
May nocht knaw weill the property,
The anger, na the wrcchit doom
That is couplit to foul thirldom.   [thraldom

But gif he had assayit it,   [experienced thraldom
Than all perquer he suld it wit;   [*par coeur* . . . know
And suld think freedom mair to prize   [more
Than all the gold in warld that is . . .

John Barbour (1316–95)
The Brus

Liberty

Liberty . . . is the most native and delightful right of man, without which
he is capable of no other right; for bondage excemeth man from the account
of persons, and brings him in rather among things *quae sunt in patrimonio
nostro*. And the encroachments upon, and injuries against, the right of
liberty, of all others are the most bitter and atrocious . . .

Though liberty be the most precious right, yet it is not absolute, but
limited . . . by the will of God and our obediential obligations to him, and
to men, by his ordinance. And though man hath power of his own person,
yet hath he no power of his own life, or his members, to dispose of them at
his pleasure, either by taking away his life, or amputation, or disabling, of
any member, either by himself, or by giving power to any other so to do,
unless it be necessary for preserving the whole; but he is naturally obliged

435

to God to maintain his life. So likewise men may be restrained or constrained
by others, without encroachment upon the law of liberty, in the pursuance
of other obediential obligations ... But in matters of utility and profit,
where the natural liberty is not hemmed in with an obligation, there, unless
by his own delinquency or consent, man cannot justly be restrained, much
less constrained, upon pretence of his utility of profit; for liberty is far preferable to profit; and, in the matter of utility, every man is left to his own
choice, and cannot, without injury to God and man, be hindered to do what
he pleaseth, or be compelled to do what he pleaseth not, in things wherein
he is free.

> Sir James Dalrymple, 1st Viscount Stair (1619–95)
> *Institutions of the Law of Scotland*

Liberty

See the smoking bowl before us!
  Mark our jovial ragged ring!
Round and round take up the chorus,
  And in raptures let us sing.

Chorus
A fig for those by law protected!
  Liberty's a glorious feast!
Courts for cowards were erected,
  Churches built to please the priest.

What is title? what is treasure?
  What is reputation's care?
If we lead a life of pleasure,
  'Tis no matter how or where!
    A fig, etc.

With the ready trick and fable,
  Round we wander all the day;
And at night, in barn or stable,
  Hug our doxies on the hay.
    A fig, etc.

Does the train-attended carriage
  Thro' the country lighter rove?
Does the sober bed of marriage
  Witness brighter scenes of love?
    A fig, etc.

Life is all a variorum,
  We regard not how it goes;
Let them cant above decorum
  Who have characters to lose.
    A fig, etc.

Here's to budgets, bags, and wallets!
  Here's to all the wandering train!
Here's our ragged brats and callets!
  One and all cry out—Amen!

    Chorus
A fig for those by law protected!
  Liberty's a glorious feast!
Courts for cowards were erected,
  Churches built to please the priest.

Robert Burns (1759–96)
from *The Jolly Beggars*

Loving Your Country

The natural love of your native cuntre suld be inseparablye rutit in your
hartis, considerand that your lives, your bodies, your habitatione, your
friends, your livings and sustenance, your hail, your pace, your refuge, the
rest of your eild [age] and your sepulture is in it.

Anonymous
The Complaynt of Scotland, 1549

To Be Put in Ony Public Hous

Dreid God and luve him faithfully,
Have faith in Christ ay constantly,
And, with they nichtbour, charity;
For grace on God ay call,
Obey and serve the Queen truly,
Keep justice, peace and unity,
Fra all sort of seditioun flee,
And do reason til all.   [always apply reason

Hate pride, envy and lechery,
All ire, sweirness and gluttony,   [reluctance
Avarice and idolatry,

All treason and debates,
Luve virtue, richt and honesty;
In charitable deeds exercit be,
All leifsome promise keep justly   [lawful
Til all manner of staits.   [estates of society

Keep you fra prodigality,
Oppressioun, wrang and cruelty,
And fra all vice and vanity,
And grund you upon truth;
Haunt guid and honest company,
Use wise counsel and gravity,
Do all your things discreitly,
And of the puir have ruth.

Sir Richard Maitland of Lethington (1496–1586)

A Good Tongue to Plead In

It may seem a paradox to others, but to me it appears undeniable, that the
Scottish idiom of the British tongue is more fit for pleading than either the
English idiom or the French tongue; for certainly a pleader must use a
brisk, smart, and quick way of speaking; whereas the English, who are a
grave nation, use a too slow and grave pronunciation, and the French a too
soft and effeminate one. And therefore, I think the English is fit for harangue-
ing, the French for complimenting, and the Scots for pleading. Our pronunciation is like ourselves, fiery, abrupt, sprightly, and bold; their greatest
wits being employed at Court, have indeed enriched very much their
language as to conversation; but all ours bending themselves to study the
law, the chief science in repute with us, hath much smoothed our language as
to pleading: And when I compare our law with the law of England, I perceive
that our law favours more pleading than theirs does; for their statutes and
decisions are so full and authoritative, that scarce any case admits pleading,
but (like a hare killed in the seat) 'tis immediately surprised by decision or
statute.

Nor can I enough admire why some of the wanton English undervalue
so much our idiom, since that of our gentry differs little from theirs; nor
do our commons speak so rudely as those of Yorkshire. . . . Their language is invented by courtiers, and may be softer, but ours by learned men
and men of business, and so must be more massy and significant; and for
our pronunciation, beside what I said formerly of its being more fitted to the
complexion of our people than the English accent is, I cannot but remember
them, that the Scots are the nation under heaven who do with most ease
learn to pronounce best the French, Spanish, and other foreign languages,

and all nations acknowledge that they speak the Latin with the most intelligible accent; for which no other reason can be given, but that our accent is natural, and has nothing, at least little, in it that is peculiar. I say not this to asperse the English, they are a nation I honour, but to reprove the petulancy and malice of some amongst them who think they do their country good service when they reproach ours.

Sir George MacKenzie (1639–91)
Preface to *Pleadings*

Look up to Pentland's Tow'ring Tap

Look up to Pentland's tow'ring tap,
  Buried beneath big wreaths o' snaw,
O'er ilka cleugh, ilk scar an' slap,
  As high as ony Roman wa'.

Driving their ba's frae whins or tee,
  There's no ae gowfer to be seen;
Nor douser fouk, wysing a-jee
  The byas bouls on Tamson's green.

Then fling on coals, an' ripe the ribs,
  An' beek the house baith but an' ben;
That mutchkin-stoup it hauds but dribs,
  Then let's get in the tappit hen.

Guid claret best keeps out the cauld,
  An' drives awa the winter soon:
It maks a man baith gash an' bauld,
  An' heaves his saul ayont the moon.

Leave to the gods your ilka care;
  If that they think us worth their while,
They can a rowth o' blessings spare,
  Which will our fashious fears beguile.

For what they hae a mind to do,
  That will they do, shou'd we gang wud;
If they command the storms to blaw,
  Then upo' sight the hailstanes thud.

But soon as e'er they cry, Be quiet,
  The blatt'ring winds daur nae mair move,

But cour into their caves, an' wait
  The high command o' supreme Jove.

Let neist day come as it thinks fit,
  The present minute's only ours;
On pleasure let's employ our wit,
  An' laugh at fortune's feckless pow'rs.

                                        Allan Ramsay (1686–1758)

Edinburgh Manners

*In 1724, General George Wade, military land commander during the 1715
rising, was sent to the Highlands to pacify the unruly clansmen by opening up
communications. He achieved this end by building forty stone bridges and many
miles of metalled roads, inspiring the couplet:*

> *Had you seen these roads before they were made,
> You would lift up your hands and bless General Wade.*

*Accompanying Wade to the Highlands was Edward (or Edmund) Burt,
who seems to have acted as an accountant. On his way to take up his post,
Burt, who left a series of letters describing in somewhat acidulated terms his
Highland experiences, stopped off at Edinburgh.*

Being a stranger, I was invited to sup at a tavern. The cook was too filthy an
object to be described; only another English gentleman whispered me and
said, he believed, if the fellow was to be thrown against the wall, he would
stick to it.

Twisting round and round his hand a greasy towel, he stood waiting to
know what we would have for supper, and mentioned several things himself;
among the rest, a *duke*, a *fool*, or a *meer-fool*. This was nearly according to
his pronounciation; but he meant a duck, a fowl, or a moor-fowl, or grouse.

We supped very plentifully, and drank good French claret, and were
very merry till the clock struck ten, the hour when every-body is at liberty,
by bent of the city drum, to throw their filth out at the windows. Then the
company began to light pieces of paper, and throw them upon the table to
smoke the room, and, as I thought, to mix one bad smell with another.

Being in my retreat to pass through a long narrow *wynde* or alley, to go
to my new lodgings, a guide was assigned to me, who went before me to
prevent my disgrace, crying out all the way, with a loud voice, 'Hud your
haunde.' The throwing up of a sash, or otherwise opening a window, made
me tremble, while behind and before me, at some little distance, fell the
terrible shower.

Well, I escaped all the danger, and arrived, not only safe and sound,
but sweet and clean, at my new quarters; but when I was in bed I was

forced to hide my head between the sheets; for the smell of the filth, thrown out by the neighbours on the back side of the house, came pouring into the room to such a degree I was almost poisoned with the stench.

Edmund Burt (d. 1755)
Letters from a Gentleman in the North of Scotland to His Friend in London

The Decline of the Guid Scots Tongue

The Scots language written by the Makars—Henryson, Dunbar, Lindsay and others—from the fifteenth to the end of the sixteenth century, had common Germanic roots with English. The eighteenth-century revivalists—Ramsay, Fergusson, Burns and others—and later the novelists Scott and Galt, used a version which, though it still contained many unique words and turns of phrase, had moved syntactically nearer English. The Scots Renaissance revival of the twentieth century—MacDiarmid, Goodsir Smith, Alexander Scott and others—has exploited, often movingly and brilliantly, a dictionary-reinforced Scots from which the tide of popular usage is shrinking, showing no likelihood of returning.

From the moment James VI and I went south to take up his English throne, the Scot whose English was inferior to that of his southern competitor for position or job, felt himself to be at a disadvantage; hence the efforts of men like Boswell and James Beattie studiously to rid their speech of Scoticisms. That the language survived to produce in our own day 'A Drunk Man Looks at the Thistle' and 'Under the Eildon Tree' is little short of miraculous when we read the interim report of its decline during the middle years of the eighteenth century by the scholarly laird of Ochtertyre, in the parish of Kincardine-in-Menteith, James Ramsay.

Though nothing is more difficult to be traced than the variations of dialect, it may be taken for granted that, in proportion as the English classics gained ground, and the intercourse with our southern neighbours increased, many words and phrases, taken from favourite authors, or collected from conversation, would be substituted in place of Scottish ones. But in the first stages of that matter, the sounds of vowels and of particular combinations of consonants, together with tones and accents of speech, were likely to undergo little change. Meanwhile the conversation of the learned, the fair, and the gay, though it had something of a Doric cast sufficient to disgust an English ear, was not devoid of elegance and propriety, being perfectly different from the language of the vulgar in town and country. Where learning and polished manners prevail, people of fashion have their own standard, which is perpetually shifting. No wonder then, that, amidst those lesser changes, the bulk of our country people at that period should still be fond of their native tongue, which could aptly express manly sense or delicate sentiment in a way to please their audience, and persons whom they were most solicitous to please. Though no fault could be found with Scotsmen who had lived long in England or the colonies for speaking like an Oxonian or a native of St James's parish, they were not envied for this accomplishment. But people were disposed to make themselves merry with their untravelled countrymen who spoke an English *a priori* which no Englishman could understand, being a compound of affectation and pomposity. There were, however, a few families who, by living much in England or with English people, had by perseverance dropped the greater part of their Scotticisms, which they considered as solecisms or barbarisms . . .

Besides the colloquial Scotch spoken in good company, there was likewise the oratorical, which was used by judges, lawyers, and clergymen, in their several departments. In this, perhaps, there was even greater variety than in the other; but it may be concluded, that such as wished to excel in their public appearances, strove to bring their speeches or sermons some degrees nearer pure English than their ordinary talk. The first, indeed, was a drift of language, appropriated to churches or court of justice; the other, an easy natural one, which could be used either in a drawing-room, or in a tavern over a bottle of wine.

> John Ramsay of Ochtertyre (1736–1814)
> *Scotland and Scotsmen*

What Makes a Good Workman

Adam Smith, a Kirkcaldy man, was educated at Glasgow University, from whence he proceeded to Balliol College, Oxford, on a Snell Exhibition. After leaving Oxford in 1746, he lectured on English Literature at Edinburgh University, before being appointed first, to the Chair of Logic at Glasgow, and two years later to that of Moral Philosophy. In 1764 he became private tutor to the young Duke of Buccleuch, from whom Smith received a pension. He also became a Commissioner of Customs in Scotland, thus augmenting his annuity of £300 a year. His 'Theory of Moral Sentiments' is no longer taken very seriously, but his 'Inquiry into the Nature and Causes of the Wealth of Nations,' clearly and forcefully written, has remained necessary reading to student economists.

People of the same trade seldom meet together even for merriment and diversion but the conversation ends in a conspiracy against the public, or in some contrivance to raise prices. It is impossible, indeed, to prevent such meetings by any law which either could be executed, or would be consistent with liberty and justice. But though the law cannot hinder people of the same trade from sometimes assembling together, it ought to do nothing to facilitate such assemblies, much less to render them necessary.

A regulation which obliges all those of the same trade in a particular town to enter their names and places of abode in a public register, facilitates such assemblies. It connects individuals who might never otherwise be known to one another, and gives every man of the trade a direction where to find every other man of it.

A regulation which enables those of the same trade to tax themselves in order to provide for their poor, their sick, their widows and orphans, by giving them a common interest to manage, may also render such assemblies necessary.

An incorporation not only renders them necessary, but makes the act of the majority binding upon the whole. In a free trade an effectual combination cannot be established but by the unanimous consent of every single trader, and it cannot last any longer that every single trader continues of the same mind. The majority of a corporation can enact a bye-law with proper penalties, which will limit the competition more effectually and more durably than any voluntary combination whatever.

The pretence that corporations are necessary for the better government of the trade is without foundation. The real and effectual discipline which is exercised over a workman is not that of his corporation but that of his customers. It is the fear of losing his employment which restrains his frauds and corrects his negligence. An exclusive corporation necessarily weakens the force of this discipline. A particular set of workmen must then be employed, let them behave well or ill. It is upon this account that in many large incorporated towns no tolerable workmen are to be found, even in some of the most necessary trades.

Adam Smith (1722–90)
The Wealth of Nations

Mediaeval Oatcakes

Under the flaps of his saddle, each man carries a broad plate of metal; behind the saddle, a little bag of oatmeal. When they have eaten too much of the sodden flesh and their stomach appears weak and empty, they place this plate over the fire, mix with water their oatmeal, and when the plate is heated, they put a little of the paste upon it, and make a thin cake, like a cracknel or biscuit, which they eat to warm their stomachs: It is therefore no wonder that they perform a longer day's march than any other soldiers.

Jean Froissart (1338–1404)
Chronicle

Scots Delicacies

Now we are upon the article of cookery, I must own, some of their dishes are savoury, and even delicate; But I am not yet Scotchman enough to relish their singed sheep's head and haggis, which were provided, at our request, one day at Mr Mitchelson's, where we dined. The first put me in mind of the history of Congo, in which I had read of negroes' heads sold publicly in the markets; the last, being a mess of minced lights, livers, suet, oatmeal, onions, and pepper, enclosed in a sheep's stomach, had a very sudden effect upon mine, and the delicate Mrs Tabby changed colour; when the cause of our disgust was instantaneously removed at the nod of our entertainer.

The Scotch, in general, are attached to this composition with a sort of natural fondness as well as to their oatmeal bread; which is presented at every table, in thin triangular cakes, baked upon a plate of iron, called a girdle; and these many of the natives, even in the higher ranks of life, prefer to wheaten bread, which they have here in perfection.

Tobias Smollett (1721–71)
Humphry Clinker

Highland Hospitality

When beginning to descend the hill towards Loch Lomond we overtook two girls, who told us we could not cross the ferry till evening, for the boat was gone with a number of people to Church. One of the girls was exceedingly beautiful; and the figures of both of them, in great plaids falling to their feet, their faces only being uncovered, excited our attention before we spoke to them: but they answered us so sweetly that we were quite delighted. At the same time they stared at us with an innocent look of wonder. I think I never heard the English language sound more sweetly than from the mouth of the elder of these girls, for she stood at the gate answering our enquiries, her face flushed with the rain; her pronunciation was clear and distinct; without difficulty, yet slow, like that of a foreign speech . . .

We were glad to be housed, with our feet on a warm hearth-stone: and our attendants were so active and good-humoured, that it was pleasant to have to desire them to do anything. The younger was a delicate and unhealthy-looking girl: but there was an uncommon meekness in her countenance, with an air of premature intelligence, which is often seen in sickly young persons. The other moved with unusual activity, which was chastened very delicately by a certain hesitation in her looks when she spoke, being able to understand us but imperfectly. They were both exceedingly desirous to get me what I wanted to make me comfortable. I was to have a gown and petticoat of the mistress's; so they turned out her whole wardrobe upon the parlour floor, talking Erse to one another and laughing all the time. It was long before they could decide which of the gowns I was to have: they chose at last, no doubt thinking it was the best, a light-coloured sprigged cotton, with long sleeves, and they both laughed when I was putting it on, with the blue linsey petticoat; and one or the other, or both together, helped me to dress, repeating at least half a dozen times, 'You never had on the like of that before.' They held a consultation for several minutes over a pair of coarse woollen stockings, gabbling Erse as fast as their tongues could move, and looking as if uncertain what to do: at last, with great diffidence they offered them to me, adding, as before, that I had never worn 'the like of them.'

The hospitality we had met on this our first entrance to the Highlands and on this day, the innocent merriment of the girls with their kindness to us, and the beautiful figure and face of the elder, comes to my mind whenever I think of the ferry house and the waterfall of Loch Lomond, and I never think of the two girls but the whole image of that romantic spot is before me, a living image, as it will be to my dying day.

Dorothy Wordsworth (1771–1855)
A Tour in Scotland

Highland Funeral

Yesterday we were invited to the funeral of an old lady, the grandmother of a gentleman in this neighbourhood, and found ourselves in the midst of fifty people, who were regaled with a sumptuous feast, accompanied with the music of a dozen pipers. In short, this meeting had all the air of a grand festival; and the guests did such honour to the entertainment, that many of them could not stand when they were reminded of the business on which we had met. The company forthwith taking horse, rode in a very irregular cavalcade to the place of internment, a church, at the distance of two long miles from the castle. On our arrival, however, we found we had committed a small oversight in leaving the corpse behind; so that we were obliged to wheel about and met the old gentlewoman half-way, carried upon poles by the nearest relations of her family, and attended by the *coronach*, composed of a multitude of old hags, who tore their hair, beat their breasts, and howled most hideously.

At the grave the orator or *senachie* pronounced the panegyric of the defunct, every period being confirmed by a yell of the *coronach*. The body was committed to the earth, the pipers playing a pibroch all the time, and all the company standing uncovered. The ceremony was closed with a discharge of pistols; then we returned to the castle, resumed the bottle, and by midnight there was not a sober person in the family, the females excepted. The squire and I were, with some difficulty, permitted to retire with the landlord in the evening; but our entertainer was a little chagrined at our retreat; and afterward seemed to think it a disparagement to his family, that not above an hundred gallons of whisky had been drunk upon such a solemn occasion.

Tobias Smollett
Humphry Clinker

The Importance of National Character

Would the British Empire become stronger were it possible to annul and dissolve all the distinctions and peculiarities, which flow out of circumstances, historical events and differences of custom and climates? Every ropemaker knows that three distinct strands, as they are called, incorporated and twisted together, will make a cable ten times stronger than the same quantity of hemp, however artificially combined into a single twist of cord. The reason is obvious to the meanest capacity. If one of the strands happen to fail a little, there is a three-fold chance that no imperfection will occur in the others at the same place, so that the infirm strand may give way a little. Yet the whole remains trustworthy. For God's sake, let us remain as Nature made us.

We would not become better subjects or more valuable members of our common empire, if we all resembled each other like so many smooth shillings. Let us love and cherish each other's virtues—bear with each other's failings—be tender with each other's prejudices, be scrupulously regardful of each man's rights. Lastly, let us know each other's improvements, but never before they are needed or demanded.

Sir Walter Scott (1771–1832)
The Letters of Malachi Malagrowther

Jeanie Deans Before Queen Caroline

Jeanie Deans has travelled to London to plead for her sister, Effie, who has been condemned to death for alleged child-murder. She addresses Queen Caroline.

My sister, my puir sister Effie, still lives, though her days and hours are numbered!—She still lives, and a word of the King's mouth might restore her to a broken-hearted auld man, that never, in his daily and nightly exercise, forgot to pray that his Majesty might be blessed with a long and prosperous reign, and that his throne, and the throne of his posterity, might be established in rightousness. O, madam, if ever ye kend what it was to sorrow for and with a sinning and suffering creature, whose mind is sae tossed that she can be neither ca'd fit to live or die, have some compassion on our misery!—Save an honest house from dishonour, and an unhappy girl, not eighteen years of age, from an early and dreadful death! Alas! it is not when we sleep soft and wake merrily ourselves, that we think on other people's sufferings. Our hearts are waxed light within us then, and we are for righting our ain wrangs and fighting our ain battles. But when the hour of trouble comes to the mind or to the body—and seldom may envisage your Leddyship—and when the hour of death comes, that comes to high and low—lang and late may it be yours—O! my Leddy, then it isna what we hae dune for oursells, but what we hae dune for others, that we think on maist pleasantly. And the thoughts that ye hae intervened to spare the puir thing's life, will be sweeter in that hour, come when it may, than if a word of your mouth could hang the haill Porteous mob at the tale of ae tow.

Sir Walter Scott
The Heart of Midlothian

The New Lanark Experiment

In 1819 the Poet Laureate, Robert Southey, visited the model village and cotton mill set up by David Dale and continued by his son-in-law Robert Owen. This had been constructed on humane lines from the implementation of practical measures of factory reform and education, and the application of the principle of co-operative shopping. Southey, who as a young man had dreamed of founding a 'Pantisocracy' in the Lake District, had by now come to terms with the realities of practical life.

A large convent is more like a cotton mill than it is like a college—that is to say such, convents as have been built since the glorious age of ecclesiastical architecture, and these are by far the greater number. They are like great infirmaries, or manufactories; and these mills which are three in number, at a distance might be mistaken for convents, if in a Catholic country. There are also several streets, or rather rows of houses for the persons employed there; and other buildings connected with the establishment. These rows are cleaner than the common streets of a Scotch town, and yet not quite so clean as they ought to be. Their general appearance is what might be looked for in a Moravian settlement.

I had written to Owen from Inverary; and he expected us, he said, to stay with him a week, or at the very least three days; it was not without difficulty that we persevered in our purpose of proceeding the same evening to Douglas Mill.

He led us thro' the works with great courtesy, and made as full an exhibition as the time allowed. It is needless to say anything more of the mills than that they are perfect in their kind, according to the present state of mechanical science, and that they appear to be under admiral management; they are thoroughly clean, and so carefully ventilated, that there was no unpleasant smell in any of the apartments. Everything required for the machinery is made upon the spot, and the expense of wear and tear is estimated at £8,000 annually. There are stores also from which the people are supplied with all the necessaries of life. They have a credit there to the amount of 16/- a week each, but they may deal elsewhere if they choose. The expenses of what he calls the moral part of the establishment, he stated at £700 a year.

But a large building is just completed, with ball and concert and lecture rooms, all for 'the formation of character'; and this must have required a considerable sum, which I should think must surely be set down to Owen's private account, rather than to the cost of the concern. . . .

Owen in reality deceives himself. He is part-owner and sole Director of a large establishment, differing more in accents than in essence from a plantation: the persons under him happen to be white, and are at liberty by law to quit his service, but while they remain in it they are as much under his absolute management as so many negro-slaves. His humour, his vanity, his kindliness of nature (all these have their share) lead him to make these *human machines* as he calls them (and too literally believes them to be) as happy as he can, and to make a display of their happiness. And he jumps at once to the monstrous conclusion that because he can do this with 2210 persons, who are totally dependant upon him—all mankind might be governed with the same facility. *Et in Utopia ego.* But I never regarded man as a machine; I never believed him to be merely a material being; I never for a moment could listen to the nonsense of Helvetius, nor suppose, as Owen does, that men may be cast in a mould (like the other parts of his mill) and take the impression with perfect certainty. Nor did I ever disguise from myself the difficulties of a system which took for its foundation the principal of a community of goods. On the contrary I met them fairly, acknowledged them, and rested satisfied with belief (whether erroneous or not) that the evils incident to such a system would be infinitely less than those which stare us in the face under the existing order. But Owen reasons from his cotton mills to the whole empire. He keeps out of sight from others, and perhaps from himself, that his system, instead of aiming at perfect freedom, can only be kept in play by absolute power. Indeed, he never looks beyond one of his own ideal square villages, to the rules and proportions of which he would square the human race. *The formation of character!* Why the end of his institutions would be, as far as possible, the destruction of all character. They tend directly to destroy individuality of character and domesticity— in the one of which the strength of man consists, and in the other his happiness. The power of human society, and the grace, would both be annihilated.

Robert Southey (1774–1843)
Journal of a Tour in Scotland 1819

Work and Happiness

All work, even cotton-spinning, is noble; work is alone noble: be that here said and asserted once more. And in like manner too, all dignity is painful; a life of ease is not for any man, nor for any god. The life of all gods figures itself to us as a Sublime Sadness,—earnestness of Infinite Battle against Infinite Labour. Our highest religion is named the 'Worship of Sorrow'. For the son of man there is no noble crown, well worn or even ill worn, but is a crown of thorns!—These things, in spoken words, or still better, in felt instincts alive in every heart, were once well known.

Does not the whole wretchedness, the whole Atheism as I call it, of man's ways, in these generations, shadow itself for us in that unspeakable Life-philosophy of his: The pretension to be what he calls 'happy'? Every pitifulest whipster that walks within a skin has his head filled with the notion that he is, shall be, or by all human and divine laws ought to be 'happy'. . . . The prophets preach to us, Thou shalt be happy; thou shalt love pleasant things, and find them. The people clamour, Why have we not found pleasant things? . . .

The only happiness a brave man ever troubled himself with asking much about was, happiness enough to get his work done. . . . It is, after all, the one unhappiness of a man, That he cannot work; that he cannot get his destiny as a man fulfilled. Behold, the day is passing swiftly over, our life is passing swiftly over; and the night cometh, wherein no man can work. The night once come, our happiness, our unhappiness,— it is all abolished; vanished, clean gone; a thing that has been. . . . But our work,—behold that is not abolished, that has not vanished: our work, behold, it remains or the want of it remains;—for endless Times and Eternities, remains; and that is now the sole question with us forevermore! Brief brawling Day, with its noisy phantasms, its poor paper-crowns tinsel-gilt, is gone; and divine everlasting Night, with her star-diadems, with her silences and her veracities, is come! What hast thou done, and how? Happiness, unhappiness: all that was but the wages thou hadst; thou hast spent all that, in sustaining thyself hitherward; not a coin of it remains with thee, it is all spent, eaten: and now thy work, where is thy work? Swift, out with it; let us see thy work!

Thomas Carlyle (1795–1881)
Past and Present

The Genius of the Scottish People

Anyone who studies the portions of the *Waverley* novels concerned with sociology and economics will be struck not only with a plain sagacity which we could equal in England, but with the digested accuracy and theoretical completeness which they show. There appears to be in the genius of the Scottish people—fostered no doubt by the abstract metaphysical education of their universities—a power of reducing human actions to formulae or principles.

Walter Bagehot (1826–77)
Literary Studies

Todd

My father's white uncle became
Arthritic and testamental in
Lyrical stages. He held cardinal sin
Was misuse of horses, then any game

Won on the sabbath. A Clydesdale
To him was not bells and sugar or declension
From paddock, but primal extension
Of rock and soil. Thundered nail

Turned to sacred bolt. And each night
In the stable he would slaver and slave
At cracked hooves, or else save
Bowls of porridge for just the right

Beast. I remember I lied
To him once, about oats: then I felt
The brand of his loving tongue, the belt
Of his own horsey breath. But he died,

When the mechanised tractor came to pass.
Now I think of him neighing to some saint
In a simple heaven or, beyond complaint,
Leaning across a fence and munching grass.

Stewart Conn (b. 1936)

Dour Passions

Gourlay is a proud and grasping man. He builds up his business and property by greed and terrorises and torments his family. Then, just as he is ruined by his own greed and lust for power, his son comes home, having been thrown out of

the university for drunkenness. There is a terrible scene. Young Gourlay gets
drunk and involved in a row at the local. At home his father waits to torment
him and jeer at him further.

He would pass the time till the prodigal came back—and he was almost
certain to come back, for where could he go in Barbie?—he would pass the
time, by trying to improve the appearance of the house. He had spent
money on his house till the last, and even now, had the instinct to embellish
it. Not that it mattered to him now, still he could carry out a small improvement he had planned before. The kitchen was ceiled in dark timber, and on
the rich brown rafters there were wooden pegs and bars, for the hanging of
Gourlay's sticks and fishing rods. His gun was up there, too, just above the
hearth. It had occurred to him about a month ago, however, that a pair of
curving steel rests, that would catch the glint from the fire, would look
better beneath his gun than the dull pegs, where it now lay against a joist.
He might as well pass the time by putting them up.

The bringing of the steps, light though they were, was too much for
Janet's weak frame, and she stopped in a fit of coughing, clutching the ladder
for support, while it shook to her spasms.

'Tuts, Jenny, this'll never do,' said Gourlay, not unkindly. He took the
ladder away from her and laid his hand on her shoulder. 'Away to your bed,
lass! You maunna sit up so late.'

But Janet was anxious for her brother, and wanted to sit up till he came
home. She answered, 'Yes,' to her father, but idled discreetly, to consume
the time.

'Where's my hammer?' snarled Gourlay.

'Is it no by the clock?' said his wife wearily. 'Oh, I remember, I remember!
I gied it to Mrs Webster to break some brie-stone, to rub the front door-step
wi'. It'll be lying in the porch!'

'Oh, aye, as usual,' said Gourlay; 'as usual!'

'John!' she cried in alarm, 'you don't mean to take down the gun, do ye?'

'Huts, you auld fule, what are you skirling for? D'ye think I mean to
shoot the dog? Set back on your creepie, and make less noise, will ye?'

Ere he had driven a nail in the rafter John came in, and sat down by the
fire, taking up the great poker, as if to cover his nervousness. If Gourlay
had been on the floor he would have grappled with him there and then. But
the temptation to gloat over his victim from his present height was irresistible.
He went up another step, and sat down on the very summit of the ladder, his
feet resting on one of the lower rounds. The hammer he had been using was
lying on his thigh, his hand clutched about its haft.

'Aye man, you've been takin a bit walk, I hear!'

John made no reply, but played with the poker. It was so huge, owing to
Gourlay's whim, that when it slid through his fingers, it came down on the
muffled hearthstone with a thud like a paviour's hammer.

'I'm told you saw the Deacon on your round? Did he compliment you on
your return?'

At the quiet sneer a lightning-flash shewed John that Allardyce had quizzed him, too. For a moment he was conscious of a vast self-pity. 'Damn them, they're all down on me,' he thought. Then a vindictive rage against them all took hold of him, tense, quivering.

'Did you see Thomas Brodie when you were out?' came the suave inquiry.

'I saw him,' said John, raising fierce eyes to his father's. He was proud of the sudden firmness in his voice. There was no fear in it, no quivering. He was beyond caring what happened to the world or him.

'Oh, you saw him,' roared Gourlay, as his anger leapt to meet the anger of his son. 'And what did he say to you, may I spier? . . . Or maybe I should spier what he did. . . . Eh?' he grinned.

'By God, I'll kill ye,' screamed John, springing to his feet, with the poker in his hand. The hammer went whizzing past his ear. Mrs Gourlay screamed and tried to rise from her chair, her eyes goggling in terror. As Gourlay leapt, John brought the huge poker with a crash on the descending brow. The fiercest joy of his life was the dirl that went up his arm, as the steel thrilled to its own hard impact on the bone. Gourlay thudded on the fender, his brow crashing on the rim.

At the blow there had been a cry as of animals, from the two women. There followed an eternity of silence, it seemed and a haze about the place, yet not a haze, for everything was intensely clear, only it belonged to another world. One terrible fact had changed the Universe. The air was different now; it was full of murder. Everything in the room had a new significance, a sinister meaning. The effect was that of an unholy spell.

As through a dream Mrs Gourlay's voice was heard crying on her God.

John stood there, suddenly weak in his limbs, and stared, as if petrified, at the red poker in his hand. A little wisp of grizzled hair stuck to the square of it, severed, as by scissors, between the sharp edge and the bone. It was the sight of that bit of hair that roused him from his stupor—it seemed so monstrous and horrible, sticking all by itself to the poker. 'I didna strike him so hard,' he pleaded, staring vaguely, 'I didna strike him so hard! Now that the frenzy had left him, he failed to realize the force of his own blow. Then with a horrid fear on him, 'Get up, faither,' he entreated, 'get up, faither; oh man, you micht get up!'

Janet, who had bent above the fallen man, raised an ashen face to her brother, and whispered hoarsely, 'His heart has stopped, John; you have killed him!'

Steps were heard coming through the scullery. In the fear of discovery Mrs Gourlay shook off the apathy that held her paralyzed. She sprang up, snatched the poker from her son, and thrust it in the embers.

'Run, John; run for the doctor,' she screamed.

'Oh, Mrs Webster, Mrs Webster, I'm glad to see ye. Mr Gourlay fell from the top o' the ladder, and smashed his brow on the muckle fender.'

George Douglas Brown (1869–1902)
The House with the Green Shutters

Success

The author of this nationally uncharacteristic outburst was three parts Scottish laird, one part Spanish hidalgo, though by temperament Scots through and through. In 1887 he was sent to prison for taking part in a demonstration on behalf of oppressed workers in Trafalgar Square. In later life he became associated with the cause of Scottish Nationalism, and was elected Lord Rector of Glasgow University. His 'Beattock for Moffat' features in every representative collection of Scottish short stories.

Success, which touches nothing that it does not vulgarise, should be its own reward. In fact, rewards of any kind are but vulgarities.

We applaud successful folk, and straight forget them, as we do ballet-dancers, actors and orators. They strut their little hour, and then are relegated to peerages, to baronetcies, to books of landed gentry, and the like.

Quick triumphs make short public memories. Triumph itself only endures the time the triumphal car sways through the street. Your nine days' wonder is a sort of five-legged calf, or a two-headed nightingale, and of the nature of a calculating boy—a seven months' prodigy, born out of time to his own undoing and a mere wonderment for gaping dullards who dislocate their jaws in ecstasy of admiration and then start out to seek new idols to adore. We feel that, after all, the successful man is fortune's wanton, and that good luck and he have but been equal to two common men. Poverty, many can endure with dignity. Success, how few can carry off, even with decency and without baring their innermost infirmities before the public gaze.

Caricatures in bronze and marble, and titles made ridiculous by their exotic style we shower upon all those who have succeeded, in war, in literature, or art; we give them money, and for a season no African Lucullus in Park Lane can dine without them. Then having given we feel that we have paid for service rendered, and generally withhold respect.

For those who fail, for those who have sunk still battling beneath the muddy waves of life, we keep our love, and that curiosity about their lives which makes their memories green, when the cheap gold is dusted over, which once we gave to success.

How few successful men are interesting! Hannibal, Alcibiades, with Raleigh, Mithridates, and Napoleon, who would compare them for a moment with their mere conquerors?

The unlucky Stuarts, from the first poet king slain at the ball play, to the poor mildewed Cardinal of York, with all their faults, they leave the stolid Georges millions of miles behind, sunk in their pudding and prosperity. The prosperous Elizabeth, after a life of honours, unwillingly surrendering her cosmetics up to death in a state bed, and Mary laying her head upon the block at Fotheringay after the nine and forty years of failure of her life (failure except of love), how many million miles, unfathomable seas, and sierras upon sierras separate them?

And so of nations, causes and events. Nations there are as interesting in decadence, as others in their ten-percentish apogee are dull and commonplace. Causes, lost almost from the beginning of the world, but hardly yet despaired of, as the long struggle betwixt rich and poor, which dullards think eternal, but which will one day be resolved, either by the absorption of the rich into the legions of the poor, or vice versa, still remain interesting, and will do so whilst the unequal combat yet endures.

R. B. Cunninghame Graham (1852–1936)
Rodeo

Lo! A Child Is Born

I thought of a house where the stones seemed suddenly changed
And became instinct with hope, hope as solid as themselves.
And the atmosphere warm with that lovely heat,
The warmth of tenderness and longing souls, the smiling anxiety
That rules a home where a child is about to be born.
The walls were full of ears. All voices were lowered.
Only the mother had the right to groan or complain.
Then I thought of the whole world. Who cares for its travail
And seeks to encompass it in like lovingkindness and peace?
There is a monstrous din of the sterile who contribute nothing
To the great end in view, and the future fumbles,
A bad birth, not like the child in that gracious home
Heard in the quietness turning in its mother's womb,
A strategic mind already, seeking the best way
To present himself to life, and at last, resolved,
Springing into history quivering like a fish,
Dropping into the world like a ripe fruit in due time.—
But where is the Past to which Time, smiling through her tears
At her new-born son, can turn crying: 'I love you?'

Hugh MacDiarmid (1892–1978)

The Quality of Glasgow Drinking

The majority of Glasgow pubs are for connoisseurs of the morose, for those who relish the element of degradation in all boozing and do not wish to have it eliminated by the introduction of music, modernistic fitments, arty effects, or other extraneous devices whatsoever. It is the old story of those who prefer hard-centre chocolates to soft, storm to sunshine, sour to sweet. True Scots always prefer the former of these opposites. That is one of our principal differences from the English. We do not like the confiding, the intimate, the ingratiating, the hail-fellow-well-met, but prefer the unapproachable, the hard-bitten, the recalcitrant, the sinister, the malignant, the sarcastic, the saturnine, the cross-grained and the cankered, and the howling wilderness to the amenities of civilization, the irascible to the affable, the prickly to the smooth. We have no damned fellow feeling at all, and look at ourselves with the eye of a Toulouse Lautrec appraising an obscene old toe-rag doing the double-split.

Hugh MacDiarmid (1892–1978)
The Uncanny Scot

Contentment

Let me, if I may, be ever welcome to my room in winter by a glowing hearth, in summer by a vase of flowers; if I may not, let me then think how nice they would be, and busy myself in my work. I do not think the road to contentment lies in despising what we have not got. Let us acknowledge all good, all delight that the world holds, and be content without it.

George Macdonald (1824–1905)
Annals of a Quiet Neighbourhood

The Old School Tie

Alexander Dow (d. 1779) fled Scotland after a duel, joined the Indian army, and became a distinguished scholar. He wrote a play, 'Zingis', and a 'History of Hindustan'.

Dow was a Scotch adventurer, who had been bred at the school of Dunbar, his father being in the Customs there, and had run away from his apprenticeship at Eyemouth and found his way to the East Indies, where, having a turn for languages, which had been fostered by his education, he soon became such a master of the native tongue as to accelerate his preferment in the army, for he soon had the command of a regiment of Sepoys. He was a sensible and knowing man of very agreeable manners and of a mild and gentle disposition. As he was telling us that night, that, when he had the charge of the Great Mogul, with two regiments under his command at Delhi, he was tempted to dethrone the monarch and mount the throne in his stead, which he said he could easily have done. When I asked him what prevented him from yielding to that temptation, he gave me this memorable answer, that it was reflecting on what his old schoolfellows at Dunbar would think of him for being guilty of such an action.

Alexander Carlyle (1722–1805)
Autobiography

Youth

Youth itself shows small variation from year to year. Its principal characteristics are unchanging as the tides.

However diffident its individuals may be, youth in the mass thinks no small beer of itself. It believes its pronouncements to be of importance. It demands a voice in the reconstituting of society. A breaking, ill-modulated, ridiculous voice it is, but it is the instrument preferred by youth to the eyes, ears, brain, and muscles. Youth despises and derides its elders, holding that they can neither paint, sing, hew marble, or rule the State. It admits to its leadership, however, certain men advanced in years but arrested in development, afflicted with madness, boys who won't grow up. It imitates the gaucheries and frantic behaviour of these afflicted persons as if they were the ritual gestures of some high priest. Only those who practise such ape-like conduct are acceptable to youth. Only those are modern. Only those are original. Originality is the important thing. And it is well known that there are certain clearly stereotyped methods of being original. That is why all modern paintings look exactly alike. It is not because it is easier to use paint as if you had never seen it before that youth composes these disarrangements of howling colour and infantile drawing. It is because somebody else has done it before them. . . .

Youth is greatly interested in psychology, or the study of the Soul. The Soul first began to attract attention about a quarter of a century ago when Dr Freud at Heaven's command arose from out the azure main. He discovered a thing called the Unconscious, which is a kind of consciousness; just as non-existence is a kind of existence and no bananas are really quite a lot. Psychology is singularly adapted for the use of youth, because it has a large vocabulary and is, in its essence, a grand, riotous, complicated, smutty story. It also moves along tram lines and is dressed in a uniform. Youth, terrified by the rearing, multitudinous manifestations of life all round it, feels safe with psychology.

There is a great deal more to be said about youth, but very little in its favour. Its most attractive qualities—its only attractive qualities—are innocence and physical beauty. But these are not in themselves sources of illimitable interest.

O. H. Mavor, 'James Bridie' (1888–1957)
Mr Bridie's Alphabet for little Glasgow highbrows

Tradition

'Heh! young folk arena what they were':
Wheeng'd the auld craw to his cronie:
'Sic galivantin here and there,
Sic wastrie and aye wantin mair;
Their menners far frae bonnie.

'Eh me! it's waur and waur they get
In gumption and decorum:
And sma' respec' for kirk or state.'
Wi' that the auld craw wagg'd his pate
As his faither did afore him.

William Soutar (1898–1943)

Scotland the What?

Six men out of seven who applied to us for executive jobs withdrew their application when they learned that the job was in Scotland

*Report by a firm of Management Consultants, quoted
in 'The Glasgow Herald'*

Scotland's image? You must be joking!
The less said about that, the better.
Bagpipes and haggis; tourist-broking
half-rainbow framed. A dead letter
dropped out of Europe's circulation.
Rounds of soliciting applause
for each enticed investing nation.
Ragbag of pound notes, ancient laws
and sour religion. Land whose thrust
once fashioned factories and ships
that shaped a reputation's trust.
A past that's locked by tightened lips
relaxing sentimental farce.
History's biggest little thinkers;
adjusting deferential blinkers
where politics and patronage speak
louder than risk or principle.

Quick takers-on of petty pique
that reasoning proves unconvincible.
Proud worshippers of the dull and thick
confusing numbers with perception.
Romanticists whose ultimate trick
is swallowing their self-deception.
Scotland's image? The hell with it!
I love; I hate; I curse; I care
that we should let ourselves submit
might be to *what we think we were.*

Tyrell McConall (b. 1941)

Scotland's Future

Although Sir Compton Mackenzie's rectoral address to the students of Glasgow University was delivered in 1932, it has an oddly modern ring.

Never before was the world apparently so full of opportunities. Never before, if individual happiness and complete self-expression matter, has it been so empty. Do you plan to be a politician? Statesmanship is now a profession. You need no longer trouble to stimulate a detached and disinterested patriotism. You will not be expected to rise above place-hunting. Your career will depend on the skill with which you can mingle impudence on the hustings with modesty on the back benches. If you should be fortunate enough to represent a Scottish constituency you will be able to give up to party what was meant for country, and you will call the sacrifice a realization of larger issues. But I must not single out the profession of politics for what will be seeming a calculated sneer without making haste to present the profession of letters as an equally soulless affair. The necessity of pleasing the many is become as urgent for the man of study as for the man of state, and, when a poet's music demands as much economic consideration as his wife, the divine fire is too often regulated by the price of fuel. It was never so easy as it is nowadays to earn a living by the pen: it was never so difficult to win a life. The freedom of the artist is an illusion. Failure and success are alike synonyms of bondage. Some of you will be thinking I have chosen for a peg on which to hang the dark cloak of pessimism two professions which are essentially self-indulgent and for the choice of which a man or woman must pay the penalty of disillusionment. I chose them as more likely examples of your hearts' desire than the many professions into which you will drift because they seem to offer the most obvious way of fitting yourselves into the huge economic jigsaw of modern life. For every one of you that becomes a teacher, a physician, a lawyer, a civil servant, or what is called a man of business, because he wants to be that above everything else, there will be ten who become one or the other because it will solve a parental problem or provide a quick independence. Malicious word! Even among the technical professions, where a more deliberate choice may be presumed, the future will always be at the mercy of 'rationalization', that latest poison-gas of a cynical industrialism, to which I shall apply the searing phrase of Tacitus for an earlier manifestation of barbarous expediency. *Solitudinem faciunt: pacem appellant*. They make a desert: they call it peace.

But set on one side the problem of your livelihood and contemplate the world you will presently enter, not as competitors in the struggle for existence, but as cool observers. As each year goes by that world becomes a little smaller. New achievements in rapid flight make it possible to suppose that before you die you may go round the world in eighty hours with more ease than Jules Verne's hero went round it in eighty days. Long before that, however, wireless and television will have made even such a brief voyage tiresome, for you will have already heard and seen the whole world from your own armchairs. There will be so much to titillate your attention when you are not slaving at a desk in the service of some machine invented to serve mankind that you may lose the habit of reading, and perhaps the ability to read anything except the jargon of commercial exchange. Even illustrated newspapers with a few headlines may be extinct before any of you have reached the century of years which with the perfection of hygiene most of you may reasonably expect to reach. Art in any sense in which we use the word today will be confined to the efforts of architects to pack people into their huge concrete hives, of dramatists to stimulate with coloured stereoscopic films the appetites of a satiated and incurious public, and of musicians to translate industry into rhythm by volumes of electrical sound.

The task of education will be to create various group-minds and to take care that the group-mind thus created shall never advance beyond a fixed condition, so that it may not interfere with other group-minds. Recreation will still be provided by various forms of ball games, and as members of the British group of commercial interests you will recall, not without pride, that Britons taught the rest of the world to play association football. The relentless onset of knowledge will have finally disposed of the myth of immortality; but by offering artificial rejuvenation together with a normal expectancy of a century of life, or even longer, it will justify the old proverb that a bird in the hand is worth two in the bush. I might add that there will be few actual birds left in the air, few fish left in the sea, and though by the enclosure of municipal parks a certain amount of wild life will be preserved for the amusement of those who on holidays cannot find room at the football matches, there will be few animals elsewhere except rats. . . .

There will be no poverty. There will be no disease. Physical pain will not be allowed. Mental agony will not be able to exist in that rich ennui. The commodities of the world will be equitably distributed; and there will be hot and cold water laid on in every room. To be sure, nobody in posterity will be able to call his soul his own; but that will not greatly matter, because by then it will have been definitely established that nobody possesses such an exclusively personal piece of property.

Sir Compton Mackenzie (1883–1972)
My Life and Times

Auld Lang Syne

Should auld acquaintance be forgot,
   And never brought to mind?
Should auld acquaintance be forgot,
   And auld lang syne?

      For auld lang syne, my dear,
        For auld lang syne,
      We'll tak a cup o' kindness yet
        For auld lang syne!

And surely you'll be your pint-stoup,   [pay for...two-quart
   And surely I'll be mine;   measure
And we'll tak a cup o' kindness yet
   For auld lang syne!

We twa hae run about the braes,
   And pu'd the gowans fine;   [daisies
But we've wandered mony a weary fit   [foot
   Sin auld lang syne.

We twa hae paidl'd in the burn,
   Frae morning sun till dine;
But seas between us braid hae roar'd
   Sin auld lang syne!

And there's a hand, my trusty fiere,
   And gie's a hand o' thine;
And we'll tak a right guid-willie waught   [draught
   For auld lang syne.

      For auld lang syne, my dear,
        For auld lang syne,
      We'll tak a cup o' kindness yet
        For auld lang syne!

Robert Burns (1759–96)

L'ENVOI

The Traveller Has Regrets

The traveller has regrets
For the receding shore
That with its many nets
Has caught, not to restore,
The white lights in the bay,
The blue lights on the hill,
Though night with many stars
May travel with him still,
But night has nought to say,
Only a colour and shape
Changing like cloth shaking,
A dancer with a cape
Whose dance is heart-breaking,
Night with its many stars
Can warn travellers
There's only time to kill
And nothing much to say:
But the blue lights on the hill,
The white lights in the bay
Told us the meal was laid
And that the bed was made
And that we could not stay.

G. S. Fraser (1915–1980)

INDEX OF AUTHORS

465